MATTHEW, Volume 2

(Chapters 8-13)

THE TEACHER'S OUTLINE & STUDY BIBLE™

MATTHEW, Volume 2

(Chapters 8-13)

THE TEACHER'S OUTLINE & STUDY BIBLE™

NEW TESTAMENT

KING JAMES VERSION

Leadership Ministries Worldwide
Chattanooga, TN

The Teacher's Outline & Study Bible™ is written for God's people to use both in their personal lives and in their teaching. Leadership Ministries Worldwide wants God's people to use *The Teacher's Outline & Study Bible™*. The purpose of the copyright is to prevent the reproduction, misuse, and abuse of the material.

May our Lord bless us all as we live, preach, teach, and write for Him, fulfilling His great commission to live righteous and godly lives and to make disciples of all nations.

Please address all requests for information or permission to:
Leadership Ministries Worldwide
PO Box 21310
Chattanooga, TN 37424-0310
Ph.# (423) 855-2181 FAX (423) 855-8616 E-Mail info@outlinebible.org
http://www.outlinebible.org

Library of Congress Catalog Card Number: 94-073070
International Standard Book Number: 1-57407-059-2

PRINTED IN THE U.S.A.

PUBLISHED BY LEADERSHIP MINISTRIES WORLDWIDE

1 2 3 4 5 01 02 03 04

LEADERSHIP MINISTRIES WORLDWIDE

DEDICATED

To all the men and women of the world who preach and teach the Gospel of our Lord Jesus Christ and to the Mercy and Grace of God

- Demonstrated to us in Christ Jesus our Lord.

"In whom we have redemption through His blood, the forgiveness of sins, according to the riches of His grace." (Eph. 1:7)

- Out of the mercy and grace of God His Word has flowed. Let every person know that God will have mercy upon him, forgiving and using him to fulfill His glorious plan of salvation.

"For God so loved the world, that he gave His only begotten Son, that whosoever believeth in Him should not perish, but have everlasting life. For God sent not his son into the world to condemn the world, but that the world through him might be saved." (Jn. 3:16-17)

"For this is good and acceptable in the sight of God our Saviour; who will have all men to be saved, and to come unto the knowledge of the truth." (1 Tim. 2:3-4)

7/00

The Teacher's Outline & Study Bible®

is written for God's servants to use in their study, teaching, and preaching of God's Holy Word.

- To share the Word of God with the world.
- To help the believer, both minster and layman alike, in his understanding, preaching and teaching of God's Word
- To do everything we possibly can to lead men, women, boys and girls to give their hearts and lives to Jesus Christ and to secure the eternal life which He offers.
- To do all we can to minister to the needy of the world.
- To give Jesus Christ His proper place, the place the Word gives Him. Therefore, no work of Leadership Ministries Worldwide will ever be personalized.

ACKNOWLEDGMENTS

Every child of God is precious to the Lord and deeply loved. And every child as a servant of the Lord touches the lives of those who come in contact with him or his ministry. The writing ministries of the following servants have touched this work, and we are grateful that God brought their writings our way. We hereby acknowledge their ministry to us, being fully aware that there are so many others down through the years whose writings have touched our lives and who deserve mention, but the weaknesses of our minds have caused them to fade from memory. May our wonderful Lord continue to bless the ministries of these dear servants and the ministries of us all as we diligently labor to reach the world for Christ and to meet the desperate needs of those who suffer so much.

THE GREEK SOURCES

1. *Expositor's Greek Testament*, Edited by W. Robertson Nicoll. Grand Rapids, MI: Eerdmans Publishing Co., 1970.

2. Robertson, A.T. *Word Pictures in the New Testament*. Nashville, TN: Broadman Press, 1930.

3. Thayer, Joseph Henry. *Greek-English Lexicon of the New Testament*. New York: American Book Co.

4. Vincent, Marvin R. *Word Studies in the New Testament*. Grand Rapids, MI: Eerdmans Publishing Co., 1969.

5. Vine, W.E. *Expository Dictionary of New Testament Words*. Old Tappan, NJ: Fleming H. Revell Co.

6. Wuest, Kenneth S. *Word Studies in the Greek New Testament*. Grand Rapids, MI: Eerdmans Publishing Co., 1953.

THE REFERENCE WORKS

7. *Cruden's Complete Concordance of the Old & New Testament*. Philadelphia, PA: The John C. Winston Co., 1930.

8. Josephus' *Complete Works*. Grand Rapids, MI: Kregel Publications, 1981.

9. Lockyer, Herbert. *All the Men of the Bible*. Grand Rapids, MI: Zon dervan Publishing House, 1958.

10. _______. *All the Miracles of the Bible*. Grand Rapids, MI: Zondervan Publishing House, 1961.

11. _______. *All the Parables of the Bible*. Grand Rapids, MI: Zondervan Publishing House, 1963.

12. _______. *The Women of the Bible*. Grand Rapids, MI: Zondervan Publishing House, 1967.

13. *Nave's Topical Bible*. Nashville, TN: The Southwestern Co., 1921.

14. *The Amplified New Testament*. (Scripture Quotations are from the Amplified New Testament, Copyright 1954, 1958, 1987 by the Lockman Foundation. Used by permission.)

15. *The Four Translation New Testament* (Including King James, New American Standard, Williams - New Testament in the Language of the People, Beck - New Testament in the Language of Today.) Minneapolis, MN: World Wide Publications, 1966.

16. *The New Compact Bible Dictionary*, Edited by T. Alton Bryant. Grand Rapids, MI: Zondervan Publishing House, 1967.

17. *The New Thompson Chain Reference Bible.* Indianapolis, IN: B.B. Kirkbride Bible Co., 1964,

THE COMMENTARIES

18. Barclay, William. *Daily Study Bible Series*. Philadelphia, PA: Westminster Press, 1958.

19. Bruce, F.F. *The Epistle to the Colossians*. Westwood, NJ: Fleming H. Revell Co., 1968.

20. _______. *The Epistle to the Hebrews*. Grand Rapids, MI: Eerdmans Publishing Co., 1964.

21. _______. *The Epistles of John*. Old Tappan, NJ: Fleming H. Revell Co., 1970.

22. Criswell, W.A. *Expository Sermons on Revelation*. Grand Rapids, MI: Zondervan Publishing House, 1962-66.

23. Greene, Oliver. *The Epistles of John*. Greenville, SC: The Gospel Hour, Inc., 1966.

24. _______. *The Epistles of Paul the Apostle to the Hebrews*. Greenville, SC: The Gospel Hour, Inc., 1965.

25. _______. *The Epistles of Paul the Apostle to Timothy & Titus*. Greenville, SC: The Gospel Hour, Inc., 1964.

26. _______. *The Revelation Verse by Verse Study*. Greenville, SC: The Gospel Hour, Inc., 1963.

27. Henry, Matthew. *Commentary on the Whole Bible*. Old Tappan, NJ: Fleming H. Revell Co., n.d.

28. Hodge, Charles. *Exposition on Romans & on Corinthians*. Grand Rapids, MI: Eerdmans Publishing Co., 1972-1973.

29. Ladd, George Eldon. *A Commentary on the Revelation of John*. Grand Rapids, MI: Eerdmans Publishing Co., 1972-1973.

30. Leupold, H.C. *Exposition of Daniel*. Grand Rapids, MI: Baker Book House, 1969.

31. Newell, William R. *Hebrews, Verse by Verse*. Chicago, IL: Moody Press, 1947.

32. Strauss, Lehman. *Devotional Studies in Philippians*. Neptune, NJ: Loizeaux Brothers, 1959.

33. ______. *Colossians & 1 Timothy*. Neptune, NJ: Loizeaux Brothers, 1960.

34. ______. *The Book of the Revelation*. Neptune, NJ: Loizeaux Broth ers, 1964.

35. *The New Testament & Wycliffe Bible Commentary*, Edited by Charles F. Pfeiffer & Everett F. Harrison. New York: The Iverson Associates, 1971. Produced for Moody Monthly. Chicago Moody Press, 1962.

36. *The Pulpit Commentary*, Edited by H.D.M. Spence & Joseph S. Exell. Grand Rapids, MI: Eerdmans Publishing Co., 1950.

37. Thomas, W.H. Griffith. *Hebrews, A Devotional Commentary*. Grand Rapids, MI: Eerdmans Publishing Co., 1970.

38. ______. *Studies in Colossians & Philemon*. Grand Rapids, MI: Bak er Book House, 1973.

39. *Tyndale New Testament Commentaries*. Grand Rapids, MI: Eerdmans Publishing Co., Began in 1958.

40. Walker, Thomas. *Acts of the Apostles*. Chicago, IL: Moody Press, 1965.

41. Walvoord, John. *The Thessalonian Epistles*. Grand Rapids, MI: Zondervan Publishing House, 1973.

OTHER SOURCES

42. *Contemporary Illustrations for Preachers, Teachers, and Writers*. Craig B. Larson, Editor. Grand Rapids, MI: Baker Books, 1996.

43. Draper, Edythe. *Draper's Book of Quotations for the Christian World*. Wheaton, IL: Tyndale House Publishers, Inc., 1992.

44. Hewett, James S. *Illustrations Unlimited.* Wheaton, IL: Tyndale House Publishers, Inc., 1988.

45. *Illustrations for Biblical Preaching*. Michael P. Green, Editor. Grand Rapids, MI: Baker Book House, 1996.

46. *INFOsearch Sermon Illustrations*. Arlington, TX: The Computer As sistant, 1-888-868-9029, 1986-1996.

47. Laurie, Greg. *Life. Any Questions?* Dallas, TX: Word Publishing, 1995.

48. *Leadership Journal*. Carol Stream, IL: Christianity Today, Inc.

49. Lucado, Max. *A Gentle Thunder*. Dallas, TX: Word Publishing, 1995.

50. ______. *The Great House of God*. Dallas, TX: Word Publishing, 1997.

51. *Preaching Today*. Carol Stream, IL: Christianity Today, Inc.

52. Robinson, Haddon . *Biblical Preaching*. Grand Rapids, MI: Baker Book House, 1980.

53. Rowell, Edward K. *Fresh Illustrations for Preaching and Teaching*. Grand Rapids, MI: Co-published by Christianity Today, Inc., and Baker Books, 1997.

54. Samra, Cal and Rose. *Holy Humor*. Mastermedia Limited, Nashville, TN: Thomas Nelson Publishers, 1996.

55. Sculley, John. Odyssey. New York, NY: Harper & Row, 1987.

56. Swindoll, Charles. *Living Above the Level of Mediocrity*. Waco, TX: Word Books, 1987.

57. *The Florence News Journal.* Florence, SC, Nov.27, 1996. 310 S. Dargan Street, 29506

MISCELLANEOUS ABBREVIATIONS

&	=	And
Bckgrd.	=	Background
Bc.	=	Because
Circ.	=	Circumstance
Concl.	=	Conclusion
Cp.	=	Compare
Ct.	=	Contrast
Dif.	=	Different
e.g.	=	For example
Et.	=	Eternal
f.	=	Following
Govt.	=	Government
Id.	=	Identity or Identification
Illust.	=	Illustration
K.	=	Kingdom, K. of God, of Heaven
No.	=	Number
N.T.	=	New Testament
O.T.	=	Old Testament
Pt.	=	Point
Quest.	=	Question
Rel.	=	Religion
Resp.	=	Responsibility
Rev.	=	Revelation
Rgt.	=	Righteousness
Thru	=	Through
V.	=	Verse
Vs.	=	Verses

HOW TO USE

THE TEACHER'S OUTLINE AND STUDY BIBLE™ (TOSB)

To gain maximum benefit, here is all you do. Follow these easy steps, using the sample outline below.

1 STUDY TITLE

2 MAJOR POINTS

3 SUBPOINTS

4 COMMENTARY, QUESTIONS, APPLICATION, ILLUSTRATIONS
(Follows Scripture)

	B. The Steps to Peace (Part II): Prayer & Positive Thinking, 4:6-9
1. Peace comes through prayer a. The charge: Do not worry or be anxious b. The remedy: Prayer 1) About everything 2) With requests 3) With thanksgiving c. The promise: Peace 1) Peace that passes all understanding 2) Peace that keeps our hearts & minds	6 Be careful for nothing; but in every thing by prayer and supplication with thanksgiving let your requests be made known unto God. 7 And the peace of God, which passeth all understanding, shall keep your hearts and minds through Christ Jesus.
2. Peace comes through positive thinking a. The charge: Think & practice things that are... 1) True 2) Honest 3) Just 4) Pure	8 Finally, brethren, whatsoever things are true, whatsoever things are honest, whatsoever things are just, whatsoever things are pure, whatsoever things are lovely, what-

1. First: Read the **Study Title** two or three times so that the subject sinks in.
2. Then: Read the **Study Title** and the **Major Points** (Pts.1,2,3) together quickly. Do this several times and you will quickly grasp the overall subject.
3. Now: Read both the **Major Points** and **Subpoints**. Do this slower than Step 2. Note how the points are beside the applicable verse, and simply state what the Scriptures saying—in Outline form.
4. Read the **Commentary**. As you read and re-read, pray that the Holy Spirit will bring to your attention exactly what you should study and teach. It's all there, outlined and fully developed, just waiting for you to study and teach.

TEACHERS, PLEASE NOTE:

⇒ Cover the **Scripture** and the **Major Points** with your students. Drive the **Scripture** and **Major Points** into their hearts and minds.

(Please continue on next page)

⇒ Cover *only some of the commentary* with your students, not all (unless of course you have plenty of time). Cover only as much commentary as is needed to get the major points across.

⇒ Do NOT feel that you must…
- cover all the commentary under each point
- share every illustration
- ask all the questions

⇒ An abundance of commentary is given so you can find just what you need for…
- your own style of teaching
- your own emphasis
- your own class needs

PLEASE NOTE: It is of utmost importance that you (and your study group) grasp the Scripture, the Study Title, and Major Points. It is this that the Holy Spirit will make alive to your heart and that you will more likely remember and use day by day.

MAJOR POINTS include:

APPLICATIONS:
Use these to show how the Scripture applies to everyday life.

ILLUSTRATIONS:
Simply a window that allows enough light in the lesson so a point can be more clearly seen. A suggestion: Do not just "read" through an illustration if the illustration is a story, but learn it and make it your own. Then give the illustration life by communicating it with *excitement & energy*.

QUESTIONS:
These are designed to stimulate thought and discussion.

A CLOSER LOOK:
In some of the studies, you will see a portion boxed in and entitled: "A Closer Look." This discussion will be a closer study on a particular point. It is sometimes too detailed for a Sunday School class session, but more adaptable for personal study or an indepth Bible Study class.

PERSONAL JOURNAL:
At the close of every lesson, there is space for you to record brief thoughts regarding the impact of the lesson on your life. As you study through the Bible, you will find these comments invaluable as you look back upon them.

Now, may our wonderful Lord bless you mightily as you study and teach His Holy Word. And may our Lord grant you much fruit: many who will become greater servants and witnesses for Him.

REMEMBER!

The Teacher's Outline & Study Bible™ is the only study material that actually outlines the Bible verse by verse for you right beside the Scripture. As you accumulate the various books of *The Teacher's Outline & Study Bible™* for your study and teaching, you will have the Bible outlined book by book, passage by passage, and verse by verse.

The outlines alone makes saving every book a must! (Also encourage your students, if you are teaching, to keep their student edition. They also have the unique verse by verse outline of Scripture in their version.)

Just think for a moment. Over the course of your life, you will have your very own personalized commentary of the Bible. No other book besides the Bible will mean as much to you because it will contain your insights, your struggles, your victories, and your recorded moments with the Lord.

> **"Study to show thyself approved unto God, a workman that needeth not to be ashamed, rightly dividing the word of truth" (2 Tim.2:15).**
>
> **"All scripture is given by inspiration of God, and is profitable for doctrine, for reproof, for correction, for instruction in righteousness: that the man of God may be perfect, throughly furnished unto all good works" (2 Tim.3:16-17).**

A SPECIAL NOTE FOR THE BIBLE STUDY LEADER

Dear Teacher:

The teaching material you hold in your hands gives your church the *maximum flexibility* in scheduling for the church year or for any Bible study program. *The Teacher's Outline and Study Bible*™ (TOSB) has been designed to help you in your teaching ministry. The wealth of material makes the TOSB the most unique Bible study material anywhere. The name says it all:

⇒ *The Teacher's* has been designed just for you, God's dear servant, the teacher of God's Holy Word.

⇒ *Outline* makes the material unique as every verse has been outlined—point by point—subject by subject—just for you.

⇒ *Study* allows you, the teacher, to study commentary that has been developed and has drawn upon over forty different sources. At your disposal are well-thought-out points that explain in simple language what the Scripture means. Suggestions for opening and closing each lesson assure that your students will be caught up from the beginning to the end. Practical points of application help you to bring the truth to whatever level of student you are teaching. Gripping illustrations have been interspersed through each lesson, illustrations guaranteed to hold the attention of your students as you drive home the point. Finally, questions that are thought-provoking and discussion-oriented are a part of *every* major point in the lesson. Imagine—all the benefits of the time spent collecting this study material are right in *your* hands, waiting for you to glean what *you need* for your next lesson.

⇒ *Bible* is the foundation of *The Teacher's Outline and Study Bible*™. God's Holy Word, outlined for you—verse by verse, point by point, subject by subject—gives you, the teacher, the great advantage of having God's Word outlined, explained, made practical, and illustrated.

NOTE: As you have no doubt noticed, this particular book is a large one. Please do not let the size of the book or the size of the studies overwhelm you or keep you from teaching the full counsel of God's Word. If you prefer not to follow a self-paced schedule, we offer two different lesson plans (following) to help you in your planning.

A ONE QUARTER OR THIRTEEN-WEEK LESSON PLAN

A SPECIAL NOTE FOR THE BIBLE STUDY LEADER

The teaching material you have before you gives your church the *maximum flexibility* in scheduling for the church year or for any Bible study program. If you prefer not to follow a self-paced schedule, please note that the contents of this study (Matthew, Volume Two) can be taught in **thirteen weeks** using the following lesson plan: [TIP: Study *all* of the material. Teach only what you have time to share.]

QUARTER #1 [13 WEEKS]
To Begin Your Exciting Study, Follow This Simple
LESSON PLAN FOR MATTHEW 8:1-13:52

V. THE MESSIAH'S GREAT AUTHORITY AND POWER REVEALED IN WORD AND WORK, 8:1-9:34

WEEK #	LESSON TITLE	SCRIPTURE TEXT	PAGE NUMBER
1	*"Jesus the Healer"*	Mt.8:1-17	3
2	*"Jesus the Lord"*	Mt.8:18-34	28
3	*"Jesus the Savior"*	Mt.9:1-17	54
4	*"Jesus the One Who Meets Man's Desperate and Hopeless Needs"*	Mt.9:18-34	78

VI. THE MESSIAH'S MESSENGERS AND THEIR MISSION, 9:35-10:42

WEEK #	LESSON TITLE	SCRIPTURE TEXT	PAGE NUMBER
5	*"The Messiah's Mission, Call, and Commission to His Disciples"*	Mt.9:35-10:15	95
6	*"The Messiah's Warning and Encouragement for the Persecuted"*	Mt.10:16-42	126

VII. THE MESSIAH'S VINDICATION OF HIS MESSIAHSHIP, 11:1-30

WEEK #	LESSON TITLE	SCRIPTURE TEXT	PAGE NUMBER
7	*"The Messiah's Vindication of His Messiahship"*	Mt.11:1-30	154

VIII. THE MESSIAH'S DEFENSE OF HIMSELF AGAINST OPPONENTS, 12:1-50

WEEK #	LESSON TITLE	SCRIPTURE TEXT	PAGE NUMBER
8	*"The Messiah (Jesus) and Man Are Greater Than Any Religion"*	Mt.12:1-21	185
9	*"The Messiah is Man's Answer to Everything"*	Mt.12:22-50	209

A ONE QUARTER OR THIRTEEN-WEEK LESSON PLAN

IX. THE MESSIAH'S PARABLES DESCRIBING THE KINGDOM OF HEAVEN, 13:1-52

A TWO QUARTER OR TWENTY-SIX WEEK LESSON PLAN

A SPECIAL NOTE FOR THE BIBLE STUDY LEADER

The contents of this study (Matthew, Volume Two) can also be taught in **twenty-six weeks** using the following lesson plan: [TIP: Study *all* of the material. Teach only what you have time to share.]

QUARTERS #1 and #2 [26 WEEKS]
To Begin Your Exciting Study, Follow This Simple
LESSON PLAN FOR MATTHEW 8:1-13:52

V. THE MESSIAH'S GREAT AUTHORITY AND POWER REVEALED IN WORD AND WORK, 8:1-9:34

VI. THE MESSIAH'S MESSENGERS AND THEIR MISSION, 9:35-10:42

VII. THE MESSIAH'S VINDICATION OF HIS MESSIAHSHIP, 11:1-30

A TWO QUARTER OR TWENTY-SIX WEEK LESSON PLAN

VIII. THE MESSIAH'S DEFENSE OF HIMSELF AGAINST OPPONENTS, 12:1-50

WEEK #	LESSON TITLE	SCRIPTURE TEXT	PAGE NUMBER
13	*"Defense 1: Messiah is Greater than Religion"*	Mt.12:1-8	185
14	*"Defense 2: Man is Greater than Religion"*	Mt.12:9-13	194
15	*"Defense 3: Messiah is the Chosen Servant of God"*	Mt.12:14-21	202
16	*"Defense 4: Messiah is of God's Kingdom and House"*	Mt.12:22-30	209
17	*"Defense 5: A Man's Words Determine His Destiny"*	Mt.12:31-37	219
18	*"Defense 6: Messiah's Answer to an Evil Generation or to Apostates"*	Mt.12:38-45	226
19	*"Defense 7: Messiah's Answer to Doubting Relatives"*	Mt.12:46-50	235

IX. THE MESSIAH'S PARABLES DESCRIBING THE KINGDOM OF HEAVEN, 13:1-52

WEEK #	LESSON TITLE	SCRIPTURE TEXT	PAGE NUMBER
20	*"The Parable of the Sower: How a Man Receives the Gospel and the Parable of the Sower Explained"*	Mt.13:1-9, 18-23	243
21	*"The Messiah's Reasons for Speaking in Parables: Who Receives and Who Loses"*	Mt.13:10-17	252
22	*"The Parable of the Wheat and the Tares: The Question of Evil—Why It Exists and the Parable of the Wheat and the Tares Explained"*	Mt.13:24-30, 36-43	260
23	*"The Parable of the Mustard Seed"*	Mt.13:31-32	270
24	*"The Parable of Leaven: The Transforming Power of the Gospel and the Messiah's Purpose for Speaking in Parables"*	Mt.13:33-35	278
25	*"The Parable of the Hidden Treasure: Giving Up All for Christ and the Parable of the Merchant Man and the Pearl of Great Price: Giving Up All for Christ"*	Mt.13:44-46	294
26	*"The Parable of the Dragnet and the Parable of the Householder"*	Mt.13:47-52	304

"

Go ye therefore, and teach all nations

" (Mt.28:19)

OUTLINE OF MATTHEW, Volume 2
(Chapter 8-13)

THE TEACHER'S OUTLINE & STUDY BIBLE™ is *unique*. It differs from all other study Bibles & sermon resource materials in that every passage and subject is outlined right beside the Scripture. When you choose any *subject* below and turn to the reference, you have not only the Scripture, but you also discover the Scripture and subject *already outlined for you—verse by verse*.

For a quick example, choose one of the subjects below and turn over to the Scripture, and you will find this marvelous help for faster, easier, and more accurate use.

A suggestion: For the quickest overview of Matthew, first read *all the major titles* (V, VI, VII, etc.), then come back and read the subtitles.

OUTLINE OF MATTHEW, Volume 2
(Chapters 8-13)

Page

THE GOSPEL ACCORDING TO
MATTHEW

INTRODUCTION

AUTHOR: Matthew. The Bible in no place says that Matthew is the author; however, the evidence for Matthew's authorship is strong.

1. Early writers have always credited the Gospel to Matthew. William Barclay quotes one of the earliest church historians, a man named Papias (A.D. 100), as saying, "Matthew collected the sayings of Jesus in the Hebrew tongue."[1] Irenaeus (about A.D. 175), the saintly bishop of Lyons, wrote: "Matthew also issued a written Gospel among the Hebrews in their own dialect, while Peter and Paul were preaching at Rome and laying the foundations of the church" (Irenaeus, *Against Heresies*, 3.1.1).

2. Matthew was qualified to write the Gospel. He had been a tax collector which means that he was involved in large business transactions. A study of the Gospel shows that the author had an interest in figures, large numbers (Mt.18:24; 28:12), and statistics (Mt.1:17). The detailed messages of Jesus point to a man experienced with shorthand which he had apparently used in business transactions. Very little is given in the Scripture about Matthew.
   a. He was one of the twelve apostles (Mk.2:14).
   b. He left all to follow Christ (Lk.5:27-28).
   c. He introduced his friends to Christ by inviting them to a feast which he gave in honor of Christ (Lk.5:29).

DATE: Uncertain. A.D. 50-70. It was written some years after Jesus' ascension, but before A.D. 70.

1. The fall of Jerusalem, A.D. 70, is prophetic (Mt.24:1f).
2. The statements such as "unto this day" (Mt.27:8) and "until this day" (Mt.28:15) suggest a date sometime after Jesus' ascension, but not too far in the distant future.
3. The scattering of the Jerusalem Church due to persecution (Acts 8:4) suggests a date sometime after the ascension. A Gospel would not have been necessary so long as the church and apostles were together.
4. The quote by Irenaeus points to Matthew writing during Nero's reign, "while Paul and Peter were in Rome."

TO WHOM WRITTEN: The Gospel was written originally to the Jews. However, it breathes a message for all, a message proclaiming the Messianic hope of the world for the Great Deliverer.

PURPOSE: To show that Jesus is the Messiah, the Savior and King prophesied by the Hebrew prophets.

Matthew is a strong book, a book written to force belief in Jesus. Matthew sets out to prove that all the prophecies of the O.T. are fulfilled in Jesus, the carpenter from Nazareth. It has one recurring theme: "All this was done, that it might be fulfilled which was spoken by the prophets, saying...." This is repeated approximately sixteen times, and there are ninety-three O.T. quotations.

SPECIAL FEATURES:

1. Matthew is *The Ecclesiastical Gospel*. Down through the centuries, Matthew has been widely used by the church. Its material is arranged primarily by subjects, not by a strict chronological sequence. It is somewhat a topical arrangement of the ministry and

---

[1] William Barclay. *The Gospel of Matthew*, Vol.1. "The Daily Study Bible." (Philadelphia, PA: The Westminster Press, 1956), p.xxi.

teachings of Jesus. As such, it has been extremely useful to the church: as an apology to defend the faith, as a handbook of instructions for new believers, and as a book of worship to read in church services.

2. Matthew is *The Teaching Gospel*. Much of Jesus' teaching is arranged so that it can be easily taught and easily lived. This material is clearly seen in five sections.

a. The Sermon on the Mount (Mt.5-7).
b. The Messiah's messengers and their mission (Mt.9-10:42).
c. The Messiah's parables (Mt.13).
d. The Messiah's disciples and their behavior toward one another (Mt.18).
e. The Messiah's prophecy of His return and the end of time: the great Olivet discourse (Mt.24-25).

3. Matthew is *The Royal Gospel* or *The Kingdom Gospel*. The heart of Matthew's Gospel is that Jesus is King. Jesus is the Son of David, the greatest of Israel's kings. He is the fulfillment of the Messianic prophecies that foretold the coming of a King like unto David.

a. His genealogy shows Him to be David's son by birth (Mt.1:1-17).
b. He was born King of the Jews (Mt.2:2).
c. He was called the King of David time and time again (Mt. 9:27; 15:22; 20:30; 21:9, 15; 22:42).
d. He personally claimed the power of a king by overriding the law: "I say unto you...." (Mt.5:21-22, 27-28, 31-32, 33-34, 38-39, 43-44).
e. He dramatically showed Himself to be King by His triumphal entry into Jerusalem (Mt.21:1-11).
f. He deliberately accepted the title of King before Pilate (Mt.27:11).
g. His cross bore the title, "King of the Jews" (Mt.27:11).
h. He claimed the supreme power of the King of Kings, "All power is given unto me" (Mt.28:18).
i. The word "Kingdom" is used fifty-four times and "Kingdom of Heaven" thirty-two times.

4. Matthew is *The Apocalyptic Gospel*. Among the Gospels, it has the most comprehensive account of the Lord's return and of the end time (Mt.24-25).

5. Matthew is *The Gospel of the Church*. It is the only Synoptic Gospel that mentions the church (Mt.16:13-23; 18:17; cp. Mk.8:27-33; Lk.9:18-22).

6. Matthew is *The Gospel of the Jew*. Matthew never failed to show that Jesus fulfills O.T. prophecy. He makes more than one hundred allusions or quotations from the O.T. He is determined to compel the Jew to believe that Jesus is the Messiah.

MATTHEW 8:1-4

	CHAPTER 8 **V. THE MESSIAH'S GREAT AUTHORITY & POWER REVEALED IN WORD & WORK, 8:1-9:34** **A. Jesus Heals a Leper: Cleansing the Most Defiled, 8:1-4** (Mk.1:40-45; Lk.5:12-16)	2 And, behold, there came a leper and worshipped him, saying, Lord, if thou wilt, thou canst make me clean. 3 And Jesus put forth his hand, and touched him, saying, I will; be thou clean. And immediately his leprosy was cleansed. 4 And Jesus saith unto him, See thou tell no man; but go thy way, show thyself to the priest, and offer the gift that Moses comanded for a testimony unto them.	**2. The leper: The unclean** a. He came to Jesus b. He worshipped c. He asked & trusted for cleansing **3. The Lord Jesus** a. He touched b. He said, "I will" c. He cleansed **4. The cleansed man** a. He must beware of pride, of boasting b. He must obey the Law
1. Multitudes followed Jesus	When he was come down from the mountain, great multitudes followed him.		

Section V
THE MESSIAH'S GREAT AUTHORITY AND POWER REVEALED IN WORD AND WORK, Matthew 8:1-9:34

Study 1: **JESUS HEALS A LEPER: CLEANSING THE MOST DEFILED**

Text: **Matthew 8:1-4**

Aim: To learn a wonderful truth: Christ can cleanse the foulest person and make him clean.

Memory Verse:

"And, behold, there came a leper and worshipped him, saying, Lord, if thou wilt, thou canst make me clean" (Mt.8:2).

INTRODUCTION

What is the dirtiest thing you have ever had to touch? Was it…

- a baby's soiled diaper?
- a child covered with mud?
- a homeless person who had not bathed for a long time?

It is our nature to avoid things that are dirty or unclean. As a general rule, even unclean people are avoided. Experience has shown that it takes a lot of effort (and sometimes a strong stomach) to clean a baby whose diaper has reached its limits. But because the baby cannot help himself, we must clean him. A child who has splashed around in the mud needs help before he can come inside the house. A homeless person, whose very presence usually repels people, needs the intervention of others to overcome his circumstances. As we will soon discover, the unclean person does not repel Christ. Instead, He is drawn to those who need His cleansing power.

This passage is a beautiful picture of spiritual cleansing. It is the power of Jesus to heal and cleanse the most defiled person.

MATTHEW 8:1-4

OUTLINE:
1. Multitudes followed Jesus (v.1).
2. The leper, the most unclean and defiled person (v.2).
3. The Lord Jesus (v.3).
4. The cleansed man (v.4).

1. MULTITUDES FOLLOWED JESUS (v.1).

They followed because they were astonished at His teaching. The people were stricken, stirred, aroused, and moved by the Lord's teaching. Jesus astonished the crowd for two reasons.
1. His message was unique.
2. His authority was strikingly different. Note the words given earlier.

> **"He taught them as one that had authority, and not as the scribes" (Mk.1:22).**

QUESTIONS:
1. What kind of leader (whether preacher, teacher, or otherwise) are you typically drawn to?
   ____One who has a charismatic personality?
   ____One who apologizes for teaching the truth?
   ____One who teaches one thing but does something entirely different?
   ____One who applies the truth of God's Word to everyday life?
2. The crowds followed Jesus because they were astonished at His teaching. What are some teachings of Christ that astonish you?

2. THE LEPER: THE MOST UNCLEAN AND DEFILED PERSON (v.2).

The leper dramatically demonstrates that no person is too unclean, polluted, dirty, or sinful to come to Jesus Christ. Note three significant points.

1. The leper came to Jesus. He came despite what people thought. He came…
   - despite being "utterly unclean" (Ro.3:23; cp. 3:10-18)
   - despite being considered dead (Eph.2:1; 4:18; 1 Jn.5:12)
   - despite being an outcast and ostracized by people
   - despite being considered polluted and incurable by people

2. The leper worshipped Jesus. The word worship means to reverence; to pay homage. The attitude of reverence and worship was shown by bowing. The leper was desperate and knew his desperate plight. He was not allowed to approach within six feet of anyone. However, he rushed up to Jesus and fell prostrate before Jesus' feet, worshipping Him. The leper demonstrated *two significant things* by rushing up to and worshipping Jesus:
   ⇒ His desire and willingness to break away from the world and its restrictions
   ⇒ His acknowledgment that Jesus was worthy of worship

3. The leper asked and trusted Jesus for cleansing. The leper did not ask merely to be healed, but he asked to be cleansed. He wanted to be restored, that is, made whole and *saved completely*. He wanted all the rights and privileges of a whole man. He wanted to be completely restored with men (socially) and with God (religiously).

The words "If thou wilt" show two things:

a. It shows great faith in Jesus. The leper believed that Jesus had the power to heal him; it was just a matter of Jesus choosing to cleanse him.

b. It shows that the leper appealed to Jesus' heart, not to His power. He believed and knew Jesus had the power. What was needed was for the leper to touch Jesus' heart. In essence what the leper asked for was the love and the power of God.

> **"Even as the Son of man came not to be ministered unto, but to minister, and to give his life a ransom for many" (Mt.20:28).**

APPLICATION:

1) The leper asked to be cleansed. God says that all men must ask if they wish to be cleansed. "Whosoever shall call upon the name of the Lord shall be saved" (Ro.10:13).

> **"That if thou shalt confess with thy mouth the Lord Jesus, and shalt believe in thine heart that God hath raised him from the dead, thou shalt be saved. For with the heart man believeth unto righteousness; and with the mouth confession is made unto salvation" (Ro.10:9-10).**

2) The leper did two things that we must all do when we ask Christ to cleanse us.
   ⇒ He genuinely trusted Christ: believed in Him and His power.
   ⇒ He offered himself to Christ: bowed and received the love and power of Christ to cleanse him.

3) Not every leper came to Jesus for cleansing, just as every generation has its unbelievers who do not come to Him for cleansing.
   ⇒ Some just do not trust Jesus. They do not believe in Him nor in His power.
   ⇒ Some know about Jesus but are unwilling to offer themselves to Him. They are unwilling to bow before Him and receive His love and power.

ILLUSTRATION:

How clean does a person have to be before Christ will accept him? What can a person do in order to be clean?

Pat had struggled all her life to be good—good enough to please her parents, her teachers, and everyone else. She even tried to be good enough to please God. But no matter how hard she tried, she always came short. Pat was destined to a life of self-condemnation until a friend named Jimmy made a suggestion.

"Pat, take a clean white shirt and do your best to dirty it up with soil from your yard. After you cake it with dirt and mud, take it inside to your sink and wash it out by hand." Pat carefully followed Jimmy's instructions, taking a white shirt and grinding the dirt and mud in. Then Pat scrubbed and scrubbed—but to no avail. The dirt stains remained no matter how much she scrubbed. After many washings, she threw up her hands and said, "No matter what I do, it won't come clean!" And as those words left her mouth, the impact of what she had said echoed in her soul. "No matter what I do, it won't come clean." The truth of God's Word had finally penetrated her heart. She could not cleanse herself; only Christ could cleanse her. Right there by her kitchen sink, she gave up and gave in to God, asking Him to cleanse her dirty heart.

QUESTIONS:

1. Have you trusted Christ to cleanse you? What faults or traits do you have that might keep you from doing so? What difference would conversion to Christ make in your life?
2. God is after more than just healing our physical aches and pains. In what areas of your heart do you need His healing touch today?

A CLOSER LOOK #1

(8:2) **Leprosy**: William Barclay points out that leprosy was the most terrible and greatly feared disease in the day of Jesus. It was disfiguring and sometimes fatal. In the Bible leprosy is a type of sin.[1]

1. The leper himself was considered *utterly unclean*—physically and spiritually. He could not approach within six feet of any person including family members. "His clothes shall be rent, and his head bare, and he shall put a covering upon his upper lip, and shall cry, 'Unclean, unclean'" (Lev.13:45).

2. He was judged as being *dead*—the living dead. He had to wear a black garment so he could be recognized as being among the *dead*.

3 He was banished as an outcast, totally ostracized from society—earthly and heavenly. "All the days wherein the plague shall be in him he shall be *defiled*; he is *unclean*; he shall *dwell alone*; *without the camp* shall his habitation be" (Lev.13:46). He could not live within the walls of any city; his dwelling had to be outside the city gates.

4. He was thought to be polluted, incurable by any human means whatsoever. God and His power alone could cure him. (Note how Jesus proved His Messiahship and deity by healing the leper.)

Imagine the anguish and heartbreak of the leper, being completely cut off from family, friends, and society. Imagine the emotional and mental pain. There are other recorded instances of lepers being healed (cp. Mt.10:8; 11:5; Mk.1:40; Lk.7:22; 17:12; and perhaps Mt.26:6; cp. Mk.14:3).

QUESTIONS:
1. If possible, imagine yourself in the shoes of a leper today. What impact would it have on your life?
2. There are many "untouchables" in society today. Who do you think they are and what can you do to reach them for Christ?

A CLOSER LOOK #2

(8:2) **Jesus Christ**: this is the first healing miracle performed by Jesus in Matthew. Christ proved two things when He healed the leper.

1. Jesus proved Himself to be God, to possess the power of God. The people knew no one could cure a leper but God (2 Ki.5:7).

2. Jesus proved Himself to be the Messiah, the Savior of the world. He not only pronounced the leper cured, as the priests did; He *cleansed* the leper. He took the man's leprosy (sin) away; He cleansed the man thoroughly and completely.

3. THE LORD JESUS (v.3).

The heart of Jesus was deeply touched by the leper. The sight just gripped His heart. The man's condition was wretched. Just imagine...

- his body full of sores
- his flesh eaten away
- his loneliness
- his desperation
- his alienation
- his emptiness
- his helplessness

1. Jesus "touched" the leper. Note that before saying a word, Jesus reached out for the man: He "put forth His hand, and touched him." When no one else would, Jesus reached out for the most defiled. How long had it been since anyone had touched him? Weeks? Months? Years?

---

1 William Barclay. *The Gospel of Matthew*, Vol.1, p.300.

"But when he saw the multitudes, he was moved with compassion on them, because they fainted, and were scattered abroad, as sheep having no shepherd" (Mt.9:36).

APPLICATION:
So many will not touch the *most defiled*. They will have nothing to do with them. They shun and avoid them. Too often, even when the defiled wander into church, the church gets rid of them as soon as possible. So many in the church have little time for the defiled. They neglect and leave them where they are. Too many believers and too many churches have lost the sense of mission to reach the most defiled.

2. Jesus said, "I will." These words say several significant things about Jesus.
   a. Jesus was not willing for the most defiled to perish (2 Pt.3:9).
   b. Jesus did not have to be urged to help the most defiled. The most defiled simply had to approach Jesus with a sincere heart.
   c. Jesus did not have to be paid to help the most defiled. The leper did nothing but come to Jesus, believing that Jesus would cleanse him.

"How God anointed Jesus of Nazareth with the Holy Ghost and with power: who went about doing good, and healing all that were oppressed of the devil; for God was with him" (Acts 10:38).

APPLICATION:
"I will." The mission of Jesus Christ is to seek and to save that which is lost, no matter how defiled (Lk.19:10; Mt.9:12-13; 20:28). The church is called to the very same mission (Jn.20:21). Jesus Christ said go—go to "every creature," to every human being (Mk.16:15; cp. Mt.28:19-20).

3. Jesus cleansed. The leper had acknowledged Jesus' power. Now he received that power: he was cleansed physically and ceremonially, that is, religiously and spiritually. Note that Jesus cleansed the man immediately. He did not hesitate; there was no waiting. The man meant business with Jesus; he genuinely wanted to be cleansed. Jesus knew his sincerity, so He cleansed him immediately. The idea is that He cleansed him *through and through* (cp. Ps.5:7; 1 Jn.1:9).

APPLICATION:
Every man must be cleansed and washed from his sins.

"And now why tarriest thou? arise, and be baptized, and wash away thy sins, calling on the name of the Lord" (Acts 22:16).

QUESTIONS:
1. There is great healing in the act of touching a person who needs Christ. Who are you most willing to touch in the name of Christ:
   ____The person who looks like you do?
   ____The person who thinks like you do?
   ____The person who has the same social status that you do?
   ____The person who is needy and destitute, regardless of his status or looks?
2. Jesus loves everyone, even the most unclean and defiled person. In your day-to-day life, what can you learn from Christ's example?
3. As you look at your own life, what do you need Jesus to wash from your heart and life today?

A CLOSER LOOK #3

(8:1-4) **Healing—Suffering**: this leper was healed. In looking at miraculous healings the question is often asked, "Why are all faithful believers not healed when they are sick and ask for healing? Some walk ever so faithfully before God and they believe that God does heal; they have as much faith, if not more faith, than some who are healed. Why then are they not also healed?"

The reason is God. When God looks at our requests, He considers at least four things.

1. God's glory. Would granting the request bring the greatest glory to God's name?
2. Our good, not only physically, but spiritually. What particular spiritual grace or quality do we need to learn: endurance, self-control, trust, dependence?
    a. Spiritually, within ourselves: will granting our request strengthen us more spiritually? Which way will our faith and trust in God grow more?
    b. Spiritually, without ourselves: how does God now want to use us—as a constant prayer warrior? As an unbelievable testimony to His empowering spiritual strength, no matter the physical condition? Consider something else: What do the people need with whom God wants to use us? What is the best way for God to reach them—by demonstrating His strength in and through our trial? No matter what some may claim, the power of God is often more forcibly seen by manifesting itself through infirmities and weaknesses.

> **"For this thing I besought the Lord thrice, that it might depart from me. And he said unto me, My grace is sufficient for thee: for my strength is made perfect in weakness. Most gladly therefore will I rather glory in my infirmities, that the power of Christ may rest upon me" (2 Cor.12:8-9).**

3. God's wisdom. He knows what is needed by whom; when it is needed, for whom it is needed, where it is needed, how it is needed, why it is needed.
4. God's mercy. He wills above all else for men to know His mercy. He does whatever is needed to demonstrate His mercy to men. Sometimes walking through the trials of life reveals His mercy more; sometimes removing the trials reveals His mercy more. He chooses the best way for both the sufferer and those who surround him.

QUESTIONS:

1. The question that has puzzled many believers is "why are all sick people not healed?" If someone posed this question to you, how would you respond?
2. Do you personally know someone who was miraculously healed? What were the circumstances behind this miracle?
3. It is easy to put God in a box and limit Him to what He can and cannot do. What limits do you put upon God concerning His power to heal?

4. THE CLEANSED MAN (v.4).

After the leper had been cleansed, he still needed to do two things—two things that every genuine believer must do.

1. The cleansed man had to be aware of pride. The leper had been cleansed and delivered from the pit of defilement. Yet, many uncleansed lepers still remained in the pit. Jesus knew this man's heart, knew that he stood in danger of temptation, the temptation of self-importance. He could easily have gone about saying what is so often heard: "Here, but for the grace of God, go I." Of course, *this was true*. But to go about proclaiming such would have tended to separate him apart as *more favored* than others, and he was not a favorite of God. God has no favorites. He was just a man who had been desperately unclean and whom Christ had cleansed. The cleansed man *needed to pro-*

claim Christ and His cleansing power, not his own cleansing. He deserved nothing, especially the grace of God; therefore, he had no reason to profess, "But for the grace of God...." Such would have been self-centered, prideful, and boastful. Jesus wanted to prevent such a profession.

ILLUSTRATION:
No person is safe from the tentacles of pride. Even after we are on the mountaintop of the greatest blessing, we will soon fall if we do not guard ourselves against pride.

When the English explorer Sir Frances Drake returned from his fifth voyage around the world, he was caught in a storm on the River Thames. As his vessel was tossed about and appeared ready to run aground, the old mariner clenched his fist and said, "Can it be that I who have braved the dangers of the seven seas must now come home and be drowned in a ditch?"[2]

Sir Frances Drake forgot to include God in his formula for success and fell into the trap of pride in the end. We must be careful. Satan often attacks when we least expect it.

2. The cleansed man had to obey the law. Why? Because the healing of a leper was a most unlikely event. If it ever happened, there was a detailed list of laws and rituals the leper had to go through. These rituals gave the priests time to confirm the cure. The rituals were considered to be a thanksgiving offering to God (Lev.14:1-32; cp. 13:38-59). Jesus charged the leper to make his offering to God and to receive the certificate that he was cleansed. Jesus told the man to obey the law for two reasons.
   a. He cared deeply for the cleansed man. He wanted him to be restored, accepted, and reunited with his family and friends. They would accept him only if he was proven to be cured.
   b. He wanted the man to respect God's law and to walk in it for the remainder of his life.

"Jesus answered and said unto him, If a man love me, he will keep my words: and my Father will love him, and we will come unto him, and make our abode with him" (Jn.14:23).

QUESTIONS:
1. How can pride be a danger to the person whom God has touched? What can you do to guard yourself from spiritual pride?
2. Why did Christ insist that the healed leper show himself to the priest? What practical lesson can you gain from this example?

SUMMARY:

Jesus Christ came to cleanse people from their sins. Only He can do this. Any attempt to cleanse yourself is futile. All you can do is ask Christ to cleanse your heart. If you ask, He will cleanse you—completely and wholly. Remember these important points from the lesson:

1. Multitudes followed Jesus. Why was this so? Because His message and authority were strikingly different.

2 *INFOsearch Sermon Illustrations* (Arlington, TX: The Computer Assistant, 1-888-868-9029, 1986-1996).

2. The leper, the most unclean, came to Jesus, asking and trusting Him to cleanse him. The leper dramatically demonstrates that no person is too unclean, too polluted, too dirty, or too sinful to come to Jesus Christ.
3. The Lord Jesus touched and willingly cleansed the man. His heart was deeply affected by the leper, just as He is deeply moved by our needs. Jesus desires to touch and cleanse us just as He did the leper.
4. After the leper had been cleansed, he still needed to do two things—two things that every genuine believer must do:
   ⇒ The cleansed man had to be aware of pride.
   ⇒ The cleansed man had to obey the religious law, thus proving to others that God was at work in his life.

PERSONAL JOURNAL NOTES
(Reflection & Response)

1. The most important thing that I learned from this lesson was:

2. The area that I need to work on the most is:

3. I can apply this lesson to my life by:

4. Closing Statement of Commitment:

B. Jesus Heals a Centurion's Servant: Receiving & Rejecting Men, 8:5-13
(Lk. 7:1-10)

1. Jesus' great power was aroused to receive the rejected
   a. By the centurion's humility
      1) Begged a Jew
      2) Called Jesus *Lord*
      3) Jesus' response: "I will"
   b. By the centurion's sense of unworthiness
   c. By the centurion's love for a slave
   d. By the centurion's great faith
      1) In Jesus' supreme authority & power
      2) In Jesus as Sovereign Lord (v.8)

2 Jesus' great power was aroused to embrace all nationalities
   a. The Roman centurion
   b. The "many" from every place, from all nations

3 Jesus' great power will reject the unbelieving

4. Jesus' great power proved His Messiahship

5 And when Jesus
was entered into Ca-
pernaum, there came
unto him a centurion,
beseeching him,
6 And saying, Lord,
my servant lieth at
home sick of the pal-
sy, grievously tor-
mented.
7 And Jesus saith
unto him, I will come
and heal him.
8 The centurion an-
swered and said,
Lord, I am not worthy
that thou shouldest
come under my roof:
but speak the word
only, and my servant
shall be healed.
9 For I am a man un-
der authority, having
soldiers under me:
and I say to this man,
Go, and he goeth;
and to another,
Come, and he com-
eth; and to my ser-
vant, Do this, and he
doeth it.
10 When Jesus heard
it, he marvelled, and
said to them that fol-
lowed, Verily I say
unto you, I have not
found so great faith,
no, not in Israel.
11 And I say unto
you, That many shall
come from the east
and west, and shall
sit down with Abra-
ham, and Isaac, and
Jacob, in the king-
dom of heaven.
12 But the children
of the kingdom shall
be cast out into outer
darkness: there shall
be weeping and
gnashing of teeth.
13 And Jesus said
unto the centurion,
Go thy way; and as
thou hast believed, so
be it done unto thee.
And his servant was
healed in the self-
same hour.

Section V
THE MESSIAH'S GREAT AUTHORITY AND POWER REVEALED IN WORD AND WORK, Matthew 8:1-9:34

Study 2: JESUS HEALS A CENTURION'S SERVANT: RECEIVING AND REJECTING MEN

Text: **Matthew 8:5-13**

Aim: To fully understand the impact of Christ's power on believers and on unbelievers.

Memory Verse:
"The centurion answered and said, Lord, I am not worthy that thou shouldest come under my roof: but speak the word only, and my servant shall be healed" (Mt.8:8).

MATTHEW 8:5-13

INTRODUCTION

> *A valuable painting had been purchased by F. W. Boreham called "The Chess Player." It portrayed Satan playing the game with a young opponent, and the man's soul was at stake. The game had progressed to the point where it was the novice's turn, and there seemed to be no move he could make that would not mean defeat for him. Awful despair was on his face as he realized his soul was lost, and Satan was grinning as he anticipated victory. A champion player who had come to view the canvas studied the picture for a time and then called for a chessboard. Placing the pieces in exactly the same position as in the painting, he said, "I'll take the young man's place." He then made a move that showed how the devil's captive could have won and been set free.*[1]

In the same sense, Jesus Christ has reached into our world and has taken our place. Christ reached across the barrier between our sin and God's holiness and saved us.

This is a great passage showing that Jesus is definitely the Messiah (v.13). He has the Messianic power to receive men (v.10-11) and to reject men (v.12). He can receive any man who truly trusts Him, no matter how far away the man may be or how many barriers may seem to stand in the way. As Messiah, He also has the power to reject the unbelieving (v.12).

Note the deep emotion felt by Jesus throughout this experience. He was aroused to make the statements He made and to prove His Messianic power (v.5-7, 10-13). Matthew's apparent purpose in recording this miracle was to show that Jesus did possess the Messianic power to do two things.

1. Jesus possessed the power to receive any man, regardless of the barrier. He could span every conceivable barrier.
    a. The ideological barrier: the centurion was a man *rejected*, despised, and hated by the Jews; yet Jesus could reach him and meet his need.
    b. The physical barrier: the centurion's servant was desperately ill and some miles away, yet Jesus could reach the servant. His power could span all the physical barrier, no matter how far away or how severe the condition.
    c. The spiritual barrier: the centurion was a Gentile, considered by the Jews to be lost spiritually, an alien and an enemy to the people of God. But Jesus had the power to reach the man, to pierce the spiritual barriers of his soul and save him.
2. Jesus possessed the power to reject any man, even those who professed to be children of the kingdom, that is, the religious (v.12).

The great faith of the centurion aroused Jesus to show the above. Jesus strongly demonstrated that He receives any man who truly believes, but He rejects those who do not believe, no matter who they are.

OUTLINE:

1. Jesus' great power was aroused to receive the rejected (v.5-9).
2. Jesus' great power was aroused to embrace all nationalities (v.10-11).
3. Jesus' great power will reject the unbelieving (v.12).
4. Jesus' great power proved His Messiahship (v.13).

1. JESUS' GREAT POWER WAS AROUSED TO RECEIVE THE REJECTED (v.5-9).

1. Jesus' power was aroused by the centurion's humility. The man's humility is seen in two most unusual acts.

---

1 *INFOsearch Sermon Illustrations* (Arlington, TX: The Computer Assistant, 1-888-868-9029, 1986-1996).

a. He was a Gentile and a Roman officer, yet he came to a Jew for help. Approaching a Jew was socially unacceptable and unheard of for a Gentile, but being an officer of Rome made it worse. Jesus knew that the centurion had great courage and humility to approach Him for help.
b. The centurion came to Jesus as "Lord," acknowledging His superior being and Messiahship. He approached Him as the One who could meet his need. Note several things.
   ⇒ He *knew and confessed* that he had a need, a need that other men could not meet. Knowing and confessing are both essential when a person really wants a need to be met.
   ⇒ He knew where to go and to whom to go in order to have his need met.
   ⇒ He was willing to do all he could to have his need met. He then trusted Jesus to satisfy his need.

"The LORD is nigh unto them that are of a broken heart; and saveth such as be of a contrite spirit" (Ps.34:18; see also Is.57:15).

Jesus' response to the centurion's cry for help was forceful: "I will." These words declare that Jesus will span and overcome all the barriers and divisions of men to meet a man's need (see point 1 of the Introduction—Mt.8:5-13). He will meet the need of anyone who truly trusts Him: master or servant, nobleman or commoner, parent or child, rich or poor, man or woman, saint or sinner, saved or doomed, capable or helpless, assured or hopeless. Jesus has no favorites. He does not favor one person over another.

"There is no respect of persons with God: but in every nation he that feareth him, and worketh righteousness, is accepted with him" (Acts 10:34-35).

APPLICATION 1:
The greatest of men must approach Jesus *begging*, totally dependent upon Him. There is no other way. Position, power, fame, wealth, and social acceptability must be laid aside. Our thoughts cannot be focused on self or social acceptability, but only upon Christ and His power if we wish Him to meet our need.

APPLICATION 2:
Our thoughts—what our minds are upon—reveal the sincerity of our hearts when approaching Jesus.
1) If our thoughts are focused on self and social acceptability, then our sincerity is weak and lacking. Jesus knows we care more for this world than for Him.
2) If our thoughts are focused on Him and His power, then Jesus knows that we are really depending upon Him to help us, regardless of what others may think or say.

QUESTIONS:
1. A person's position or title can be either a stumblingblock or a stepping stone when seeking Christ. What are the special challenges that a person of influence faces when confronted by Christ?
2. When you pray to the Lord, are you ever tempted to focus upon what you want Him to do instead of being focused upon Him? What can you do to discipline yourself to stay focused upon God?

2. Jesus' power was aroused by the centurion's sense of unworthiness. The centurion did not say, "My servant is not worthy to have you come"; but he said, "I am not worthy." A sense of *personal unworthiness* gripped him. Jesus Christ is the Sovereign

Lord. He alone is the One who has the power to meet our needs. Therefore, we have to confess our inadequacy and unworthiness to have the Lord help us.

> **"And whosoever shall exalt himself shall be abased; and he that shall humble himself shall be exalted" (Mt.23:12; see also Lk.14:11; 18:14).**

APPLICATION:
Socially speaking, the greater proclaimed his inferiority to the lesser. Society considered the centurion greater than the poor preacher from Nazareth. But the centurion humbly confessed a deep unworthiness before Christ. He saw something of God in Christ, something that caused him to humble himself before Christ.
1) We are to see God in Christ.
2) We are to see value in every man, the value that God puts upon even the poorest and most unacceptable. We are to humble ourselves before all, no matter how it may hurt.

> **"Let nothing be done through strife or vainglory; but in lowliness of mind let each esteem other better than themselves. Look not every man on his own things, but every man also on the things of others" (Ph.2:3-4).**

ILLUSTRATION:
It takes a truly humble person to put the needs, hopes, and dreams of others before his own selfish ways. The rules that the world plays by exalt self at the expense of others. The contrary ways of God's kingdom are illustrated by this striking example.

> *The television coverage of the 1984 Summer Olympic Games gave the world some memorable experiences. One of those moments occurred in a commercial that appeared prior to the games. It featured world record holder Bob Beamon seated in front of his TV set. He turned to the camera and said, "Back in the Olympic Games of 1968, I set a world record in the long jump. At the time, some people said no one would ever jump that far again. Well, over the years I've enjoyed sitting in front of my television set and watching them try. But now there's a new kid, I'm told, who might have a chance of breaking my record. Well, there's just one thing I have to say about that." At this point the viewer is set up for some kind of self-centered, defiant comment. Instead, Beamon's face softened, and in a most believable way he said, "I hope you make it, kid."*[2]

Our greatest personal accomplishments can come only when we humble ourselves before God. Who are you pulling for to make it to heaven?

3. Jesus' power was aroused by the centurion's love—his love for a slave. The centurion was pouring out his heart for another person (intercessory prayer). In the eyes of society the person should have been meaningless to him, yet the man meant much to him. He loved this *meaningless* person, this slave.

APPLICATION 1:
What a lesson for us! The great need is for intercessory prayer and love for all, no matter who they are and what others may think.

> **"Thou shalt love thy neighbour as thyself" (Mt.22:39).**

---

2 *INFOsearch Sermon Illustrations* (Arlington, TX: The Computer Assistant, 1-888-868-9029, 1986-1996).

"This is my commandment, That ye love one another, as I have loved you" (Jn.15:12).

APPLICATION 2:
The believer is to love. He is not only to love those close to him, but he is to love all. The centurion loved a slave. Our love can be measured by the centurion's love.

1) How much do we carry the needs of our loved ones to the Lord?
2) How much do we carry the needs of slaves, those alien to us, to the Lord?
3) How much do we look after and care for those of our own household, whether aged and disabled parents or children or spouse (see A CLOSER LOOK # 2—Mt.8:8)?

4. Jesus' power was aroused by the centurion's great faith. The centurion believed in the great power of Jesus to span and to overcome all barriers—even the barrier of time and space. What great faith!

The centurion illustrated perfectly what faith is (Heb.11:6).

⇒ It is believing that *Christ is*: that He is sovereign Lord. All power is subject to Him (Heb.11:6; cp. Mt.8:6).

⇒ It is believing that "Christ is a rewarder of those that diligently seek Him" (Heb.11:6 cp. Mt.8:8-9).

Note that the centurion had diligently sought Christ, believing Christ could meet his need. Many believers so seek the Lord, but what made the centurion's faith so much greater was his belief that the *Word of Christ* was all that was needed. Christ did not have to be present for the need to be met. As a centurion he had authority over men. All he had to do was issue an order and it was carried out, whether he was present or not. He was a sovereign commander. He was saying, "How much more are you, O' Lord. But speak the word only, and my need shall be met." Forceful—powerful: a great lesson on faith for all.

"But without faith it is impossible to please him: for he that cometh to God must believe that he is, and that he is a rewarder of them that diligently seek him" (Heb.11:6).

APPLICATION:
The centurion's faith was great because it was a personal faith in Jesus...

- in Jesus' supreme authority and power
- in Jesus as Sovereign Lord over all: all men and all nature. Note this included himself, a soldier of Rome, the conquering nation; it also included space and time and the physical corruption of disease (cp. Jer.23:23-24). He believed Jesus to be Lord over both the kingdom of nature and the kingdom of heaven.

QUESTIONS:

1. How often are your prayers intercessory, focused on the needs of other people? Is intercessory prayer the duty of only certain people? Why or why not?
2. What is the key to having the same kind of faith that the centurion displayed before Jesus?

A CLOSER LOOK #1
(8:5-9) **Centurion**: an officer in the Roman armed forces. He commanded about one hundred soldiers. To the Jew, the centurion had three things against him: he was bitterly hated because he was non-Jewish, a Gentile; he was of the nation that had conquered Palestine, Rome; and he was a member of the armed and occupying force.

Note the following references to centurions in the New Testament. Every time a centurion is mentioned, it is with honor.

1. There was the centurion who had great faith in the power of Jesus (Matthew 8:5).

2. There was the centurion who recognized Jesus hanging on the cross as the Son of God (Matthew 27:54).

3. There was the centurion Cornelius, who was the first Gentile convert to the Christian church (Acts 10:22).

4. There was the centurion who recognized that Paul was a Roman citizen and rescued him from the rioting mob (Acts 23:17-23).

5. There was the centurion who took steps to deliver Paul from being murdered after being informed of the Jews' plan (Acts 24:23).

6. There was the centurion whom Felix ordered to escort and look after Paul (Acts 24:23).

7. There was the centurion who escorted Paul on his last journey to Rome. He treated Paul with great courtesy and accepted him as the leader when the storm struck the ship (Acts 27:43).

The structure of the Roman military was built around the Roman legion which consisted of 6000 men.

⇒ The Roman legion was divided into cohorts: each cohort had 600 soldiers. This means there were ten cohorts in each legion.

⇒ The cohort was divided into centuries. Each century had 100 men and was led by a centurion. The centurions were the backbone of the Roman legions. They were the leaders in closest contact with the men; therefore, they were the officers upon whom the top brass depended so heavily.[3]

A CLOSER LOOK #2

(8:8) **Slave—Care—Love—Intercession**: this is the only recorded time in Scripture where a person came to Jesus in behalf of a slave or servant. There were several times when parents brought children (Mt.9:18-34; Lk.7:11-18; Jn.4:46-54) and friends brought friends (Lk.18:26), but this soldier and officer brought his servant. Note that the slave, being sick with palsy, would have been completely helpless and useless to the centurion. He was disabled for his work, yet the centurion took care of him. He had not *rejected* him, sent him to some other home, or put him under someone else's care. He had personally *received* the slave with open arms and was looking after him. This was bound to have affected Jesus dramatically.

Jesus used this occasion to strongly demonstrate a much needed lesson: He receives any man who truly believes and rejects any man who does not believe, no matter who he is.

2. JESUS' GREAT POWER WAS AROUSED TO EMBRACE ALL NATIONALITIES (v.10-11).

1. Jesus' power embraced the Roman centurion: Jesus *opened* His heart and arms and *embraced* the centurion. This He did despite the fact that the man was despised and rejected as a Gentile. (Imagine! He was not just a Gentile, but a Roman and a soldier, a citizen and soldier of the nation that enslaved the Jews.) Jesus not only received the centurion, He commended him for his faith. Note: He did not commend him for who he was nor for what he had done as a soldier.

APPLICATION 1:

True belief is a rare thing. Not many truly believe, yet belief in Jesus Christ is one of the greatest qualities of human life—a quality ignored, neglected, and in some cases denied.

---

3 William Barclay. *The Gospel of Matthew*, Vol.1., p.306.

APPLICATION 2:
There are times when recognition and commendation are to be given. But again, note for what: it is for spiritual strength. However, caution should always be exercised lest the temptation of pride and self-importance sets in.

2. Jesus has the power to embrace the "many" from every place, from all nations (see A CLOSER LOOK # 3—Mt.8:11).

> **"Go ye therefore into the highways, and as many as ye shall find, bid to the marriage" (Mt.22:9; see also Jn.7:37).**

APPLICATION:
Who are to be saved? The centurion's faith stirred deep emotion within Christ, emotion so strong that He claimed several things.
1) Many shall come—just as the centurion had come—by faith (Gal.3:14; Eph.2:8-9; cp. Ro.4:11-12, 16).
2) Many shall come—just as the centurion had come—from everywhere, the east and the west (Rev.7:9; 21:24; cp. Mt.24:3).
3) Many shall sit down with Abraham and Isaac and Jacob in heaven (Heb.2:10).

A CLOSER LOOK #3
(8:11) **Gentiles, Conversion**: Jesus used the centurion's great faith to predict a great revival among Gentiles in the future. We, of course, are in the midst of this great Gentile conversion, the Gentile conversion so clearly predicted by our Lord on the memorable day of the centurion's conversion.

1. The centurion had something unusual. He had whatever had given Abraham and Isaac and Jacob their entrance into heaven. *He had faith*. He was a Gentile, not a son of Abraham by birth, but he had just become a son of Abraham by faith (Ro.4:11-12.)

2. The centurion was to do something unusual. He was to "sit down" with Abraham and Isaac and Jacob in heaven. Jesus was saying that salvation shall come to the Gentiles.

3. The centurion was an illustration, a foreshadowing of the coming conversion of the Gentiles.

QUESTIONS:
1. How willing are you to embrace or accept a person who is despised by others? Are you as open as you should be?
2. Do you think Christ ever marvels at your faith? Is that a goal for which every believer should strive?

3. JESUS' GREAT POWER WILL REJECT THE UNBELIEVING (v.12).

The judgment of unbelievers is to be terrible. Note: Jesus predicted that the Jews who persist in unbelief will perish. They will be rejected by God, despite the fact they had been chosen to be the children of God and had been given so many privileges.

1. There will be *outer darkness*: a region, a habitation, a place of pitch black that forbids any sight whatsoever. It is a place without light and without any hope of light whatsoever. It is a place of utter darkness in which one lives completely incapacitated, helpless, and hopeless. It is far away from the splendor, glory, and brightness of God's presence. It is being cast into the gloom and blackness of the outer world. It is misery, the misery of a lost soul.

> **"But the children of the kingdom shall be cast out into outer darkness: there shall be weeping and gnashing of teeth" (Mt.8:12; see also Mt.22:13).**

2. There will be *weeping*: loud grief, mourning, groaning, wailing, and floods and floods of tears.

3. There will be *gnashing of teeth*: grinding the teeth; biting in hostility, bitterness, and indignation; spitefully snapping the teeth. It is rage, fury, and despair because nothing can be done. A person's state is permanently determined.

> **"And cast ye the unprofitable servant into outer darkness: there shall be weeping and gnashing of teeth" (Mt.25:30; see also Ps.112:10).**

APPLICATION:
Entrance into heaven is based upon one thing and one thing only: faith in Christ. Heritage, godly parents or children, religious profession, baptism, or church membership—all are useless without faith. Without faith, man has only the judgment of God to look forward to.

ILLUSTRATION:
We live in a world that places too much faith in man and what man has created—as this story pointedly illustrates:

> *Many years ago a party of mountain climbers began the dangerous descent of one of the peaks in the Swiss Alps. The first man in the line lost his foothold and slipped over the ledge. The next two men were dragged after him, but the experienced climbers above braced themselves and stood firm to bear the shock. However, when the rope ran its length, the cord snapped like a thread. Horrified, the climbers saw their friends spreading their arms and legs in a hopeless attempt to stop their slide over the precipice as they fell to their death on the great glacier 4,000 feet below. For half an hour the other three remained in terrified silence—petrified with fear. Finally they nerved themselves to continue their perilous descent. Hours later they arrived in Zematt to tell their sad story. When the climbers examined the rope to find out why it had not held, they were shocked at what they discovered. True Alpine Club rope has a red strand running through it, but this rope did not have that distinguishing thread. It was a weak substitute.*[4]

QUESTIONS:
1. Eternal separation from God should be a compelling motivation for anyone to get right with God. And yet, so many people still reject Christ and do not believe. In your opinion, why does a person risk hell instead of accepting Christ?
2. A lot of people do not believe in a literal hell. What Scriptures can you use to help convey the reality and horror of it?

4. JESUS' GREAT POWER PROVED HIS MESSIAHSHIP (v.13).

His great power to meet the centurion's request proved His unlimited power as Messiah. Just as Jesus encouraged the centurion, Jesus often encourages us when we seek Him in behalf of others. Jesus said to the centurion, "As you believe, so it shall happen." It was almost like a blank check. In other words, the amount we receive depends on our faith in Him, depends on what we ask!

QUESTIONS:
1. What is the greatest thing you have ever seen God do? Does the power of Christ guarantee you will receive everything you ask for? Why or why not?
2. Is your faith in God what it should be? What would you expect to happen if you prayed and acted with greater faith?

---

4 *INFOsearch Sermon Illustrations* (Arlington, TX: The Computer Assistant, 1-888-868-9029, 1986-1996.)

MATTHEW 8:5-13

SUMMARY:

As we walk throughout life, we are confronted with a choice: either to trust in God's keeping power or trust in man's strength. The way to benefit from the power of Christ is clear, but not always easy: we must ask in faith—trusting. What barriers are you facing today that keep you from trusting Christ? Remember what Jesus' great power did:

1. Jesus' great power was aroused to receive the rejected.
2. Jesus' great power was aroused to embrace all nationalities.
3. Jesus' great power was aroused to reject the unbelieving.
4. Jesus' great power proved His Messiahship.

PERSONAL JOURNAL NOTES
(Reflection & Response)

1. The most important thing that I learned from this lesson was:

2. The area that I need to work on the most is:

3. I can apply this lesson to my life by:

4. Closing Statement of Commitment:

	C. Jesus Heals Peter's Mother-in-Law: Jesus' Power & Its Purpose, 8:14-17 (Mk.1:29-34; Lk.4:38-41)	arose, and ministered unto them. 16 When the even was come, they brought unto him many that were pos- sessed with devils: and he cast out the spirits with his word, and healed all that were sick:	**2. Purpose 2: To meet the needs of the multitude**
1. Purpose 1: To meet the needs of individuals & families a. He visited Peter's home b. He healed Peter's mother-in-law: She arose & served	14 And when Jesus was come into Pe- ter's house, he saw his wife's mother laid, and sick of a fever. 15 And he touched her hand, and the fever left her: and she	17 That it might be fulfilled which was spoken by Esaias the prophet, saying, Him- self took our infirmi- ties, and bare our sicknesses.	**3. Purpose 3: To prove His Messiahship** a. He bore the ultimate cause of disease b. He bore each fresh illness

Section V
THE MESSIAH'S GREAT AUTHORITY AND POWER REVEALED IN WORD AND WORK, Matthew 8:1-9:34

Study 3: JESUS HEALS PETER'S MOTHER-IN-LAW: JESUS' POWER AND ITS PURPOSE

Text: Matthew 8:14-17

Aim: To make a strong commitment, a commitment to minister more and more to a needy world.

Memory Verse:

"That it might be fulfilled which was spoken by Esaias the prophet, saying, Himself took our infirmities, and bare *our* sicknesses" (Mt.8:17).

INTRODUCTION

What kind of attitude do you have when it comes to serving others? If a typical day in your life could be given a book title, which title comes closest to describing you?

1. *Cinderella:* "I'll serve others until my Prince Charming comes along and takes me away to a life of ease where I will live happily ever after."
2. *Moby Dick:* "I feel like I'm being swallowed up by people who always demand something from me."
3. *Prince and the Pauper:* "I'd give anything to switch with someone who has it better than I do."
4. *Robinson Crusoe:* "A deserted island with someone to serve me looks better all the time."
5. *Snow White and the Seven Dwarfs:* "Hi-ho, hi-ho, it's off to serve I go."

One of the purposes for which Jesus came to earth was to meet the needs of individuals and families. The experience in Peter's home shows this.

Jesus was entering Peter's home in order to rest. It was the Sabbath and He had just been ministering in the synagogue, teaching and healing (Mk.1:29; Mk.1:21-34). On the way to Peter's home, He encountered a desperate plea to heal the centurion's servant.

MATTHEW 8:14-17

Now He was tired, very tired; He needed rest. Yet when He entered the home, there was another demand made upon Him. Another person needed help.

How often Jesus must have felt that He could not put one foot in front of the other! He desperately felt the need to collapse into bed, but He went on. Note several things.

1. This was an individual in a single home. There was no crowd, no publicity, no recognition. There was only a simple lady, lying sick in bed.

2. This was the very purpose for which Jesus came: to minister. He loved and had the power to help, so He helped. He did what He could when He could, forgetting all about Himself.

> **"The Son of man came not to be ministered unto, but to minister" (Mt.20:28; see also Lk.19:10).**

OUTLINE:

1. Purpose 1: to meet the needs of individuals and families (v.14-15).
2. Purpose 2: to meet the needs of the multitude (v.16).
3. Purpose 3: to prove His Messiahship (v.17).

1. PURPOSE 1: TO MEET THE NEEDS OF INDIVIDUALS AND FAMILIES (v.14-15)

Christ demonstrated this purpose in two acts.

1. Jesus visited Peter's home as He visited the homes and families of many who ministered with Him. He had a very special care and love for families. Note the individuals involved in this home:

   a. The husband, Peter.
   b. The wife.
   c. The mother-in-law.
   d. The brother-in-law, Andrew.
   e. The friends, James and John (Mk.1:29f).

Also remember the attention Jesus gave to little children (Mt.18:1-4; 19:13-15; Lk.9:46-48; 18:15-17).

> **"For where two or three are gathered together in my name, there am I in the midst of them" (Mt.18:20).**

APPLICATION 1:
No individual or family is too poor or unimportant for Jesus to visit and help. He cares for all.

APPLICATION 2:
Who were Peter's wife and mother-in-law? This is the only time they are mentioned. They represent the quiet and unknown believers. Note that the individual person and family are most important to Jesus. He is not after the recognition of a crowd. He did not serve only when it would gain Him recognition. He willingly ministered quietly, unbeknown to others. He will meet our needs quietly, when we are all alone and unknown to the world.

2. Jesus healed Peter's mother-in-law.

   a. Note what immediately grabbed the attention of Jesus when he entered Peter's house: "He saw his [Peter's] wife's mother...sick of a fever." *Need* grabbed Jesus' attention. His very purpose on earth was to focus on the needs of individuals and families. He cared about their needs, including their sicknesses (cp. Mt.9:18-34; Lk.7:11-17; Jn.4:46-54).

b. Note what Jesus did: He "touched her." There is something special about a touch between individuals.
   1) There is a communication of warmth, tenderness, and caring.
   2) There is also a communication of power when we touch and pray. This power is an infusion of real assurance and confidence over whatever is being prayed. We are assured that "we have the petitions that we desired of Him."

> **"And this is the confidence that we have in him, that, if we ask any thing according to his will, he heareth us: and if we know that he hear us, whatsoever we ask, we know that we have the petitions that we desired of him" (1 Jn.5:14-15).**

c. Note what Peter's mother-in-law did: she arose and began to serve the Lord immediately.
   1) She had been sick with a fever, and she could have sat around for a while claiming weakness and the need to regain her strength.
   2) She was not the head of the house. She could have waited to follow the head or wife of the house. But note: she did neither; she immediately arose and began serving her Lord.

> **"The aged men [must] be sober, grave, temperate, sound in faith, in charity, in patience. The *aged women likewise*, that they be in behaviour as becometh holiness, not false accusers, not given to much wine, teachers of good things" (Tit.2:2-3).**

APPLICATION 1:
What a lesson for us!

- When Jesus touches us, we need to get up immediately and begin serving.
- When Jesus touches us with power, it is not to make us feel important. His touch of power is for service not for feelings of self-importance.
- When Jesus touches us with power, we are not to wait until others begin serving. We are to get up ourselves and launch the ministry of reaching others for the Lord.

Peter's mother-in-law had been favored with the wonderful power of the Lord. She could have felt important enough to be exempt from the menial duties. She could have joined the others waiting to be served.

APPLICATION 2:
"He touched her." Jesus' purpose on earth was to touch individuals and families. There is no question that His touch affected Peter's mother-in-law. She got up and ministered. But His touch was bound to have affected the others also. A touch intimately communicates what a person is trying to say to another person.

ILLUSTRATION:
There are two classes of people in the world today: those who help others and those who do not. Some people live a long, long time before they discover the true meaning of their life here on earth.

> *Here is the losing and finding of life in a person. Marian Preminger was born in Hungary in 1913, raised in a castle with her aristocratic family, surrounded with maids, tutors, governesses, butlers, and chauffeurs. Her grandmother, who lived with them, insisted that whenever they traveled, they take their own linen, for she believed it was beneath their dignity to sleep between sheets used by common people.*

While attending school in Vienna, Marian met a handsome young Viennese doctor. They fell in love, eloped, and married when she was only eighteen. The marriage lasted only a year, and she returned to Vienna to begin her life as an actress.

While auditioning for a play, she met the brilliant young German director, Otto Preminger. They fell in love and soon married. They went to America soon thereafter, where he began his career as a movie director. Unfortunately and tragically, Hollywood is a place of dramatic illustrations of people "biting, devouring, and consuming" one another. Marian was caught up in the glamour, lights, and superficial excitement and soon began to live a sordid life. When Preminger discovered it, he divorced her.

Marian returned to Europe to live the life of a socialite in Paris. In 1948 she learned through the newspaper that Albert Schweitzer, the man she had read about as a little girl, was making one of his periodic visits to Europe and was staying at Gunsbach. She phoned his secretary and was given an appointment to see Dr. Schweitzer the next day. When Marian arrived in Gunsbach she discovered he was in the village church playing the organ. She listened and turned pages of music for him. After a visit he invited her to have dinner at his house. By the end of the day she knew she had discovered what she had been looking for all her life. She was with him every day thereafter during his visit, and when he returned to Africa he invited her to come to Lambarene and work in the hospital.

Marian did—and found herself. There in Lambarene, the girl who was born in a castle and raised like a princess, who was accustomed to being waited on with all the luxuries of a spoiled life, became a servant. She changed bandages, bathed babies, fed lepers — and became free. Marian wrote her autobiography and called it All I Ever Wanted Was Everything. *She could not get the "everything" that would satisfy and give meaning until she could give everything. When she died in 1979, the New York Times carried her obituary, which included this statement from her: "Albert Schweitzer said there are two classes of people in this world—the helpers, and the nonhelpers. I'm a helper."* [1]

QUESTIONS:

1. Jesus spent a lot of time visiting people in their homes. What were some of His reasons for doing this? What lessons from this can you apply to your own life?
2. Why is "touch" such a powerful thing between individuals?
3. What response does Christ expect from you when He touches your life?

A CLOSER LOOK #1

(8:14) **Peter**: note these facts about Peter's home life and family tree.

1. Peter had a wife. He was to live some forty or more years, so he and his wife were probably newlyweds when Christ called him. Interestingly, tradition says that Peter's wife served with him in the ministry. William Barclay quotes a touching picture by Clement of Alexandria who said that she was martyred with Peter: "On seeing his wife led to death, Peter rejoiced on account of her call and her conveyance home, and called very encouragingly and comfortingly, addressing her by name, 'Remember thou the Lord.'"[2] There is strong evidence that Peter was martyred by crucifixion in Rome. Tradition says he felt so unworthy to be crucified like his Lord that he begged to be crucified upside down.

2. Peter had a house. He was formerly from Bethsaida (Jn.1:44). Here he is seen in Capernaum. After Jesus called him to be an apostle, he probably moved to Caper-

---

1 *Illustrations Unlimited.* James S. Hewett, Editor. (Wheaton, IL: Tyndale House Publishers, Inc., 1988), p. 359.

2 *Stromateis* 7:6. Quoted by William Barclay. *The Gospel of Matthew*, Vol.1, p.313.

naum where the headquarters of Jesus was located.

3. Peter looked after his mother-in-law. Apparently she was old and widowed and needed to be cared for by her children. Peter demonstrated real compassion and a tenderness of heart in allowing her to live with his family.

4. Peter opened his home to guests. Mark says that the home was that of Peter and Andrew; however, it was probably owned by Peter, since his wife and mother-in-law are mentioned. Note that Jesus, James, and John were being entertained by Peter as guests (Mk.1:29f). It is possible that Jesus stayed at Peter's home when in Capernaum, and that Peter's home was Jesus' headquarters.

5. Peter's father was Jona or Jonah (Jn.21:15-17). He had at least one brother, Andrew (Jn.1:41).

2. PURPOSE 2: TO MEET THE NEEDS OF THE MULTITUDE (v.16).

Note three things.

1. Jesus was tired; he was finally getting some rest. But the people heard He was in town and their needs were desperate. They began to gather at the door begging Him to help them.
   a. He was faced with man's unceasing cry for help.
   b. He gave up His rest in order to help. He walked on earth for that very purpose.
   c. He turned no one away. He "healed all." As long as there was one person who needed Him, He helped.

2. Jesus was desperately needed by the world, as pictured in this scene. Not all the city came, just as all the world does not come today. But some did come. Who? Those who knew and confessed their need for His help.
   a. It is for the ones who are "lost" that He has come.

   > **"For the Son of man is come to seek and to save that which was lost" (Lk.19:10).**

   b. It is for the ones who are "sick," the ones who need the Physician, that He has come.

   > **"But go ye and learn what that meaneth, I will have mercy, and not sacrifice: for I am not come to call the righteous, but sinners to repentance" (Mt.9:13; see also Mt.20:28).**

   c. It is for all who would "come" that He has come.

   > **"Come unto me, all ye that labour and are heavy laden, and I will give you rest" (Mt.11:28).**

3. Jesus had the power to help all. The word "all" is emphasized. There was no need—no matter how desperate—that His power could not reach.
   a. His power could "cast out the spirits" of evil (demons). He proved His power over Satan. He had the power to overthrow and destroy Satan.

   > **"Now is the judgment of this world: now shall the prince of this world be cast out" (Jn.12:31; see also Heb.2:14; 1 Jn.3:8).**

   b. His power could meet *all* needs, no matter how desperate. Note the words, "He healed all." The emphasis is upon *all*.

   > **"How God anointed Jesus of Nazareth with the Holy Ghost and**

with power: who went about doing good, and healing all that were oppressed of the devil; for God was with him" (Acts 10:38).

QUESTIONS:
1. A picture of Jesus' humanity is seen in His physical fatigue—He was tired. When you are weary, how do you respond when needy people demand your immediate attention?
2. What kind of people need Jesus Christ?
3. Is there anyone whom Christ cannot help? Is there anything that Jesus Christ cannot do? Explain your answers.

3. PURPOSE 3: TO PROVE HIS MESSIAHSHIP (v.17).

Jesus was the Messiah. His ministry was beyond question a fulfillment of the Scriptures that predicted the Messiah. This is clearly seen in that He is the "Ideal Servant of God"; that is, He did not just heal our sicknesses as any other minister, but He "Himself took our infirmities, and bore our sicknesses." This means at least two things.

1. He bore our infirmities and sicknesses to the ultimate degree when He died on the cross for us. It was there that He bore them (see A CLOSER LOOK *# 2*—Mt.8:17 for discussion). (Cp.Jn.1:29.)
2. He bore each fresh illness in a way that will never be understood.
   a. Each need that stood before Him was *a reminder* that He had to bear the sin of the world. He knew what it meant to bear the sin of the world and all that it was to include. So seeing the needs of men standing before Him reminded Him of the suffering He was to bear.
   b. Each need that He met was a foretaste of the cross. The thought of what He had to bear was upon His mind day by day and hour by hour as He went about ministering. This was bound to weigh ever so heavily upon Him.
      ⇒ Mark says that *virtue*, that is, power, went out of Him when He healed (Mk.5:30; cp.Lk.8:46).
      ⇒ He sighed heavily at one miracle (Mk.7:34).
      ⇒ He experienced deep emotion when raising Lazarus from the dead (Jn.11:33).

The following is a simple yet descriptive way to picture how Jesus bore our sins for us.

1. He bore our sins *for us*: "in His own body on the tree" (1 Pt.2:24; cp. Is.53:4-6).

> **"Who his own self bare our sins in his own body on the tree, that we, being dead to sins, should live unto righteousness: by whose stripes ye were healed" (1 Pt.2:24).**

2. He bore our sins *off and from us*: removed, lifted them off us. He has "carried away" our sins (Mt.8:17). "He has cast our sins into the depths of the sea" (Mic.7:19) and as far as "the east is from the west" (Ps.103:12).

> **"He will turn again, he will have compassion upon us; he will subdue our iniquities; and thou wilt cast all their sins into the depths of the sea" (Mic.7:19; see also Ps.103:12).**

3. He bears our sins *with us*. He can be "touched with the feelings of our infirmities" (Heb.4:15-16).

> **"For we have not an high priest which cannot be touched with the feeling of our infirmities; but was in all points tempted like as we are, yet without sin. Let us therefore come boldly unto the throne of grace,**

that we may obtain mercy, and find grace to help in time of need" (Heb.4:15-16).

APPLICATION:
There is only one sure provision for the needs of the human soul: Jesus Christ. Our needs cannot be met...
- by philosophy and psychology
- by mental and physical health

Jesus Christ alone is "the way, the truth, and the life" (Jn.14:6). When we turn to Him, then we will come to know the *comfort and support* needed to walk through life.

ILLUSTRATION:
Why does Jesus Christ have the right to lay claim on our lives? Why does He have the right to require believers to serve Him as Lord and Savior? For the answer, we have only to look at His nail-scarred hands.

"Would you take a bullet for the President?" That is the question that everyone who seeks a career as a member of the Secret Service must answer. On March 30, 1991, the answer to this question was put to a dramatic test. As President Ronald Reagan exited from a Washington hotel, he was attacked by a crazed man, John Hinkley, Jr. As the shots were fired, the President's bodyguards went into action. Reagan was pushed toward the car door as one of his bodyguards shielded the President with his body, taking the lethal bullet that was meant to assassinate Reagan, saving his life. Fortunately, the Secret Service agent survived his injury.

In the same sense, Jesus Christ took the bullet of sin for us. Christ spread His arms open wide, bearing the brunt of sin's impact for us. Unlike the heroic Secret Service agent, Christ's brave act cost Him His life. The nail prints on His hands and feet are a lasting reminder of His great love for us.

Hands that formed the world in which we live
Hands that care for our deepest need and will always give
Hands that reached into our darkened lives of sin
Hands that bear the scars of love, now we are born again

A CLOSER LOOK #2
(8:17) **Disease—Sickness—Corruption**: the ultimate cause of corruption is sin and evil in the world (Gen.2:15-3:7). An imperfect and corruptible world produces the seed of imperfection and incompleteness. It produces the seed of aging and deterioration until finally all waste away. Imperfection, sin, and disease are just the way of a world that is imperfect. The seed of corruption eats away until all become diseased and sick and ready for the grave. But this is the object of the glorious gospel, to proclaim...
- that Jesus bore the world's corruption, its disease and sickness (Ro.8:19-23; cp. Is.53:4).
- that Jesus bore the sins and evil of men (1 Pt.2:24).

Jesus also promises to intervene and recreate a new heaven and earth—a new heaven and earth that will be incorruptible and eternal (2 Pt.3:10-13; Rev.21:1f). He furthermore promises that the man who believes in Him has everlasting life and will be a citizen of the new heavens and earth. The believer will never be condemned to corruption and death, but he passes from death to life the very moment he trusts Jesus Christ as his Savior (Jn.5:24).

MATTHEW 8:14-17

QUESTIONS:
1. What day-to-day consequences do sin and evil produce in the world today?
2. What does it mean to you personally that Jesus Christ takes your infirmities and bears your sins on a daily basis?

SUMMARY:

Being a servant of Christ is one of the greatest purposes and motivations a person can have. Jesus has set the standard for living a life full of purpose. Your great task is to learn from His shining example.

Purpose 1: to meet the needs of individuals and families. Christ demonstrated this purpose in two acts.
- ⇒ Jesus visited Peter's home, as He visited the homes and families of many who ministered with Him. He had a very special care and love for families.
- ⇒ Jesus healed Peter's mother-in-law.

Purpose 2: to meet the needs of the multitude. As long as there was one person who needed Him, He helped.

Purpose 3: to prove the Messiahship of Christ. His ministry was beyond question a fulfillment of the Scriptures that predicted the Messiah. This is clearly seen in that He is the "Ideal Servant of God."

PERSONAL JOURNAL NOTES
(Reflection & Response)

1. The most important thing that I learned from this lesson was:

2. The area that I need to work on the most is:

3. I can apply this lesson to my life by:

4. Closing Statement of Commitment:

	D. Jesus Attracts People: The Cost of True Discipleship, 8:18-22 (Lk.9:57-62)	goest.	mined
		20 And Jesus saith unto him, The foxes have holes, and the birds of the air have nests; but the Son of man hath not where to lay his head.	c. Jesus demanded more 1) Accept Him as the Son of Man 2) Live a life of selflessness 3) Abandon all
1. The multitude was attracted	18 Now when Jesus saw great multitudes about him, he gave commandment to depart unto the other side.	21 And another of his disciples said unto him, Lord, suffer me first to go and bury my father.	**3. The average disciple was attracted** a. He hesitated b. He had divided attention
2. The scholar was attracted a. He willed to follow b. He was deter-	19 And a certain scribe came, and said unto him, Master, I will follow thee whithersoever thou	22 But Jesus said unto him, Follow me; and let the dead bury their dead.	c. Jesus demanded more d. Immediate loyalty e. A sense of urgency

Section V
THE MESSIAH'S GREAT AUTHORITY AND POWER REVEALED IN WORD AND WORK,
Matthew 8:1-9:34

Study 4: JESUS ATTRACTS PEOPLE: THE COST OF TRUE DISCIPLESHIP

Text: Matthew 8:18-22

Aim: To learn the essential requirements of being a true disciple of Christ.

Memory Verse:

INTRODUCTION

People who are serious about searching for truth are attracted by several things:

⇒ They want something that works.
⇒ They want something that is real.
⇒ They want something that is an improvement over what they currently have.

Look at your life for a moment. Does your faith "work"? Is your Christianity "real"? Is your life as a believer appealing enough to attract others to follow? Is it an improvement over what the world has to offer?

Jesus Christ attracts people. He has made such an impact upon the world that human history itself measures its years by the date of His birth and death (BC—before Christ, and AD—anno Domini, in the year of the Lord). Jesus predicted: "And I, if I be lifted up from the earth [the cross], will draw all men unto me" (Jn.12:32).

OUTLINE:

1. The multitude was attracted (v.18).
2. The scholar was attracted (v.19).
3. The average disciple was attracted (v.21-22).

1. THE MULTITUDE WAS ATTRACTED (v.18).

Note that the multitude gathered about Jesus because they had desperate needs, and He was meeting their needs out of a heart of deep compassion (cp. Mt.8:16-17). The whole countryside and surrounding towns were swarming with people who had heard that He was in Capernaum, and they had flocked to Him. They were attracted to what they were hearing, ever hoping to have their needs met.

APPLICATION 1:
People often come to Jesus Christ because of *what they can get out of Him*. Men have a faint idea and some understanding that He can meet needs, so when they face bad situations they come to Him and to the church for help. Jesus said it well:

> **"Jesus answered them and said, Verily, verily, I say unto you, Ye seek me, not because ye saw the miracles, but because ye did eat of the loaves, and were filled" (Jn.6:26; cp. Jn.6:5-26).**

APPLICATION 2:
There are several reasons why the multitude is attracted to Jesus.

1) Some like what they see: lives are changed for good; people are helped; ministry is carried on for the public good; and good works abound. Some people agree with what is being done—at least in spirit—and they are perfectly willing to be identified with such a movement.
2) Some profess Christ and belong to a church because of the image and social standing it brings. Professing Christ, even if it is done quietly or silently, opens doors. Membership in Christ's church is even listed and expected by some employers when hiring personnel. Belonging to a church helps to show a well-rounded and moral person. Some just want the image that profession of faith conveys.
3) Some follow Christ and His church because of family and friends. They are urged to belong to a church; therefore, they profess and attend—some regularly, others irregularly.
4) Some feel more comfortable following Christ and attending church. Their consciences would bother them if they did not profess Him and attend church at least occasionally. They profess and attend only enough to feel comfortable and to keep their consciences subdued.
5) Some have a faint understanding of God. They want to be approved and accepted by Him. They know that they must show some interest in Him if they wish Him to show interest in them, looking after and caring for them. So they profess Him and attend church as much as they deem necessary in order to secure His approval and care.
6) Some have seen God's power to change lives and to deliver through terrible trials. It may have been in the life of a family member, a friend, a fellow employee, a relative, or a distant acquaintance. But the power of Christ was clearly evident. Thus, they know that Christ and His church might be able to help them when trouble comes.
7) Some believe Jesus is the Savior, the promised Messiah, and they want to be identified with Him. So they follow Him and His church.

What the multitude missed is stated very pointedly by Christ in answer to the multitude's question.

> **"What shall we do, that we might work the works of God? Jesus answered and said unto them, This is the work of God, that ye believe on Him whom He hath sent" (Jn.6:28-29).**

Christ also gave another forceful answer on another occasion.

> **"And He said to them all, If any man will come after me, let him deny himself, and take up His cross daily, and follow me" (Lk.9:23).**

ILLUSTRATION:
Many people exist in darkness without even knowing it. They are unaware of the value of living in the light. For this reason, we must shine brightly for Christ. The light that shines consistently will eventually draw others to the light of Christ.

> *In order to convince the people of Philadelphia of the advantages of street lighting, Benjamin Franklin decided to show his neighbors how compelling a single light could be. He bought an attractive lantern, polished the glass, and placed it on a long bracket that extended from the front of his house. Each evening as darkness descended, he ignited the wick. His neighbors soon noticed the warm glow in front of his residence. Even those living farther down the street and in the next block were attracted by Franklin's light. Passers-by found that the light helped them to avoid tripping over protruding stones in the roadway. Soon others placed lanterns in front of their homes, and eventually the city recognized the need for having well-lighted streets.*[1]

QUESTIONS:
1. Is the light of your life attracting your neighbors to Christ? Or would they be shocked to find out you are a Christian?
2. There are many reasons why people are attracted to Jesus Christ. What originally attracted you to seek Him?

2. THE SCHOLAR WAS ATTRACTED (v.19).

Note that this man was a disciple, a follower of Jesus (v.21). The scholar believed Jesus to be the most superior teacher he had ever seen. He himself was a teacher by profession, and he was enormously attracted to the teaching ability of Jesus.

1. The scholar yearned to follow Jesus. The depth of his desire was most unusual, for there was constant conflict between Jesus and the scholar's professional peers.
   a. Jesus opposed the legalistic traditions of the Scribes and other religionists, strongly opposed them. He said so in no uncertain terms, condemning them with such language that only God Himself would dare use (cp. Lk.11:37-54; see A CLOSER LOOK # 1—Mt.8:19).
   b. The Scribes opposed Jesus with deep hostility, even to the point of plotting to kill Him (Lk.11:52-54; Jn.7:1f).
2. The scholar proclaimed his willingness to go anyplace. Note his words: he said he *was willing* to go anyplace. This too is most unusual, for he worked in a quiet atmosphere where he could copy and teach the law. Being around Jesus, who was surrounded by multitudes of people including children, was anything but quiet.
3. Jesus demanded more: being willing to follow Jesus was not enough. Being willing to go to the ends of the earth was not enough. Jesus said three things were essential for the man to become a disciple.
   a. The man had to accept Jesus as the Son of Man (see A CLOSER LOOK # 2—Mt.8:20).
   b. The man had to know personal poverty, that is, Jesus demands total abandonment of self. He demands first place in a person's life, the surrender of all material goods and things under His control. A slave's will and possessions must be subjected to his lord. The Christian is a slave who follows the Lord Jesus as absolute Lord, or else he does not follow Him at all.

> **"Then Peter began to say unto him, Lo, we have left all, and have followed thee" (Mk.10:28).**

   c. The man had to abandon all: for Christ and His mission—*all he was and had.*

---

1 *INFOsearch Sermon Illustrations* (Arlington, TX: The Computer Assistant, 1-888-868-9029, 1986-1996).

MATTHEW 8:18-22

"And he said to them all, If any man will come after me, let him deny himself, and take up his cross daily, and follow me. For whosoever will save his life shall lose it: but whosoever will lose his life for my sake, the same shall save it" (Lk.9:23-24).

APPLICATION 1:
Some scholars, the intelligencia of the world—the teacher, the wealthy, the famous, the powerful—desire to follow Jesus; but they stumble at the demands that require *more*.

1) Some stumble over confessing Jesus to be *the Son of Man*. Every belief and doctrine that points to His deity is questioned and doubted or even denied. They have difficulty doing what Jesus told this Scribe to do: follow Him as *the Son of Man*, as God's very own Son, begotten of Him (Jn.3:16). They suggest problems with the virgin birth and Incarnation, with the godly power and miraculous works, with the death, resurrection, ascension, exaltation, and with the spiritual and intercessory ministry of Jesus Christ. They are attracted to Him as the greatest of all teachers, but they are just unwilling to follow Him as *the Lord*, as God Himself incarnate in human flesh.
2) Some stumble over personal poverty. Giving and working diligently in order to give more is foreign to them. Giving to the point that they would have to trust Christ for the necessities of life is unknown (cp. Mt.1:24-34). They have allowed the world to influence them. They seek the material security and comfort of this world. They save, lay up, and insure. They ignore the fact that this world's wealth fluctuates up and down and is subject to collapse ever so quickly because of the unexpected. They excuse their hoarding with the interpretation that a person must be *willing* to give all he has, not really give it. They feel that it is the willingness to give that Jesus is really after. A person does not necessarily have to give it all. However, this argument fails to see a critical point. What Christ says to the scholar, He says to all:
   ⇒ "Being willing is not enough. You must give all. *Being willing is following and doing*. I have no luxuries, not even a place to lay my head. I have given all. You must give all if you wish to follow me." (Cp. Mt.19:16-22.) Few of us are willing to pay this kind of price to follow Christ. Are you? Am I? Are we willing to give *all we are and have*?
3) Some stumble over total abandonment of themselves and their possessions

APPLICATION 2:
Many are committed, but their commitments are *self-commitments* not Christ-commitments. We must realize that self-commitment involves great willingness, determination, and discipline—so much so that people often follow through in a great way. But self-commitment is not enough for Christ. There has to be a total commitment *to the Son of Man*, abandoning all of self and all of the world for Him and His cause.

QUESTIONS:
1. A lot of people are intrigued by the man Jesus Christ and His teachings, but they have no interest in becoming one of His disciples. What does total commitment really mean? Why does Christ require total commitment from His disciples?
2. If a "willingness" was all that it took to follow the Lord, more people would be on their way to heaven. But no matter how willing a person is, he still must act upon his willingness. What is the key to putting faith in action?
3. Is it possible for a person to be committed to a religious organization but not to Christ? How can you identify and witness to this type of person?
4. Have your material possessions ever hindered you from following Christ more fully? How and why?

A CLOSER LOOK #1

(8:19) **Scribe**: the Scribes were a profession of men sometimes called lawyers. They were some of the most devoted and committed men to religion in all of history and were of the sect known as the Pharisees. However, every Pharisee was not a Scribe. A Scribe was more scholarly, more highly trained than the average Pharisee.

1. The Scribes copied the written law, the Old Testament Scriptures. In their copying function, they were strict copiers, meticulously keeping count of every letter in every word. This exactness was necessary, for God Himself had given the written law to the Jewish nation. Therefore, the law was not only the very Word of God, it was the greatest thing in the life of the Jewish nation. It was considered the most precious possession in all the world; consequently, the Jewish nation was committed to the preservation of the law (Neh. 8:1-8). A young Jew could enter no greater profession than the profession of Scribes.

2. The Scribes studied, classified, and taught the moral law. This function brought about the Oral or Scribal Law that was so common in Jesus' day. It was the law of rules and regulations. There were, in fact, so many regulations that over fifty large volumes were required when they were finally put into writing. The great tragedy was that through the centuries, the Jews began to place the Oral law over the written law.

The Scribes felt that the law was God's final word. Everything God wanted man to do could be deduced from it; therefore, they drew out of the law every possible rule they could and insisted that life was to be lived in conformity to these rules. Rules were to be a way of life, the preoccupation of a man's thoughts. At first these rules and regulations were taught by word of mouth; however, in the third century after Christ, they were put into certain writings.

The Halachoth: rules that were to govern the ritual of worship

The Talmud: made up of two parts

⇒ The Mishnah: sixty-three discussions of various subjects of the law

⇒ Germara: the sacred legends of the people

Midrashim: the commentaries on the writings

Hagada: thoughts on the commentaries

A CLOSER LOOK #2

(8:20) **The Son of Man**: Jesus is not only what an ordinary man is, a son of man; Jesus is what every man ought to be, the Son of Man Himself. He is the Ideal Man, the Representative Man, the Perfect Man, the Pattern, the Embodiment of everything a man ought to be. Jesus Christ is the perfect picture of a man. Everything God wants a man to be is seen perfectly in Jesus Christ (cp. Jn.1:14; Col.2:9-10; Heb.1:3).

The title also means the Ideal Servant of man. It stresses His sympathy for the poor, the broken-hearted, the captive, the blind, the bruised, the outcast, the bereaved (cp.Lk.4:18). Jesus is the Pattern, the Model, the Perfect Example of concern and caring. He served and set a perfect example of how every man ought to serve other men.

Jesus calls Himself "the Son of Man" about eighty times. It is His favorite term. The title "Son of Man" is probably based upon the Son of Man in Daniel (Dan.7:13-14). Scripture also gives a picture of Jesus as the heavenly Son of Man contrasted with Adam as the earthly Man (1 Cor.15:45-47). Each serves as a Representative Man for the human race in God's plan for world history.

"But that ye may know that the Son of man hath power on earth to forgive sins, (then saith he to the sick of the palsy,) Arise, take up thy bed, and go unto thine house" (Mt.9:6).

QUESTIONS:

1. What positive contributions did the Scribes make during the time of Christ? What did they do that placed the Jewish people into bondage? What lessons can the modern Bible student learn from the Scribes?
2. It is hard for a person to follow Christ with total abandonment. Who is the most committed person that you know? What traits are seen in him/her that can help you follow Christ more closely?

3. THE AVERAGE DISCIPLE WAS ATTRACTED (v.21-22).

The call of God came to this man, yet he hesitated. Note three facts.

1. His hesitation was legitimate. Caring for parents is essential. His father was either already dead or on the verge of death. He was legitimately needed.

2. His problem was divided attention. When he felt God's call, he looked at his situation and did not yield immediately. What happened is what so often happens. The man's circumstances and problems overwhelmed him. He wanted to wait and to handle them. Then as soon as the problems were handled, he would go and follow Jesus.

> **"If any man come to me, and hate not his father, and mother, and wife, and children, and brethren, and sisters, yea, and his own life also, he cannot be my disciple. And whosoever doth not bear his cross, and come after me, cannot be my disciple" (Lk.14:26-27).**

3. Jesus demanded more. He saw through the man's partial commitment. He saw his lack of trust in God. Christ expects us to care for our parents (1 Tim.5:3-8); but He demands an immediate response, an immediate loyalty, demands that we put Him first and follow Him with a sense of urgency.

> **"Jesus saith unto them, My meat is to do the will of him that sent me, and to finish his work" (Jn.4:34).**

APPLICATION 1:
Some reject and subdue the call of God, using their parents or family as the excuse. These are warned and the words to them are serious: they are "not worthy of me," Christ says (Mt.10:37-39).

APPLICATION 2:
All excuses are inadequate. God knows what He is doing when he calls a person. What He wants is trust, total trust. Think about it: there is no better time to call a person than when he faces some unusual trial or circumstance. What better time for a person to demonstrate and to be taught complete trust?

APPLICATION 3:
Note two critical matters.

1) A called person can use anything as an excuse to delay God's call. That is the point of recording this disciple's experience. His excuse was the most legitimate excuse possible: to care for his family. All other excuses carry less weight.
2) A called person is to let the world take care of worldly matters (2 Tim.2:4). He is to follow Christ immediately with a great sense of urgency.

A CLOSER LOOK #3
(8:21-22) **Discipleship**: the words of this disciple show that he sensed *a call* from God. He is characteristic of many who call Jesus "Lord" with their mouths, but fail to make Him Lord of their lives. They have heard the call of Jesus and have a desire to follow

Him, but they put off the actual act of obedience. They allow other concerns to prevent immediate discipleship. They deceive themselves, thinking there will be a more convenient time later on. It is possible that this man's father was living, but elderly, needing his son to care for him. He was merely asking Jesus to wait until his father died and no longer needed his attention—a commendable request. The element of abandonment and complete trust was simply missing. When there is movement within a person's heart to follow Jesus, the moment must be grasped.

QUESTIONS:

1. What effect do circumstances have upon a person's responding to God's call?
2. You cannot hide behind a shallow confession or a lofty title. The person who truly wants to follow Christ must be totally committed to Him. What do you need to do today that will make you a more committed believer?
3. What are some of the more common excuses a person uses in order to avoid or delay God's call? Why are all excuses to God inadequate?
4. When is the best time to respond to the call of God? Why?

SUMMARY:

Jesus Christ reaches out and attracts people to Himself from every level of society. His irresistible love acts like a Divine magnet that pulls the human heart to Himself. The challenge for each believer is to be a strong testimony for Christ, a testimony that will attract others to Christ. The believer's testimony is to be so strong that...

1. The multitude will be attracted to Christ.
2. The scholar will be attracted to Christ.
3. The average disciple will be attracted to Christ.

PERSONAL JOURNAL NOTES
(Reflection & Response)

1. The most important thing that I learned from this lesson was:

2. The area that I need to work on the most is:

3. I can apply this lesson to my life by:

4. Closing Statement of Commitment:

MATTHEW 8:23-27

	E. Jesus Calms a Storm: Conquering Fear & Nature, 8:23-27 (Mk.4:35-41; Lk.8:22-25)	25 And his disciples came to him, and awoke him, saying, Lord, save us: we perish.	**4. A desperate approach: Lord, awake—save us**
1. A basic fact: True disciples follow Him no matter what	23 And when he was entered into a ship, his disciples followed him.	26 And he saith unto them, Why are ye fearful, O ye of little faith? Then he arose, and rebuked the winds and the sea; and there was a great calm.	**5. A challenging question** a. Why are you so fearful? b. Why so little faith? **6. A strong, powerful deliverance: A great calm**
2. A fearful experience: A great storm arose **3. A terrifying discovery: Man is not able to handle the situation**	24 And, behold, there arose a great tempest in the sea, insomuch that the ship was covered with the waves: but he was asleep.	27 But the men marvelled, saying, What manner of man is this, that even the winds and the sea obey him!	**7. A marvelous purpose** a. To prove who He is b. To strengthen faith c. To demonstrate His care for all

Section V
THE MESSIAH'S GREAT AUTHORITY AND POWER REVEALED IN WORD AND WORK, Matthew 8:1-9:34

Study 5: JESUS CALMS A STORM: CONQUERING FEAR AND NATURE

Text: **Matthew 8:23-27**

Aim: To gain more and more confidence in God's ability to grant peace through any storm of life.

Memory Verse:

"And he saith unto them, Why are ye fearful, O ye of little faith? Then he arose, and rebuked the winds and the sea; and there was a great calm" (Mt.8:26).

INTRODUCTION

The human mind is often attacked by fear, all kinds of fears. For instance:

⇒ If I fail to perform adequately, I will lose the position or job or be considered a loser.
⇒ If I begin this business, it might fail.
⇒ If I fly in an airplane, it might crash.
⇒ If I speak up, I might be thought ignorant or be ridiculed.
⇒ If I follow the Lord, life might get really hard.

But ask yourself this question: If Christ is truly the Lord of all, what power should fear have over you? This leads us to a most important point: when we go through the storms and fears of life, it is vital that we place our trust in Jesus Christ, not in self and not in the things of this world. Only Christ can give peace in place of fear. This is clearly seen in this important portion of Scripture.

What was the purpose of this experience? Why was a storm allowed to arise on the sea with Christ in the boat? The answer is given in v.27. And what a marvelous purpose it was: to stir His people to ask, "What manner of man is this?" He proved again that He is the Messiah! Calming the storm did three things.

1. It demonstrated who He is: the Sovereign Lord who has all power—even power over nature.
2. It strengthened the belief of His followers: belief in Him as the Messiah and in His personal care as their Savior.
3. It gave to all generations a picture of His care and power—His care and power to deliver through all the storms of life (trials and fearful experiences).

OUTLINE:

1. A basic fact: true disciples follow Him no matter what (v.23).
2. A fearful experience: a great storm arose (v.24).
3. A terrifying discovery: man is not able to handle the situation (v.24).
4. A desperate approach: Lord, awake—save us (v.25).
5. A challenging question (v.26).
6. A strong, powerful deliverance: a great calm (v.26).
7. A marvelous purpose (v.27).

1. A BASIC FACT: TRUE DISCIPLES FOLLOW HIM NO MATTER WHAT (v.23).

The words "His disciples followed Him" are significant. His disciples followed Him wherever He went. They had made a genuine commitment; they were now committed to following Him regardless of the circumstances and the cost. We have some idea of the sacrifice His disciples made through a glimpse into Peter's family (Mt.8:14-17). Remember, Peter and the others had left home, seldom to return, at least for any length of time. Just imagine the cost, the enormous sacrifice it was for them and their families!

> **"So likewise, whosoever he be of you that forsaketh not all that he hath, he cannot be my disciple" (Lk.14:33).**

APPLICATION 1:
How many are willing to follow Jesus regardless of circumstances, cost, and the sacrifice demanded?

> **"He that loveth father or mother more than me is not worthy of me: and he that loveth son or daughter more than me is not worthy of me. And he that taketh not his cross, and followeth after me, is not worthy of me" (Mt.10:37-38).**

APPLICATION 2:
Not everyone follows Jesus. It was only a short distance around the lake (twelve miles) and only eight miles across. Jesus could have easily walked around the lake, but He chose to go by sea in order to rest and to share this experience with the disciples. But note: there is nothing said about the multitudes following Him now, not as they had followed after the Sermon on the Mount (8:1). Why were they not following?

1) The extra distance? (The effort required to follow Jesus was just too demanding.)
2) The potentially dangerous storms as one journeyed? (The journey to follow Jesus involved too many storms of abuse and ridicule, persecution and questions.)

3) The cost of passage? (The cost of following Jesus required too much sacrifice, the denial of too many creature comforts.)
4) The unbelief and dislike of His miracles and claims?

QUESTIONS:
1. What kinds of situations would keep you from following the Lord?
2. The person who really loves Jesus Christ will follow Him—no matter the circumstance. When is the most difficult time for you to follow Christ?
3. What is the greatest sacrifice you have made in order to follow Christ?

2. A FEARFUL EXPERIENCE: A GREAT STORM AROSE (v.24).

This was a most fearful experience; the apostles' very lives were threatened (v.25). The waves were covering the boat (v.24). It was, so to speak, a trial of trials. If Jesus could teach them His care through this experience, they would know He could take care of them through any storm or trial.

Note three things.
1. The storm arose quickly, unexpectedly: "Behold, there arose."
2. The storm was great: the waves were covering the boat.
3. The storm was life-threatening: "we perish" (v.25).

"Yet man is born unto trouble, as the sparks fly upward" (Job 5:7; see also Job 14:1).

APPLICATION 1:
We face many storms throughout life, fearful storms.
1) Some storms swoop down upon us totally unexpectedly. There is no warning, no sign of their coming. But they come, and as long as we follow Jesus, they will come.
2) Some storms are great. Their waves and repercussions slash against us. They overwhelm us and threaten to engulf us.
3) Some storms are life-threatening. We see no escape, no way out, no deliverance. There seems to be no way to carry on, not in the present circumstances.

APPLICATION 2:
Nature itself can appear calm and secure; it can seem serene and safe. But its storms can arise quickly, unexpectedly. Some persons are frightened by the storm's billowing clouds rolling in upon one another, the roar of thunder, the flash of lightning, and the torrent of rain. It is dangerous and life-threatening to anyone who is not sheltered and protected.

The picture is also true with some of the trials of life—trials which everyone has or will have. What we need is the shelter and protection of Jesus Christ Himself.

QUESTIONS:
1. Think about your life for a moment. What is the greatest storm that has ever come your way? How did you react to this storm?
   ____Did you panic?
   ____Did you blame God for the storm?
   ____Did you cry out for God to help you?
2. What good results can come from the storms of life?

A CLOSER LOOK #1

(8:24) **Sea of Galilee—Lake Gennesaret—Sea of Tiberias**: a fresh-water lake in northern Palestine. At its widest points it was only about 13 miles north to south and 8 miles east to west. It would not be called a sea today because of its small size. There are several important facts to note about the Lake.

1. The Lake was known by several names: the Sea of Galilee (Mt.4:18; 15:29; Mk.1:16; 7:31), the Sea of Tiberias (Jn.6:1; 21:1), the Lake of Gennesaret (Lk.5:1), and simply the "Sea" (Jn.6:16-25) or the "Lake" (Lk.5:2; 8:22). In the Old Testament, it was called the Sea of Chinnereth (meaning heart-shaped, Num.34:11; Dt.3:17; Josh.13:27) or Chinneroth (Josh.12:3; 1 Ki.15:20).

2. The Lake was surrounded by some of the richest and most heavily populated areas of Palestine. Large towns flourished along its shores, towns which play a prominent role in Scripture: Capernaum (Mt.4:12-13), Bethsaida (Mk.6:45), Chorazin (Lk.10:13), Magdala (Mt.15:39), Gadara (Mk.5:1).

3. The Lake was subject to violent storms. It sat 680 feet below sea-level, which gave the Lake a warm climate; but it was in a pocket-like basin surrounded by steep, fast-rising hills (2000 feet high) and funnel-like mountains. The funnels or deep ravines running down through the mountains have resulted from eons of erosion. When cold-fronts move in with their fierce winds, the cold whips through the funnel-like gorges and mixes with the warm temperatures of the Lake. Unpredictable and terrifying storms result (Mt.8:23-27; Mk.4:35-41; Lk.8:22-25).

3. A TERRIFYING DISCOVERY: MAN IS NOT ABLE TO HANDLE THE SITUATION (v.24).

The terrifying discovery was twofold.

1. They, the seasoned and self-confident fishermen, were unable to handle this particular storm. Note these facts about the disciples and the storm.
   a. They were seasoned fishermen. They knew the sea and the boat; they knew how to handle themselves in the midst of any situation or trial. The same is true with many of us. We are seasoned at living and in handling the storms of life. We feel that no trial or situation can overcome us or be beyond our control. We are completely self-sufficient, or so we think and feel.
   b. They were face-to-face with a storm so severe that they were not able to save themselves. No doubt, they had faced storms before, but they had never confronted a situation as terrifying as this severe storm. Everyone of us will face a *storm that terrifies* us some day. The *terrifying storm* will be beyond our control. We will not be able to save ourselves.
   c. They were frightened and terrified. They were completely helpless and hopeless, left to themselves. When the terrifying storm hits us, it will also leave us fearful, helpless, and hopeless.
   d. They apparently had tried to handle the storm without Jesus until the situation got out of control (cp. v.25). This, of course, is the root of the problem in many of our situations: lack of trust and faith in Christ and failing to call upon Him soon enough to prevent desperation.

2. They were without the immediate help of Jesus. To them, He was asleep. Jesus was present, yet He seemed so far away; He seemed asleep. He was out of reach, unaware of their desperate plight, unconscious of their need—so the disciples thought. How often our lack of trust and sin cause us to feel that the Lord is unaware, out of reach, and untouched by our need.

> **"O our God, wilt thou not judge them? for we have no might against this great company that cometh against us; neither know we what to do: but our eyes are upon thee" (2 Chron.20:12).**

MATTHEW 8:23-27

ILLUSTRATION:

Jesus has promised never to leave us nor forsake us, but we tend to forget His promise when the storms of life overwhelm us. We need to remember this one great truth: God's help is not hindered by the size of the storm. He is always working, even in the midst of the storm—a fact we often overlook. This fictional story illustrates this very thing.

> *It was flash flood season in a small rural community. As torrential rains came down, water began to spill over the banks of the river and onto the property of one homeowner after another. One man even climbed to the roof of his house to be rescued.*
>
> *Neighbors in rowboats paddled by the man and cried out, "Do you want to ride with us?" "No thanks, I'm waiting for the Lord to save me."*
>
> *As the water began to rise and lick the eaves of the house, a speedboat filled with rescuers was dispatched to take him to dry land. "Get in our boat... time is wasting!" Once again, the man looked at the water and then looked up and replied, "Thanks, but no thanks. I'm waiting for the Lord to save me."*
>
> *By this time the water had begun to dampen his feet and quickly rose up his leg. From a distance, he saw a helicopter coming in his direction. By the time the helicopter had gotten to his house, the water was chest-deep and rapidly rising. A ladder came falling down from the helicopter. "Get on the ladder!" came the urgent instructions from the bullhorn. The man thought about it and just waved the helicopter away, "No thanks, I'm waiting for the Lord to save me."*
>
> *The storm was quickly over, but too late for the stubborn man. As he stood before the Pearly Gates, he was irritated and had only one question: "Listen here, I was trusting you to save me! Where were you?!*
>
> *A calm voice behind the Gates replied: "I sent you rowboats, a speedboat and a helicopter. What more do you want?"*

We must never forget—sometimes Jesus Christ sends the ordinary to do the obvious!

QUESTIONS:

1. A lot of people have a false sense of security—a belief that they can handle anything that comes their way. Why are people unable to handle everything that comes to them? When are you most tempted to handle things without the Lord?
2. When do you feel that Jesus is not available to help you? What should you do when you feel like this?

4. A DESPERATE APPROACH: LORD AWAKE—SAVE US (v.25).

Why did the disciples call upon Jesus now? Why not earlier?

⇒ The situation was totally *out of control*, beyond their ability to handle.

⇒ They were about to perish and die.

⇒ They had waited and waited, trying over and over to handle the situation themselves. They were prideful men: big, sturdy, capable, and seasoned in their profession. They had always handled every situation before; they could handle this one, or so they thought.

In the final analysis, the disciples confessed their need. They broke through their pride and came to Jesus. But note: they had almost waited too late, humanly speaking (v.24-25). Jesus *stirred Himself* and heard their confession.

APPLICATION:
Note these significant lessons.

1) Imminent danger can drive us to Christ, but we need to remember three critical things.
   a) We can wait too long. We can die and slip into eternity before we know it.
   b) We run a terrible risk in waiting. We overlook something: a person who decides to wait until the last minute is not all that sincere about Christ, and Christ knows it.
   c) We waste a lifetime of *living—really living in all the fullness of life*. Abundant life comes only through Christ—the life that brings unbelievable confidence and assurance, security and self-worth, love and joy, peace and rest.

   "I am come that they might have life, and that they might have it more abundantly" (Jn.10:10).

2) There is one ingredient so often missed in asking Christ to save us, one ingredient that determines whether we are heard or not: a true sense of need—a desperate plea for help beyond ourselves—a crying out to the Lord Himself—a diligent seeking.

   "But without faith it is impossible to please him: for he that cometh to God must believe that he is, and that he is a rewarder of them that diligently seek him" (Heb.11:6).

3) Their cry included the steps necessary for Christ to save them.
   a) They believed He could save them: so they came to Him.

      "For God so loved the world, that he gave his only begotten Son, that whosoever believeth in him should not perish, but have everlasting life" (Jn.3:16).

   b) They confessed their need to be saved, that they were perishing.

      "For all have sinned, and come short of the glory of God" (Ro.3:23; see also Ro.6:23).

   c) They cried out in desperation for Christ to save them.

      "For whosoever shall call upon the name of the Lord shall be saved" (Ro.10:13; see also Ro.10:9-10).

4) A desperate cry that will not quit will awaken the Lord to our need. No matter what it may be, persevering in prayer will awaken Him and bring the answer.

   "Ask, and it shall be given you; seek, and ye shall find; knock, and it shall be opened unto you: for every one that asketh receiveth; and he that seeketh findeth; and to him that knocketh it shall be opened" (Mt.7:7-8).

MATTHEW 8:23-27

QUESTIONS:
1. In what ways can pride prevent you from asking the Lord for help?
2. When you become desperate, what is usually your first reaction:
   ____Do you make a quick decision on your own?
   ____Do you become paralyzed, unable to act?
   ____Do you ask the Lord for help?

5. A CHALLENGING QUESTION (v.26).

The disciples were going through two human experiences, but *they were aware of only one*: the experience of terrible fear. What they failed to see was completely hidden to them. They were experiencing the root cause of fear: little faith. Their trust in Christ (that their lives were completely in His keeping and under His care) was lacking. Their trust was incomplete and immature. They were not sure that He was aware of their desperate need. But He was, just as He is aware of all needs—always. He was the One who asked, "Why are ye fearful?" It was as though He was shocked at their lack of faith. (See A CLOSER LOOK # 2—Mt.8:26.)

> **"Verily I say unto you, If ye have faith as a grain of mustard seed, ye shall say unto this mountain [trial], Remove hence to yonder place; and it shall remove; and nothing shall be impossible unto you" (Mt.17:20).**

APPLICATION:
Note several lessons.
1) Christ was not disturbed with their calling and interrupting His sleep. He was disturbed with their fear and lack of trust. He is never disturbed with our crying out to Him.
2) There is no excuse for a disciple's fear. Of all people, believers are supposed to be the persons trusting Him, knowing that He is looking after their lives. Believers are to know the supernatural strength of Christ; they are supposed to walk through all things courageously, even death.
3) The disciples neglected Christ. They could have prevented much of their problem if they had gone to Christ earlier. As pointed out previously, they were trying to handle the situation by themselves, confident of their own ability. How often we walk in self-confidence, not paying enough attention to the Lord and His care. We *always* need to be calling upon Him, not waiting until the last moment, expecting Him to step in and meet our emergencies (1 Pt.5:7; Eph.6:18).
4) Christ rebukes fear and unbelief. Fear and unbelief dishonor Him. It says to the world that Christ is not enough, that He is not strong enough, does not care enough, does not love enough to look after us in our trouble and sin. How foolish we are (Jn.3:16; 1 Pt.5:7; Mt.11:28-30)!
5) Faith is to be several things.
   ⇒ Faith is to be the foundation of our lives, not a beam for emergency support.
   ⇒ Faith is to be the flow of our behavior, not the serum for emergencies.
   ⇒ Faith is to be the permeating thought of our mind, not the sporadic thought aroused by need.
   ⇒ Faith is to be the constant plea of our heart, not the occasional cry of desperation.
6) Storms and trials can lead to terrible discouragement and fear...
   - fear that one has gone too far for recovery
   - fear that no one really cares
   - fear that one is a stumblingblock and a burden to others
   - fear that there is no real reason for living

But there is hope—*in Christ*. He is *The Great Deliverer* from fear. In fact, He is The Great Deliverer from all trials and temptations.

> **"There hath no temptation taken you but such as is common to man: but God is faithful, who will not suffer you to be tempted above that ye are able; but will with the temptation also make a way to escape, that ye may be able to bear it" (1 Cor.10:13).**

QUESTIONS:

1. When is Christ most likely to ask you, *"Where is your faith?"*
2. What do you know about God that assures you of His safe-keeping—even during a dangerous storm of life?
3. Is there a proper time and place for fear in your life? Why or why not? How can you know when fear is to be replaced by faith?

A CLOSER LOOK #2

(8:26) **Fear**: fear can be a good thing as well as a bad thing. Fear sometimes causes us to respond with more vigor and strength, intelligence and wisdom, well beyond ourselves. Fear can make us face three things.

1. Fear can make us face the reality about ourselves: what we really are, who we really are, and why we really are here.

2. Fear can make us face our desperate need: that we are not perfect nor completely self-sufficient, self-contained, or adequate for all things. We are not the summit of existence nor the epitome of what man should be. Humanism and humanistic philosophy (that man is all) are not the crowning glory of behavior and thought. We desperately need to face that fact. No matter how well we behave or how high we think, we still have terrible storms that fall upon us, engulfing us like waves of the ocean rolling in one upon another. And then the final wave that no man can handle, the great tidal wave of death, drowns the breath of life out of us. We must face the fact...

- that there are desperate needs that must be handled
- that we are incapable of handling them ourselves

3. Fear can make us face our need for help beyond ourselves. In facing death, we are as helpless as the disciples were. We cannot stop death. When it is time, we die. Note this fact as well: just like the disciples, we need help all the time. We may not confess our need, but the *need for Christ* is always hounding us whether we recognize it or not. We may walk day by day in our own strength and ability, but there would be a tremendous difference if we trusted Christ to save us.

⇒ Things would not discourage or frighten us.

> **"And we know that all things work together for good to them that love God, to them who are the called according to his purpose" (Ro.8:28).**

⇒ Life would be smoother and more peaceful.

> **"Peace I leave with you, my peace I give unto you: not as the world giveth, give I unto you. Let not your heart be troubled, neither let it be afraid" (Jn.14:27).**

⇒ Life would bear so much more fruit.

> **"But the fruit of the Spirit is love, joy, peace, longsuffering, gentleness, goodness, faith, meekness, temperance: against such there is no law" (Gal.5:22-23).**

⇒ Assurance, confidence, and hope would abundantly flood our hearts and minds.

"And hope maketh not ashamed; because the love of God is shed abroad in our hearts by the Holy Ghost which is given unto us" (Ro.5:5; cp. 5:1-5).

QUESTIONS:
1. What effect does fear have upon your life?
2. If you truly place your trust in Christ, what are the benefits promised to you?

6. A STRONG, POWERFUL DELIVERANCE: A GREAT CALM (v.26).

Christ is the Sovereign Lord over all nature. He can do what He wills for any of us. When He arose and rebuked the storm, then there was an instantaneous calm. But note this: the disciples misread both the situation and Christ's presence. When they awoke Christ, Christ pointed out their fear immediately—even before He arose and answered their need.

This says something of critical importance: all the problems of the world are known by Christ and providentially overruled by Him. He does not have to rush to meet them. Problems should not be a danger or threat to us as the children of God. This does not mean that we will not suffer or die, nor that we do not have to bear terrible trials. The disciples had to experience this storm and they had to experience many other storms. But Christ was with them, and He is always with us. He will strengthen and carry us through all the storms of life. In fact, as with the disciples, God uses the storms of life to teach us more and more trust in Him. If there were no trials, there would be no need to trust Him.

How often we misread the presence of Christ, thinking He is out of reach. And how often we misread the storm, thinking it is out of His control. The problem is, we are not walking close enough to Him to be conscious of His presence and care. He will speak and calm the storm at the very best time, after everyone has learned what they are supposed to learn through the storms.

"But Jesus beheld them, and said unto them, With men this is impossible; but with God all things are possible" (Mt.19:26).

APPLICATION 1:
Christ arises when He is called upon. When we really mean what we pray, He arises to His feet in our behalf. He stands and confronts the situation head-on, meeting our needs beyond what we ask, in the very best way possible.

"Likewise the Spirit also helpeth our infirmities: for we know not what we should pray for as we ought: but the Spirit itself maketh intercession for us with groanings which cannot be uttered" (Ro.8:26).

APPLICATION 2:
Note two things.
1) Christ can calm any storm of life for us.
2) Christ can strengthen us to go through any storm of life.

"Blessed be God, even the Father of our Lord Jesus Christ, the Father of mercies, and the God of all comfort; who comforteth us in all our tribulation, that we may be able to comfort them which are in any trouble, by the comfort wherewith we ourselves are comforted of God" (2 Cor.1:3-4).

QUESTIONS:
1. If you really believe Christ has control over nature, how can you explain all the violent weather to unbelievers?
2. Are you going through a violent storm right now? How has Christ promised to help you through it?

7. A MARVELOUS PURPOSE (v.27).

The disciples marveled; they had never seen anything like it—even the winds and seas obeyed Him.

1. They now knew more about what it meant to call Him "Lord." He was the sovereign Lord who possessed all power over nature—the same power that the prophets of old proclaimed for God.

2. They also knew more about what it meant to trust Him and His Word. He was able to control even the elements of nature. They could now depend upon His power to do whatever was needed. In Him, the power was available to control all things and to do all things.

> **"Verily, verily, I say unto you, He that believeth on me, the works that I do shall he do also; and greater works than these shall he do; because I go unto my Father" (Jn.14:12).**

ILLUSTRATION:
The longer a believer walks with God and experiences His power firsthand, the greater the view of God's sovereignty. The Christian who has walked with God through storm after storm has learned that God is always big enough.

> *Bedtime had come for the little girl whose first day of kindergarten was coming up. She was excited and anxious at the same time. As her Daddy read her a bedtime story, she was fascinated with the idea that God is BIG. "Daddy, just how big is God? Is He bigger than our house? Is He bigger than my school? Is He bigger than our town? Is He bigger than a mountain? Is He...?" Her father cut her off and simply said, "Sweetie, God is always bigger than your biggest need!"*

QUESTIONS:
1. What is the most spectacular thing you have seen God do? What are some quiet ways He shows His control over life?
2. As you reflect upon your life, when has God's faithfulness been most evident to you?

SUMMARY:

When the storms of life threaten to drown you, you must remember that Jesus Christ is the Lord of every storm and He will use each storm to strengthen your faith in Him. Believers in every generation must know the timeless principles of these points:

1. A basic fact: true disciples follow Christ no matter what. His disciples followed Him wherever He went. They had made a genuine commitment; they were now committed to following Him regardless of the circumstances and the cost.
2. A fearful experience: a great storm. The apostles' very lives were threatened (v.25). The waves were covering the boat (v.24). It was, so to speak, a trial of trials. If Jesus could teach them His care through this experience, they would know He could take care of them through any storm or trial.

MATTHEW 8:23-27

3. A terrifying discovery: man is not able to handle the situation. The seasoned and self-confident fishermen were unable to handle this particular storm.
4. A desperate approach: Lord, awake—save us. The disciples confessed their need. They broke through their pride and came to Jesus. But note: they had almost waited too late, humanly speaking (v.24-25).
5. A challenging question. The disciples were not sure that Christ was aware of their desperate need. But He was, just as He is aware of all needs—always. He was the One who asked, "Why are ye fearful?" It was as though He were shocked at their lack of faith.
6. A strong, powerful deliverance: a great calm. Christ is the Sovereign Lord over all nature. He can do what He wills for any of us. He arose and rebuked the storm—then there was an instantaneous calm.
7. A marvelous purpose. The disciples marveled; they had never seen anything like it—even the winds and seas obeyed Him.

PERSONAL JOURNAL NOTES
(Reflection & Response)

1. The most important thing that I learned from this lesson was:

2. The area that I need to work on the most is:

3. I can apply this lesson to my life by:

4. Closing Statement of Commitment:

MATTHEW 8:28-34

	F. Jesus Casts out Demons: Saving Men, 8:28-34 (Mk.5:1-20; Lk.8:26-40)	sought him, saying, If thou cast us out, suffer us to go away into the herd of swine.	
1. Jesus went where no other men would go a. Among the evil possessed b. Among the dead c. Among the fierce	28 And when he was come to the other side into the country of the Gergesenes, there met him two possessed with devils, coming out of the tombs, exceeding fierce, so that no man might pass by that way.	32 And he said unto them, Go. And when they were come out, they went into the herd of swine: and, behold, the whole herd of swine ran violently down a steep place into the sea, and perished in the waters.	**2. Jesus saved those whom no other men could reach** a. The power of His word: "Go" b. The result: Demons were expelled & exorcised
d. Among the defiant	29 And, behold, they cried out, saying, What have we to do with thee, Jesus, thou Son of God? art thou come hither to torment us before the time?	33 And they that kept them fled, and went their ways into the city, and told every thing, and what was befallen to the possessed of the devils.	**3. Jesus was rejected again by covetous men** a. The covetous heard of the Lord's presence and behavior
e. Among the malicious—the devourers—the destroyers	30 And there was a good way off from them an herd of many swine feeding. 31 So the devils be-	34 And, behold, the whole city came out to meet Jesus: and when they saw him, they besought him that he would depart out of their coasts.	b. The covetous felt nothing in common with Him: "When they saw Him" c. The covetous rejected and expelled Him

Section V
THE MESSIAH'S GREAT AUTHORITY AND POWER REVEALED IN WORD AND WORK, Matthew 8:1-9:34

Study 6: JESUS CASTS OUT DEMONS: SAVING MEN

Text: Matthew 8:28-34

Aim: To gain a deeper understanding of the wonderful and powerful deliverance of Jesus Christ.

Memory Verse:

"For the Son of man is come to seek and to save that which was lost" (Luke 19:10).

INTRODUCTION

Just one look at the news—whether on television, radio, or in the newspaper—would convince even the most optimistic that this world is in desperate shape. Our communities are littered with people who are pushing drugs and killing innocent bystanders. There are young teenagers joining gangs that loot, intimidate, and even kill. Is anyone ever considered to be hopeless, to be beyond the reach of God's redemptive saving power? One of the greatest examples of God's grace is the story of Nicki Cruz and David Wilkerson. This classic story is told in the book *The Cross and the Switchblade*.

As you may recall, Wilkerson was the young, zealous preacher who came to the inner city looking for the lost. Cruz was a feared gang leader who stalked the crime-filled streets of New York City. What brought this hardened criminal to Christ? It was the gospel—the gospel of God's love for the lost. David Wilkerson was willing to put his own life at risk in order to bring men like Nicki Cruz to the saving knowledge of Jesus Christ. What can we learn from this story? No matter how bleak the situation looks, no one—absolutely no one—is beyond God's saving power.

Throughout history, Jesus Christ has made it a point to reach into the deep, dark places of the world to save men, women, boys, and girls from the certainty of hell. The point is this: no one is beyond hope—not even the most vile and corrupt person imaginable. Christ came to save sinners—all sinners—whoever and wherever they are.

OUTLINE:

1. Jesus went where no other men would go (v.28-31).
2. Jesus saved those whom no other men could reach (v.32).
3. Jesus was rejected again by covetous men (v.33-34).

A CLOSER LOOK #1

(8:28-34) **Evil Spirits—Demons—Satan***:* the Bible teaches that there are beings in the spiritual world who are evil just as there are men in this world who are evil. The Bible calls these beings "*evil spirits*." Note that the very word *evil* is used in their name, which describes exactly what their nature and mission are. "Evil spirits" apparently have a leader called *the evil one*. He is sometimes called by other names describing the terrible work he is out to do in defiance of God.

Some deny a *force of evil* in an unseen world, whereas the person who accepts the Bible as the authoritative Word of God accepts what the Bible teaches about their presence.

Those who deny evil spirits feel that a civilized and scientific society knows better; it is just too intelligent to accept *evil beings* in an unseen world who have the power to possess, obsess, and oppress men. Three primary reasons lead to this conclusion.

1. The existence of evil spirits in an unseen world cannot be scientifically proven.
2. The behavior of what is called *evil spirits* seems to exist more and to be more marked in unscientific societies that tend to stress evil spirits.
3. The behavior of those *possessed* is thought to be nothing more than mental illness.

There are huge problems with the denial of an evil spirit behind the seen world. The denial leaves much unanswered.

1. How can *mental illness* explain such behavior as is witnessed so often upon the scene of human history? Consider Hitler and other mass murderers who committed atrocities against so many people. Realistically, several facts militate against much of the behavior being ascribed to mental illness.
   a. There is the fact that many who did so much evil were nurtured in the arms of mothers or someone else who did care. Mental illness points out deviations from healthy rearing. But realistically, the deviations can come nowhere close to matching the terrible atrocities. And the deviation from normal behavior does not always vary that much until the terrible atrocity is committed.
   b. A human being who is mentally ill cannot move among sound people for too long without being found out. True mental illness cannot fake that much and that often. Its behavior deviates often enough that others know that a person is acting extremely abnormal. A mentally ill person can be detected and reached out to by caring people.

c. A person who is mentally ill cannot move among a large number of sound leaders and convince them all to commit atrocity after atrocity. Realistically, there has to be more than mental illness behind inhuman behavior that is so deceiving (blinding) and so terribly destructive.

2. The claim that *demon-like behavior* exists more in unindustrialized societies has two faults.

a. Such a claim is disputable, although probably true. But the point is this: a scientific society that is dominated by unbelief is bound to ascribe abnormal behavior to whatever it feels causes the defect. Therefore...

- abnormal behavior is frequently ascribed to mental illness
- severe abnormal behavior is marked up as unexplainable or due to a complete diverse (split) personality

However, claiming that something is unexplainable or coming up with a new name does not do away with reality, the truth of what actually exists. (There is not that much difference between the psychological belief in two complete personalities within a body and Scriptural belief which also says that two persons can *possess* a body—the man himself and an evil spirit.)

b. The Bible claims that the evil spirits of the unseen world are highly intelligent and deceptive.

⇒ When a man thinks he "walks in light" (is enlightened or scientific), the Bible says the evil one fashions himself into an angel of light and uses strategies of light. Therefore, men would naturally call abnormal behavior by some natural or humanistic term as *mental illness* (2 Cor.11:14-15; Eph.6:11).

⇒ When a person believes in evil spirits and opens his life to such spirits, the evil one uses the strategies of what men call *dark spirits*.

1. JESUS WENT WHERE NO OTHER MEN WOULD GO (v.28-31).

1. Jesus went among the evil-possessed. These two men were as possessed with evil as any had ever been. (Cp. Mark and Luke to have a complete picture of their plight.) They were so possessed and acted so insane that no man would dare reach out with a helping hand. In fact, no man dared go near them. Yet God cares for all and cares equally. And He wants His people to care and to reach out to all no matter how bad their condition. Christ went where no men dared to go. He went among those who were *possessed with devils*.

2. Jesus went among the dead. Note two things.

a. These men lived among the tombs, in the graveyard.

b. These men represented *the living dead*—all men without Christ are "dead in their sins." The difference between the two possessed men and all others is that they were the picture of the worst of the living dead. They show just how far away some can slide from God and from their families and friends. They can be so possessed with evil that they are completely cut off both from God and man, living as though among the dead (cp. Eph.2:1-3; 5:14; Col.2:13).

> **"It was meet that we should make merry, and be glad: for this thy brother was dead, and is alive again; and was lost, and is found" (Lk.15:32).**

APPLICATION:

Note two things.

1) Where the depth of evil can lead: among the dead. The men came "out of the tombs."

2) How far a person can go in giving himself over to *evil* or *devils*: he can literally ruin his life. He can become so cut off from others that he lives as "among the dead."

3. Jesus went among the fierce. Some men are dangerous; they are so given over to evil that they are a threat to everyone. The two possessed men were "exceeding fierce." They threatened any who passed by.

APPLICATION:
Why do men become fierce and dangerous?

1) Some give themselves over to evil step by step. They grow more evil over a period of time, walking so long in pride and envy, selfishness and lust that they rebel against giving of themselves. They react with malice and revenge against any who go contrary to their wishes. Sensual stimulation and material things—as well as wealth, recognition, and power—become the ambition and focus of their lives. They become obsessed and possessed, reacting with anger against any position or relationship that does not give way to their desires.
2) Some become so self-centered that they react violently if they do not receive the attention and recognition they desire or get what they want. They behave so selfishly that they become "possessed with devils."
3) Some give themselves over to evil to the extent that they become possessed with evil. They are capable of acting and reacting so coldly that others become nothing but pawns to do their bidding. If anyone expresses a different position, they become an immediate threat.
4) Some are ignored, neglected, rejected, and abused to the point that they withdraw and become subject to being possessed with the negative reactions of evil: self-centeredness, self-pity, anger, hostility, malice, bitterness, revenge, and on and on.

   When the heart is not filled with God, it is filled with self and evil, and it sometimes becomes angry and fierce against people and positions. There is no exception; everyone without God experiences some anger and fierceness during their journey without God. Some go so far as to become possessed with *an evil spirit of fierceness*.

4. Jesus went among the defiant. Men rebel against God; and rebellion in God's eyes is defiance, that is, rejection of Him and His will. These men rebelled and were as resistant as men can be. Note three facts.

a. They protested Jesus' presence: "cried out" in defiance against His presence. How many of us protest and have times that we do not want God's presence?
b. They recognized Him as the Son of God. They recognized something that many today refuse to acknowledge.
c. They acknowledged a day of torment, of judgment yet to come. They did something many try to deny.

APPLICATION:
Note several important lessons.

1) It is not the knowledge that God exists that makes a person a child of God. It is love: love of God and love of man. The person who truly reaches out for God and for man is born of God.

> **"Thou believest that there is one God; Thou doest well: the devils also believe, and tremble" (Jas.2:19).**

2) Evil spirits have nothing to do with Christ. Christ did not come to save fallen angels, but fallen men. Christ went to a graveyard to save these two men. He

will go anyplace to save anyone. How much more should we be willing to go anyplace to reach fallen men?

> **"To wit, that God was in Christ, reconciling the world unto himself, not imputing their trespasses unto them; and hath committed unto us the word of reconciliation. Now then we are ambassadors for Christ, as though God did beseech you by us: we pray you in Christ's stead, be ye reconciled to God" (2 Cor.5:19-20).**

3) Some men react against Jesus Christ just as these evil spirits did.
   a) They can call Jesus Christ the Son of God and have nothing to do with Him.
   b) They can acknowledge a day of torment and still have nothing to do with Him.
   c) They can reject Him, protest His presence, oppose His right to control their lives, rebel against His interference, even hate Him and feel animosity toward Him.
4) Some men may be nagged with the question: Do we have anything to do with God? Man is the concern of God, and the fact that a person may be nagged with the question is a good sign. Such a man can find God and find deliverance if he will diligently seek God.

> **"And ye shall seek me, and find me, when ye shall search for me with all your heart" (Jer.29:13).**

5. Jesus went among the malicious, the devourers, the destroyers. The evil spirits are said to be the ones speaking here. They recognized Jesus' sovereignty. Note how the *evil spirits* thought and worked.
   a. They were indwelling and hurting these men physically, mentally, and spiritually.
   b. They wished (if exorcised from human bodies) to hurt other men by damaging and destroying their property.
   c. They wished (if exorcised) to keep other men from Christ by destroying their property and having them blame God for the devastation and loss.

> **"The devil, as a roaring lion, walketh about, seeking whom he may devour" (1 Pt.5:8).**

ILLUSTRATION:
Jesus Christ did not shy away from going to the "hard places" of ministry in order to save a soul. His example is a strong challenge to us all.

> *Years ago Oliver Cromwell, the great British leader, faced a crisis: a shortage of metal for making coins. Cromwell sent his troops on a mission to find the precious metal.*
>
> *After searching the local cathedral, Cromwell's soldiers reported, The only precious metal to be found was in the statues of the saints standing in the corners of the churches. Cromwell's famous, but blunt, instructions were then given: Well, then, melt down the saints and put them into circulation!*

Sometimes we have to go to strange places and do strange things to reach our desired goal.

> **"Even as the Son of man came not to be ministered unto, but to minister, and to give his life a ransom for many" (Mt.20:28).**

QUESTIONS:
1. Believers are naturally more comfortable sharing the gospel with people who are non-threatening. But how can we move beyond this and follow the example of Jesus by going into the hard places and meeting the most difficult people?
2. What things in your society cause a person to become possessed by evil spirits?
3. What can you personally do to help prevent the spread of evil in your home, your community, your world?

2. JESUS SAVED THOSE WHOM NO OTHER MEN COULD REACH (v.32).

1. There is the power of His Word. The devil's power may be great, but the Word of Christ is omnipotent (all-powerful).

> **"And Jesus came and spake unto them, saying, All power is given unto me in heaven and in earth" (Mt.28:18).**

2. There is the result of His Word. The men were saved and the evil spirits were cast out of the men. Christ has the power to deliver and save. All He has to do is say, "Go," and whatever evil dwells in a man is gone. The man is delivered from all evil—its presence, guilt, and consequences. The man is "saved to the utmost" (Heb.7:25).

> **"As thou hast given him power over all flesh, that he should give eternal life to as many as thou hast given him" (Jn.17:2).**

APPLICATION:
Some people may seem hopeless to us. They may rage and rebel against God, even defy Him, but Christ can and will reach them. We just need to go to them in the name of our Lord, for He has the power to deliver and save. The power of Christ is able and all sufficient, sufficient enough to meet any need. The evil spirits were two of the worst ever described, yet they were expelled and the men were delivered. This is the very purpose of this experience. It is a demonstration of Christ's power to save men who are gripped by the depths of darkness.

QUESTIONS:
1. Have you personally ever had to use God's Word to confront evil or evil spirits? How did you do it? What was the outcome?
2. How can you go about using God's Word to challenge evil spirits when dealing with someone else? Do you need special preparation to do so?

A CLOSER LOOK #2
(8:32) **Evil Spirit**: a question needs to be asked about the swine that were killed (Mt.8:30-32). There were about two thousand of them (Mk.5:13). Why were they killed? As this is discussed, it should be noted that Christ did not kill them. He, of course, knew they would be killed; but the evil spirits were the ones who drove them wildly over the cliff. Why did Christ allow the owners to suffer such a great loss?

There are several possible answers.

1. It was a visible sign that the two possessed men were truly saved and freed from the evil spirits. Everyone knew beyond question that the two were possessed. Only a dramatic act could give unquestionable proof.

2. It was to convince those who did not believe in evil spirits that there are most definitely evil spirits who do possess bodies. (Unbelievers such as the Sadducees and other liberal thinkers of the day needed to see the truth.)

3. It was to teach obedience and holiness. It was against the law for a Jew to own and eat swine (Lev.11:7; cp. Is.65:3-4; 66:17). If the owners were Jews (and they probably were), they were sinning against the law. Jesus was thereby teaching that His presence demanded holiness and obedience to the law.

4. It was to teach the value of a human soul. The two possessed men were of far more value than any amount of material wealth, and even more so if the wealth was gained by illegal means.

5. It was to attract the attention and open the door for the evangelization of the surrounding district. No doubt the news of the Messiah's presence and power would spread, stirring people to open their hearts to receive the message of the healed demoniacs (Lk.8:38-40).

6. It was to drive home Jesus' holiness and to arouse the people to acknowledge it; thereby the seeking and honest heart would be open for salvation (Lk.8:38-40).

7. It was to awaken covetous men to the fact that they were gripped by greed. They were doomed unless they forsook their material possessions and turned to the Messiah (Mt.19:16-26). This could have been the best way and the only chance for them to be awakened to their need and to the power of Christ to deliver them.

8. It was to show the true nature of evil spirits.

3. JESUS WAS REJECTED AGAIN BY COVETOUS MEN (v.33-34).

1. The covetous men heard of the Lord's presence and behavior. The herd-keepers ran into the city to report what had happened. Note: the whole city went out to meet Him and all reacted against the loss of the wealth. Nothing was acknowledged of the good done.

   a. There was good in that a great deliverance had taken place. Two hopeless men had been healed and delivered.
   b. There was good in the truth about the swine. Whatever was behind the destruction of the swine, it was for the good of all involved (see A CLOSER LOOK # 2—Mt.8:32).

2. The covetous men felt nothing in common with Christ. "When they saw Him," they saw only a man standing there who had destroyed their property. They were blind to the glorious work and deliverance of the two possessed men. Salvation was not on their minds—business was. Their thoughts were engulfed in their material loss, not in heaven's gain.

APPLICATION 1:
When covetous men see the Lord, they feel nothing in common with Christ and His demand for self-denial.

APPLICATION 2:
The Lord's attitude and demands toward material possessions are stringent. A covetous man is either forced to repent, that is, turn from his materialism, or to outrightly reject Christ (Mt.19:16-22).

3. The covetous men rejected and expelled Christ. They did not come to be saved by the Messiah, but to banish Him. They banished Him who had the power to drive out all the evil forces that had gripped their lives and that were leading them down the road to material destruction.

"Love not the world, neither the things that are in the world. If any man love the world, the love of the Father is not in him. For all

that is in the world, the lust of the flesh, and the lust of the eyes, and the pride of life, is not of the Father, but is of the world" (1 Jn.2:15-16).

ILLUSTRATION:
There are many covetous or greedy people who miss out on the glory of God, miss out on His work of salvation in the lives of sinners. Why? Because they look in the wrong places.

> *An article in a San Francisco newspaper reported that a young man who once found a $5 bill on the street resolved that from that time on he would never lift his eyes while walking. The paper went on to say that over the years he accumulated, among others things, 29,516 buttons, 54,172 pins, 12 cents, a bent back, and a miserly disposition, but he also lost something—the glory of sunlight, the radiance of the stars, the smiles of friends, and the freshness of blue skies.*[2]

What is your habit: to look down or to look up and see the Lord at work?

QUESTIONS:
1. The miracles of Christ are often ignored by people with covetous hearts. What things come to your mind about people who have ignored what Christ has done for them?
2. Why would a covetous person reject Christ?
3. What are the consequences to the covetous person, or any person, who rejects Christ?

SUMMARY:

Jesus Christ has come to save people, even the most desperate, most vile person in the world. There is no such thing as being *more saved* or *more lost*. A sinner without Christ is totally lost, but a person who allows Christ to save him is totally saved. The lessons from this Scripture are far reaching for the believer who wants to follow the Lord's example:

1. Jesus went where no other men would go.
2. Jesus saved those whom no other men could reach.
3. Jesus was rejected again by covetous men.

PERSONAL JOURNAL NOTES
(Reflection & Response)

1. The most important thing that I learned from this lesson was:

2. The area that I need to work on the most is:

3. I can apply this lesson to my life by:

4. Closing Statement of Commitment:

---

2 *INFOsearch Sermon Illustrations* (Arlington, TX: The Computer Assistant, 1-888-868-9029, 1986-1996).

MATTHEW 9:1-8

CHAPTER 9

G. Jesus Heals a Paralyzed Man: Forgiving Sin, 9:1-8
(Mk.2:1-12; Lk.5:17-26)

1. Jesus left Gadara & entered His own city—Capernaum

2. Jesus' power to forgive sins was demonstrated
   a. The friends' deep care: Brought their friend to Jesus
   b. The friends' great faith
   c. Jesus' compassion: Forgave the man's sins

3. Jesus' power to forgive sins was questioned: Silently accused of blasphemy

4. Jesus' power to forgive sins was proven
   a. He revealed something: He knew their rejection
   b. He suggested something: A test
   c. He did something: He healed the man
   d. He commanded something: Go

5. Jesus' power to forgive sins brought glory to God

And he entered into
a ship, and passed
over, and came into
his own city.
2 And, behold, they
brought to him a
man sick of the pal-
sy, lying on a bed:
and Jesus seeing
their faith said un-
to the sick of the
palsy; Son, be of
good cheer; thy
sins be forgiven
thee.
3 And, behold, cer-
tain of the scribes
said within them-
selves, This man
blasphemeth.
4 And Jesus knowing
their thoughts said,
Wherefore think ye
evil in your hearts?
5 For whether is easi-
er, to say, Thy sins be
forgiven thee; or to
say, Arise, and walk?
6 But that ye may
know that the Son of
man hath power on
earth to forgive sins,
(then saith he to the
sick of the palsy,)
Arise, take up thy
bed, and go unto
thine house.
7 And he arose, and
departed to his
house.
8 But when the mul-
titudes saw it, they
marvelled, and glori-
fied God, which had
given such power
unto men.

Section V
THE MESSIAH'S GREAT AUTHORITY AND POWER REVEALED IN WORD AND WORK, Matthew 8:1-9:34

Study 7: JESUS HEALS A PARALYZED MAN: FORGIVING SIN

Text: Matthew 9:1-8

Aim: To grasp the real power of Jesus to forgive sins.

Memory Verse:

"But that ye may know that the Son of man hath power on earth to forgive sins, (then saith he to the sick of the palsy,) Arise, take up thy bed, and go unto thine house" (Mt.9:6).

INTRODUCTION

Have you ever had to stand in line for a long time to get something you wanted or needed?

⇒ Waiting for a seat in a restaurant?
⇒ Waiting in line to buy something?
⇒ Waiting your turn to get a driver's license or renewal?
⇒ Waiting to buy a ticket for a popular concert or sporting event?

What we are willing to stand in line for says a lot about our priorities. In the case of the paralytic's four friends, their motive for coming to Jesus was driven by the friend's sickness and by their faith in Christ's ability to touch the sick man. As this beautiful story of commitment records, these men were willing to wait for the only One who could help.

OUTLINE:

1. Jesus left Gadara and entered His own city—Capernaum (v.1).
2. Jesus' power to forgive sins was demonstrated (v.2).
3. Jesus' power to forgive sins was questioned: He was silently accused of blasphemy (v.3).
4. Jesus' power to forgive sins was proven (v.4-7).
5. Jesus' power to forgive sins brought glory to God (v.8).

A CLOSER LOOK #1

(9:1-8) **Jesus Christ, Deity—Forgiveness**: note several things about this experience.

1. The experience must have embarrassed the sick man, indicated by the wording of Jesus' response, "Son, be of good cheer." His friends had not waited their turn, and the sick man was unable to stop them. He was probably expecting a rebuke.

2. The experience touched the heart of Jesus in a very special way. It revealed a persistent faith that would not be stopped until it had accomplished its end. The friends had a faith that would not quit, no matter what.

3. The experience caused Jesus to reveal and speak the thoughts that are ever on His mind: "Son, be of good cheer; thy sins are forgiven thee." His words are ones of compassion, affection, endearment, sympathy, encouragement, assurance, and forgiveness.

4. The experience gave Jesus the unique opportunity to prove His Messiahship: that He is the Son of Man. Note that Jesus did not say "I," but "the Son of Man has power [authority] on earth to forgive sins." The people were familiar with the title "the Son of Man" (cp. Dan.7:13-14). Every phrase is important.

   a. The Son of Man is given "authority," that is, dominion and power, over a kingdom that is open to all people.
   b. The Son of Man is "given power [authority] over earth" now as well as in the future.
   c. The Son of Man's power includes the power to forgive as well as the power to rule and reign.

1. JESUS LEFT GADARA AND ENTERED HIS OWN CITY—CAPERNAUM (v.1).

The Gadarenes had asked Jesus to leave (cp. Mt.8:34). There is no record of His ever entering their coasts again. He obeyed their wish.

APPLICATION:
Jesus' experience with the Gadarenes is a warning to every man, city, and nation. He will not force Himself upon any person or society. What a contrast with the people of Capernaum and the paralyzed man of this story.

QUESTIONS:

1. Have you ever tried to force the gospel on someone who did not want to hear it? What was the outcome?
2. There are people throughout society who ask Jesus Christ to leave, people in...
   - families
   - schools
   - governments
   - even churches

   What happens to people who ask Christ to leave?

MATTHEW 9:1-8

2. JESUS' POWER TO FORGIVE SINS WAS DEMONSTRATED (v.2).

1. There was the friends' deep care. They brought their disabled friend to Christ. Note four facts.

a. The man was disabled. He was helpless; therefore, he was without hope. But his friends cared deeply for him.
b. The friends displayed a very special care, one that was deeper than that of mere friendship (Mark and Luke show this). They were obsessed with the mission to get this disabled friend to Jesus. They not only went to the friend and made his bed as an act of ministry and service; but they went to him, made a pallet, and then *brought him to Jesus*.
c. The friends acknowledged Jesus' power to help. They did not approach Him with an attitude of *maybe He could help*, but that He *could* and *would* help. They did not question His power.
d. The friends persisted even to the point of rudeness (Lk.11:5-10; 18:1-8). They would not be stopped (cp. Mark and Luke).

> **"We then that are strong ought to bear the infirmities of the weak, and not to please ourselves" (Ro.15:1; see also Gal.6:2).**

APPLICATION 1:
All men are disabled and sick spiritually. Therefore, we must strive to possess the same three qualities as the friends of the disabled did:
1) We must be obsessed with the mission of getting the disabled to Christ. We must cling to the helpless and hopeless until we can get them to Christ.
2) We must acknowledge Christ's power to help—beyond any question.
3) We must persist and persevere until we get the disabled to Christ.

APPLICATION 2:
We cannot save our friends. No man can forgive another man's sins or heal a man, but we *can bring a man to Christ* for salvation and deliverance.

2. There was the friends' great faith. Note the words, "their faith": it was *their faith* that saved this man, both the faith of the disabled man and that of his friends. *Their faith* was great and persistent. What is great faith?

a. Great faith is focusing one's belief on Jesus Christ. It is centering one's attention and conviction on Christ; that He alone is the answer to the needy and the helpless of the world, no matter who they are.
b. Great faith is acknowledging that a need does exist and must be met.
c. Great faith is doing all one can do to meet the need. These men did all they could do. They made a great effort. They went to the disabled friend's house, made a pallet, and carried him to Jesus.
d. Great faith persists until the need is met.

> **"And I say unto you, Ask, and it shall be given you; seek, and ye shall find; knock, and it shall be opened unto you. For every one that asketh receiveth; and he that seeketh findeth; and to him that knocketh it shall be opened" (Lk.11:9-10).**

APPLICATION 1:
Jesus will never fail to acknowledge persistent faith. He saw the faith of these men; He could not miss it. Their faith had caused them to persist—quitting was unthinkable. They persisted until they reached Him.

APPLICATION 2:
The faith of friends carries some weight and has a bearing on the salvation of the hopeless and helpless. It was *their faith* that saved this man. We must go out of

the walls of our churches and homes to bring the helpless and hopeless to Christ. Christ will honor our belief and trust in Him. He will save those whom we bring.

ILLUSTRATION:
Acts of compassion are often by-passed for the "bottom line" of personal cost: *what will it cost me to do this for you?* There have been many opportunities for showing compassion lost by most of us. But here is one story where this was not the case:

In 1975 a child named Raymond Dunn, Jr., was born in New York State. The Associated Press reports that at his birth, a skull fracture and oxygen deprivation caused severe retardation. As Raymond grew, the family discovered further impairments. His twisted body suffered up to twenty seizures per day. He was blind, mute, immobile. He had severe allergies that limited him to only one food: a meat-based formula made by Gerber Foods.

In 1985, Gerber stopped making the formula that Raymond lived on. His mother scoured the country to buy what stores had in stock, accumulating cases and cases, but in 1990 her supply ran out. In desperation, she appealed to Gerber for help. Without his particular food, Raymond would starve to death.

The employees of the company listened. In an unprecedented action, volunteers donated hundreds of hours to bring out old equipment, set up production lines, obtain special approval from the USDA [United States Drug Administration], and produce the formula—all for one special boy.

In January 1995, Raymond Dunn, Jr., known as the Gerber Boy, died from his physical problems. But during his brief lifetime he called forth a wonderful thing called compassion.[1]

QUESTIONS:
1. Every lost person needs someone who cares enough to bring him to Christ. Are you willing to make that kind of commitment to someone—whether family, friend, or stranger?
2. What obstacles keep you from bringing people to Christ?
3. How can your faith contribute to a person's salvation?

3. There was Jesus' compassion. The greatest need this crippled man had was to be forgiven his sins. Therefore, this was the first thing Jesus did. This was the most important thing. But remember, faith is necessary for one's sins to be forgiven, and thankfully these friends and the disabled man already had faith.

> **"Him hath God exalted with his right hand to be a Prince and a Saviour, for to give repentance to Israel, and forgiveness of sins" (Acts 5:31).**

APPLICATION 1:
Jesus has compassion for all men—even the rude. But He has a special compassion for a person whose faith genuinely seeks and believes in Him. What He looks for and sees in a man is *faith*, faith that causes a man to seek after Him with all his heart.

1) These men were no doubt considered rude for breaking into line. They were probably thought selfish and self-centered by pushing ahead. But their hearts

---

1 Cited by Larry A. Payne in *Fresh Illustrations for Preaching and Teaching* by Edward K. Rowell. (Grand Rapids, MI: Co-published by Christianity Today, Inc., and Baker Books, 1997), p.24.

were crying out in desperation for their friend.
2) The disabled man was probably embarrassed, but he was also desperate, so he was willing to bear the humiliation.

APPLICATION 2:
Jesus did not conduct His services by ceremony and ritual. These men interrupted whatever He was doing. Why? Because they had need and were desperately seeking His help. Ceremony and ritual can never replace compassion. The church needs to keep itself open to the message of compassion, and compassion should always supersede ceremony and ritual. Need should always be met before ceremony and ritual. This is a known fact but a revolutionary practice.

A CLOSER LOOK #2
(9:2) **Forgiveness**: to send off, to send away. The wrong is cut out, sent off, and sent away from the wrongdoer. The sin is separated from the sinner. There are four main ideas in the Biblical concept of forgiveness.

1. There is the idea of why forgiveness is needed. Forgiveness is needed because of wrongdoing and guilt and the penalty arising from both (cp. Ro.3:23; 6:23; 8:1).
2. There is the idea of a *once-for-all* forgiveness, a total forgiveness. A man is *once-for-all* forgiven when he receives Jesus Christ as his Savior. Belief in Jesus Christ is the only condition for being forgiven *once-for-all* (Eph.1:7; Ro.4:5-8).
3. There is the idea of forgiveness that maintains fellowship. Fellowship exists between God as Father and the believer as His child. When the child does wrong, the fellowship is disturbed and broken. The condition for restoring the fellowship is a confession and a forsaking of the sin (Ps.66:18; Pr.28:13; 1 Jn.1:7).
4. There is the idea of a *releasing from guilt*. This is one of the differences between man forgiving a man and God forgiving a man. A man may forgive a person for wronging him, but he can never remove the guilt that his friend feels. And often he cannot remove the resentment he feels within his own heart. Only God can remove the guilt and assure the removal of resentment, and God does both. God forgives and erases the guilt and resentment (Ps.51:2, 7-12; 103:12; 1 Jn.1:9).

QUESTIONS:
1. Do you find it difficult to accept or receive forgiveness from God? Why or why not?
2. Forgiveness and guilt are meshed together. Is it possible to be forgiven by another person yet still have terrible feelings of guilt? What is the only way guilt can be removed from your life?

3. JESUS' POWER TO FORGIVE SINS WAS QUESTIONED: HE WAS SILENTLY ACCUSED OF BLASPHEMY (v.3).

Note: it was the religionists who *thought* that Jesus could not forgive sins, and the thought was whispered among themselves. They accused Jesus of blasphemy, of claiming to do what only God could do—forgive sins. Many think this even today. In the inner recesses of their hearts, many people do not think Jesus can truly forgive sin. They have the *thought*, the *doubt*, and perhaps even *whisper* or *hint* to others, that He is not really the Son of God, the One who has the power to forgive sins.

APPLICATION:
The innermost belief of many today is a paradox.
1) Many do not believe that Jesus Christ is truly living, that He is the Son of God, God incarnate in human flesh, who arose from the dead and is seated at the right hand of God.

2) Many who disbelieve, however, do accept Jesus Christ to be one of the greatest teachers who ever lived. The paradox with this position is that it makes Christ the biggest fraud in all history, for He did claim to be the Son of God and to possess the power of God to forgive sins.

> **"For God so loved the world, that he gave his only begotten Son, that whosoever believeth in him should not perish, but have everlasting life" (Jn.3:16).**

QUESTIONS:
1. Religionists—those who put their trust in religion instead of in Christ—do not believe that Christ can forgive a person's sins. Why does this view place so many people in bondage?
2. Why is it so important for Christ to have the power to forgive sins?

4. JESUS' POWER TO FORGIVE SINS WAS PROVEN (v.4-7).

Note four steps.

1. Jesus revealed something: He knew the rejection of the religionists. The Scribes' *evil* was their thinking that Jesus, the Son of God, was not of God, that He did not have the power to forgive sins (v.4). The crowd at least recognized His power as being the power of God, but not the Scribes and religionists. In their pride and hardness of heart, they rejected Him and refused to ascribe any authority to Him. He knew exactly what they were thinking.

APPLICATION 1:
Christ knows all our thoughts. No thought and no imagination are hidden from Him (cp. Mt.12:25; Lk.6:8; 9:47; Jn.2:25).

APPLICATION 2:
Thoughts that deny Jesus' deity are evil. Jesus has but one question for the unbeliever: "Wherefore think ye evil in your hearts?" (v.4).

2. Jesus suggested something: a test. It is much easier to say something than to do something. Therefore, Jesus suggested that He be put to the test, that He prove His deity by act and not just by word. Note two things.

a. Jesus was acknowledging that *profession only* was inadequate evidence for a claim. Action is also needed. Jesus proved that He was not just speaking words, not just professing to have the power of God to forgive sins. He forcefully spoke and the man arose.

b. Jesus' purpose was to demonstrate that the Son of Man has power to *forgive sins*. God has committed all judgment into the hands of Jesus, a judgment that either forgives or condemns a person.

> **"For the Father judgeth no man, but hath committed all judgment unto the Son: That all men should honor the Father. He that honoreth not the Son honoreth not the Father which hath sent him" (Jn.5:22-23).**

3. Christ did something: He healed the man. Christ proved His deity and Messiahship. This miracle and all others miracles prove two things.

a. His miracles prove exactly what He was claiming: that He is truly the Messiah, the Son of Man, the Son of the living God. He has the power to forgive sins.

b. His miracles prove that God does care: He cared enough to send His only Son into the world to heal and to save the needy and the hopeless.

> **"And Jesus came and spake unto them, saying, All power is given unto me in heaven and in earth" (Mt.28:18).**

APPLICATION:
Note that Christ did not argue with the religionists. His purpose was to heal and to save the needy, not to argue who He is and by whose authority He possesses the power of God.
1) He revealed His Divine knowledge, His omniscience: "Why think ye?"
2) He revealed His Divine power, His omnipotence: "Arise, take up thy bed, and go...." What a lesson for pastors, churches, and denominations today! How we need to cease arguing and begin carrying out the real mission God has called us to do.

4. Christ commanded something: go to thy house. Why did Christ send the man to his house? Our homes are to be the first recipients of our witness. But the very opposite is too often true; our homes are often overlooked and neglected. Note two facts about the saved man that can teach us a clear lesson.
a. He had been a burden to his loved ones.
b. He could now be a servant who could minister to his loved ones.

> **"And the things that thou hast heard of me among many witnesses, the same commit thou to faithful men, who shall be able to teach others also" (2 Tim.2:2).**

QUESTIONS:
1. Have you ever asked Christ to prove something to you? Have you ever asked Him to prove...
   ___His love for you?
   ___His control over your circumstances?
   ___His provision for you?
2. Do you think Christ performs miracles today? What evidence supports your opinion?

5. JESUS' POWER TO FORGIVE SINS BROUGHT GLORY TO GOD (v.8).

From this one verse, we can draw three important lessons by looking at the applications below:

APPLICATION 1:
Two things should stir unbelievers to glorify God.
1) The fact that the Messiah has really come: "God so loved the world that He gave His only begotten Son that whosoever believeth in Him should not perish but have everlasting life" (Jn.3:16).
2) The fact that unbelievers can be forgiven their sins, that is, saved: "He is able to save them to the uttermost that come unto God by Him, seeing He ever liveth to make intercession for them" (Heb.7:25).

APPLICATION 2:
Note several warnings.
1) A person can glorify God and still not be saved. The multitudes glorified God, yet they did not receive forgiveness of sins.

2) A person can marvel at Christ, but he may fail to believe that Christ is truly the Son of God.
3) A person can believe that Jesus Christ was only a man who was given the power of God while on earth, but this person will never be saved as long as he denies that Jesus is the Son of God (Jn.3:16; cp. Mt.10:33).

"By him therefore let us offer the sacrifice of praise to God continually, that is, the fruit of our lips, giving thanks to his name" (Heb.13:15; see also Ps.22:23; Ps.67:3).

ILLUSTRATION:
The greatest miracle of all is when a sinner has been forgiven by Christ. We must learn the truth that He and He alone has the power to grant forgiveness. We can neither buy nor earn forgiveness, and we never deserve it.

A little boy came to the Washington Monument and noticed a guard standing by it. The little boy looked up at the guard and said, "I want to buy it." The guard stooped down and says, "How much do you have?" The boy reached into his pocket and pulled out a quarter. The guard said, "That's not enough." The boy replied, "I thought you would say that." So he pulled out nine cents more. The guard looked down at the boy and said, "You need to understand three things. First, thirty-four cents is not enough. In fact, $34 million is not enough to buy the Washington Monument. Second, the Washington Monument is not for sale. And third, if you are an American citizen, the Washington Monument already belongs to you."

We need to understand three things about forgiveness. First, we cannot earn it. Second, it is not for sale. And third, if we accept Christ, we already have it.[2]

QUESTIONS:
1. Think of the last time something caused you to glorify God. What impact did it have on you? On others?
2. How can a person glorify God but not be saved?

SUMMARY:

Jesus was moved by the great faith of the four men who carried their sick friend to Him. The challenge that each believer faces is to have a faith that is grounded in Christ and resting upon His promises. Do you have a persistent faith, a faith that does not quit? History is the true indicator that proves the value of persistent faith in the life of the believer. This Scripture reinforces this great truth. Refresh your memory with this momentous story:

1. Jesus left Gadara and entered His own city—Capernaum. But note why He left Gadara: The Gadarenes had asked Jesus to leave. He obeyed their wish, never to return again.
2. Jesus' power to forgive sins was demonstrated as He reached out to the disabled man.
3. Jesus' power to forgive sins was questioned by the religionists: He was silently accused of blasphemy.

---

2 *Illustrations Unlimited.* James S. Hewett, Editor, p.218-219.

4. Jesus' power to forgive sins was proven.
5. Jesus' power to forgive sins brought glory to God.

PERSONAL JOURNAL NOTES
(Reflection & Response)

1. The most important thing that I learned from this lesson was:

2. The area that I need to work on the most is:

3. I can apply this lesson to my life by:

4. Closing Statement of Commitment:

MATTHEW 9:9-13

1. The sinner who needed a Savior a. Jesus saw a man b. Jesus called the man c. The man acted: He arose & followed Jesus **2. The sinner who introduced his sinful friends to the Savior** a. He entertained Jesus & his sinful friends	**H. Jesus Calls Matthew: Receiving Sinners, 9:9-13** (Mk.2:14-17; Lk.5:27-32) 9 And as Jesus passed forth from thence, he saw a man, named Matthew, sit- ting at the receipt of custom: and he saith unto him, Follow me. And he arose, and followed him. 10 And it came to pass, as Jesus sat at meat in the house, behold, many publi- cans and sinners came and sat down with him and his dis-	ciples. 11 And when the Pharisees saw it, they said unto his disci- ples, Why eateth your Master with publicans and sin- ners? 12 But when Jesus heard that, he said unto them, They that be whole need not a physician, but they that are sick. 13 But go ye and learn what that meaneth, I will have mercy, and not sacri- fice: for I am not come to call the righteous, but sinners to repentance.	b. The religionists questioned Jesus' fellowshipping with sinners **3. The Savior who saved the sinner: His mission** a. He came to be where the spiritually sick are b. He came to have mercy, not to gain sacrifice c. He came to call men to repentance

Section V
THE MESSIAH'S GREAT AUTHORITY AND POWER REVEALED IN WORD AND WORK, Matthew 8:1-9:34

Study 8: JESUS CALLS MATTHEW: RECEIVING SINNERS

Text: **Matthew 9:9-13**

Aim: To learn exactly why Christ came to earth: to save sinners from their sin.

Memory Verse:

"I say unto you, that likewise joy shall be in heaven over one sinner that repenteth, more than over ninety and nine just persons, which need no repentance" (Luke 15:7).

INTRODUCTION

How does it make you feel…

- when you have been overlooked for the party that everyone else has been invited to attend?
- when you are sick and nobody calls to see how you are feeling?
- when your job keeps you from participating in what others are doing?
- when everything that you do seems to be unappreciated?

There are few human emotions more intense and painful than the feeling of not being included, of being rejected. This is particularly true in the context of a sinner who is cut off from God. This rejection, the rejection of not having fellowship with God, is much more serious than being overlooked for a superficial social event. The main theme of the Bible is that of redemption, of God seeking and bringing lost sinners to repentance. We need to remember that the lost are blinded to the need for Christ. God has called us to go to sinners, to those who are spiritually sick, and bring them to Jesus. We can learn how this is done by studying this important portion of Matthew's life.

MATTHEW 9:9-13

This is one of the most heart-warming and touching scenes in all the Bible. It is Matthew's personal testimony.

Imagine him sitting and writing about the experiences of so many others that we have just read about in chapters 1-8. Now he comes to his own personal experience. He was a man who was bitterly opposed, talked and gossiped about and even hated—not by just a few, but by everyone. He was so detested that he was classified with the worst of sinners (Lk.15:1). He was a tax-collector for a conquering nation. He had become wealthy by extortion, so wealthy that he was able to own a house large enough to handle a huge crowd and a large feast. He was immoral, unjust, money-hungry, and worldly-minded. He cared more for possessions and wealth than for people. Through the years he had become hard, bitter and, worst of all, without love, purpose, meaning, and significance in life. There is, of course, so much more; yet he covers it all in these few simple verses.

What is so heart-warming and touching is that he shares his own personal conversion in one simple verse, and then he moves on to share how Jesus came to save sinners such as himself. He does not talk about himself nor about the details of his sin and shame, but He lifts up Jesus and the glorious salvation Jesus came to bring. He emphasizes not his own conversion, but the fact that Jesus came to save all tax-collectors and sinners such as himself.

OUTLINE:

1. The sinner who needed a Savior (v.9).
2. The sinner who introduced his sinful friends to the Savior (v.10-11).
3. The Savior who saved the sinner: His mission (v.12-13).

A CLOSER LOOK #1

(9:9-13) **Matthew—Tax-Collector**: Jesus "saw a man," a sinner who needed a cause. The people saw not a man, but Matthew, a tax-collector for the Romans. They hated him and all other tax-collectors. There are three reasons why tax-collectors were so bitterly hated.

1. They served the Roman conquerors. Most tax-collectors were Jews, but in the people's eyes they had denied their Jewish heritage and betrayed their country. They were thus ostracized, completely cut off from Jewish society and excommunicated from Jewish religion and privileges.
2. They were cheats, dishonest and unjust men. Most tax-collectors were extremely wealthy. The Roman government compensated tax-collectors by allowing them to collect more than the percentage required for taxes. Tax-collectors greedily abused their right, adding whatever percent they wished and felt could be collected. They took bribes from the wealthy who wished to avoid taxes, fleeced the average citizen, and swindled the government when they could.
3. They were assuming rights that belonged only to God. In the eyes of the Jews, God and the ruling High Priest were considered to be the head of Jewish government. Therefore, taxes were to be paid only to God and His government. To pay taxes to earthly rulers was an abuse and a denial of God's rights. Therefore, tax-collectors were excommunicated from Jewish religion and privileges. They were accursed, anathema.

1. THE SINNER WHO NEEDED A SAVIOR (v.9).

Note Matthew's conversion.

1. Jesus "saw a man" named Matthew. Jesus saw where he was sitting and what he was doing. He saw everything about Matthew. He saw his heart, his mind, his thoughts, his hurt, his pain, his loneliness, his lack of purpose and meaning in life. He saw a useless life, a life being wasted. He "saw a man," a man who needed a Savior, a Savior who could meet every need of his existence.

2. Jesus called the man. He dramatically said, "Follow me." It was forceful and to the point. There were to be no questions asked, no hesitations, no buts, no allowances, no half-heartedness, no delayed decision.

Again, the command was forceful and to the point. The man was to follow at once, without hesitating. It was either immediate and total commitment or nothing.

> **"Come unto me, all ye that labour and are heavy laden, and I will give you rest. Take my yoke upon you, and learn of me; for I am meek and lowly in heart: and ye shall find rest unto your souls. For my yoke is easy, and my burden is light" (Mt.11:28-30).**

3. The man acted: he arose and followed Jesus. He got up and left all to follow Him. Of course, sometime after this initial encounter he acted responsibly and took care of his business affairs, resigning his position in a responsible manner. But when the call first came, he immediately began to follow Christ. He left all and committed himself totally to Christ.

> **"So likewise, whosoever he be of you that forsaketh not all that he hath, he cannot be my disciple" (Lk.14:33).**

APPLICATION 1:
Matthew was a working man, very industrious. He was not lazy or slothful. Apparently he was dissatisfied with his profession, but he was working, and working hard. Jesus has no room for the lazy and the soft.

APPLICATION 2:
A dramatic change took place in Matthew.
1) Jesus' call was clear and forceful, unequivocal: "Follow me."
2) Matthew's response was clear and forceful, unequivocal: he arose and followed Christ.

ILLUSTRATION:
Christ came to save sinners, all sinners—no matter their status or profession in life. But only those who respond to His call will be plucked out of the treacherous waters of sin.

> *If a person were to fall into ten feet of water, would he drown? The depth of the water is not really the issue. It is what a person does after he falls in the water that counts. If he comes up out of the water he can be saved, but if he stays under he's doomed.*
>
> *The same is true for people on the path of life. Those who fall into sin and choose to stay there are doomed to hell, but those who fall and choose to get up can be saved to eternal life!*

QUESTIONS:
1. Christ extends His hand to us (and all sinners) every day. What step must *you* take to be rescued?
2. Christ sees not only our sins, but also our needs. Is there any sin too big, any need too great for Him to meet? Why do we so often live as if our problems are too big for him to handle?
3. Why is it so important to respond to God's call immediately? Is there any harm in waiting?

2. THE SINNER WHO INTRODUCED HIS SINFUL FRIENDS TO THE SAVIOR (v.10-11).

1. Matthew entertained Jesus and his sinful friends. The very first thing Matthew did was witness to his friends. He arranged a "great feast" for Jesus to share with his sinful friends (Lk.5:29). The witnessing session was apparently very fruitful: "there were many, and they followed Him" (Mk.2:15).

> **"Then said Jesus to them again, Peace be unto you: as my Father hath sent me, even so send I you" (Jn.20:21).**

APPLICATION 1:
All the apostles set a *dynamic example in witnessing*. They all began to witness immediately upon their conversion. How often we fail and come short in witnessing to our sinful friends.

APPLICATION 2:
A new convert should not boast in his past, but in Jesus. However, this is too often not the case. Many emphasize their past sins—sins such as materialism, immorality, drunkenness, and pride—instead of Jesus. But note that Matthew does no writing about his former life. He lifts up Jesus Christ, not his past life and wealth. He does not even mention his wealth or his house nor that he had planned a "great feast" for Christ and his sinful friends. Mark and Luke are the ones who tell us this. What a lesson in modesty and humility!

APPLICATION 3:
Note several important lessons.
1) Jesus went where the sinners were. He did not avoid or shy away from them. He sought them out.
2) Sinners felt comfortable coming to Jesus. They did not shy away nor feel unwelcomed.
3) Jesus had meals with sinners, immoral people whom society and religionists rejected and avoided.
4) Jesus reached out to sinners, to witness to them. Look at the scene here: there was a large feast and a party of immoral characters, and Jesus was right in the midst of them. Of course, the purpose of the feast was for Jesus to bear witness. This is important: we are to be out in the world witnessing to sinful men, but we are not to be of the world.

2. The religionists questioned Jesus' fellowship with sinners. They (the Pharisees) "saw it"; that is, they saw Jesus sitting and eating with sinners. It is almost as if they were waiting and watching for wrongdoing so they could pounce on Him.

The religionists did not speak to Jesus Himself, but to His disciples. They would not dare approach Him personally, but they readily attacked Him through those closest to Him. Perhaps there was an attempt to turn His followers away from Him as is often the case in day-to-day life.

APPLICATION 1:
Many love to hear news that is bad, tragic, or immoral. In fact, the more immoral and unjust, the juicier the attack, the talk, and the gossip in their minds.

APPLICATION 2:
The temperate, the disciplined, the moral, the strict, the law-abiding, the religious so often find it difficult to understand and forgive those who fail. They simply cannot comprehend how a person can be so undisciplined and live such an

immoral life. How often do we convey the idea that God has nothing to do with sinners?

APPLICATION 3:
The self-disciplined and religious are sometimes the most judgmental and censorious. A judgmental and censorious spirit does more to hurt people than any other single thing. But note what God says: the person who judges and censors others shall be shut out of the Kingdom of God (Ro.2:1-3).

QUESTIONS:
1. Are you at ease introducing your lost friends to Christ? What is the key to witnessing to your lost friends?
2. People often tend to give more glory to Satan's work in their past life than to God's glorious deliverance and salvation. What do you stress the most when you share your testimony—Satan's damage or God's healing?
3. How comfortable are sinners who are in your presence?
   ___They feel condemned.
   ___They feel talked down to.
   ___They feel that you are somehow different, but approachable.
   ___They feel that you hate their sin but love them personally.

3. THE SAVIOR WHO SAVED THE SINNER: HIS MISSION (v.12-13).

Two things are being said in these two verses.

First, Matthew was testifying that he, the sinner, and his sinful friends were spiritually sick, and they needed the mercy of God. They needed a Savior and they believed that Jesus was that Savior. They believed that Jesus had come to save them.

Second, Jesus was warning the religionists and those who think they are more acceptable to God than others...

- Jesus warned that He came to be where the spiritually sick are. He had come to earth for the same purpose that a physician sets up an office or enters a home: to help the sick. However, just like the physician, Jesus can minister only to the sick who call upon Him or come to Him for healing.
- Jesus warned that He came to have mercy on people, not to lead people to make sacrifices in religious worship. He came to show and bestow mercy upon sinners, upon any person who knows that he is a sinner and desires the mercy and acceptance of God.
- Jesus warned that He came to call sinners to repentance. If a person does not know that he needs changing (repentance), Jesus cannot help him. But if he knows he is a sinner and wants to be changed, Jesus can lead him to repentance (to change).

Note that the threefold purpose of Jesus is given.

1. Jesus came to be where the spiritually sick are.

> **"Even as the Son of man came not to be ministered unto, but to minister, and to give his life a ransom for many" (Mt.20:28; see also Lk.19:10).**

APPLICATION 1:
Sin is a sickness. All have sinned (Ro.3:23); therefore all are spiritually sick and need healing by the Great Physician. But a man must acknowledge his sickness and ask the physician for help if he wishes to be healed.

APPLICATION 2:
Many are walking about with the fatal disease of sin, but they are...

- ignoring it
- neglecting it
- feeding it
- denying it
- abusing it

APPLICATION 3:
Sin, the sickness of the spirit, is always curable (Ro.10:13). It is fatal if unchecked, but no one need ever die from it. How foolish to have a fatal disease that is curable and not seek the cure!

2. Jesus came to have mercy, not to gain sacrifice.

"For I desired mercy, and not sacrifice; and the knowledge of God more than burnt offerings" (Hos.6:6).

APPLICATION:
God's call is to mercy, not to sacrifice. Sacrifice and gifts are wanted by God, but they are not enough. A person can make one sacrifice after another and continually give gifts and still not please God. What God wants first of all is a person's life, all that a person is and has. Once God has the person's life, He has all he is. God wants to have mercy, to forgive and to cleanse and to make the person acceptable for heaven.

3. Jesus came to call men to repentance.

"I tell you, Nay: but, except ye repent, ye shall all likewise perish" (Lk.13:3).

APPLICATION 1:
Jesus does not call the self-righteous and the self-satisfied. Why? Because they feel they are already *good enough* to be acceptable to God. Jesus calls sinners to repentance who are deeply aware of their need for a Savior (1 Tim.1:15), for a changed life (2 Cor.5:17).

APPLICATION 2:
Note the person whom Jesus calls.
1) The person who is spiritually sick.
2) The person who needs mercy.
3) The person who is a sinner.
4) The person who needs repentance.

ILLUSTRATION:
When God calls a person to repentance, it is always based upon His great mercy. The call to repentance expects an instant response of obedience. It is not a time to negotiate a better deal with God.

Two men were shipwrecked. One of them started to pray, "Dear Lord, I've broken most of the Commandments. I've been an awful sinner all my days. Lord, if you'll spare me I'll..."

The other one shouted, "Hold on, don't commit yourself. I think I see a boat coming!"[2]

---

2 *INFOsearch Sermon Illustrations* (Arlington, TX: The Computer Assistant, 1-888-868-9029, 1986-1996).

MATTHEW 9:9-13

QUESTIONS:

1. We often forget that Christ came to save the spiritually sick: all who confess to be sinners, all who know they are under a death sentence. Where can the spiritually sick be found? What is your responsibility toward them?
2. In very practical terms, what does it mean to repent?
3. Through Christ, repentance is the lifeline to salvation. Can a person pick and choose when to repent? Can a person be saved without repenting?

A CLOSER LOOK #2

(9:13) **Repentance**: Christ preached repentance. Repentance means to change; to turn; to change one's mind; to turn one's life. It is turning away from sin and turning toward God. It is putting sin out of one's thoughts and behavior. It is resolving never to think or do a certain thing again. (Cp. Mt.3:2; Lk.13:2-3; Acts 2:38; 3:19; 8:22; 26:20.) The change is turning away from lying, stealing, cheating, immorality, cursing, drunkenness, and the other so-called glaring *sins of the flesh*. But the change is also turning away from *the silent sins of the spirit* such as self-centeredness, selfishness, envy, bitterness, pride, covetousness, anger, evil thoughts, hopelessness, laziness, jealousy, and lust.

SUMMARY:

Jesus Christ came to save us from sin and death, to call us *to repentance*. The question that every one of us must ask is this: Have I responded to Christ? Have I obeyed Him and repented? Any answer but "yes" is the greatest of human tragedies. Matthew reminds us of his own testimony of salvation:

1. He was the sinner who needed a Savior.
2. He was the sinner who introduced his sinful friends to the Savior.
3. Jesus Christ was the Savior who saved him, the sinner.

PERSONAL JOURNAL NOTES
(Reflection & Response)

1. The most important thing that I learned from this lesson was:

2. The area that I need to work on the most is:

3. I can apply this lesson to my life by:

4. Closing Statement of Commitment:

         1. John's disciples questioned Jesus about fasting: Jesus gave three illustrations **2. The Bridegroom: A new life & age of joy** a. His presence brings joy b. His prediction: Death	**I. Jesus Answers a Question about Fasting: Ushering in a New Age & Covenant, 9:14-17** (Mk.2:18-22; Lk.5:33-39) 14 Then came to him the disciples of John, saying, Why do we and the Pharisees fast oft, but thy disci- ples fast not? 15 And Jesus said unto them, Can the children of the bride- chamber mourn, as long as the bride- groom is with them? but the days will	come, when the bridegroom shall be taken from them, and then shall they fast. 16 No man putteth a piece of new cloth unto an old garment, for that which is put in to fill it up taketh from the garment, and the rent is made worse. 17 Neither do men put new wine into old bottles: else the bottles break, and the wine runneth out, and the bottles per- ish: but they put new wine into new bot- tles, and both are pre- served.	c. His death will bring fasting **3. The new cloth: A stronger life and age** a. The new is stronger b. The old is weaker **4. The new & old wine: A new life & age of more power** a. The new would burst the old bottles b. Both are to be preserved

Section V
THE MESSIAH'S GREAT AUTHORITY AND POWER REVEALED IN WORD AND WORK, Matthew 8:1-9:34

Study 9: JESUS ANSWERS A QUESTION ABOUT FASTING: USHERING IN A NEW AGE AND COVENANT

Text: **Matthew 9:14-17**

Aim: To make sure you have received the new life offered by Christ.

Memory Verse:

"Neither do men put new wine into old bottles: else the bottles break, and the wine runneth out, and the bottles perish: but they put new wine into new bottles, and both are preserved" (Matthew 9:17).

INTRODUCTION

Many a young child has received "hand-me-downs" from an older sibling or family friend. Whether they be shirts, pants, or a winter coat, the older clothes can usually be worn at least a few more times before becoming dust rags. No longer in "new and mint condition," these clothes are useful, but are not intended to last for a long time. Of these hand-me-downs, some shirt or coat becomes a favorite—even after it is worn out. The color is faded, the worn spots have become holes, and the threads are frayed. To get rid of such a favorite garment is very difficult, but it is necessary. In the same sense, spiritual children become accustomed to old garments, to old ways of doing things. Putting on anything new is resisted. In this particular portion of Scripture, Christ will address the need for each one of us to carefully examine and put on the new things that He has in store for us.

The question of fasting had already been answered by Jesus (Mt.6:16-18), but John's disciples were not aware of it. It is important to see a little of the background of this passage in order to understand what is really happening.

1. John was in prison with the threat of capital punishment hanging over his head. His disciples were naturally concerned. They were fasting often in his behalf, asking God to deliver him, and they could not understand why Jesus and His disciples had not joined in fasting for John's release. John's disciples had been taught by John to fast and to fast often (Jn.11:18). They were also deeply steeped in Jewish religious practices which demanded much fasting. Jesus seemed to break the traditional ritual of fasting; therefore, they could not understand how He could be the Messiah and be so irreligious.

2. What Jesus did was enlarge the question of fasting to include all religious ceremonies and rituals, rules and regulations. He used three illustrations to show that He was ushering in a new life, a new age, and a new covenant between God and man. The truth of the old religion and its practices was to be preserved; they were not to be done away with (v.17). However, now there was to be a greater truth, a truth that superseded all former truth. He had been *sent by God* to bring a new life to man. Note that the focus of this new life was His presence, the presence of the Bridegroom. Christ is the Bridegroom of the new age, the new life, and the new covenant. He is the Bridegroom of the church.

OUTLINE:

1. John's disciples (v.14).
2. The Bridegroom: a new life and age of joy (v.15).
3. The new cloth: a stronger life and age (v.16)
4. The new and old wine: a new life and age of more power (v.17).

1. JOHN'S DISCIPLES (v.14).

John's disciples questioned Jesus about fasting (see Introduction above for discussion). Note two things.

1. John's disciples were criticizing, grumbling, and complaining. Why? Because Jesus' disciples were not doing what John's disciples thought they should do. Jesus' disciples were not fasting in prayer and asking God to deliver John from prison, nor were they fasting two times a week as all religionists were supposed to do. Simply stated, they felt that Jesus' disciples were living *loose lives,* not following the rules and regulations of religion.

APPLICATION:
How often we criticize those who veer away from the traditions and rules that we practice and find easy to keep. While most men are disciplined in some areas, they are also undisciplined in others. It is easy to criticize another man's weakness while overlooking our own. (Cp. Mt.7:1-5.) Much division and damage are done by murmuring among God's people!

2. Jesus answered the question about fasting by giving three illustrations.

QUESTIONS:

1. Are you ever tempted to criticize another believer who worships God in a different way from you? What causes believers to criticize others from different denominations or parts of the Body of Christ?
2. Where there are differences in the way religion is practiced, what is your obligation—to yourself, to others, to God?

2. THE BRIDEGROOM: A NEW LIFE AND AGE OF JOY (v.15).

The first illustration is that of the Bridegroom. The Bridegroom pictures a new life and age of *joy*. The illustration is clear. During the marriage festivities of a bridegroom, as long as the bridegroom is present, his attendants rejoice. It is a joyful, festive time. Jesus was teaching several lessons.

⇒ He is the Bridegroom (cp. Jn.3:29). The children are the attendants or children of the bridegroom.

⇒ His presence is an occasion for joy and rejoicing. His presence is what makes the difference in a life. If He is present, there is no reason to mourn. He brings joy and rejoicing to life (Ps.16:11; Jn.15:11; Ph.4:4; 2 Cor.6:10).

⇒ His presence was going to be removed; then His disciples would mourn His absence and there would be cause for fasting.

Note three significant points.

1. Jesus' presence brings joy. The age of the Messiah was often pictured as a joyful occasion. It was often compared to the festivities surrounding a marriage feast. Jesus was saying that He was the Bridegroom who was ushering in the Messianic Age. The Messiah brought a *new age* and a *new life* to man, an age of joy and liberation (salvation). It is a new age and life that supersedes the mechanical and external rituals and ceremonies of religion. It is an age that brings God's presence down to man and lays the emphasis on God's presence, not on ritual and ceremony.

"I am come that they might have life, and that they might have it more abundantly" (Jn.10:10).

APPLICATION:

The presence of Jesus Christ gave the disciples a sense of God's presence. His presence filled them with love, joy, and peace (Gal.5:22-23). It infused them with a conviction and confidence of living forever in God's presence. Therefore, they had no need to be fasting in order to gain a closer walk and a deeper consciousness of God's presence. They were already walking close to Him.

The same is true of us. When we are aware of the Bridegroom's presence and walking close to Him, there is not as much need to be fasting. It is a time of praise, rejoicing, and service. But when the Bridegroom seems to be far away, when we are not so conscious of His presence and not walking as closely as we should, then we need to fast and seek His presence and power.

2. Jesus' prediction was that He would die. Jesus was predicting His death by violent means. He was to "be taken from them." Note several things.

a. His death enabled His Spirit to be present with all believers around the world (Jn.14:16-18).

"Nevertheless I tell you the truth; It is expedient for you that I go away: for if I go not away, the Comforter will not come unto you; but if I depart, I will send him unto you" (Jn.16:7).

b. His death brought sorrow to the hearts of all who saw it and understood it. But it brought joy soon after, for there was the knowledge that He lives forevermore.

"Verily, verily, I say unto you, That ye shall weep and lament, but the world shall rejoice: and ye shall be sorrowful, but your sorrow shall be turned into joy. A woman when she is in travail hath sorrow, because her hour is come: but as soon as she is delivered of the child, she remembereth no more the anguish, for joy that a man is born into

the world. And ye now therefore have sorrow: but I will see you again, and your heart shall rejoice, and your joy no man taketh from you" (Jn.16:20-22).

c. His death and its cleansing power can be *forgotten* (2 Pt.1:9). The Lord's presence can fade from a person's consciousness. A person can become so busy and preoccupied with the affairs of the world that he loses his sensitivity to the Lord's presence. At such times, the person needs to get alone with God. His concern should be so great that neither food nor sleep matter; nothing matters except regaining the consciousness of God's presence.

"But he that lacketh these things is blind, and cannot see afar off, and hath forgotten that he was purged from his old sins" (2 Pt.1:9).

3. Jesus' death brought fasting.

APPLICATION:
His death caused the first disciples to fast. It ought to cause us to fast also:
⇒ when we first learn of His death and what it really means.

"For God so loved the world, that he gave his only begotten Son, that whosoever believeth in him should not perish, but have everlasting life" (Jn.3:16).

⇒ when we are forcibly reminded that He died for us. Such times should be heartrending times, precious times of prayer and fasting for other believers.
⇒ when we have allowed His presence to slip out of our minds for some length of time. At such times we need to get alone and meditate upon His death, allowing nothing to interfere, including food.

"Watch and pray, that ye enter not into temptation: the spirit indeed is willing, but the flesh is weak" (Mt.26:41).

QUESTIONS:
1. Jesus has promised that His presence will bring joy to His people. What is missing if a believer is not experiencing that joy? How can a person draw closer to God?
2. Why is it so important to remember the Lord's death on the cross? In what ways can you keep the Lord's death and sacrifice in the forefront of your mind?
3. Why should a person fast? How often should a person fast? What does God want to do in the heart of any believer who fasts for the right reasons?

3. THE NEW CLOTH: A STRONGER LIFE AND AGE (v.16).

The second illustration is that of the new cloth. The new cloth illustrates a stronger life and age. Jesus was saying two things.

1. He was ushering in a new life and age which was stronger than the old life and age.

2. He could not take His teachings and patch up the old teaching. It would not only *detract* from the good of the old, but it would cause a *tear* that would be greater than what was going to naturally happen. There was going to be a tear in the old religion and teaching, a natural tear that occurs when any new age or movement is launched in a major way. But the tear would be greater if He attempted to patch up the old, causing the followers of the old to react even more violently and quickly than what they would have.

"But as many as received him, to them gave he power to become the sons of God, even to them that believe on his name: which were born, not of blood, nor of the will of the flesh, nor of the will of man, but of God" (Jn.1:12-13).

APPLICATION 1:
There was a tear, a pulling apart between Jesus and the *old religion* with its rituals and ceremonies. He was saying that the tear would have been much greater if He had adopted the old and reformed it. Both the new and old would have been useless, no good for any man to wear. The true religion would have been drastically torn and unsuitable to clothe a man (cp. such passages dealing with righteousness as 2 Cor.5:19-20; Ph.3:4-16, esp.5-7, 9).

APPLICATION 2:
Many people are attached to *formal religion,* putting their trust in its ceremonies and rituals. Going through the mechanics of religion is what is thought to be important. A person feels that he is acceptable to God as long as he worships God and that anyone who says otherwise or attempts to change the tradition of religion is radical and fanatic.

APPLICATION 3:
The following statements are tragically true.
⇒ Many worship tradition, not God.
⇒ Many worship ritual, not God.
⇒ Many worship religion, not God.
⇒ Many worship ceremony, not God.
⇒ Many worship fellowship, not God.

"Having a form of godliness, but denying the power thereof: from such turn away" (2 Tim.3:5).

A CLOSER LOOK #2
(9:16) **Jesus' Life—Reformation**: Christ brings an adventuresome life. New wine skins were elastic and would expand as the gas of fermenting wine built up pressure. Old wine skins were hardened and would not expand, but rather would explode under pressure. Jesus said that He was bringing a new elasticity to life: a new expansion, a new adventure, a new excitement, a new life.

"Therefore if any man be in Christ, he is a new creature: old things are passed away; behold, all things are become new" (2 Cor. 5:17).

ILLUSTRATION:
It is human nature to cling to what is old and familiar. This has been noted in the course of human events concerning new inventions.

Listen to these examples of inventions and ideas that some people said "couldn't be done" so they resisted the new.

1. The first successful cast-iron plow, invented in the United States in 1797, was rejected by New Jersey farmers under the theory that cast iron poisoned the land and stimulated the growth of weeds.

2. An eloquent authority in the United States declared that the introduction of the railroad would require the building of many insane asylums, since people would be driven mad with terror at the sight of locomotives rushing across the country.

3. In Germany it was proved by "experts" that if trains went at the frightful speed of 15 miles an hour, blood would spurt from the travelers' noses and passengers would suffocate when going through tunnels.

4. Commodore Vanderbilt dismissed Westinghouse and his new air brakes for trains, stating, "I have no time to waste on fools."

5. Those who loaned Robert Fulton money for his steamboat project stipulated that their names be withheld for fear of ridicule were it known they supported anything so "foolhardy."

6. In 1881, when the New York YWCA announced typing lessons for women, vigorous protests were made on the grounds that the female constitution would break down under the strain.

7. Men insisted that iron ships would not float, that they would damage more easily than wooden ships when grounding, that it would be difficult to preserve the iron bottom from rust, and that iron would deflect the compass.

8. Joshua Coppersmith was arrested in Boston for trying to sell stock in the telephone. "All well-informed people know that it is impossible to transmit the human voice over a wire."

9. The editor of the Springfield Republican refused an invitation to ride in an early automobile, claiming that it was incompatible with the dignity of his position.[1]

QUESTIONS:

1. How would you describe your Christian life:
   ___I'm all patched up and leaking like a sieve.
   ___I've still got a patch or two of old traditions that I just can't let go of yet.
   ___I've allowed the Lord to replace everything with a new cloth (life).
2. Are all traditions wrong? Which ones are of the Lord and which ones are not? What is the ultimate authority for deciding what tradition is right or wrong?

4. THE NEW AND OLD WINE: A NEW LIFE AND AGE OF MORE POWER (v.17).

The third illustration is the new and old wine. The new and old wine illustrates a new life and age of *more power*. Christ was saying two things.

1. The new wine would burst the old bottles. The new life and age which He ushered in had too much gas, energy, and power for the old bottles. The pressure would burst the old bottles. There was just too much power.

> **"And what is the exceeding greatness of his power to us-ward who believe, according to the working of his mighty power, which he wrought in Christ, when he raised him from the dead, and set him at his own right hand in the heavenly places, far above all principality, and power, and might, and dominion, and every name that is named, not only in this world, but also in that which is to come: and hath put all things under his feet, and gave him to be the head over all things to the church, which is his body, the fulness of him that filleth all in all" (Eph.1:19-23).**

2. The answer to handling old and new wine is to preserve the good of both. The old religion was not to be cast aside. It had some strengths and some benefits. The answer was not to reform it, but to fulfill it by ushering in a new life and age. The old bottles (restrictions) were not strong enough to contain the new life which Christ was bringing in.

---

1 *Illustrations Unlimited.* James S. Hewett, Editor, p. 407.

"For he hath made him to be sin for us, who knew no sin; that we might be made the righteousness of God in him" (2 Cor.5:21).

APPLICATION 1:
The new wine would have been lost if it had been put into the old bottles of religion. There would be no new life or age, no hope for man whatsoever (2 Cor.5:17).

APPLICATION 2:
We must not let the traditions of the old way bring about our death. Our rituals, ceremonies, and religion will die apart from the new life in Jesus Christ. Even we will die apart from His new life. Our traditions, our religion can keep us from Him by focusing our attention upon them instead of upon God.

ILLUSTRATION:
The religious traditions of men usually have sincere, innocent beginnings. The great problem comes when the tradition replaces the real reason for religion: having a fresh, on-going relationship with God. This humorous story makes a striking point.

A devout Christian who had a cat used to spend several minutes each day at prayer and meditation in his bedroom. He read a portion of Scripture and a devotional book, followed by a period of silent meditation and prayer. As time went on his prayers became longer and more intense.

He came to cherish this quiet time in his bedroom, but his cat came to like it, too. She would cozy up to him, purr loudly, and rub her furry body against him. This interrupted the man's prayer time, so he put a collar around the cat's neck and tied her to the bedpost whenever he wanted to be undisturbed while at prayer. This didn't seem to upset the cat, and it meant that the man could meditate without interruption.

Over the years, the daughter of this devout Christian had noted how much his devotional time had meant to him. When she began to establish some routines and patterns with her own family, she decided she should do as her father had done. Dutifully she, too, tied her cat to the bedpost and then proceeded to her devotions. But time moved faster in her generation and she couldn't spend as much time at prayer as did her father.

The day came when her son grew up and wanted to make sure that he preserved some of the family traditions which had meant so much to his mother and his grandfather. But the pace of life had quickened all the more and there simply was no time for such elaborate devotional proceedings. So he eliminated the time for meditation, Bible reading, and prayer. But in order to carry on the religious tradition, each day while he was dressing he tied the family cat to the bedpost.

Thus forms become more important than the faith they are meant to convey.[2]

Has anything in *your* religious ritual replaced your relationship with Christ?

A CLOSER LOOK #3
(9:17) **Covenant**: the new life and age is the new covenant Christ came to establish between God and man. The old covenant was a written law; the new covenant is the Spirit of God Himself. The old covenant was written words and letters, a written document, a set of laws that men had to obey (Exodus 24:1-8). The fact to note is this: the law was external; it sat outside man and insisted that man subject himself to the rule and obey it.

2 *Illustrations Unlimited.* James S. Hewett, Editor, p. 437.

MATTHEW 9:14-17

The new covenant is different, entirely distinct. It is internal, within man. It is a personal relationship with God, a relationship that is created by God Himself. When a person believes in God's Son, God places His Spirit in the heart of the person, and the person becomes a Spirit-filled person.

> **"But the Comforter, which is the Holy Ghost, whom the Father will send in my name, he shall teach you all things, and bring all things to your remembrance, whatsoever I have said unto you" (John 14:26).**

QUESTIONS:

1. The new life that Christ offers is one that grows and has no limits. How can you be sure you are not restricting that growth in your life?
2. What have you tried to contain in old wine skins (in the old ways of doing things) that has blown up in your face?
3. Why must a person get rid of the old life for the new?

SUMMARY:

Jesus Christ has come to give us new life. This new life is not to be found in the old traditions of religion, but in Jesus Christ Himself. How is your relationship with Him? The blessings of having a new way of living in Christ are spelled out through these important points:

1. John's disciples questioned Jesus about fasting. In answering them, Jesus Christ used three illustrations that pointed to the new life He was creating for mankind.
2. Illustration number one: The Bridegroom: a new life and age of joy.
3. Illustration number two: The new cloth: a stronger life and age.
4. Illustration number three: The new and old wine: a new life and age of more power.

PERSONAL JOURNAL NOTES
(Reflection & Response)

1. The most important thing that I learned from this lesson was:

2. The area that I need to work on the most is:

3. I can apply this lesson to my life by:

4. Closing Statement of Commitment:

1. **The hopeless cry for life (Part 1)**
   a. The man: A ruler & a father
      1) Hopeless: Death
      2) Attitude: Worship
      3) Request: Touch her
      4) Faith: "Shall live"
   b. Jesus' response: Arose & followed
2. **The secret hope for health**
   a. The woman
      1) Hopeless: Ostracized
      2) Attitude: Unworthy
      3) Faith: "I shall be whole"
   b. Jesus' response
      1) "Turned": Responded to her
      2) "Saw": Had compassion
      3) Called her "Daughter": Adopted her
      4) Made her whole by His power
3. **The hopeless cry for life (Part 2)**
   a. The trying delay: Jesus finally arrived
   b. The atmosphere: Noisy
   c. The strong demand

J. Jesus Heals Several People: Meeting Man's Desperate & Hopeless Needs, 9:18-34

(Mk.5:21-43; Lk.8:41-56; 11:14-15)

18 While he spake these things unto them, behold, there came a certain ruler, and worshipped him, saying, My daughter is even now dead: but come and lay thy hand upon her, and she shall live.

19 And Jesus arose, and followed him, and so did his disciples.

20 And, behold, a woman, which was diseased with an issue of blood twelve years, came behind him, and touched the hem of his garment:

21 For she said within herself, If I may but touch his garment, I shall be whole.

22 But Jesus turned him about, and when he saw her, he said, Daughter, be of good comfort; thy faith hath made thee whole. And the woman was made whole from that hour.

23 And when Jesus came into the ruler's house, and saw the minstrels and the people making a noise,

24 He said unto them, Give place: for the maid is not dead, but sleepeth. And they laughed him to scorn.

25 But when the people were put forth, he went in, and took her by the hand, and the maid arose.

26 And the fame hereof went abroad into all that land.

27 And when Jesus departed thence, two blind men followed him, crying, and saying, Thou Son of David, have mercy on us.

28 And when he was come into the house, the blind men came to him: and Jesus saith unto them, Believe ye that I am able to do this? They said unto him, Yea, Lord.

29 Then touched he their eyes, saying, According to your faith be it unto you.

30 And their eyes were opened; and Jesus straitly charged them, saying, See that no man know it.

31 But they, when they were departed, spread abroad his fame in all that country.

32 As they went out, behold, they brought to him a dumb man possessed with a devil.

33 And when the devil was cast out, the dumb spake: and the multitudes marvelled, saying, It was never so seen in Israel.

34 But the Pharisees said, He casteth out devils through the prince of the devils.

   d. The daughter's death
   e. The mourner's reaction: Scorn
   f. The power of Jesus' hand
   g. The result of His power
4. **The unceasing cry for sight**
   a. The men followed Jesus
      1) Acknowledged His Messiahship
      2) Cried for mercy
      3) Sought after Him
   b. Jesus' response: A readiness to help
      1) His question
      2) His touch
      3) His power: Based on faith
   c. Jesus' instruction: Focus on me, not on the miracle nor on self
5. **The quiet approach for sanity & speech**
   a. A demon-possessed man brought by others
   b. Jesus' response: He healed
6. **The reaction to Jesus' power**
   a. The people: Were amazed
   b. The religionists: Called Jesus devil-possessed

MATTHEW 9:18-34

Section V
THE MESSIAH'S GREAT AUTHORITY AND POWER REVEALED IN WORD AND WORK, Matthew 8:1-9:34

Study 10: JESUS HEALS SEVERAL PEOPLE: MEETING MAN'S DESPERATE AND HOPELESS NEEDS

Text: **Matthew 9:18-34**

Aim: To arouse yourself to trust Christ, even in the darkest of times.

Memory Verse:

"And when he was come into the house, the blind men came to him: and Jesus saith unto them, Believe ye that I am able to do this? They said unto him, Yea, Lord. Then touched he their eyes, saying, According to your faith be it unto you" (Mt.9:28-29).

INTRODUCTION

One of Hollywood's most endearing movies is the classic directed by Frank Capra *"It's a Wonderful Life."* Even these many years later, the impact of Capra's film continues to convey some of life's most important lessons:

⇒ Good can overcome evil.
⇒ Money does not guarantee happiness.
⇒ People are important and are placed here on earth by God's design.
⇒ Relationships are important and are not to be taken for granted.
⇒ The events of this world—both the good and the bad—are not unknown to God and He is always in control.
⇒ No matter how bad things might seem to be, the power of hope will help a person persevere.
⇒ The impossible becomes possible as long as there is hope.

This passage includes four examples of people who had desperate, hopeless needs. They demonstrate two things: Christ is beyond question the Messiah, "the Son of David" (v.27); and Christ has the power to meet our desperate, hopeless needs, even the need of conquering death.

OUTLINE:

1. The hopeless cry for life (Part 1) (v.18-19).
2. The secret hope for health (v.20-22).
3. The hopeless cry for life (Part 2) (v.23-26).
4. The unceasing cry for sight (v.27-31).
5. The quiet approach for sanity and speech (v.32-33).
6. The reaction to Jesus' power (v.33-34).

A CLOSER LOOK #1

(9:18-34) **Faith**: the things God wants from men are the very same things a parent wants from a child—faith and trust, love and dependence. God wants a man to believe and trust Him, to love and depend upon Him. This is clearly seen throughout this passage.

1. God responds to true faith. God does whatever good a person asks if that person really believes in Him and in His power. And amazingly, the request can be *in behalf of another person*. God will touch the life of another person because we pray in faith (cp. Mt.8:5-13).

a. The daughter was raised from the dead because of the father's faith (Mt.9:18, 25).
b. The hemorrhaging woman was healed and saved because of her own faith (Mt.9:21-22).
c. The two blind men received their sight because of their own persistent faith (Mt.9:29-30).
d. The dumb man possessed by an evil spirit was delivered and received his sanity because of the faith of others (Mt.9:32-33).

2. Our faith is only as strong as *the object of our faith*. The power of faith does not rest in a person's own faith but in God and God alone (Mk.6:30). Christ can do anything no matter what it is, but the question is, will He? It always depends upon two things.

a. Is the request good? Is it good for all, both for the people involved and for the world? And is it good for God Himself and His glory? Only God can know if a request is good; that is, does it embrace good for all persons involved. This is what is meant by asking according to His will. But note this: a great deal of what is good (His will) is already revealed to us in His Word. We can ask according to His Word and He will answer—if we truly believe.
b. Is the request really asked in faith? Do we really believe that God can and will do the good that we ask?

> **"But without faith it is impossible to please him: for he that cometh to God must believe that he is, and that he is a rewarder of them that diligently seek him" (Heb.11:6).**

QUESTIONS:

1. When circumstances become overwhelming, why are people tempted to place their faith in earthly things instead of in the Lord? What kinds of earthly things do people place their faith in?
2. God responds to true faith. What is *true faith*? How can you distinguish between true faith and mere profession?

1. THE HOPELESS CRY FOR LIFE (PART 1) (v.18-19).

The man who cried for help was a ruler and a father. Luke says that the ruler's name was Jairus. He oversaw the administration of the synagogue at Capernaum. The synagogue ruler was an elected position among the religious leaders. The person was highly respected, both capable and popular, a person who wielded great power. He determined who was to teach in the synagogue worship and supervised the whole operation. He was one of the most important men in a community.

Jairus' daughter was only twelve years old. Jairus was a man of strong courage who loved his daughter deeply. He showed remarkable strength of character in approaching Jesus, for he went against the tide of the other religionists who were violent in their thoughts against Jesus. The other religionists would no doubt react against Jairus. Only a sense of desperation would stir him to approach Jesus, and then he would approach Him only as a last resort. It was the desperate need of his daughter that drove Jairus to Jesus.

1. Note four things about the man and his desperation.

a. His hopelessness: he was so hopeless that he interrupted Jesus while Jesus was preaching and teaching. His young daughter was dead, gone forever. Again, he loved his daughter, apparently loved her more deeply than most. He stood up against the world, that is, against the censoring and hostility of his peers. He was an elected official by the religious elders; therefore, he was probably risking his position by coming to Christ. Only an unusual love and belief would have driven him to approach Jesus in the face of so much opposition (cp. Mt.9:34).

> **"For all those things hath mine hand made, and all those things have been, saith the LORD: but to this man will I look, even to him that is poor and of a contrite spirit, and trembleth at my word" (Is.66:2).**

APPLICATION:
One thing should always receive priority over everything else—the cry of a hopeless and helpless person. When the hopeless and helpless approach us, we should immediately stop and go to them, doing what we can. Prayer, study, preaching—all are to take a back seat to helping those who have need. Note: the need Jesus met was immediate and urgent. There was not even time to say a word. Jesus was silent. He simply responded by arising and going as requested.

b. His attitude: he worshipped Jesus; he fell down at the Lord's feet. Remember this was a distinguished man, an elected official who oversaw the administrative responsibilities of the most important institution in a Jewish city—the synagogue. He was a dynamic example of how leaders should approach Christ: in humility, worship, and faith.

> **"Whosoever therefore shall humble himself as this little child, the same is greatest in the kingdom of heaven" (Mt.18:4).**

APPLICATION 1:
We will never know the mercy of Christ until we humble ourselves and become as little children (Mt.18:3).

APPLICATION 2:
Too often, the desperate needs of loved ones drives us into a state of helplessness and hopelessness, depression and self-pity. The need may be severe illness, terrible trouble, or death. However, despair is not the answer to desperate needs. The answer is to lift up our heads to Jesus for the salvation of our loved ones. We are to come before Christ and ask Him to help us. He never turns away.

c. His request: he asked Jesus to come and touch his daughter.

> **"He shall call upon me, and I will answer him: I will be with him in trouble; I will deliver him, and honour him" (Ps.91:15).**

APPLICATION:
We must ask Jesus for *His touch*—to *touch us*, to *touch our need*—and He will.

d. His faith: "She shall live." This man was a man of great faith. He believed that if Jesus would just come to his home, his daughter would live. He believed Christ could raise her from the dead.

APPLICATION:
Note two lessons.

1) This is the same great faith that we must have.
   a) We must believe that Jesus can meet our desperate needs.
   b) We must believe that Jesus can raise us up from the dead (Jn.6:39-40, 44, 54; 1 Cor.15:12-58; 1 Th.4:13-18).

2) This man was driven to Jesus by a tragic event. God uses tragedy to drive us to Jesus. Every man should approach Jesus in times of tragedy, but he should approach in a spirit of worship and belief—truly believing and trusting that Jesus will help.

"And all things, whatsoever ye shall ask in prayer, believing, ye shall receive" (Mt.21:22).

2. Note Jesus' response to the father's desperation: Jesus arose and acted by following the man, by going to his house where the need was. There was no hesitation whatsoever.

"Call unto me, and I will answer thee, and show thee great and mighty things, which thou knowest not" (Jer.33:3).

APPLICATION:
Note three lessons.

1) The ruler was so desperate that he interrupted Jesus while Jesus was preaching and teaching. Jesus did not stop him nor rebuke him. He said nothing. He simply *responded to the man's* desperate and hopeless cry. Jesus always receives and responds to a man...
   - who is desperate
   - who confesses his hopelessness and helplessness
   - who acknowledges his need and believes that Jesus can help

2) Jesus never turns from a desperate man who comes to Him. In fact, He does not even hesitate to help the man. He will not even take the time to speak. He will arise and follow the desperate man to meet his need. Jesus is ever ready to help. He longs to help.
3) Note that Jesus will visit us wherever our need is. In this event, Jesus left his meeting and the opportunity to preach and teach in order to meet the desperate need. What a lesson for us! How much we need to learn what the priorities really are!

ILLUSTRATION:
People in the world today are looking for someone to care for them-to really care. In the busyness of life, we often become focused upon our rigid schedules and not upon the needs of hurting people who come our way.

It was a day that would not be forgotten. At the dawn of a popular holiday, David was faced with his own mortality. Wracked with chest pain, David and his wife Pat hurried to the hospital. The first diagnosis was not good: a massive heart attack that required emergency bypass surgery. Worry, anxiety, fright, shock: all these emotions ran through Pat's mind as she awaited the outcome. But Pat was surrounded by friends who held her, listened to her, prayed with her, and comforted her during those critical hours. Despite their previous agenda for the busy holiday weekend, Pat and David's many friends dropped their plans to minister to them in their time of need.

What do you do for people in their hour of need? Are you too busy to help? Too tired? Too self-absorbed?

QUESTIONS:
1. Try to place yourself in Jairus' place. Would you have approached Christ in the same way he did? Would you have done anything differently?
2. What social pressures did Jairus face? Are these same pressures in your society today? If so, what are they and how should the believer respond to them?
3. Do you ever feel that God is too busy to be bothered by your troubles? Why is God never too busy for you?

2. THE SECRET HOPE FOR HEALTH (v.20-22).

The woman had been hemorrhaging for twelve years (see A CLOSER LOOK # 2—Mt.9:20). She was desperately hopeless, feeling ashamed, embarrassed, and unworthy. According to the law, she was not to be in the crowd surrounding Jesus at all. Instead, she was supposed to be isolated. Nevertheless, her desperation drove her to Jesus. She felt that Jesus would never touch her because she was unclean. Yet, she had heard so many wonderful things about Him that she believed if she could only touch His garment, even without His knowing it, she would be healed. Imagine her great faith! Jesus' response was fourfold.

1. *Jesus turned* to the woman. There was no way Jesus could have felt the touch to His robe. He was being pressed and jostled by the crowd, yet when she stepped up behind Him and touched His robe, He knew. How?

a. Her faith touched Him. It is faith that touches Jesus. Faith will never go unnoticed nor be ignored by Jesus.

> **"And saying, The time is fulfilled, and the kingdom of God is at hand: repent ye, and believe the gospel" (Mk.1:15).**

b. Virtue (power and life) went out from Jesus into her. When a person places his faith in Jesus and His power, it touches Jesus, and Jesus infuses His virtue (His power and life) into that person. That is what life and salvation are all about: the infusion of God's virtue, power, and life into the spirit of man.

> **"Being born again, not of corruptible seed, but of incorruptible, by the word of God, which liveth and abideth for ever" (1 Pt.1:23).**

APPLICATION:
Jesus stopped and turned to the woman. To Jesus, the most important work in all the world is meeting a person's need. The more desperate the need, the more Jesus wants to stop and face the need. Nothing will keep Him from stopping and turning to a person who comes to Him in desperation.

> **"That it might be fulfilled which was spoken by Esaias the prophet, saying, Himself took our infirmities, and bare our sicknesses" (Mt.8:17; see also Is.53:4).**

2. *Jesus saw* the woman. He saw her desperation, her confession of hopelessness, her need, her faith; and His heart went out to her from the depths of compassion.

APPLICATION:
The Lord cares for all, no matter how rejected, cut off, or ostracized. A person may be considered unclean, dirty, polluted, contaminated, lost forever; but that person is precious to our Lord. His heart goes out in tenderness and care to the greatest of sinners.

"For we have not an high priest which cannot be touched with the feeling of our infirmities: but was in all points tempted like as we are, yet without sin. Let us therefore come boldly unto the throne of grace, that we may obtain mercy, and find grace to help in time of need" (Heb.4:15-16).

3. *Jesus adopted* the woman. He called her "daughter" and adopted her into the family of God. Speaking to her in behalf of the Father, He immediately gave her the assurance that she was accepted by God and that God would help her. Note also that Jesus said, "be of good cheer." She experienced the consolation and assurance of God immediately.

Note: When a person really comes to God in desperation, God immediately gives a sense and a knowledge of adoption and comfort. He gives such a release from pressure and desperation that the person's spirit sighs and revels in the new found peace.

"But as many as received him, to them gave he power to become the sons of God, even to them that believe on his name" (Jn.1:12).

4. *Jesus made* her whole. His virtue (power and life) was infused into her and she was saved and made whole. She had feared facing Jesus because she feared being rebuked. She was wrong. Jesus longed to heal the desperate among the people. No person is too dirty for Him. In fact, the more unclean a person is, the more He wants to cleanse and make him whole. Imagine such a Savior!

"Even as the Son of man came not to be ministered unto, but to minister, and to give his life a ransom for many" (Mt.20:28).

QUESTIONS:

1. The woman whom Jesus healed had been sick for twelve years. When you pray, do you ever get discouraged and feel like giving up if the answer is not immediate? How can you be encouraged to keep on praying when the answer seems so far away?
2. It is important that Christ be touched by your faith. How is this achieved?
3. God knows everything about you and what is takes to meet your need. If this is true, why does God still require you to seek Him and ask Him for help?

A CLOSER LOOK #2

(9:20) **Man, Rejected—Religion, Rejected by**: the woman afflicted with an uncontrollable hemorrhage was considered unclean. No one could touch her or anything she touched. She was ostracized and cut off from society, excommunicated from religious observances. If she was married, she was to be divorced (cp. Lev.15:25-27). The fact of this woman's uncleanness had sunk deeply into her mind, for she had been outcast from society and family—left all alone for twelve years. She had gone to every doctor she knew or had ever heard about, and not one was able to help her (Mt.5:26). She was now poor, for she had spent all she had seeking to find a cure. She had daily experienced the pit of loneliness, unacceptance, and low self-esteem. She was nothing even in her own eyes. Therefore, in approaching Jesus she felt both embarrassment and unworthiness. Her hemorrhaging was a personal and intimate matter that was too embarrassing to be discussed before people, and she felt Jesus would never touch her because of her uncleanness.

Despite all this, she had exactly what it took to get help from God: a desperation and a belief that Jesus Christ could help. We can picture her wondering, "What am I to do? He will not greet me; I am unclean." But all of a sudden she knew: "If I may but touch His garment, I shall be whole." And she was. Her faith made her whole.

Symbolically, her disease is a clear picture of what sin does. It cuts a person off from God and from true fellowship with believers (Is.59:2). The only means of restoration is to come to Jesus even as she did.

In contrast to what men do when they are confronted with the unclean, Jesus responds; He does not ostracize. Jesus calls us unto Himself; He does not divorce us. Jesus adopts; He does not excommunicate us.

QUESTIONS:
1. Have you ever been too embarrassed to ask for God's help? Why?
2. How does Christ respond to unclean, sinful people who cry out to Him? How does His response contrast with that of men who are repulsed by unclean people?

3. THE HOPELESS CRY FOR LIFE [PART 2] (v.23-26).

Again, this desperate cry was by the ruler and father in behalf of his daughter. There are several significant facts to note.

1. The trying delay (v.20-22). Why did Jesus allow the woman to delay Him? No need is greater than the need arising from death. Jesus knew that the ruler's desperation was bound to grow more uneasy by allowing the woman to delay Him. But He also knew that the ruler's confidence and assurance would be strengthened by seeing Him meet the woman's need. Perhaps the man needed to be strengthened. Whatever the reason for allowing the delay, Jesus knew.

APPLICATION:
Jesus always knows what is best for us and when to meet our need. We should not become fearful, questioning and unbelieving when our needs are not immediately met. Jesus is going to meet the need of anyone who approaches Him in humility and faith.

2. The atmosphere in the ruler's house. The atmosphere was noisy, the grief loud.

APPLICATION:
Note two lessons.
1) Loud noise and grief do not create the proper atmosphere for Jesus to work and meet our needs. We should rid ourselves of such distraction—get quiet, meditate, pray, and trust the Lord to do His work.
2) The world suffers and endures loud noise and grief because it has no hope over death. But the Lord longs to meet the grief of the believer's heart with the quiet assurance and hope He has given. Assurance is the promise given to the believer who truly hopes in the Lord (Tit.2:13).

3. The strong demand. Jesus demanded a quiet, prayerful atmosphere. He said, "give place," depart, go, be gone with the noise and loud grief. There is no room for this behavior in the face of faith.

APPLICATION:
We are seldom conscious of Jesus attempting to comfort us in the midst of noise and loud mourning.

4. The daughter's death. She was dead, and Luke says unmistakably that the people *laughed Jesus to scorn* "knowing that she was dead" (Lk.9:53). Mark says that certain ones even came to meet the ruler and said, "thy daughter is dead" (Mk.5:35). Men dread and fear death, so they soften its thought by calling it *sleep*.

5. The mourners' reaction. They scorned Jesus. They knew what death was because they were around death all the time, especially the paid mourners. It was the practice of the wealthy to pay professional mourners to grieve over the death of their loved ones. In this case, there was no question Jairus' daughter was dead and not asleep.

There is also the possibility that the mourners scorned Jesus to discourage the ruler from allowing Jesus to help. They knew somewhat of Him and His power because Capernaum was His home, the center of His ministry. If He raised Jairus' daughter, they would lose their work and payment.

APPLICATION:
Most men scoff at the idea of Jesus raising the dead (cp. 1 Cor.15:12f; 15:35f; 2 Pt.3:3f. These passages will show clearly the questions that cause men to scoff.)
1) Men often mock and scorn what they do not understand.
2) We must believe and trust and confess with Paul, "O the depth of the riches both of the wisdom and knowledge of God! how unsearchable are His judgments, and His ways past finding out!" (Ro.11:33).

6. The power of His hand. The description of our Lord's power is both beautiful and assuring.
a. "He went in." He will always *come in* to us wherever we are, if our hearts will only reach out to Him as the ruler's heart did. We may be disabled, but He will come to help us.
b. He "took her by the hand." He reached to infuse His power and life into her. He will infuse His power and life into us if we will only call upon Him.
c. He raised her up: "she arose." Jesus will raise us up, meeting our desperate needs on this earth, and He will also raise us up in the last day. (Cp. Jn. 5:22-30.)

> **"And Jesus came and spake unto them, saying, All power is given unto me in heaven and in earth" (Mt.28:18).**

APPLICATION:
Jesus' power can and will touch any needs.
1) He can touch the most desperate needs of all—the needs arising from the death of loved ones.
2) He can touch the desperate needs of people through our intercession. Our loved ones may be helpless even as this young daughter was, but if we will pray, Jesus will use His sovereign power to touch their need.

7. The result of His power. Jesus' fame was spread abroad. The raising of the dead was proof that Jesus was the Messiah (see A CLOSER LOOK # 1—Mt.9:18-34; cp. Mt.10:9; A CLOSER LOOK # 1—11:5). The people talked and talked about His power, but note how many still did not believe. They still refused to commit their lives to Him. How precious are those of succeeding generations who have not seen, yet believe.

> **"Jesus saith unto him, Thomas, because thou hast seen me, thou hast believed: blessed are they that have not seen, and yet have believed" (Jn.20:29).**

QUESTIONS:
1. Have you ever felt neglected or forgotten by God? Why is it important to trust God for the things that you cannot yet see?
2. People typically scorn the life and works of Jesus Christ. How can you protect your own faith when you live or work in the midst of scoffers?
3. Why are miracles no guarantee that a lost person will be convinced to follow Christ?

4. THE UNCEASING CRY FOR SIGHT (v.27-31).

This cry came from two blind men who were apparently sitting beside the road begging. In Jesus' day most blind men were beggars. These two blind men overheard what had been happening. A chord was struck in their hearts, so they began to follow Jesus, crying out as fast as they could shout, "Thou Son of David, have mercy on us."

1. Note that they took the very steps necessary to have their needs met.
   a. They acknowledged that Jesus was the Messiah, the Savior of the world. This is seen in the title they used for Jesus, "Thou Son of David" (see A CLOSER LOOK # 3—Mt.9:27 for more discussion).

   APPLICATION:
   The men were blind. They could not see what Jesus was doing. They could only hear.
   1) The lost are blind. They cannot see; they cannot understand.
   2) The lost can only hear.

   > **"Faith cometh by hearing, and hearing by the Word of God" (Ro.10:17).**

   Hearing the gospel is the only hope for the lost. It is imperative that we go and proclaim the Word to them.

   b. They cried for mercy. These men did what we must do if we wish God to have mercy upon us.
   ⇒ The blind men "believed the report" about the Messiah (Ro.10:16). They could only hear the report; they could not see what was happening.
   ⇒ They personally cried out for mercy, accepting and confessing that Jesus was the Messiah.

   > **"This poor man cried, and the LORD heard him, and saved him out of all his troubles" (Ps.34:6).**

   APPLICATION:
   God is rich in mercy (Eph.2:4-5). He will have mercy on any who genuinely cry to Him for mercy.

   c. They fought their way to him. They persisted and went after what they wanted. Note that Jesus did not stop immediately. He knew their hearts just as He knows everyone's heart. He knew they needed to grow in desperation. They needed to be so desperate that they would cast themselves upon Him totally. They had apparently not reached that point. So He, who is all-wise, walked on as though He did not hear them. And all the while they clawed their way through the crushing crowd, shouting at the top of their voices, becoming more and more desperate and more and more ready to take the great leap of saving faith.

   APPLICATION:
   Note three lessons.
   1) The men persisted and kept after Jesus. After following Him right up to the house where He had entered, they somehow gained entrance. The point is, they would not give up until Jesus helped them.
   2) Persistence, a true cry for help, is not rudeness to Jesus. How many have been interrupted in their homes and counted it rudeness? How we need to learn that the first order of the day is to minister!

3) The two blind men helped each other. They began together and fought together to get to Jesus. What a lesson for us when we confront need! Believers with common needs can help each other reach Jesus.

> **"And ye shall seek me, and find me, when ye shall search for me with all your heart" (Jer.29:13).**

QUESTIONS:
1. Why is it so important to verbally share the gospel with the spiritually blind?
2. What practical lessons can you apply to your own life from the example of these blind men?

2. *Jesus' response* was compassionate and forceful. There was an unmistakable readiness to help. This is seen in three acts.

a. Jesus questioned the two blind men: "Believe ye that I am able to do this?" Jesus stands ready to help—always. There is never a time when He is not ready to help, but there is a prerequisite to His helping. There is one qualification: "Believe ye that I am able to do this?"

APPLICATION:
Many balk at the question of faith: "Believe ye that I am able to do this?"
1) Some do not believe at all.
2) Some doubt that Jesus has the power or interest to help.
3) Some ignore and could care less.
4) Some follow after Jesus and even ask for mercy, but they never *commit their lives* in faith to Christ. They believe mentally that He is the Messiah, the Son of God, but they lack one essential: they do not act on what they profess. They have never turned over their lives to the One they say they trust. A person has not trusted Christ unless he has entrusted his life into Jesus' keeping.

> **"But without faith it is impossible to please him: for he that cometh to God must believe that he is, and that he is a rewarder of them that diligently seek him" (Heb.11:6).**

b. Jesus touched the two men. Note the tender touch of Jesus. These men could see nothing; they had a special need, so Jesus met their need in a special way.

APPLICATION:
Jesus always meets every facet of our need. He touches all who sincerely come to Him in whatever way they need to be touched. This fact should make every man come to Him. There is no need, no special problem existing, that He cannot meet.

> **"Call unto me, and I will answer thee, and show thee great and mighty things, which thou knowest not" (Jer.33:3).**

c. Jesus exerted His power: He healed them, but it was based on their faith.

APPLICATION:
Note four lessons.
1) Their *faith in Christ and His power* brought about their healing.
   ⇒ It did not take works, but faith.
   ⇒ It did not take health, but faith.
   ⇒ It did not take money, but faith.
   ⇒ It did not take friends, but faith.
   ⇒ It did not take social acceptance or position, but faith.

2) Jesus knows our faith and He knows how to grow our faith. Note how He grew the faith of these men. Whatever we need to develop a strong faith, whether trial or test or immediate blessing, God will bring that experience into our lives (Ro.8:28f; Ph.1:29; 1 Pt.4:12-13).
3) What a blessed thought! Jesus receives our faith, accepts it, and acts on what we believe.
4) This is a warning: no man is dealt with according to his profession. He is dealt with according to his faith: "But without faith, it is impossible to please Him...." (Heb.11:6).

"And all things, whatsoever ye shall ask in prayer, believing, ye shall receive" (Mt.21:22).

3. *Jesus' instruction* to these men was a charge that is often needed. It is especially needed by believers who experience the miraculous touch of Jesus' power. The charge was "see no man know it"; in other words, be humble. Christ wanted these men to set a dynamic example of humility. Therefore, Jesus charged them to keep quiet. He knew the inner recesses of their hearts and minds just as He knows all men's. Apparently, they had hearts that would tend toward boasting in their miracle and in the change brought about in their lives.

APPLICATION:
Note two lessons.
1) There was danger in being so blessed by Jesus. Pride and self-importance could easily set in. They could think of themselves more highly than they ought to think.
2) There is a fine line between honoring Jesus and honoring oneself in a testimony. The heart makes the difference and only God knows the heart. *But He does know*. How often we boast and glory in such phrases as...
   - what a change has been wrought in my life
   - but for the grace of God there go I
   - what a terrible sinner I was

In and of themselves these phrases can and often do bring glory to God. But often they draw attention to the sinner and the sin instead of to God.

"For I say, through the grace given unto me, to every man that is among you, not to think of himself more highly than he ought to think; but to think soberly, according as God hath dealt to every man the measure of faith" (Ro.12:3).

QUESTIONS:
1. Jesus is willing and able to help any person who calls out to Him. Too often believers do not cry out to God for help because they feel their problems are just too great for anyone—including God—to handle. Is there anything too big for God to handle? Are you guilty of not taking your problems to the Lord? How can you change your attitude about asking God for help?
2. Why is faith the only thing that Christ responds to?

A CLOSER LOOK #3
(9:27) **Jesus Christ, Son of David—Names—Titles**: Jesus was the Davidic heir—He was qualified to be the Messianic King. God had given to David and His seed (the Messiah) the promise of eternal government (2 Sam.7:12; Ps.39:3f; 132:11).

The Jews believed these promises of God. Therefore Jesus, "who is called Christ" (Mt.1:16), was the promised Son of Abraham, the promised Son of David (Mt.1:1).

Note how often Jesus was called the son of David. (Cp. M.12:23; 15:22; 20:30-31; 21:9, 15; Acts 2:29-36; Ro.1:3; 2 Tim.2:8; Rev.22:16.) It was the common title and popular concept of the Messiah. Generation after generation of Jews looked for the promised deliverer of Israel. The people expected Him to be a great general who would deliver and restore the nation to its greatness. In fact, they expected Him to make the nation the center of universal rule. He would, under God, conquer the world and center the glory and majesty of God Himself in Jerusalem. And from His throne, the throne of David, He would execute "the Messianic fire of judgment" upon the nations and peoples of the world.

1. The Messianic King was prophesied.

> **"He shall build a house for my name, and I will stablish the throne of his kingdom for ever" (2 Sam.7:13).**

2. Jesus Christ is the Messianic King.

> **"Where is he that is born King of the Jews? for we have seen his star in the east, and are come to worship him....And thou Bethlehem, in the land of Juda, art not the least among the princes of Juda: for out of thee shall come a Governor, that shall rule my people Israel" (Mt.2:2, 6).**

5. THE QUIET APPROACH FOR SANITY AND SPEECH (v.32-33).

Note how quietly this event is placed in the midst of the other miracles, but the lessons are pointed.

1. There was the man.
   a. He was brought by others.
   b. He needed help desperately: he was demon-possessed, that is, possessed by an evil spirit.

> **"And I say unto you, Ask, and it shall be given you; seek, and ye shall find; knock, and it shall be opened unto you. For every one that asketh receiveth; and he that seeketh findeth; and to him that knocketh it shall be opened" (Lk.11:9-10).**

APPLICATION:
Note four lessons.

1) Many have to be brought if they are ever to come. They are too weak in spirit, mind, or body to come on their own. They will not come unless they are brought.
2) We must go after the needy in order to bring them. Many would come...
   - if we would simply visit and go after them.
   - if we would make friends with them and nurture them along the way.
3) Some are possessed by the wrong spirit, that is, not by God's Spirit. Spiritually, they are dull in their knowledge of Christ. They have no awareness, no consciousness, no understanding whatsoever of the delivering power that is in Christ. The fact that there is a Savior is totally foreign to them.
4) Some are gripped by the deepest form of evil, demon-possession. They desperately need to be brought to Christ (cp. Mt.8:28-34; Lk.8:26-40.)

2. There was Jesus' response. He healed the man.

> **"Now unto him that is able to do exceeding abundantly above all that we ask or think, according to the power that worketh in us" (Eph.3:20).**

APPLICATION:
Note how much power Jesus has.
1) He can touch the life of a person because of the faith of another. Intercessory prayer and faith are God's way for many to be reached.
2) He can break the greatest of bondages—even the grip and power of Satan when Satan totally possesses the life of a person.

A CLOSER LOOK #4
(9:32-34) **Evil Spirits**: evil spirits are demons. There is only one devil. However, there are many evil or unclean spirits or demons, and the New Testament has much to say about them.

The characteristics of demons other than the ones given in the outline above are said to be as follows:

1. They are spirits (Mt.12:43-45).
2. They are Satan's emissaries (Mt.12:26-27).
3. They know their fate is to be eternal doom (Mt.8:29; Lk.8:31).
4. They affect man's health (Mt.12:22; 17:15-18; Lk.13:16). Apparently, demon-possession is to be distinguished from mental illness.
5. They seduce men to a false religion of hardship or austerity (1 Tim. 4:1-3).
6. They seduce men to depart from the faith (1 Tim. 4:1).
7. They are cast out of people (exorcism) in the name of Jesus Christ (Acts 16:18).
8. They will participate in the apocalyptic or threatening judgment which is coming upon the earth (Rev. 9:1-11, 20).

Evil spirits are enemies of Christ and of man. As such, they oppress, possess, and obsess people. (1) They delude the world and blind people to Christ (Eph. 2:2). (2) They attack theology (1 Tim. 4:1-3). (3) They attack society (Rev. 9:3, 20-21). (4) They attack individuals (Lk.8:29). (5) They influence people to commit the sins of demon-worship, idolatry, sorcery, fornication, theft, murder, and much more (Rev. 9:20-21).

The believer's defense is the Lord. The believer must pray and fast and take on the armor of God in order to stand against the power of evil spirits.

QUESTIONS:
1. Who needs your help in coming to Jesus? What do you need to do to bring that person or persons to Christ?
2. How would your life be different if you gave yourself completely over to the power of Christ?
3. What experience have you had or heard about with evil spirits? Why are they so dangerous to the believer?

6. THE REACTION TO JESUS' POWER (v.33-34).

The people were amazed. They witnessed what they called the wonderful work of God, wonder after wonder. But note: not all believed. Despite the amazing work of God, only a few truly trusted Him.

The religionists hated Christ. They were hostile toward Him, vehemently so. They were guilty of the unpardonable sin.

> **"The heart is deceitful above all things, and desperately wicked: who can know it?" (Jer.17:9).**

ILLUSTRATION:
Some people—no matter the evidence, no matter the proof, no matter the facts—refuse to acknowledge God's power in the world today. But creation itself cries

out and testifies to the wonderful work of God—a work that cannot always be explained by human reason.

An arrogant young man was conversing with some agnostic friends in a hotel lobby. "I will not believe anything I cannot understand," he exclaimed. "Nor will I," said another. A Christian who had been speaking to them about their souls inquired, "Gentlemen, do I understand that you won't believe anything you can't comprehend?" "That's right!" "Well," said the Bible-believing young witness, "while riding over to the hotel this morning, I saw some geese in a field eating grass. Some pigs, sheep, and cows were doing the same. The grass when digested turns to feathers on the geese, to bristles on the swine, to wool on the sheep, and to hair on the cows. Do you believe that?" They agreed they did. "Yes, you believe it," said the Christian, "but do you really understand it?" The young men fell silent, for they realized there were mysteries in this life that they had to accept even though they could not rationalize their answers.[2]

QUESTIONS:
1. So many people are closed-minded to God's work in the world. Why are some people so hardened to God?
2. Just as Christ and His works are scoffed at, so the believer, as Christ's representative on earth, will be scoffed at. Have you experienced being rejected by the scoffers of the world?

A CLOSER LOOK #5

(9:34) **Satan**: Satan is called "the great dragon…that old serpent." His name is *Lucifer*. He was probably one of the highest angels ever created by God, but he fell because of selfishness and pride (Is.14:12; cp. 1 Tim. 3:6.) He is "an angel of light" with such deceptive and seductive power that even some ministers follow him, ministers who are "transformed as the ministers of righteousness" (2 Cor. 11:14-15). Throughout Scripture Satan is described as follows:

1. He is "the god of this world" who blinds men's minds (2 Cor. 4:4).
2. He is "the prince of this world" (Jn.12:31; Jn.14:20; Jn.16:11) and "the prince of the power of the air" (Eph.2:2; Eph.6:12).
3. He is Satan, which means the adversary (1 Chron. 21:1; Job 1:6; Job 2:1-6; Zech. 3:1; Mt.4:10; Mk.1:13; Lk.4:8; Jn.13:27; Acts 5:3; Acts 26:18; Ro.16:20).
4. He is the devil, which means the slanderer (Mt.4:1, 5, 8, 11; Lk.4:2-6, 13; 1 Peter 5:8; Rev. 20:2).
5. He is the deceiver of the whole world (2 Cor. 11:3; Rev. 12:9).
6. He is the tempter (Mt.4:3; 1 Th. 3:5).
7. He is the evil one (Mt.6:13; Mt.13:19, 38).
8. He is the father of lies (Jn.8:44).
9. He is the accuser of the brethren (Rev. 12:10).
10. He is a murderer (Jn.8:44).
11. He is called Beelzebub (Mt.12:24; Mk.3:22; Lk.11:15).
12. He is called Belial (2 Cor. 6:15).
13. He is called Abaddon (Rev. 9:11).
14. He is called the angel of the bottomless pit (Rev. 9:11).
15. He is called Apollyon (Rev. 9:11).
16. He is called the enemy (Mt.13:39).
17. He is called the gates of hell (Mt.16:18).
18. He is called the great red dragon (Rev. 12:3).

---

2 *INFOsearch Sermon Illustrations* (Arlington, TX: The Computer Assistant, 1-888-868-9029, 1986-1996).

19. He is called a lying spirit (1 Kings 22:22).
20. He is called that old serpent (Rev. 12:9; Rev. 20:2; cp. Gen.3:4, 14; 2 Cor. 11:3).
21. He is called the power of darkness (Col. 1:13).
22. He called the prince of devils (Mt.12:24).
23. He is called the ruler of the darkness of this world (Eph.6:12).
24. He is called the spirit that works in the children of disobedience (Eph.2:2).
25. He is called the unclean spirit (Mt.12:43).
26. He is called the wicked one (Mt.13:19, 38).

Satan's purpose in making war against God is twofold.

1. Satan's purpose is power and worship, to receive as much of the power and worship of the universe as possible (Isaiah 14:12-17; Ezk.28:11-17). He goes about this in three ways.

- ⇒ He opposes and disturbs God's work in the world (Isaiah 14:12-17; Ezk.28:11-17; Job 1:6; Job 2:1-6; Mt.4:10; Mk.1:13; Lk.4:8; Rev. 12:7-9).
- ⇒ He discourages believers through various strategies (Lk.22:31; Eph. 6:10-12).
- ⇒ He arouses God's justice against people by leading people to sin and to deny and rebel against God. And when they do, God's justice has to act and judge people to the fate of their choice: that of living with Satan eternally (see note—Mt.12:25-26;Jn.13:31-32).

2. Satan's purpose is to hurt and cut the heart of God. Why? Because God has judged and condemned him for rebelling against God. Therefore, Satan does all he can to get back at God. The best way he can do this is to turn the hearts of people away from God, leading them to sin and to follow the way of evil.

However, Christ has broken Satan's power by two acts.

1. By never giving in to the devil's temptation (Mt.4:1-11) and by never sinning (2 Cor. 5:21). Christ overcame sin. He was righteous; He was perfect.
2. By destroying the devil's power of death. Christ was not held by physical or spiritual death (Hebrews 2:14-15). He arose and ascended to God's right hand.

It is for this reason that the Bible says "greater is he that is in you, than he that is in the world" (1 Jn.4:4); and again, "If God be for us, who can be against us?" (Ro.8:31).

SUMMARY:

There is hope, great hope, for the person who is surrounded by darkness and despair. When all seems lost, hope in God will light the way. The next time your hope is waning, about to fade away—just remember the timeless truth found in these points:

1. The hopeless cry for life (Part 1). It was the desperate need of his daughter that drove Jairus to Jesus.
2. The secret hope for health. The woman with the hemorrhage had exactly what it took to get help from God: a desperation and a belief that Jesus Christ could help.
3. The hopeless cry for life (Part 2). An untimely interruption caused the cry of Jairus to become more desperate as life was escaping from his precious daughter.
4. The unceasing cry for sight from the two blind men on the roadside.
5. The quiet approach for sanity and speech for the demon-possessed man.
6. The reaction to Jesus' power. The people were amazed. They witnessed what they called the wonderful work of God, wonder after wonder. But note: not all believed. Despite the amazing work of God, only a few placed their hope in Him—only a few truly trusted Him.

MATTHEW 9:18-34

PERSONAL JOURNAL NOTES
(Reflection & Response)

1. The most important thing that I learned from this lesson was:

2. The area that I need to work on the most is:

3. I can apply this lesson to my life by:

4. Closing Statement of Commitment:

MATTHEW 9:35-38

Outline	Scripture	Scripture (cont.)	Outline (cont.)
	VI. THE MESSIAH'S MESSENGERS AND THEIR MISSION, 9:35-10:42 (Mk.6:7-13; Lk.9:1-6) **A. The Mission of the Messiah, 9:35-38**	ing every sickness and every disease among the people.	d. Message: The gospel of the Kingdom
		36 But when he saw the multitudes, he was moved with compassion on them, because they fainted, and were scattered abroad, as sheep having no shepherd.	**2. His compassion** a. Crowds fainting: Weary & bewildered b. Crowds scattered c. Crowds as sheep without a shepherd
		37 Then saith he unto his disciples, The harvest truly is plenteous, but the labourers are few;	**3. His vision** a. A great harvest b. A great need for laborers
1. His ministry a. Method: Went forth b. Place: Everywhere c. Work: Teaching, preaching, & healing	35 And Jesus went about all the cities and villages, teaching in their synagogues, and preaching the gospel of the kingdom, and heal-	38 Pray ye therefore the Lord of the harvest, that he will send forth labourers into his harvest.	c. A great need for prayer d. A great force of laborers

Section VI
THE MESSIAH'S MESSENGERS AND THEIR MISSION, Matthew 9:35-10:42

Study 1: **THE MISSION OF THE MESSIAH**

Text: **Matthew 9:35-38**

Aim: To determine how to become more focused upon the mission of the Lord.

Memory Verse:

"Then saith he unto his disciples, The harvest truly *is* plenteous, but the labourers *are* few; Pray ye therefore the Lord of the harvest, that he will send forth labourers into his harvest" (Mt.9:37-38).

INTRODUCTION

Life is full of great opportunities. But life is also filled with numerous distractions that prevent us from realizing many opportunities. We often act like a child with a brief attention span:

> *"Johnny, listen carefully to what I say. Go and tell your brother and sister it is time for dinner." With a burst of energy and a sincere desire to do as he was told, little Johnny left the kitchen and went to find his siblings. But along the way the family dog picked up his rubber ball and wanted to play. After a quick game of fetch, Johnny continued his mission to find his brother and sister. Only a few moments had gone by when Johnny passed by the television and noticed his favorite cartoon on. Settling in, his concentration was broken only when his mother came into the room. "Johnny, have you done what I asked?" "Sure Mom, I was just on the way."*

Sound familiar? Probably all of us have been through that scenario many times. But serving a cold supper because a child was distracted is a small matter when compared to what God has called us to do. When it comes to our Lord's instructions to stay focused on His mission, the stakes are life and death. We are to go into the fields and work in the Lord's harvest. Anything that distracts us from this task causes us to miss one of life's greatest opportunities—and jeopardizes the souls of countless people. The mission of the Messiah was threefold.

OUTLINE:

1. There was His ministry (v.35).
2. There was His demonstration of compassion (v.36).
3. There was His call to the greatest of all visions (v.37-38).

1. HIS MINISTRY (v.35)

The mission of Jesus Christ was to minister. Four things are covered about His ministry in this verse.

1. Jesus' method of ministry. Jesus Christ had but one method in reaching people: He "went out" after people. He did not sit back and wait for people to come to Him.

> **"For the Son of Man is come to seek and to save that which is lost" (Lk.19:10).**

APPLICATION:
We are foolish to sit back and wait for people to come to us. The vast, vast majority will not come. They do not know to come; we have to go out after them. Therefore, the very same method that Jesus used is given to us in the Great Commission.

> **"Go ye therefore, and teach all nations, baptizing them in the name of the Father, and of the Son, and of the Holy Ghost: Teaching them to observe all things whatsoever I have commanded you: and, lo, I am with you alway, even unto the end of the world. Amen." (Mt.28:19-20.)**

2. Jesus' place of ministry. Jesus literally went everywhere: in all the cities and villages (Mt.9:35), in the countryside (Mt.5:1), in the synagogues (Mt.9:35), on the mountains (Mt.5:1), by the seashore (Mt.4:18), in boats (Mt.8:23f), by graveyards (Mt.8:28f), and in homes (Mt.8:14; 9:10). There was no place where Jesus did not go to minister.

> **"Go ye therefore into the highways, and as many as ye shall find, bid to the marriage" (Mt.22:9).**

APPLICATION:
Note three striking lessons.

1) With all the means of transportation available to us today, how much more *we* should go everywhere, not neglecting mansion or slum.
2) Christ taught in the synagogues, in the existing establishments when they were open to Him. Note two things.
   ⇒ He made use of what was available, *the existing establishment*, although the people violently opposed Him.
   ⇒ He went where there was a ready audience when He had the opportunity.
3) There are places where some believers will not go to minister: the small town, the obscure village, the mill town, the inner city, out in the country, the foreign country, the north, east, west or south, the lower class, the upper class. But not so with Christ; He went everywhere.

MATTHEW 9:35-38

ILLUSTRATION:
For many believers, the Christian life is a paradox. We are challenged by the Lord to reach out to those in need, but in many cases, our hearts are just not in it. How true is this story for you?

Humorist Charles Laine, of Franklin, TN, tells this story:
Doris Laine (Charles' wife) invited some people to dinner. At the table, she turned to her six-year-old daughter and said, "Would you like to say the blessing?"
"I wouldn't know what to say," the little girl replied.
"'Just say what you hear Mommy say," the mother said.
The little girl bowed her head and said: "Dear Lord, why on earth did I invite all these people to dinner?"[1]

The true believer seeks the best way to reach out to people. He is willing to minister anywhere...even in his home!

QUESTIONS:
1. We cannot assume that people who do not know the Lord will come to church to find Him. Why is this true? What is your responsibility to the lost?
2. Jesus moved freely between the establishment and the non-traditional places where people congregated. What are some practical ways you can share your faith outside the walls of the church?

3. Jesus' work or type of ministry: teaching, preaching, and healing. Jesus had a threefold work that should serve as the primary guide for believers.
   a. He preached. He proclaimed the good news of the King, God Himself. He brought the glorious message of salvation and redemption to man.
   b. He taught. He rooted and grounded all who would receive the message. Hearing and receiving the good news were not enough. People needed to be taught.
   c. He healed. He met the physical, mental, and emotional needs of those who hurt and suffered.

> **"How God anointed Jesus of Nazareth with the Holy Ghost and with power: who went about doing good, and healing all that were oppressed of the devil; for God was with him. And we are witnesses of all things which he did both in the land of the Jews, and in Jerusalem; whom they slew and hanged on a tree" (Acts 10:38-39).**

APPLICATION 1:
Note three lessons.
1) What is preached needs to be taught and lived. Talking and preaching are not enough. What God has to say He wants taught so that men may know how to live.
2) Every believer is to proclaim, teach, and heal. Jesus never intended for the minister or pastor or preacher to do the job alone. He has commissioned every believer, and He expects every believer to be about the business of reaching and helping people.
3) Men need to hear the message, but they also need to be taught the details of the message and how to apply it to their lives. The only conceivable way men can know how to live day by day is to be taught the details of the message.

---

[1] Cal and Rose Samra. *Holy Humor*. Mastermedia Limited. (Nashville, TN: Thomas Nelson Publishers, 1996.), p.159-160.

APPLICATION 2:
When dealing with preaching, teaching, and healing, we must be aware of and guard against the potential danger of each.

1) *Preaching only* will feed only the major points of God's message to people. *Preaching only* will leave a person with a huge gap in his spiritual life. He will not know how to apply the will of God in his life day by day. Teaching is needed as well as preaching.
2) *Teaching only* leads to four errors.
   a) It only leads a person into a discussion of God's Word and its details. It misses out on the proclamation of the overview and great subjects of the Bible.
   b) It shortchanges a person in the experience of worshipping around the proclamation of the King's message.
   c) It shortchanges a person in the experience of the Holy Spirit's working through preaching (1 Cor.1:18, 21).
   d) It minimizes God's chosen method to save men. It often leads a person to feel he grows into becoming a Christian because he learns the details of God's Word. Preaching (that is, proclamation) is needed as well as teaching (that is, discussion).

> **"For the preaching of the cross is to them that perish foolishness; but unto us which are saved it is the power of God....For after that in the wisdom of God the world by wisdom knew not God, it pleased God by the foolishness of preaching to save them that believe" (1 Cor.1:18, 21).**

3) *Healing only* leads to an emphasis upon the needs of the flesh and a de-emphasis on the needs of the Spirit. It can lead to a minimizing of salvation, to stressing healing over salvation. Preaching and teaching are needed as well as healing.

4. Jesus' message: the gospel of the Kingdom. Jesus Christ was the herald of the King proclaiming the good news of His kingdom.
   a. There is a King—God Himself.
   b. There is the kingdom where the King dwells. It is called heaven, which is another dimension of being, another world. The King—His reign and power and sovereignty—rules everywhere in both heaven and earth, both the seen and unseen worlds, in both the spiritual and physical dimensions of being.

> **"For by him were all things created, that are in heaven, and that are in earth, visible and invisible, whether they be thrones, or dominions, or principalities, or powers: all things were created by him, and for him" (cp. Col.1:16).**

   c. There is the *true* herald of the King sent by the King Himself. Jesus Christ is the herald who is the perfect representative of the King. He proclaims the good news about the kingdom, a message without any falsehood, a message full of truth and hope, the hope for eternal salvation.

> **"Now after that John was put in prison, Jesus came into Galilee, preaching the gospel of the kingdom of God, and saying, The time is fulfilled, and the kingdom of God is at hand: repent ye, and believe the gospel" (Mk.1:14-15).**

MATTHEW 9:35-38

QUESTIONS:

1. The threefold work of Jesus (preaching, teaching, and healing or ministering) gives us the pattern for a balanced ministry. How would you score the balance of your own church?
   _____We do all three things well.
   _____We do two out of three.
   _____We do one out of three.
   _____We do zero out of three.
2. How would your community be different if every believer adopted Jesus' work as his own?
3. We live in a world where there are many different messages offered to man every day. How is the gospel of the Kingdom of God different from all the rest?

A CLOSER LOOK #1
(9:35) **Preaching**: to proclaim, herald, publish. The preacher is a herald or messenger who comes in the name of the King and who represents the King (cp. 2 Cor.5:20). He comes to proclaim the message of the King and *only* the message of the King. He has no message of his own. If and when he begins to proclaim his own message, he is no longer the herald or the spokesman of the King.

2. HIS COMPASSION (v.36).

The mission of Jesus Christ was to show compassion (see A CLOSER LOOK # 2—Mt.9:36). He was to express and demonstrate God's compassion, the kind of compassion all men are to have for all other men. Jesus "saw the multitudes." He saw those following Him—those in the villages, in the cities, in the countryside, in the synagogues, on the mountains, by the seashore, by the graveyards, in boats, and in homes—and He "was moved with compassion." Jesus was moved over the physical needs of men: their hunger, pain, and suffering. He was moved over the spiritual needs of men: their being lost and dead to God; their emptiness and loneliness and bewilderment; their having no purpose, meaning, or significance in life. He saw them all and He observed and studied them. No one escaped the eye or the heart of Jesus, and as He looked, He saw three things.

1. Jesus saw the crowds fainting (see A CLOSER LOOK # 3—Mt.9:36). They were weighed down and ready to collapse.
   a. Life weighed them down. Life was cruel, hard, empty, and without real purpose. Life too often seemed hopeless and worthless.
   b. Religion weighed them down.
      1) Religion laid burden after burden, demand after demand upon them. It required endless rituals, ceremonies, and rules.
      2) Religion also misled them into beliefs that really did not lead them to God. Therefore, they were not spiritually satisfied. They were *dead to God*.
   c. Sin weighed them down. They were not taught the truth but, rather, the ideas of religionists. Therefore, they were still dead in their sins (Eph.2:15). The weight of their sins still rested upon their hearts and preyed upon their minds, weakening whatever confidence and assurance they had. Their sins made them uncertain of the future.

> **"Come unto me, all ye that labour and are heavy laden, and I will give you rest. Take my yoke upon you, and learn of me; for I am meek and lowly in heart: and ye shall find rest unto your souls" (Mt.11:28-29).**

APPLICATION:
The crowds fainted, for they were deceived by their leaders, teachers, preachers, and priests. They had great confidence in them, but their leaders misled and deceived them. Therefore, they followed and lived in error, a road that led to an empty destiny. They were empty, weary, perplexed, and unsatisfied.

2. Jesus saw the crowds scattered (see A CLOSER LOOK # 4—Mt.9:36). They wandered about, not knowing which direction to go. They stopped here and there trying to find something that satisfied them, but to no avail. They were without meaning, purpose, or significance. Many turned...

- to restrictive religion (Judaism) or philosophy (Stoics)
- to loose religion (polytheism) or philosophy (Epicureans)
- to no religion (atheism) or philosophy (humanism)

However, nothing filled their inner being; nothing really satisfied, not spiritually. The human soul still ached for the truth of God.

> **"I am come that they might have life, and that they might have it more abundantly" (Jn.10:10).**

3. Jesus saw the crowds as sheep without a shepherd. They went astray, just as sheep. They had no leader who had the courage to surrender to the truth and to live by it. There was no one to teach the truth. Practically every teacher seemed to be out to fleece the sheep, to secure his own position and to build a following of his own ideas. Few led the people to God; instead, many led the people away from God. The people were as sheep without a shepherd.

> **"How think ye? if a man have an hundred sheep, and one of them be gone astray, doth he not leave the ninety and nine, and goeth into the mountains, and seeketh that which is gone astray?" (Mt.18:12).**

QUESTIONS:

1. How vast is Christ's compassion for people? Do you think it is only limited to Christians? How about the Muslim...the Buddhist...the Jew...the atheist?
2. What kinds of things tend to weigh you down—even to the point of collapse? What is God's answer to your burdens?
3. There are at least two things that are true about sheep: they have no wisdom and they have no method of defense. Every sheep needs a shepherd to lead it in life and to protect it from things that will destroy its life. How do these principles apply to your needs?

A CLOSER LOOK #2
(9:36) **Compassion**: to be moved inwardly; to yearn with tender mercy, affection, pity, and empathy. It is the very seat of a man's affections. It is the deepest movement of emotions possible, being moved within the deepest part of a person's being.

> **"Who shall separate us from the love [compassion] of Christ? shall tribulation, or distress, or persecution, or famine, or nakedness, or peril, or sword?" (Ro.8:35).**

A CLOSER LOOK #3
(9:36) **Fainted**: to grow weary, lose heart, lack courage, be fainthearted, bewildered. The word is used when a person has struggled and struggled against some trial, some sin, or stood against a barrage of insults until he can stand no more. It means that a person has undergone one ordeal after another until he is ready to collapse (Heb.12:3).

A CLOSER LOOK #4
(9:36) **Scattered**: to be cast out, laid low, thrown down, prostrated, dejected, and hopeless. Being scattered may come from experiences such as drunkenness, or struggling and fighting within and without, or being so weary that a person is simply cast down. It is being prostrated by forces within oneself or laid low by forces outside of oneself.

3. HIS VISION (v.37-38)

The mission of Christ was to share the vision of a world in desperate need. The vision of the Lord Jesus Christ is the greatest challenge known to man.

1. The vision of a great harvest. All men everywhere are fainting, weary, bewildered, scattered and are as sheep without a shepherd. But note a critical point: the Lord's vision is not only worldwide; it involves the changing of every human life on the globe (1 Pt.3:9; 2 Cor.5:17).

> **"Say not ye, There are yet four months, and then cometh harvest? behold, I say unto you, Lift up your eyes, and look on the fields; for they are white already to harvest. And he that reapeth receiveth wages, and gathereth fruit unto life eternal: that both he that soweth and he that reapeth may rejoice together" (Jn.4:35-36).**

APPLICATION 1:
The harvest is *needful work.*
1) It is great, that is, plentiful. There are fields and fields of people growing in the valleys and hills of the world (Mt.9:36).
2) It is a ripe harvest, ready and desperate to be reaped (Mt.9:36).
3) It has to be reaped in its season, that is, in its generation. There is only a short time when it can be reaped; otherwise it will rot and die in the field where it grew.

APPLICATION 2:
The harvest must be reaped or reached in every generation.
1) Everyone has only a certain season (generation, life-span) when he can be reaped. His season for being reaped is short, ever so short.
2) Everyone has a peak season, a time when he is really at his peak and ready to be harvested. It is so much more fruitful and joyful to harvest a man in his peak season than to try at other times.

APPLICATION 3:
The harvest is plentiful.
1) A harvest of children needs to be reached and taught the Word.
2) A harvest of young people needs to be reached and grounded in the Word.
3) A harvest of women needs to be reached and taught the confidence and protection of God's love.
4) A harvest of men needs to be reached and taught the strength and security of God's direction and care.

2. The vision of a great need for laborers. Christ needs people, that is, believers: men, women, boys, and girls. Laborers are few. He needs many laborers and He needs them *now*. Unless there are reapers to go forth, the harvest will die and rot upon the earth.

> **"Then saith he unto his disciples, The harvest truly is plenteous, but the labourers are few" (Mt.9:37).**

APPLICATION 1:
An unlimited amount of work is to be done, but there are so few to do it.
1) The harvest will never be reaped unless laborers go forth (Mt.28:19-20; Jn.20:21; cp. Lk.19:10).
2) The harvest will rot in the field where it grows (the earth).

APPLICATION 2:
Laborers are desperately needed for every generation.
1) The harvest is always great. The harvest is every man, woman, and child within a generation.
2) The harvest must have enough reapers to reach every living person during his or her season, that is, life-span. Just imagine—the whole population of the earth changes about every hundred years!

APPLICATION 3:
Why are there not more laborers?
1) Some reject the call of God.
2) Some postpone the call of God.
3) Some deny the call of God; they close their minds entirely.
4) Some seek a profession, a position, or a livelihood instead of really reaching out and ministering to people.
5) Some preach false gospels. They seek to propagate their own rationale and ideas instead of the truth of God.
6) Some lack enough commitment to reach out and minister.
7) Some are satisfied with the traditional and ritual approaches of religion.
8) Some are more concerned with the bureaucracy than with laboring, more concerned with carrying things on as they have always been.

QUESTIONS:
1. It is hard to see Christ's vision for the world when our attention is focused upon our own selfish motives and desires. What is the key thing that you can do in order to keep Christ's vision before your eyes?
2. Think for a moment. What is *your* role in the harvest?

3. The vision of a great need for prayer. Laborers are needed, but they must be the laborers of God, for the harvest is God's. It is totally inadequate to humanly select the laborers, lay human plans, and send laborers forth in human strength. Such human action will not get the job done alone. God's call and God's appointment are needed. Christ is saying, "Pray that God will raise up enough laborers to reach your generation, the generation for which you are immediately responsible."

> **"Ask, and it shall be given you; seek, and ye shall find; knock, and it shall be opened unto you" (Mt.7:7).**

APPLICATION 1:
Note three significant facts.
1) Christ Himself prayed all night before choosing the first laborers and before sending them out on their first missionary journey (Lk.6:12-13).

2) The number of laborers for any generation depends upon the prayers of God's people in that generation. If God's people are concerned for their generation, they pray for laborers to reach and minister to it. If they lack concern, they do not pray and laborers are few. Compare the *deadness of religion* in Christ's day and the few true laborers there had been for some four hundred years.
3) Christ first of all gave this charge to His apostles and ministers. They were to take the lead and to teach the absolute necessity of praying for laborers.

APPLICATION 2:
Note two things.
1) The harvest is the Lord's. He knows the harvest, every stem and blade of it. He knows everyone—every body and mind, act and thought, need and provision (Mt.10:30). He knows the heart as well as the most efficient and effective way to harvest the field.
2) Therefore, the laborers must be chosen, called, and enlisted by Him. Christ is the One who must send forth laborers.

APPLICATION 3:
Three things should drive us to pray with all fervency for laborers.
1) The good news, the gospel of the kingdom (Mt.9:35).
2) Compassion for the souls of men, for those who have fainted, are scattered, and are without a shepherd.
3) Love for Christ and appreciation for what He has done (2 Cor.5:14).

4. The vision of a great force of laborers. The harvest is so plentiful and ready that a great force needs to be sent forth and *sent forth now*. Note several truths in the Scripture.

a) God is "the Lord of the harvest." He is "the Husbandman" (Jn.15:1). The harvest is "the vineyard of the Lord of hosts" (Is.5:7). The world is His. He can see that it is reaped if there are enough laborers.

b) "We are laborers together with God: ye are God's husbandry" (1 Cor.3:9). God labors and we labor; we both have a part. What a glorious truth and challenge: God needs us! What a glorious privilege—we are to labor side by side with God!

APPLICATION 1:
Note several significant lessons.
1) God desires every generation to have a great force of laborers. He wills for every man, woman, and child to be reached with "the gospel of the kingdom" (Mt.9:35). He wills for none to be lost (2 Pt.3:9).
2) It is God who is to send forth laborers, not men. He is to do the selecting, calling, ordaining, and sending. Our task is to pray for laborers, and when God raises them up, we are to support them by utilizing every means possible.
3) God raises up people with very special gifts to harvest the fields.

> **"And he gave some, apostles; and some, prophets; and some, evangelists; and some, pastors and teachers" (Eph. 4:11).**

4) The harvest is God's. It is to be harvested as He says and wills, not as we may wish. No man has the right to harvest by using his own message and ideas. Christ has clearly instructed and demonstrated that "the gospel of the kingdom" is to be preached.

APPLICATION 2:
The harvest is God's. He can reap the harvest if several conditions exist.
1) If there is enough *concern* within our generation for the multitudes of people who are lost.
2) If there is enough *prayer* for laborers.
3) If there is enough *commitment* to surrender to His call to go.
4) If there is enough *dedication* to follow Him day by day and hour by hour.
5) If there is enough *faith* to believe Christ and the truth of the Scripture.
6) If there is enough *conviction* to stand true and firm through all.

ILLUSTRATION:
The urgency to go into the fields to harvest is just as real today as it was during the first century. And yet, the harvest remains plentiful, crying out for laborers.

> *Andrew Meekens, an elder in the International Evangelical Church of Addis Ababa, was one of those who died on November 23, 1996, when a high-jacked jet ran out of fuel and crashed near the Comoros Islands.*
>
> *According to survivors of the crash, after the pilot announced he would attempt an emergency landing, Meekens stood up and spoke, calming passengers on the Ethiopian Airlines flight. Meekens then presented the gospel of Jesus Christ, and invited people to respond.*
>
> *A surviving flight attendant said, "that about twenty people accepted salvation, including a flight attendant who did not survive the crash.*
>
> *'We preach as dying people to dying people.'"*[2]

Do you labor in His fields? Or do you linger on the outside watching others do the work of the harvest? Just where do you fit into the scheme of things?

QUESTIONS:
1. What role does prayer play in the Lord's harvest? How faithful are you in praying for the harvest of souls who need Christ?
2. What practical things can you do to remember to pray for those who labor in the Lord's harvest?
3. Christ has said that the harvest is plentiful, but the laborers are few. What are the obvious consequences of failing to harvest souls who are ripe?

SUMMARY:

Have you caught the vision that Christ had: the vision to harvest the lost souls of the world? It is imperative that every believer be a strong witness for Christ. God has called all of us to action, to go forth and do these three things:

1. To minister just as Jesus ministered.
2. To demonstrate compassion, the kind of compassion all people are to have for others.
3. To call men to the greatest of all visions, the vision of a great harvest and the vision of an abundance of laborers to enter the harvest of souls.

---

2 Cited in *Beacon* (1/97). SOURCE: *Fresh Illustrations for Preaching and Teaching.* Edward K. Rowell, p.55.

MATTHEW 9:35-38

PERSONAL JOURNAL NOTES
(Reflection & Response)

1. The most important thing that I learned from this lesson was:

2. The area that I need to work on the most is:

3. I can apply this lesson to my life by:

4. Closing Statement of Commitment:

1. They were called "to Him" **2. They were given power & authority**	**CHAPTER 10** **B. The Messiah's Call to His Disciples, 10:1-4** (Mk.3:13-19; Lk. 6:13-19; Acts 1:13) And when he had called unto him his twelve disciples, he gave them power against unclean spirits, to cast them out, and to heal all manner of sickness and all manner of disease.	2 Now the names of the twelve apostles are these; The first, Simon, who is called Peter, and Andrew his brother; James the son of Zebedee, and John his brother; 3 Philip, and Bartholomew; Thomas, and Matthew the publican; James the son of Alphaeus, and Lebbaeus, whose surname was Thaddaeus; 4 Simon the Canaanite, and Judas Iscariot, who also betrayed him.	**3. They were twelve in number** **4 They were made apostles** **5. They included three sets of brothers** **6. They were organized two by two for ministry**

Section VI
THE MESSIAH'S MESSENGERS AND THEIR MISSION, Matthew 9:35-10:42

Study 2: THE MESSIAH'S CALL TO HIS DISCIPLES

Text: Matthew 10:1-4

Aim: To make a fresh commitment to be faithful, faithful in becoming a fisher of men and women.

Memory Verse:

"And when he had called unto *him* his twelve disciples, he gave them power *against* unclean spirits, to cast them out, and to heal all manner of sickness and all manner of disease" (Mt.10:1).

INTRODUCTION

When you were a child, how did you respond to the question: "What do you want to be when you grow up?" This question is put to nearly every child, usually many times. Most responses fall in the categories of fame or heroism, such as an actor, a nurse, a policeman, or a fireman. As a child grows into youth and then young adulthood, the career tracks usually change at least a dozen times. But as an adult, the innocent question takes on a far more serious tone: "Now, that you have grown up, what have you become?"

Many people have grown up and become just what they wanted to be, others have not. But Jesus Christ came to raise each one of us to a new level of purpose, of great significance. As we grow up in Him, Christ has called us to be His disciples—to be "fishers of men."

OUTLINE:

There are several important facts given about their commissioning call.
1. They were called "to Him" (v.1).
2. They were given power and authority (v.1).
3. They were twelve in number (v.2).

4. They were made apostles (v.2).
5. They included three sets of brothers (v.2).
6. They were organized two by two for ministry (v.3).

1. THE DISCIPLES WERE CALLED TO CHRIST (v.1).

There are three steps in the call of the disciples to the ministry.

1. *The discipleship call.* They heard about Christ, went to hear Him, and began to follow Him just as many others did (cp. Jn.1:35f).

2. *The commitment call.* There were multitudes of people following Christ, but He noticed the unusual commitment of these twelve men. At this point He called them to the ministry: to leave all and to begin a period of special training in order to preach and teach professionally. Note Lk.6:13 where Jesus called His disciples to Him, and from among the many whom He called, "He chose twelve whom also He named apostles."

3. *The commissioning call.* Christ commissioned them to go forth with the message of salvation.

APPLICATION 1:
The disciples who had been *with Jesus* for some time had touched, talked, shared, communed, prayed, meditated, and fellowshipped with Him. They had shared and been taught the Scriptures by Him and probably had been taught how to preach and teach. They certainly had witnessed His preaching and teaching and His method of doing both. Several lessons can be learned from this.

1) Every believer needs to be *with Jesus*. We must all learn to quietly meditate and study His Word, communing with Him in prayer.
2) Every servant needs to go through a period of preparation and training before being sent forth. A servant must first be proved (1 Tim.3:10).
3) Every worker (minister) must have a personal relationship with Jesus, *being with Him day by day*. There is no substitute for the training a person receives at the feet of Jesus, learning from His Spirit as he studies His Word and communes with Him in prayer.

APPLICATION 2:
Note three lessons.

1) A person must first be trained, then he can become qualified to serve.

> **"And the things that thou hast heard of me among many witnesses, the same commit thou to faithful men, who shall be able to teach others also" (2 Tim.2:2).**

2) The major prerequisite for ministry is to be "with Jesus" learning from Him and His Word, communing with Him in prayer and in quietness.

> **"But his delight is in the law of the LORD; and in his law doth he meditate day and night" (Ps.1:2).**

3) Public ministry requires two forms of preparation or training.
   a) Private preparation with Christ: *being with Him* all alone (2 Tim.2:15).
   b) Public preparation or formal training: observing and learning from Christ as He ministers through others (Mt.5:1f; 2 Tim.2:2).

QUESTIONS:

1. There are many people who confess to be followers of Christ but are not committed to Him. What does it really mean to be committed to Christ? Are you as committed to Christ as you can be? How committed should you be? Why have you not yet made a full commitment to Christ?

2. What is the best way a believer can be prepared for public ministry? Explain your answer.

2. THE DISCIPLES WERE GIVEN POWER AND AUTHORITY (v.1).

The power to heal and cast out demons was given by Christ to prove that Christ was truly the Son of God (Mt.9:6; Jn.10:25-26). The apostles were given the same authority and power because they were being sent in His name. They were proclaiming Him and His message to be true; they were proving it by the power given them.

> **"This is a faithful saying, and worthy of all acceptation, that Christ Jesus came into the world to save sinners" (1 Tim.1:15).**

The major thing that the miracles teach is this: God truly loves and cares for us here and now, physically. His care is not only for the future and for our spiritual welfare, but His care is for our deliverance in the here and now (the Great Redeemer).

> **"Behold, I give unto you power to tread on serpents and scorpions, and over all the power of the enemy: and nothing shall by any means hurt you. Notwithstanding in this rejoice not, that the spirits are subject unto you; but rather rejoice, because your names are written in heaven" (Lk.10:19-20).**

APPLICATION:
Note three lessons.

1) A servant's power is derived from his master. The believer's authority is derived from his Lord.
   ⇒ This is great assurance. The Lord's servant does not face the world alone. He has supernatural authority and power behind him, the very power of the Lord Himself.
   ⇒ This is great responsibility. The Lord's servant has no right to strike out and act alone. He is to carry the message and deeds of the Lord, not his own message and behavior.

2) The authority and power given by the Lord *concern ministry,* not position, wealth, fame, or earthly dominion. The Lord's servant is given power to *reach out and help people.* What a lesson for the motives and actions of God's servants, both lay and clergy!
3) The power given by the Lord is directed against the devil and evil spirits that control men. It is a spiritual warfare, fought against the evil that possesses the minds and hearts of men.
   ⇒ There is the evil of false teachings and doctrines or beliefs that are always so prominent among mankind (1 Tim.4:1).
   ⇒ There is the evil of deceptive and fleshly behavior that has always enslaved men (2 Tim.3:1-7, 13).
   ⇒ There is the evil of some who rebel so much that they are given over to walk almost exclusively after the flesh (2 Pt.2:10).

ILLUSTRATION:
Jesus Christ has made available His power and authority to each believer. The danger that awaits us is when we trust in our own power and become too busy to keep our spiritual edge sharp.

> *A meteorologist and a minister never missed a weekend of golf. One weekend, just as they began to play, a thunderstorm broke out. Soaking wet, they*

retreated to the clubhouse for an hour. Still the rain came down. With no relief in sight, the preacher turned to the weatherman and said, "You would think that between the two of us, we could do SOMETHING!"[1]

The point is that we can do nothing outside of Christ's power and authority.

> **"I am the vine, ye *are* the branches: He that abideth in me, and I in him, the same bringeth forth much fruit: for without me ye can do nothing" (Jn 15:5).**

QUESTIONS:

1. Jesus gave His disciples power and authority. What kind of power and authority are available to the believer who lives today? Why do so many believers try to live under their own power and authority?
2. Can you think of some examples when the Lord's authority and power have been abused? Is this true only at a leadership level? Why is this such a serious problem in many Christian circles?
3. It is of critical importance that we identify who the real enemy is—Satan, not other believers. What practical things can you do in order to keep Satan in your sights?

A CLOSER LOOK #1

(10:1) **Power—Authority**: the Greek word means authority. Christ was giving *His own authority* to His messengers. They were sent forth by Him on His special mission; therefore, they were given His authority and power to minister.

Notice that the power to save or convert the lost was not given. Why? Only God can save and penetrate the spiritual world or dimension. Man's authority is limited to the physical world and dimension.

A CLOSER LOOK #2

(10:1) **Unclean Spirits—Evil Spirits**: evil spirits are spirits of unholy, polluted, immoral, and unjust behavior; they are spirits belonging to the ungodly realm of darkness. Two things need to be said about evil spirits at this point.

1. Christ accepts and teaches the presence and reality of evil spirits. He sent His apostles forth with the authority to cast them out.
2. Throughout human experience, most beliefs have extremes that arise and surround the actual truth. Note several facts that every thinking and honest person knows about this fact of human experience.
    a. The extremes of a belief range from extreme liberalism (denial) all the way over to extreme conservatism (superstition).
    b. The fact that some carry a belief over into superstitious behavior does not mean that there is not truth in the belief. It does not mean this any more than the denial of a belief means the belief is untrue.
    c. The fact that some may and probably do misread and carry the belief in evil spirits over into the area of the superstitious does not mean there are not evil spirits. Christ did accept their presence, and He taught the fact of their existence to His apostles.

---

[1] *Executive Speechwriter Newsletter* (n. d.), p. 4. SOURCE: *INFOsearch Sermon Illustrations* (Arlington, TX: The Computer Assistant, 1-888-868-9029, 1986-1996).

3. THE DISCIPLES WERE TWELVE IN NUMBER (v.2).

A teacher, including Christ, can adequately teach only so many. Note that Christ taught some things to the multitudes; then He taught more to a much smaller number (Mary, Martha, Lazarus, and some others); and finally He taught all things to a small band of men (the twelve apostles). We might say that He taught all He could to a small band of disciples who were to carry on His life's work (cp. Jethro's advice to Moses, suggesting that Moses organize the people into groups of ten for more efficient rule, Ex.18:17-26).

There are two thoughts at this point.

APPLICATION 1:
How much we need to heed this method that Christ followed—the method of making disciples out of a few while ministering to the many. And note: the twelve were not to be administrators for Christ. They were to be ministers for Christ, men who would do the same work of ministry that He did. They were to carry on the ministry He had begun.

APPLICATION 2:
What would happen if every minister and teacher (lay and religious) discipled just twelve persons in his lifetime, twelve who would carry on some kind of ministry? How long would it take to reach the world with the gospel?

QUESTIONS:
1. Christ chose to select only a few people to pour His life into. What was His purpose for doing this? What practical lessons can you glean from His example?
2. The person who has been discipled must also be willing to serve others—even as Christ ministered to the needy. If God led a few believers into your life over the next three years, what kind of disciples would they turn out to be?

A CLOSER LOOK #3
(10:2) **Apostles**: why did Christ select twelve special apostles instead of some other number? There are several possible reasons.

1. There were twelve tribes of Israel. Through Abraham, the Israelites had been called to be the people of God (Gen.12:1-5). Christ wanted to reach out to Israel first and to give them a last chance. Therefore, He wanted an apostle to represent each of the twelve tribes, to equal the twelve patriarchs of Israel, that is, to equal Jacob's sons. The number twelve was symbolizing that He was making an attempt to reach all Israel.

2. The Jews had been the first body of people called by God (Gen.12:1-5). Therefore, they were to be the first people called by God's Son. The twelve apostles were to be the representatives of Christ who were to bring Israel's twelve tribes to God the Father. Note an important fact: Christ said the twelve apostles were to judge the twelve tribes of Israel (Mt.19:28; Lk.22:29-30).

3. The twelve apostles were to be the patriarchs, the heads, the apostles of the new Israel (Rev.21:14; Jas.1:1; cp. Gal.6:16; cp. Ro.2:28-29).

4. THE DISCIPLES WERE MADE APOSTLES (v.2).

Note several things.

1. Christ Himself is called an apostle; that is, He was the messenger of God sent by God Himself. (Cp. Heb.3:1.)

2. These twelve men were also to be called apostles; that is, they were to be the messengers sent by Christ Himself.

3. There is a sense in which the ministers of every generation are the Lord's apostles, His very special messengers. They are the men who are sent forth by Christ to be His representatives. There is a lesson here in that God's people should respect the Lord's messenger as His special apostle. (see A CLOSER LOOK # 5, Apostle—Mt.10:2).

> **"And I will give you pastors according to mine heart, which shall feed you with knowledge and understanding" (Jer.3:15).**

A CLOSER LOOK #4

(10:2) **Apostle**: a person who is sent out. An apostle is a representative, an ambassador, a person who is sent out into one country to represent another country. Three things are true of the apostle.

⇒ He belongs to the one who has sent him out.
⇒ He is commissioned to be sent out.
⇒ He possesses all the authority and power of the one who sends him out.

The word "apostle" has both a narrow and a broad usage in the New Testament.

1. The narrow sense. It refers to the twelve apostles and to Paul as an apostle (Acts 1:21-22; 1 Cor.9:1). In this narrow sense there were at least two basic qualifications.

a. The apostle was a man chosen directly by the Lord Himself or by the Holy Spirit (cp. Mt.10:1-2; Mk.3:13-14; Lk.6:13; Acts 9:6, 15; 13:2; 22:10, 14-15; Ro.1:1). He was a man who had either seen or been a companion of the Lord Jesus.

b. The apostle was a man who had been an eyewitness of the resurrected Lord (Acts 1:21-22; 1 Cor.9:1).

2. The broad sense. The word "apostle" refers to other men who preached the gospel. It is used of two missionaries: Barnabas (Acts 14:4, 14, 17) and Silas (1 Th.2:6), and two messengers, Titus (2 Cor.8:23) and Epaphroditus (Ph.2:25). There is also a possibility that James, the Lord's brother (Gal.1:19), and Andronicus and Junia (Ro.16:7) are referred to as apostles.

In the narrow sense, the gift of an apostle was bound to die out because of the unique qualifications to receive the gift. But historically, in the broad sense, there is perhaps a sense in which the qualifications and gift itself are still given and used by the Lord. The Lord's servants of all generations must *see* the Lord and know Him intimately. Similarly, we must personally *see and experience* the power of the resurrection. Certainly there are some in every generation who have *so seen* the Lord Jesus and who *so know* and *so experience* the power of the Lord's resurrection. Perhaps the Lord Jesus endues some with the unique gift of an apostle to be used in a very special way throughout His most precious domain—the church.

QUESTIONS:

1. As you study the Scriptures and read about other apostles of the faith, what kinds of qualities did they exhibit?
2. What role does the modern-day apostle have in the church?
3. All believers, as ministers of God, are God's representatives here on earth. Can you say you truly belong to God? That the message you give to others is God's message and not your own?

5. THE DISCIPLES INCLUDED THREE SETS OF BROTHERS (v.2).

Note the influence of families upon children. Six of Christ's apostles, one half of the inner circle, were apparently from *closely knit* families. The brothers respected each other enough to listen and follow one another (cp. Jn.1:40f). The disciples who were brothers were Simon Peter and Andrew, James and John (the sons of Zebedee), and the other James and Lebbeus.

ILLUSTRATION:
One of a Christian's greatest joys is to see a family member—whether it be a child, a parent, a brother or sister, or some distant relative—respond to God's call. All the money and success in the world could not replace the satisfaction of seeing a loved one follow Christ. But the tragedy is equally as great when a family member fails to be a witness to Christ.

A young man was to be sentenced to the penitentiary for committing forgery. The judge had known him from childhood, for he was well acquainted with his father, a famous legal scholar and the author of an exhaustive study entitled The Law of Trusts. "Do you remember your father?" asked the magistrate. "I remember him well, your honor," came the reply. Then trying to probe the offender's conscience, the judge said, "As you are about to be sentenced, and as you think of your wonderful dad, what do you remember most clearly about him?" There was a pause; then the judge received an answer he had not expected. "I remember, sir, when I went to him for advice, he looked up at me from the book he was writing and said, 'Run along, boy, I'm busy!' When I went to him for companionship, he turned me away, saying, 'Run along, son; this book must be finished!' Your honor, you remember him as a great lawyer; I remember him as a lost friend." The magistrate muttered to himself, "Alas! Finished the book, but lost the boy!"[2]

What will your family do when Christ calls? Have you made time for them?

QUESTIONS:
1. Did someone in your family influence your life as a Christian? If so, in what way? If not, who did?
2. What is the relationship that other members of your family have with Christ? In what ways have you or can you influence them?
3. What benefits are there for several family members to serve Christ together?

6. THE DISCIPLES WERE ORGANIZED TWO BY TWO FOR MINISTRY (v.10:3-4).

Christ seemed to arrange the apostles two by two. Note how Matthew also groups them in pairs. Several lessons can be immediately drawn from this.

APPLICATION 1:
1) We need each other, someone with whom we can be close in fellowship and ministry.
2) We need to go forth together two by two.
3) We need to organize for ministry.

APPLICATION 2:
Note the humility that Matthew teaches. He is the writer of this great gospel, yet he demonstrates the ingredient so necessary for the servant of Christ (Ph.2:3-4; cp. Ro.12:10).
1) He mentions Thomas, his partner, before himself. The other two gospel writers place him before Thomas.

---

2 *INFOsearch Sermon Illustrations* (Arlington, TX: The Computer Assistant, 1-888-868-9029, 1986-1996).

2) He again mentions his terrible past—that he was a publican and a traitor to the Jewish nation.

QUESTIONS:

1. What practical lessons can we learn from the disciples' going out two by two? Is there any principle that you can apply to your own ministry for the Lord?
2. Within any group of believers there is the possibility that not all are faithful to the Lord. There are "Judases'" waiting for the moment to betray the cause of Christ. What is your role in this situation? What is God's role?

SUMMARY:

There is no greater privilege given to a person than to be called by Jesus Christ. There is nothing on this earth more important than to do what God calls you to do.

> *In attempting to recruit John Sculley, the 38-year-old President of Pepsi-Cola, Steve Jobs, Founder of Apple Computer, issued a tremendous challenge to Sculley. He asked: "Do you want to spend the rest of your life selling sugared water or do you want a chance to change the world?"*
>
> *What a challenge to all Christians! Are we settling for less than God's best in our lives?* [3]

1. The disciples were called "to Him."
2. The disciples were given power and authority.
3. The disciples were twelve in number.
4. The disciples were made apostles.
5. The disciples included three sets of brothers.
6. The disciples were organized two by two for ministry.

PERSONAL JOURNAL NOTES
(Reflection & Response)

1. The most important thing that I learned from this lesson was:

2. The area that I need to work on the most is:

3. I can apply this lesson to my life by:

4. Closing Statement of Commitment:

---

3 *John Sculley, Odyssey*. (New York, NY: Harper & Row, 1987), p. 90.

C. The Messiah's Commission to His Disciples, 10:5-15
(Mk.6:7-13; Lk.9:1-6)

1. Jesus sent forth His disciples, commanding them

2. First, go to Israel: To the lost of one's own house

3. Second, preach: The Kingdom of Heaven is at hand

4. Third, minister, sharing freely

5. Fourth, receive compensation
   a. Do not seek material gain
   b. Seek only to be adequately cared for

6. Fifth, seek a worthy host

7. Sixth, plan your ministry & your visits
   a. Approach cordially
   b. If accepted, share your peace
   c. If rejected, leave & symbolize judgment
   d. Rejecters are to be judged

5 These twelve Jesus sent forth, and commanded them, saying, Go not into the way of the Gentiles, and into any city of the Samaritans enter ye not:

6 But go rather to the lost sheep of the house of Israel.

7 And as ye go, preach, saying, The kingdom of heaven is at hand.

8 Heal the sick, cleanse the lepers, raise the dead, cast out devils: freely ye have received, freely give.

9 Provide neither gold, nor silver, nor brass in your purses,

10 Nor scrip for your journey, neither two coats, neither shoes, nor yet staves: for the workman is worthy of his meat.

11 And into whatsoever city or town ye shall enter, enquire who in it is worthy; and there abide till ye go thence.

12 And when ye come into an house, salute it.

13 And if the house be worthy, let your peace come upon it: but if it be not worthy, let your peace return to you.

14 And whosoever shall not receive you, nor hear your words, when ye depart out of that house or city, shake off the dust of your feet.

15 Verily I say unto you, It shall be more tolerable for the land of Sodom and Gomorrha in the day of judgment, than for that city.

Section VI
THE MESSIAH'S MESSENGERS AND THEIR MISSION, Matthew 9:35-10:42

Study 3: **THE MESSIAH'S COMMISSION TO HIS DISCIPLES**

Text: **Matthew 10:5-15**

Aim: To organize a successful strategy of evangelism for your own life.

Memory Verse:
"And as ye go, preach, saying, The kingdom of heaven is at hand" (Mt.10:7).

INTRODUCTION

There are many people who become involved in the Lord's work but want to serve according to their own rules. We live in times when human opinions often replace God's law. Some of these modern-day opinions are:

⇒ I'll serve God when it is convenient for me.
⇒ Faith is a very private thing. I would never ask anyone else about his or her relationship with God.

⇒ I'll do anything for God...as long as it is easy and not too time-consuming.
⇒ Don't offend anyone with the claims of Christianity. As long as a person believes in *something*, why turn him off with my beliefs?

Is there any wonder so many people have yet to hear the gospel? No person has ever been saved by another person's opinion. The challenge for each believer, for each true disciple of Jesus Christ, is to clearly understand what the Word of God teaches and then to faithfully act upon it.

OUTLINE:
1. Jesus sent forth His disciples, commanding them (v.5).
2. First, go to Israel, to the lost of one's own house (v.6).
3. Second, preach: preach the Kingdom of Heaven is at hand (v.7).
4. Third, minister, sharing freely (v.8).
5. Fourth, receive compensation (v.9-10).
6. Fifth, seek a worthy host for lodging (v.11).
7. Sixth, plan your ministry and visits (v.12-15).

1. JESUS SENT FORTH HIS DISCIPLES, COMMANDING THEM (v.5).

Note that Jesus did not send forth every disciple who was following Him. Only a few were chosen to serve as special messengers to devote *all their time* to preaching and ministering. Most other disciples were to be witnessing for Christ in their work and in their other daily activities.

APPLICATION 1:
A person is sent forth by Jesus; he does not choose on his own to go forth. If he does, he goes forth in his own strength and power, and cannot expect to receive the power of Christ.

APPLICATION 2:
The ministry is not a profession; it is a commission. Christ calls and commissions. The man who chooses to be a minister without a true call and commissioning of the Lord experiences four things.
1) He finds himself ministering primarily in his own strength.
2) He often finds his heart void and feels the constant pressure of having to come up with *human ideas* and *human programs*. He has difficulty maintaining a sense of meaning and purpose for both himself and his people.
3) He senses a real void and shortcoming in proclaiming the gospel and in doing the work of the ministry.
4) He often wonders what *good* is really being done. He frankly lacks the sense of a real call within; therefore, there is no *outside godly connection* to comfort and assure him that he is in God's will. He is left to seek comfort and assurance only from himself or from some other human source. There is no supernatural Spirit or power to encourage him.

ILLUSTRATION:
It is impossible to do God's work without God's help. Nevertheless, there are many people who attempt it. Being stubborn, they waste valuable time and effort just to prove a point or to do things their own way, as is comically pointed out in the following story:

> *Between two farms near Valleyview, Alberta [Canada], you can find two parallel fences, only two feet apart, running for a half mile. Why are there two fences when one would do?*

Two farmers, Paul and Oscar, had a disagreement that erupted into a feud. Paul wanted to build a fence between their land and split the cost, but Oscar was unwilling to contribute. Since he wanted to keep cattle on his land, Paul went ahead and built the fence anyway.

After the fence was completed, Oscar said to Paul, 'I see we have a fence.

"What do you mean 'we?'" Paul replied. "I got the property line surveyed and built the fence two feet into my land. That means some of my land is outside the fence. And if any of your cows sets foot on my land, I'll shoot it."

Oscar knew Paul wasn't joking, so when he eventually decided to use the land adjoining Paul's for pasture, he was forced to build another fence, two feet away.

Oscar and Paul are both gone now, but their double fence stands as a monument to the high price we pay for stubbornness.[1]

How many 'fences,' how many useless things, have you done in God's name without God's call and God's support?

QUESTIONS:
1. What is the relationship between Christ's call and Christ's power? What bearing does this have on anything you feel led to do by Christ?
2. As a layperson, does God's command to go and minister apply to you? Why or why not?

2. FIRST, GO TO ISRAEL: TO THE LOST OF ONE'S OWN HOUSE (v.6).

The offer of salvation was to go to Israel first, not to the lost of the world. Later it was to be offered to the whole world (Ro.9:30; cp. Ro.10:13; see A Closer Look # 1—Mt.10:6).

APPLICATION:
A man is to go first to his own house.
1) He is to demonstrate love for his own family and friends first. If he does not love those of his own household enough to witness to them, how can he love those whom he does not know?
2) He is to learn how to bear witness to those who are more likely to respond instead of react. Such knowledge better prepares him to face the world and its negative responses.

A CLOSER LOOK #1

(10:6) **Israel**: Jesus had several reasons for sending His messengers to Israel first. (1) Israel held a very special place in God's plans. The nation was to be given first opportunity to hear the gospel. (2) The disciples needed to concentrate their efforts right where they were lest their efforts be scattered. (3) God's method is always for a person to reach his own home and his own people first. A person is to begin his witness and work immediately, right where he lives.

> **"But ye shall receive power, after that the Holy Ghost is come upon you: and ye shall be witnesses unto me both in Jerusalem, and in all Judaea, and in Samaria, and unto the uttermost part of the earth" (Acts 1:8).**

---

1 Cited by Daren Wride. SOURCE: *Fresh Illustrations for Preaching and Teaching.* Edward K. Rowell, p.200.

A word needs to be said about Israel. Jesus was pointing out several things.

1. Israel had a very special place in God's heart. Therefore, the gospel was to be preached to Israel first.
2. Israel was as lost sheep: "My people hath been lost sheep" (Jer.50:6). Note that the Gentiles are also called "lost sheep" (1 Pt.2:25).
3. Israel's people were lost because their shepherds (teachers) let them scatter. Their teachers had not adhered to the truth.

> **"But when he saw the multitudes, he was moved with compassion on them, because they fainted, and were scattered abroad, as sheep having no shepherd. Then saith he unto his disciples, The harvest truly is plenteous, but the labourers are few; pray ye therefore the Lord of the harvest, that he will send forth labourers into his harvest" (Mt.9:36-38).**

QUESTIONS:

1. Bearing witness to one's family is usually more difficult than doing so to a stranger. What are some practical ways you can be a strong witness to your loved ones?
2. Is there ever a time when you should give up on your family?

3. SECOND, PREACH: THE KINGDOM OF HEAVEN IS AT HAND (v.7).

Note the message is a *given* message, given by the Lord Himself. The disciples were not to proclaim their own ideas nor the ideas of others. They were to preach the message *given* by the Lord. No matter the generation, the message needs to be repeated and repeated.

⇒ It is the same yesterday, today, and forever (Heb.13:8).
⇒ It was the message of Christ (Mt.4:17, 23).
⇒ It was the message of John (Mt.3:2).
⇒ It was the message of the apostles and ministers of Christ.

> **"For the kingdom of God is not meat and drink; but righteousness, and peace, and joy in the Holy Ghost" (Ro.14:17).**

QUESTIONS:

1. Modern man is often tempted to *improve* on what has been handed down by God. Is there any room for man to change the message of the gospel, to add to or take away from it?
2. What are some forces in the world that seek to divert the believer's attention away from the true gospel?

A CLOSER LOOK # 2

(10:7) **Kingdom of Heaven**: the Kingdom of Heaven and of God is revealed in four different stages throughout history.

1. There is the spiritual kingdom that is at hand; it is present right now (Mt.4:17; 12:28).
   a. The present kingdom refers to God's rule and reign and authority in the lives of believers.

> **"Who hath delivered us from the power of darkness, and hath translated us into the kingdom of his dear Son" (Col. 1:13).**

b. The present kingdom is offered to the world and to men in the person of Jesus Christ.
c. The present kingdom must be received as a little child.

> **"But when Jesus saw it, he was much displeased, and said unto them, Suffer the little children to come unto me, and forbid them not: for of such is the kingdom of God" (Mk.10:14-15).**

d. The present kingdom is experienced only by the new birth.

> **"Jesus answered and said unto him, Verily, verily, I say unto thee, Except a man be born again, he cannot see the kingdom of God" (Jn.3:3).**

e. The present kingdom is entered now and must be received now.

> **"Verily I say unto you, Whosoever shall not receive the kingdom of God as a little child, he shall not enter therein" (Mk.10:15).**

f. The present kingdom is a spiritual, life-changing blessing.

> **"For the kingdom of God is not meat and drink; but righteousness, and peace, and joy in the Holy Ghost" (Ro.14:17).**

g. The present kingdom is to be the first thing sought by believers.

> **"But seek ye first the kingdom of God, and his righteousness; and all these things shall be added unto you" (Mt.6:33).**

2. There is the professing kingdom that is also in this present age. It refers to modern-day Christianity in every generation. It pictures what the Kingdom of Heaven or professing Christianity is like and what professing Christianity will be like between Christ's first coming and His return. This imperfect state is what is called "the mysteries of the kingdom of heaven" (Mt.13:1-52, esp. 13:11).

> **"Another parable put he forth unto them, saying, The kingdom of heaven is likened unto a man which sowed good seed [good men] in his field: but while men slept, his enemy came and sowed tares [evil men] among the wheat, and went his way" (Mt.13:24-25).**

3. There is the millennial kingdom that is future. It is the actual rule of Christ or the government of Christ that is to come to this earth for a thousand years.
a. The millennial kingdom is the kingdom predicted by Daniel.

> **"And in the days of these kings shall the God of heaven set up a kingdom, which shall never be destroyed: and the kingdom shall not be left to other people, but it shall break in pieces and consume all these kingdoms, and it shall stand for ever" (Dan.2:44).**

b. The millennial kingdom is the kingdom promised to David.

> **"And when thy days be fulfilled, and thou shalt sleep with thy fathers, I will set up thy seed after thee, which shall proceed**

out of thy bowels, and I will establish his kingdom....And thine house and thy kingdom shall be established for ever before thee: thy throne shall be established for ever" (2 Sam.7:12, 16).

c. The millennial kingdom is the kingdom pictured by John.

"And I saw thrones, and they sat upon them, and judgment was given unto them: and I saw the souls of them that were beheaded for the witness of Jesus, and for the word of God, and which had not worshipped the beast, neither his image, neither had received his mark upon their foreheads, or in their hands; and they lived and reigned with Christ a thousand years. But the rest of the dead lived not again until the thousand years were finished. This is the first resurrection. Blessed and holy is he that hath part in the first resurrection: on such the second death hath no power, but they shall be priests of God and of Christ, and shall reign with him a thousand years" (Rev. 20:4-6).

4. There is the perfect kingdom of the new heaven and earth that is future.
   a. The eternal kingdom is the rule and reign of God in a perfect universe for all eternity.

"Let not your heart be troubled: ye believe in God, believe also in me. In my Father's house are many mansions: if it were not so, I would have told you. I go to prepare a place for you. And if I go and prepare a place for you, I will come again, and receive you unto myself; that where I am, there ye may be also" (Jn.14:1-3).

b. The eternal kingdom is the perfect state of being for the believer in the future.

"Now this I say, brethren, that flesh and blood cannot inherit the kingdom of God; neither doth corruption inherit incorruption" (1 Cor. 15:50).

c. The eternal kingdom is an actual place into which believers are to enter sometime in the future.

"And I say unto you, That many shall come from the east and west, and shall sit down with Abraham, and Isaac, and Jacob, in the kingdom of heaven" (Mt.8:11).

d. The eternal kingdom is a gift of God that will be given in the future.

"Fear not, little flock; for it is your Father's good pleasure to give you the kingdom" (Lk. 12:32).

A CLOSER LOOK #3

(10:7-8) **Ministers—Ministry**: the major areas of service for the apostles were twofold—the area of preaching the gospel (v.7) and the area of ministering (v.8).

The apostles were to minister and to share freely. Christ gave them His authority and power freely; therefore, they were to minister freely, not charging *special fees for special ministries* (note this is not referring to *compensation* for special ministries, but to *special fees* for special ministries, v.10). Their ministry and sharing were in four primary areas.

A CLOSER LOOK #3
(10:7-8) **Ministers—Ministry**: the major areas of service for the apostles were twofold—the area of preaching the gospel (v.7) and the area of ministering (v.8).

The apostles were to minister and to share freely. Christ gave them His authority and power freely; therefore, they were to minister freely, not charging *special fees for special ministries* (note this is not referring to *compensation* for special ministries, but to *special fees* for special ministries, v.10). Their ministry and sharing were in four primary areas.

1. They were to heal the sick. Many had physical needs; they were ill, hurting, and suffering. Some did not have enough to eat or wear or even a place to live. Some were weak and had lost the will to fight. They were hopeless and helpless, discouraged and depressed. They needed the message of the gospel.

2. They were to cleanse the lepers. Leprosy was considered a form of pollution; therefore, it was a symbol of sin. The apostles were to cleanse the lepers. They were to cleanse those who had the actual disease, and they were to preach the power of Christ to cleanse a life polluted with sin.

3. They were to raise the dead. There is no record of the apostles' raising the dead before the resurrection of Christ, but the apostles were used by God to raise many to spiritual life. The Bible says men are "dead in sins" (Eph.2:1). Therefore, the disciples were to preach the power of Christ to raise men to life eternal.

4. They were to cast out devils. Demon-possession means that a person is gripped by evil forces. When a man is gripped by an evil spirit, he is no longer in control of his life; he is controlled by the forces of evil. The disciples were to preach the power of Christ to deliver men from the spirits of evil.

QUESTIONS:
1. Most people think of the Kingdom of Heaven as being only in the future. How can you understand and explain that it is also here *now*?
2. The apostles were commissioned to preach the gospel and to minister to the needs of people. Why are both aspects essential?

4. THIRD, MINISTER, SHARING FREELY (v.8).

Two things always need to be remembered about the apostle's unusual power.

1. Their power was a given power. It came from the Lord Himself. God gives His servant the gifts and the power to preach and minister as He has called him (1 Cor.12:28f; Eph.4:11-13). The gifts and the power are of God, not of the man himself. The gifts and the power of a man come freely from God; therefore, he is freely to give all he has. All the energy and all the toil necessary are to be poured into preaching the gospel and into ministering to people.

2. Their power was to confirm that God does love and care for the world and that the message being preached was actually from God.

APPLICATION:
Ministering to the needs of people shows two things.
1) God loves and cares for people.
2) The minister is a minister of love and care.

"Even as the Son of man came not to be ministered unto, but to minister, and to give his life a ransom for many" (Mt.20:28).

QUESTIONS:
1. The power that allows the believer to share the gospel comes from God alone. In hearing preaching and teaching, how can you tell if someone's message and power are from God?
2. Power can often be an intoxicating thing. What can a person do to guard against becoming intoxicated by power?

5. FOURTH, RECEIVE COMPENSATION (v.9-10).

In financial matters Christ expected two things from His apostles and His people. First, His apostles and servants were not to spend their own money on the ministry; and second, His people were to adequately support His apostles and servants.

> **"Even so hath the Lord ordained that they which preach the gospel should live of the gospel" (1 Cor.9:14; see also Gal.6:6).**

APPLICATION 1:
The apostles, God's servants, were forbidden to accumulate estates *through the ministry*. But neither were they to spend their own money on the ministry. There were several reasons for this.
1) Their minds and hearts were to be centered on preaching the gospel and ministering to people, not on buying and selling and accumulating.
2) They were to trust God for their needs and, by such example, to teach dependence upon God (Mt.6:24-34).
3) They were to teach and depend upon God's people to provide for them (cp. 1 Cor.9:13-14).
4) They were to allow God's people the privilege of sharing in the ministry through their giving. God's people were to learn more and more trust by depending upon God to help them raise whatever funds they needed to support the ministers.

APPLICATION 2:
God's servant or laborer is worthy of being financially supported. In fact, Paul taught that God's servant was to be "counted worthy of double honor" (salary, compensation, financial support).

ILLUSTRATION:
Christianity is very practical. Those who have been called by God into full-time Christian service have bills to pay, just like everyone else does.

Workers earn it,
spendthrifts burn it,
bankers lend it,
women spend it,
forgers fake it,
taxes take it,
dying leaves it,
heirs receive it,
thrifty save it,
misers crave it,
robbers seize it,
rich increase it,
gamblers lose it …
I could use it.[2]

---

2 Richard Armour. As quoted in *Draper's Book of Quotations for the Christian World* by Edythe Draper. (Wheaton, IL: Tyndale House Publishers, Inc., 1992).

QUESTIONS:
1. The gospel is free, but the cost of sharing it is not. God's people who minister must be fairly compensated for their time. Is your church treating your pastor fairly? Other support staff? Visiting ministers? Missionaries of your church?
2. What is your part in supporting God's ministers? Is any believer exempt from helping? Why or why not?
3. What dangers does a person face when raising money for his own ministry? What safeguards should be in place?

6. FIFTH, SEEK A WORTHY HOST (v.11).

In every city and place there are some who have good reputations and some who have bad reputations. Several factors determined a worthy host.

1. A worthy host was a person with a good reputation concerning morals. Living with a person of evil and unjust morals would cause the apostles' own morals to be questioned. They were to reach out to the immoral, even as Christ did, but not to fellowship and live with them. They were to be careful in choosing their close friends.

2. A worthy host was a person with a good reputation concerning God. Some would have a spiritual interest and some would not.

3. A worthy host was a person with a good reputation concerning hospitality. Some would willingly care for strangers; others would not.

> **"Distributing to the necessity of saints; given to hospitality" (Ro.12:13; see also 1 Pt.4:9).**

APPLICATION 1:
Note several lessons.
1) The apostles were to seek out the *worthy host*. They were not to seek out the wealthy and leading citizens of a community, nor were they to seek out the best accommodations.
2) Paul sought out *God's people* when he went into a new and strange place (Acts 28:14).
3) The *good people* of a place are usually known—those whose qualities are honesty, decency, and kindness.
4) Note the lesson about the believer's *close friends*. His close friends are to be God's people—people counted worthy by God.

APPLICATION 2:
God's messenger was to stay with the same host throughout his stay in a place. He was not to seek more comfort and luxury as he came to know a place. There are several reasons for this.
1) Such action might indicate favoritism and cause jealousy.
2) Such action might indicate a materialistic, selfish, and soft mind, leading to the questioning of a person's commitment.
3) Such action distracts from a person's purpose and ministry.
4) Such action hurts and often alienates the first host.

QUESTIONS:
1. If God called you to travel and minister for Him, how could you go about seeking a worthy host?
2. If there were traveling ministers in your area, would you be known or sought out as a worthy host? If not, what could you do to become more suitable?

7. SIXTH, PLAN YOUR MINISTRY, YOUR VISITS (v.12-15).

The Lord sent His messengers forth, that is, out visiting in the houses of the city. They did not sit back waiting on the people to come to them. They went out carrying the gospel to the people.

Note the Lord told the apostles how to visit. Precise plans were laid.

1. The apostles were to approach a house cordially (v.13). Saluting, that is, approaching cordially, does several things.
   a. It communicates a friendliness and kindness which encourages an open reception.
   b. It opens the door to more conversation which the messenger can turn into a presentation of the gospel.
   c. It tells immediately whether a person is receptive or not.

> **"Put on therefore, as the elect of God, holy and beloved, bowels of mercies, kindness, humbleness of mind, meekness, longsuffering" (Col.3:12).**

APPLICATION:
The messenger is to greet and be courteous to people, not forceful, demanding, forward, or ugly.

2. If the people accepted the apostles, the apostles were to share peace (v.13). The greeting of *peace* was to be given to every home and place they approached. If the people were worthy, the messengers were to continue their message of peace. If the people were unworthy, they were to let the salutation lie alone. They were to say nothing else. They were not to continue the message of peace. They were to take the message of peace and leave without sharing it.

> **"For the kingdom of God is not meat and drink; but righteousness, and peace, and joy in the Holy Ghost" (Ro.14:17).**

APPLICATION 1:
The witnesses of the Lord must discern and make a judgment about the people to whom they are witnessing.
1) Are they kind and gracious or cold and hard?
2) Are they shy and bashful or really disinterested?
3) Are they truly receptive or just kind and gracious to everyone?
4) Are they spiritually sensitive or just interested in religious matters?

APPLICATION 2:
The Lord's witness must not waste time. He must discern as quickly as possible who is worthy and receptive.

APPLICATION 3:
The greeting of the day was "Peace be unto you." The apostles were to use the greeting as the basis of their message. They were to expand it. Their message was to be peace—*peace with God and the peace of God.*

3. If the people rejected the apostles, the apostles were to leave. The Lord's messenger and witness could expect to be rejected by some. When rejected, the messenger was to do two things.
   a. He was to leave the house or city.
   b. He was to shake the dust off his feet. This was to be a symbol that...
      - the people had lost their opportunity.

- the people's wickedness was so detestable that it polluted the very ground upon which their house or city sat.
- God would reject the people even as they had rejected Him.

APPLICATION 1:
Note that some *do* reject. They reject two things.
1) The messenger himself.
2) The messenger's words.

APPLICATION 2:
When rejected, the messenger is not to argue or force the gospel upon the person. Christ expects His messenger to leave. Note the words: "When ye depart."

4. Rejecters were to be judged (see A Closer Look # 4—Mt.10:15). Rejection of God's messenger and of the gospel condemns a person to a terrible fate. The person's judgment is to be more severe than even the judgment of Sodom and Gomorrha. Why? Because the person rejects God's very own Son. Sodom and Gomorrha never had the opportunity to hear God's Son. Our responsibility is much greater because our privilege to hear God's Son is much greater.

> **"And as it is appointed unto men once to die, but after this the judgment" (Heb.9:27).**

QUESTIONS:
1. What advantages are there for the person who plans his or her times of ministry? How important are the details when planning a ministry trip?
2. How does a modern-day believer "share peace"?
3. Have you ever been rejected because of your message about Christ? Is this something you should take personally? Why?

A CLOSER LOOK #4
(10:15) **Sodom and Gomorrha**: these two cities and their citizens are used as examples of the worst sinners (Dt.32:32; Is.1:10; Ezk.16:46; Mt.11:23-24; Lk.10:12-13; 17:29; Ro.9:29; 2 Pt.2:6; Jude 7; Rev.11:8). The cities were destroyed by fire (Gen.19:24-25) and are said to be "suffering the vengeance of eternal fire" (Jude 7).

SUMMARY:

The commission to evangelize the world with the message of the gospel has been issued to every believer. We are commissioned to go forth just as Christ sent the first disciples forth:

1. Jesus sent forth His disciples, commanding them.
2. First, go to Israel, to the lost of one's own house.
3. Second, preach: preach the Kingdom of Heaven is at hand.
4. Third, minister, sharing freely.
5. Fourth, receive compensation.
6. Fifth, seek a worthy host for lodging.
7. Sixth, plan your ministry and visits.

MATTHEW 10:5-15

PERSONAL JOURNAL NOTES
(Reflection & Response)

1. The most important thing that I learned from this lesson was:

2. The area that I need to work on the most is:

3. I can apply this lesson to my life by:

4. Closing Statement of Commitment:

	D. The Messiah's Warning of Persecution, 10:16-23
1. Two facts must be kept in mind a. You are commissioned b. You are as sheep among wolves **2. Counsel 1: Be wise & harmless, v.16**	16 Behold, I send you forth as sheep in the midst of wolves: be ye therefore wise as serpents, and harmless as doves.
3. Counsel 2: Beware of men a. The persecutors: The state & the religionists b. The reasons you will be persecuted 1) For the Lord's sake 2) To be a testimony	17 But beware of men: for they will deliver you up to the councils, and they will scourge you in their synagogues; 18 And ye shall be brought before governors and kings for my sake, for a testimony against them and the Gentiles.
4. Counsel 3: Do not worry about a defense a. God will meet your need b. God's Spirit will speak in you	19 But when they deliver you up, take no thought how or what ye shall speak: for it shall be given you in that same hour what ye shall speak. 20 For it is not ye that speak, but the Spirit of your Father which speaketh in you.
5. Counsel 4: Know that families will be divided	21 And the brother shall deliver up the brother to death, and the father the child: and the children shall rise up against their parents, and cause them to be put to death.
6. Counsel 5: Endure to the end	22 And ye shall be hated of all men for my name's sake: but he that endureth to the end shall be saved.
7. Counsel 6: Flee persecution	23 But when they persecute you in this city, flee ye into another: for verily I say unto you, Ye shall not have gone over the cities of Israel, till the Son of man be come.

Section VI
THE MESSIAH'S MESSENGERS AND THEIR MISSION, Matthew 9:35-10:42

Study 4: **THE MESSIAH'S WARNING OF PERSECUTION**

Text: **Matthew 10:16-23**

Aim: To learn how to prepare for persecution.

Memory Verse:

"Behold, I send you forth as sheep in the midst of wolves: be ye therefore wise as serpents, and harmless as doves" (Mt.10:16).

INTRODUCTION

As a believer, are you immune from persecution? Definitely not! Today, all over the world, believers are being persecuted because of their faith in Jesus Christ. Now more than ever before believers must learn how to respond to a world that hates and persecutes them. Why? Because God has a purpose for our persecution as illustrated by the life of Adoniram Judson.

MATTHEW 10:16-23

Adoniram Judson, the renowned missionary to Burma, endured untold hardships trying to reach the lost for Christ. For seven heartbreaking years he suffered hunger and privation. During this time he was thrown into Ava Prison and for 17 months was subjected to almost incredible mistreatment. As a result, for the rest of his life he carried the ugly marks made by the chains and iron shackles which had cruelly bound him. Undaunted, upon his release he asked for permission to enter another province where he might resume preaching the Gospel. The godless ruler indignantly denied his request, saying, "My people are not fools enough to listen to anything a missionary might SAY, but I fear they might be impressed by your SCARS and turn to your religion!"[1]

There is one thing true believers must know as they go forth for Christ. They are as sheep in the midst of wolves. They can expect to be persecuted, severely persecuted. They must "beware of men" (v.17).

What Christ did in this passage was warn His disciples about persecution, and as He warned them, He counseled them on how to deal with persecution.

OUTLINE:

1. Two facts must be kept in mind (v.16).
   a. Believers are commissioned: sent forth.
   b. Believers are as sheep among wolves.
2. Counsel 1: be wise and harmless (v.16).
3. Counsel 2: beware of men (v.17-18).
4. Counsel 3: do not worry about a defense (v.19-20).
5. Counsel 4: know that families will be divided (v.21).
6. Counsel 5: endure to the end (v.22).
7. Counsel 6: flee persecution (v.23).

1. TWO FACTS MUST BE KEPT IN MIND (v.16).

Two facts must be kept in mind as the believer faces persecution.

1. The believer is commissioned and sent forth by Christ. Note the words, "I send you forth." It is Christ, the Son of God, who sends us forth. There is great comfort in this fact, for Christ knows what is to face the believer. He is fully aware of the persecution that lies ahead, yet He still sends His messenger forth. Why? Because the Son of God is able to use our persecution for several ends.

   a. He is able to teach us about God's care as He protects and delivers us.
   b. He is able to teach us to trust more and more, maturing us as believers.
   c. He is able to take our suffering and touch the hearts of the persecutors, leading them to surrender their lives to Christ.
   d. He is able to use our strong example as a testimony to other believers, encouraging them to stand firm in the face of persecution.
   e. He is able to deliver us through death itself into the very presence of God.

Christ knows the importance of the message being carried forth, that is, the gospel of the kingdom. It is essential for man's salvation. Therefore, despite the rejection and persecution by many, the message must still be proclaimed so that some might be saved.

2. The believer is sent forth as a sheep in the midst of wolves. Being commissioned by Christ assures persecution. Christ sends His believer forth in the midst of a world that *will* oppose the gospel; He knows that the believer is to be persecuted. Therefore, the believer…

   • must know about and expect persecution. He must not be caught off guard when it comes.

---

1 *INFOsearch Sermon Illustrations* (Arlington, TX: The Computer Assistant, 1-888-868-9029, 1986-1996).

- must know that his persecution is but "light affliction" in comparison with the glory that lies ahead. In fact, "our light affliction, which is but for a moment, worketh for us a far more exceeding and eternal weight of glory" (2 Cor.4:17).

APPLICATION:
Every believer must know that at some time he will be looked at skeptically and suffer some abuse, ridicule, or rejection.

QUESTIONS:
1. What are the negatives and positives of being sent out in the name of Jesus Christ?
2. Have you ever been in a situation where you were persecuted? If so, how did you respond? How did God see you through the situation? If not, does it mean you are never going to face persecution?

2. COUNSEL 1: BE WISE AND HARMLESS (v.16).

The first counsel is to be wise and harmless—as wise as serpents and as harmless as doves. To be "wise as serpents" means to maneuver quietly with caution and intelligence; to maneuver with a planned strategy; to be quick in seeing danger and quick to escape from it. It means to be a person of vision and initiative, knowing one's resources, knowing when to strike and when to withdraw. It means seizing the moment when the opportunity arises to present the message, withdrawing quickly when danger threatens.

The believer is also to be like a dove: to be as gentle and harmless as a dove; to cause no damage; to be known as a symbol of peace; to be as pure, unmixed, and unadulterated as doves.

APPLICATION 1:
The Lord's people and messengers are exposed to a world of evil men (wolves). Therefore, they are to do two things.

1) Be as wise as serpents. In facing danger the serpent...
   - tries to escape
   - takes shelter out of sight if possible
   - is quiet
   - does not expose itself needlessly
   - seeks preservation first of all
2) Be as harmless as doves. The dove...
   - is mild and meek
   - bears no ill or hurt
   - is innocent and inoffensive
   - is a symbol of peace, not of war

APPLICATION 2:
The Lord's witness is to have a serpent-like mind and a dove-like spirit.

1) He is to be wise in sensing threats and to respond without reaction.
2) He is not to provoke others nor allow himself to be provoked.
3) He is to guard against being wronged and do wrong to no one.

QUESTIONS:
1. The instructions for our behavior are clear: to be as wise as serpents and as harmless as doves. How do you go about doing this? What does it really mean in everyday life?
2. Who can you look to as a model for this type of behavior? What changes can you make in your life to be a good example to others?

3. COUNSEL 2: BEWARE OF MEN (v.17-18).

The second counsel is to beware of men. Two significant points need to be studied by believers.

1. There are the persecutors. The persecutors are three in number: men in general, religionists, and the state. The believer is to beware, to be on guard and to watch—always. If the believer really lives for Christ, he is subject to being persecuted: ridiculed, rejected, disliked, hated, murmured against, abused, physically attacked, jailed, or even martyred. Who will do such things to believers?
   a. Men, people just like himself, will persecute believers. Men can, will, and do turn into brute beasts when they do not like something. Their depraved, wolf-like nature begins to manifest itself. They often attempt to hurt or destroy believers either by reputation or by force. The attack may be over a job, a position, an act, or a belief.
   b. Religionists, people in the synagogues and churches, will persecute believers. The church is full of people who have not really committed their lives to God. They do not know Him in a real and personal way. Therefore, the believer who truly lives and teaches and takes a stand for God and His righteousness is sometimes persecuted by those within the church. Why? Because they do not understand God nor His righteousness. They can become two-faced, evil speaking, gossiping, slandering, reviling, and insulting. The great tragedy is that persecution can and too often does take place within the walls of God's house.
   c. Civil authorities within the state will persecute believers. Believers all over the world always have been and always will be dragged before state authorities and persecuted.

> **"If the world hate you, ye know that it hated me before it hated you. If ye were of the world, the world would love his own: but because ye are not of the world, but I have chosen you out of the world, therefore the world hateth you. Remember the word that I said unto you, The servant is not greater than his lord. If they have persecuted me, they will also persecute you; if they have kept my saying, they will keep yours also" (Jn.15:18-20).**

APPLICATION 1:
Note three lessons about the character of religionists.

1) Religionists can be so deceived that they think they do God a service by persecuting the believer (Jn.16:2). Paul was scourged *five times* by religionists.

> **"Of the Jews five times received I forty *stripes* save one" (2 Cor. 11:24).**

2) Churches seldom like to be disturbed. When the gospel of God is preached or a real ministry for God is attempted, the church is sometimes so encrusted with formalism and the old way of doing things that it fails to see the truth. It persecutes the man of God.
3) Too often church members have persecuted the Lord's messenger and teacher. They have sometimes destroyed the messenger's ministry and reputation in a particular place. But God has always proven faithful. He has continued to use His servant—marvelously so. He will always use His persecuted servant who remains true to Him.

APPLICATION 2:
The believer is to beware of men in high positions, whether in church, state, or business. The higher the position, the more persecution can be expected.

2. There are two reasons for persecution given in this passage.
   a. The believer is persecuted for the Lord's sake or cause. The believer tries to live for Christ and to carry out His cause. The natural man, whether in the world or church, does not understand the things of God, so he opposes them.

      "Blessed are ye, when men shall revile you, and persecute you, and shall say all manner of evil against you falsely, for my sake" (Mt.5:11; see also 2 Cor.4:11).

   b. The believer is persecuted so that he might be a testimony to the persecutors. There is no greater testimony for Christ than a believer standing up for Christ in the face of persecution (cp. Acts 24:1f; 25:1f; 25:13f; 26:1f).
      1) Standing firm demonstrates the truth of the gospel. Its message of love and salvation is clearly seen by the persecutor.
      2) Standing firm gives the Holy Spirit a unique opportunity to reach the hearts of those standing by with the truth of the gospel.
      3) Standing firm is a testimony *against* the persecutors. It shows the depth of the wickedness and evil of their hearts. It shall stand as a testimony against them in the day of judgment.

         "Then shall he answer them, saying, Verily I say unto you, Inasmuch as ye did it not to one of the least of these, ye did it not to me. And these shall go away into everlasting punishment: but the righteous into life eternal" (Mt.25:45-46).

ILLUSTRATION:
While persecution usually brings to mind some physical abuse, it can just as easily be a more subtle kind that is far more damaging.

C. S. Lewis fell into grace. But instead of simply entering a monastery, he did worse. He ended up publicly explaining and openly defending his personal God to millions of listeners and readers. Such undignified behavior embarrassed the hierarchy at his college at Oxford and cost Lewis his chance of ever advancing to a higher position on the faculty there. Lewis learned that if you speak about beauty, truth or goodness, and about God as a great spiritual force of some kind, people will remain friendly. But he found that the temperature drops when you discuss a God who gives definite commands, who does definite acts, who has definite ideas and character.[2]

QUESTIONS:
1. What examples can you think of concerning religious persecution in your society? How can this strengthen (or weaken) your resolve to be a witness for Christ?
2. Some of life's greatest heartaches for the believer have come from other members of the church. How can this happen among people who supposedly know and love the Lord? What is to be the believer's response to persecution within the church?

4. COUNSEL 3: DO NOT WORRY ABOUT A DEFENSE (v.19-20).

The third counsel is not to worry about a defense. A believer is never left alone defending himself against persecution.

1. God gives what is to be said. Note: He gives the answer in the very hour it is to be spoken.

---

2 Kathryn Lindskoog. Cited in *Illustrations Unlimited.* James S. Hewett, Editor, p. 490.

"But when they deliver you up, take no thought how or what ye shall speak: for it shall be given you in that same hour what ye shall speak" (Mt.10:19).

2. God's Spirit actually does the speaking "in" the believer.
3. God stands with the believer.

"For I will give you a mouth and wisdom, which all your adversaries shall not be able to gainsay nor resist" (Lk.21:15).

APPLICATION:
When believers are called upon to defend themselves, they are often nervous and apprehensive. They wonder *how* to speak in their own defense.
1) Some may distrust their own ability. They feel incapable. They have seldom if ever appeared anywhere to defend themselves (cp. Moses, Ex.4:10-12; Jeremiah, Jer.1:6, 10).
2) Some may distrust their own emotions. They are nervous and extremely apprehensive about standing before people. Having to stand before others defending themselves increases their nervousness.

Believers need to trust God for what is to be said. This does not mean we should not be praying and thinking, but it means that God is to be trusted for the defense. There is a reason for this: only God knows the hearts of the persecutors and any others who are present. Therefore, He alone knows what needs to be said to touch their hearts or else to serve as a witness against them in the future.

QUESTIONS:
1. Are you ever concerned about what you will do or say if you are persecuted because of your faith? What assurance do these verses give you?
2. What is your responsibility when you are persecuted? What is God's responsibility?
3. What role does the Holy Spirit play in the lives of believers when they are persecuted?

A CLOSER LOOK #1
(10:20) **Holy Spirit**:
1. The Holy Spirit was given to be our companion (Jn.14:16).
2. The Holy Spirit was given to counsel us (Jn.14:26).
3. The Holy Spirit was given to give us courage for witnessing no matter the circumstances (Jn.15:26-27).
4. The Holy Spirit was given to put conviction in our lives and ministry (Jn.16:7-8).
5. The Holy Spirit was given to share the deep things of God with us (1 Cor. 2:9-10).
6. The Holy Spirit was given to pray and intercede for us and to help us pray (Ro.8:26).
7. The Holy Spirit was given to bear His fruit in us (Gal.5:22-23).
8. The Holy Spirit was given to fill us and to put a song of joy in our hearts despite circumstances (Eph. 5:18-19).
9. The Holy Spirit was given to grant us assurance that we are children and heirs of God (Ro.8:16-17).

5. COUNSEL 4: KNOW THAT FAMILIES WILL BE DIVIDED (v.21).

The fourth counsel is to know that families will be divided. A person's own family can become his greatest persecutor. Why? There are three reasons.

1. Because of the believer's commitment to Christ and His righteousness. The family often lives a worldly life and cannot understand a godly life. The family, therefore, opposes a certain member who ceases to participate in certain functions and traditions (2 Cor.6:17-18; 1 Jn.2:15-16).
2. Because of the family's orthodox religion or church. The converted family member may wish to change religions or churches. The family opposes such a move.
3. Because of the believer's commitment to Christ. The believer should become a dynamic witness, sharing the graciousness and love of the Lord. Such an active witness is sometimes an embarrassment to a family.

> **"Then Peter began to say unto him, Lo, we have left all, and have followed thee" (Mk.10:28).**

APPLICATION:
Nothing hurts more than having our own families oppose and persecute us when we make a decision to follow Christ. It hurts us deeply.

In truth, sometimes the most severe opposition comes from family members. The reason is twofold.

1) They feel their influence should be respected.
2) They feel that the whole family is affected by what its members do.

These two feelings are normal for a family, but the believer knows and has committed his life to the truth of Jesus Christ. Therefore, the believer is convinced of the family's need to be converted, not for him to deny his faith.

A genuine believer is a man of conviction, believing that Jesus Christ is truly the Messiah, the Son of the living God. He adheres to this truth, living and bearing witness to it. Since such conviction and unswerving testimony are seldom understood, they are often opposed. Because of this, a believer sometimes has to choose between obedience to Christ and obedience to his family.

QUESTIONS:
1. One of the hardest things to understand is a believer's own family turning against him. Can you relate an incidence of this? How did the believer react?
2. How can a believer prepare himself for persecution from within his family due to his commitment to Christ?

6. COUNSEL 5: ENDURE TO THE END (v.22).

The fifth counsel is to endure to the end. Again, the believer must expect persecution. All men of the world will oppose him. Why? "For my name's sake." The genuine believer lives and witnesses to the name of Christ, which is the name of righteousness and self-denial. The world and its people oppose any lifestyle that demands total self-denial. But the person who endures to the end shall be saved. Note several things.

1. There is an end to persecution. It is only temporary; it will end.
2. Endurance is possible. A believer can endure. God will sustain him through the persecution.

> **"For consider him that endured such contradiction [hostility] of sinners against himself, lest ye be wearied and faint in your minds" (Heb.12:3).**

3. Salvation and deliverance are waiting for the person who endures: a life of glory and reward.

> **"Blessed is the man that endureth temptation: for when he is tried, he shall receive the crown of life, which the Lord hath promised to them that love him" (Jas.1:12).**

APPLICATION 1:
It hurts to be the object of talk, ridicule, slander, gossip, and abuse. The believer must remember three facts.
1) He is to endure persecution for Christ's sake.
2) He is to endure persecution to assure salvation.
3) He is to endure persecution to assure a glorious reward (Jas.1:12).

ILLUSTRATION:
It is impossible to endure for long without trusting God for His strength and grace. Sometimes we call out to God as a last resort when He should be our first, middle, and last resort.

> *Vance Havner told a story about an elderly lady who was greatly disturbed by her many troubles—both real and imaginary. Finally, someone in her family tactfully told her, "Grandma, we've done all we can for you. You'll just have to trust God for the rest." A look of absolute despair spread over her face as she replied, "Oh dear, has it come to that?" Havner commented, "It always comes to that, so we might as well begin with that! God's Word tells us to bring every concern once and for all to the Lord. Since He offers to handle our problems, why not let Him?"*[3]

The next time you are persecuted, turn to God first, not last!

QUESTIONS:
1. What does it really mean to "endure to the end"? How is a believer to do this?
2. A persecuted believer is not to fear what men can do to him. What is the key to embracing this truth as your very own?

7. COUNSEL 6: FLEE PERSECUTION (v.23).

The sixth counsel is to flee persecution. Note what Christ had already told His disciples.

1. If the disciple's message was rejected, he was to leave the house or the city. He was to get out quickly and quietly.

> **"And when ye come into an house, salute it. And if the house be worthy, let your peace come upon it: but if it be not worthy, let your peace return to you. And whosoever shall not receive you, nor hear your words, when ye depart out of that house or city, shake off the dust of your feet" (Mt.10:12-14).**

2. The disciple was to be as wise as a serpent in sensing and fleeing danger (Mt.10:16).

---

3 *INFOsearch Sermon Illustrations* (Arlington, TX: The Computer Assistant, 1-888-868-9029, 1986-1996).

MATTHEW 10:16-23

Now, for a third time Christ says: "When they persecute you…flee." There are at least three reasons why Christ instructs us to flee.

1. Christ cares for us, for our safety.

> **"Casting all your care upon him; for he careth for you" (1 Pt.5:7).**

2. Christ wants other people to hear the gospel. While some are receptive, obviously others are not. Therefore, Christ says it is better to minister to those who are receptive than to cast one's pearls (the gospel) before swine (the rejecters) or to have the wolves destroy one's life.

3. Christ wants a witness against all rejecters. They need to know just how terrible their sin and shame, coldness and hardness, bitterness and enmity are against God. If a rejecter can see his true heart in this life, perhaps he will surrender to God and His love. If not, then he will see the witness of his persecution stand against him in the terrible day of judgment.

APPLICATION 1:
Courage and conviction for a cause are not automatic occurrences, but neither are they a rarity. Note two significant points about such commitment to causes:

1) In life there are two types of commitment among men.
   ⇒ First, there is a reasonable and rational commitment. Such commitment can, in fact, be so strong that it will endure persecution to death.
   ⇒ Second, there is a fanatical or hysterical commitment. Such commitment can be so unreasonable and irrational that it throws itself into martyrdom.
2) There are several things that make the believer's courage and commitment different and distinctive.
   ⇒ First, believers suffer for a commitment to *the truth* as revealed by God in His Son (Jn.3:16).

> **"For what glory is it, if, when ye be buffeted for your faults, ye shall take it patiently? But if, when ye do well, and suffer for it…this is acceptable with God" (1 Pt.2:20).**

   ⇒ Second, believers attempt to escape persecution and to prevent it. They obey Christ and flee if possible. They do not court danger and recklessness.
   ⇒ Third, believers stand for or endure persecution only when they cannot escape it. At that point, they stand firm for the Lord and His faith, trusting God to bear them through it all.

> **"For unto you it is given in the behalf of Christ, not only to believe on him, but also to suffer for his sake" (Ph.1:29; see also 2 Tim.3:12).**

APPLICATION 2:
The genuine believer will accept martyrdom for his faith, but he does not seek it. He seeks life and freedom so that he can continue to proclaim Christ. His message is a message of life and the sanctity of life. How then can he invite death?

QUESTIONS:

1. Christ tells us to run and escape from coming persecution. And yet we know of many through the centuries and even today who have been martyred. How can you know what Christ wants you to do in a particular situation?
2. Is your courage and commitment to share the gospel strong enough to bear fruit—or do people even know you are a Christian?

MATTHEW 10:16-23

SUMMARY:

The warnings to believers are stark: persecution is coming and preparation must be made. Will *you* be ready? You will if you heed the Lord's counsel:

1. Two facts must be kept in mind.
   a. Believers are commissioned: sent forth.
   b. Believers are as sheep among wolves.
2. Counsel 1: be wise and harmless.
3. Counsel 2: beware of men.
4. Counsel 3: do not worry about a defense.
5. Counsel 4: know that families will be divided.
6. Counsel 5: endure to the end.
7. Counsel 6: flee persecution.

PERSONAL JOURNAL NOTES
(Reflection & Response)

1. The most important thing that I learned from this lesson was:

2. The area that I need to work on the most is:

3. I can apply this lesson to my life by:

4. Closing Statement of Commitment:

MATTHEW 10:24-33

	E. The Messiah's Encouragement Not to Fear Persecution, 10:24-33
1. The fact of persecution a. A warning: You are not above persecution b. A privilege: You are to share the sufferings of Christ c. A surety: You are more likely to suffer persecution than Christ was	24 The disciple is not above his master, nor the servant above his lord. 25 It is enough for the disciple that he be as his master, and the servant as his lord. If they have called the master of the house Beelzebub, how much more shall they call them of his household?
2. Do not fear persecutors a. The truth will be revealed	26 Fear them not therefore: for there is nothing covered, that shall not be revealed; and hid, that shall not be known.
b. The message must be preached 1) The message given by Christ: In secret 2) Message is urgent	27 What I tell you in darkness, that speak ye in light: and what ye hear in the ear, that preach ye upon the housetops.
3. Do not fear men who kill the body a. They are unable to kill the soul b. God alone can destroy the soul & the body	28 And fear not them which kill the body, but are not able to kill the soul: but rather fear him which is able to destroy both soul and body in hell.
4. Do not fear—God cares a. He cares for the common sparrow b. He knows every injury to each sparrow c. He cares for every detail of your life d. He values you more than sparrows	29 Are not two sparrows sold for a farthing? and one of them shall not fall on the ground without your Father. 30 But the very hairs of your head are all numbered. 31 Fear ye not therefore, ye are of more value than many sparrows.
5. The conclusion: Loyalty is essential a. Confess Christ & He will confess you	32 Whosoever therefore shall confess me before men, him will I confess also before my Father which is in heaven.
b. Deny Christ & He will deny you	33 But whosoever shall deny me before men, him will I also deny before my Father which is in heaven.

Section VI
THE MESSIAH'S MESSENGERS AND THEIR MISSION,
Matthew 9:35-10:42

Study 5: **THE MESSIAH'S ENCOURAGEMENT NOT TO FEAR PERSECUTION**

Text: **Matthew 10:24-33**

Aim: To fortify your heart with confidence, confidence in God's ability to care for you during times of persecution.

Memory Verse:

"And fear not them which kill the body, but are not able to kill the soul: but rather fear him which is able to destroy both soul and body in hell" (Mt.10:28).

MATTHEW 10:24-33

INTRODUCTION

Christians are the most widely persecuted among all religious people. These are the cold, hard facts:

- ⇒ According to experts, more believers have been martyred in the twentieth century than in any other century.
- ⇒ Hundreds of thousands of believers worldwide are killed every year because of their faith in Jesus Christ.
- ⇒ In some countries it is a capital crime for a person to be converted to Christ.

The examples could go on and on. Is persecution an oddity or is it to be expected? The Bible and the personal experiences of countless believers reveal the obvious. Believers are often persecuted. They are bypassed, shunned, withdrawn from, isolated, talked about, ridiculed, mocked, considered strange, and joked about. But the persecution can go even further, involving physical abuse and even murder, depending on the society and the laws under which the believer lives. This passage is a great encouragement to the believer facing persecution. Christ said three times, "Fear not" (v.26, 28, 31). He was encouraging His disciples not to fear persecution. On the contrary, they must *expect* persecution, for He Himself was persecuted.

OUTLINE:

1. The fact of persecution (v.24-25).
2. Do not fear persecutors (v.26-27).
3. Do not fear men who kill the body (v.28).
4. Do not fear, for God cares—supremely so (v.29-31).
5. The conclusion: loyalty is essential (v.32-33).

1. THE FACT OF PERSECUTION (v.24-25).

1. There is the warning: the disciple is not above persecution. No disciple is above his master; no servant is above his lord. Therefore, the believer must expect persecution, for he shall be persecuted even as his Lord was persecuted.

APPLICATION:
If our Master and Lord has suffered persecution, so shall we. Why? Because we are His. We belong to Him. All that He is and all that He stands for is what we are and what we stand for. Whatever caused men to persecute Him, *the same is in us*. They will persecute us for the same thing and for the same reason they persecuted Him.

2. There is the privilege of persecution. The believer shares in the sufferings of Christ. Note the words, "It is enough." God has done enough for the believer. He has exalted the believer to an unbelievable height. The believer is now *just like his Master and his Lord*. God has accepted the believer as an *equal* to His own dear Son (Ro.8:16-17; Gal.4:4-7; Eph.1:5-6).

What does this mean? It means that persecution is a privilege. When we are persecuted, we are walking in the highest and most noble company possible—the company of God's dear Son.

APPLICATION 1:
Imagine! We are *called* by God's very own Son, the Master and Lord of the universe. To have God's very own Son as our Master and Lord is the highest privilege imaginable. Thus, it is a high privilege to suffer for Him. No higher call could come to a man. Christ calls us to live righteously in a world that does not want righteousness. The fact that the world reacts against us does not do away with our high calling. It only enhances our call and sets it even higher. The *evil*

behavior of the world shows just how precious and how greatly to be desired our high calling is.

> **"For unto you it is given in the behalf of Christ, not only to believe on Him, but also to suffer for His sake" (Ph.1:29; see also Acts 5:41; 9:16; Ro.8:17; Heb.11:25).**

APPLICATION 2:
Living righteously in a world that does not want righteousness assures persecution.

> **"Yea, and all that will live godly in Christ Jesus shall suffer persecution" (2 Tim.3:12).**

3. There is the surety: believers are more likely to suffer persecution than Christ was. Some believers must expect harsh persecution just as Christ suffered (1 Pt. 4:11-12). Note the words, "them of His household." We are of His household. If the Master and Lord was abused, His disciples and servants will be abused. If the world dragged the Master out to kill Him, they will drag the servant out to be killed. Whatever the world did to the Master of the house, they will do to us. Christ was persecuted terribly. They called Him Beelzebub, the god of flies and filth, the name given to describe the chief of devils. Consider three things.
   a. The terrible wickedness of some men: to be so encrusted in wickedness that they curse the Son of God.
   b. The unbelievable patience and forbearance of Christ: that He would allow Himself to be cursed and abused.
   c. The strong lesson for us: no matter how severe the persecution, Christ has gone before us. He is our forerunner; He has already suffered the depth of indignity and ridicule.

> **"For consider Him that endured such contradiction [hostility] of sinners against Himself, lest ye be wearied and faint in your minds" (Heb.12:3; see also Heb.2:17-18; 4:15-16).**

QUESTIONS:
1. No Christian is above persecution. How would you explain this fact to an unbeliever in a positive light?
2. In what way have you found persecution to be a privilege? Or heard about it? Again, how would you explain this fact to an unbeliever in a positive light?

2. DO NOT FEAR PERSECUTORS (v.26-27).

The first word of encouragement is this: do not fear persecutors. There are two major points in this statement of encouragement.

1. The truth shall be revealed; *the truth* will someday be known. God will reveal *the truth* in the day of judgment, if not before.
   a. The cloak that persecutors put upon their evil will be stripped off. It will no longer be able to be disguised. Their true character will be revealed by God and shown to all who stand in that day.
   b. The cloak that the world puts upon the believer's witness will be stripped away in that day. God will reveal the truth of the believer's witness. His testimony will be vindicated, and the persecution will be seen to have been but "a light affliction" in comparison to "the weight of glory" that will be ours (2 Cor.4:17).

c. The cloak that the world puts upon the gospel will be stripped away in that day. God will reveal that the gospel is true, and true in its entirety. The gospel will be vindicated. It will be seen and known to have been true.

The believer is not to fear what his persecutors say. He can rest assured: the day is coming when the truth will be known. The accusations, the talk, the cloaks, the disguises, the secrets of all men shall be stripped and unveiled for all to see (Ro.2:2, 6, 11, 16).

APPLICATION:

Note three lessons.

1) Believers will be vindicated. All the talk and abuse inflicted upon believers will be handled by Christ. The shunning, sneering, isolation, coldness, ugliness, abuse, and mistreatment by neighbors, fellow employees, church members, and carnal believers—all will be dealt with by God. Christ is emphatic; He speaks to the point: "Fear not persecutors: the truth is to be revealed" and dealt with.
2) We are not to fear the damage of our *character and reputation* by men. What is really in our hearts and lives—despite our shortcomings, failures, and sins—is known to God. He is going to deliver and vindicate us. He is going to restore our reputation and character and see to it that we "have [the] praise of God" (1 Cor.4:5). Therefore, we are not to fear persecutors.
3) Many believers are made *spectacles* by unbelievers both within the church and the world. But the day is coming when the truth is to be known.
   a) The true believer shall be exalted with a "far greater weight of glory" (2 Cor.4:17).
   b) The true believer shall "have [the] praise of God" Himself (1 Cor.4:5).
   c) The true believer shall "shine forth as the sun in the kingdom of [his] Father" (Mt.13:43).

2. The message must be preached. This verse is full of meaning for the messenger of Christ. Note the words, "What I tell you in darkness...What ye hear in the ear." Christ is saying three things.

a. Christ gives the message that He wants proclaimed. Christ says that it is "what I tell you" that the messenger is to hear and proclaim.
b. Christ gives His message in the quietness of being alone with His messenger. It is "in the darkness...in the ear" that Christ gives His message to the messenger. That is, Christ gives His message when the messenger gets all alone and draws close to the Lord in prayer and study of the Word.
c. The messenger is to proclaim the message "upon the housetops." Two things are meant by this.
   ⇒ The message is urgent. It is to be proclaimed loud and clear for all to hear.
   ⇒ The message is to be buzzed about, always shared and proclaimed. In the day of Christ, people sat upon their roofs (flat roofs) in the quiet of the evening and buzzed about with conversation. This is the picture Christ is painting for His disciples.

"And he said unto them, Go ye into all the world, and preach the gospel to every creature" (Mk.16:15).

ILLUSTRATION:

We are not to fear those who persecute us. God has called believers to stay focused on what He has given us to do (complete the task of the Great Commission)...and to leave the rest (our defense) to Him.

The builders of the Panama Canal faced enormous obstacles of geography, climate, and disease. Most of the construction was supervised by Colonel

George Washington Goethals. He had to endure severe criticism from many back home who predicted that he would never complete the "impossible task." But the great engineer was resolute and pressed steadily forward in his work without responding to those who opposed him. "Aren't you going to answer your critics?" a subordinate inquired. "In time," Goethals replied. "How?" the man asked. The colonel smiled and said, "With the canal!" And his answer came on August 15, 1914, when the canal opened to traffic for the first time.

If we tried to respond to all who criticize us as we follow the Lord, nothing worthwhile would be accomplished, but if we are confident we are doing God's will, we can close our ears to ridicule and press on with the work. Completing the task is often the best way to silence the critics.[1]

QUESTIONS:

1. Do you ever get angry or tempted to take action against someone who is doing evil? Where does your responsibility stop and God's start?
2. No matter the danger, we must be willing to preach the gospel "from upon the housetops." What does this mean in our society? Why is it so important to keep on preaching the gospel when faced with persecution?

3. DO NOT FEAR MEN WHO KILL THE BODY (v.28).

The second word of encouragement is this: do not fear men who kill the body. We are not to fear men (persecutors), but to fear God. The reason is simple and understandable: men can kill only the body; God can destroy both body and soul "in hell" (see A CLOSER LOOK # 1—Mt.10:28).

There are several reasons why men are not to be feared.

1. Men can kill only the body, not the soul. Their power is limited and they can go no further. They cannot touch a person's soul, a person's real being.

2. Men can only send us out of this world, not out of heaven. "To be with Christ...is far better" (Ph.1:23; 3:20-21).

3. Men can only separate us from this world, not from life. We have eternal life; death is not part of the experience of the believer. The believer does not *taste* death. Christ *tasted*, that is, experienced, death for the believer (Heb.2:9). The believer has already passed from death to life and is in the process of living forever (Jn.5:24). He is merely transferred from this world, the physical dimension of being, into the next world, the heavenly or spiritual dimension of being.

4. Men can only cut us off from worldly men and the earthly redeemed, not from the love of God and the saints in glory.

> **"Who shall separate us from the love of Christ? shall tribulation, or distress, or persecution, or famine, or nakedness, or peril, or sword?" (Ro.8:35; see also v.36-39; Pr.29:25; Is.51:12).**

APPLICATION 1:

Fearing men causes several things.

1) It causes a person to become disturbed within his heart and mind, sensing the loss of peace.
2) It causes a person to lose his fervor and his sense of commitment.
3) It causes a person to be sidetracked, to give up what he knows to be God's will, sensing the loss of mission, meaning, and purpose.

---

1 *INFOsearch Sermon Illustrations* (Arlington, TX: The Computer Assistant, 1-888-868-9029, 1986-1996).

APPLICATION 2:
There is a remedy to keep us from fearing men: fearing God. (see A CLOSER LOOK # 1—Mt.10:28).

1) God can destroy us, both body and soul, putting both "in hell." The word "destroy" does not mean that our body and soul would cease to exist, but that they would live a worthless existence—be ruined and suffer in ruin forever.
2) Christ was speaking to believers in this passage. God is to be feared much more than men are to be feared. The terror of men pales into insignificance in comparison to God's terror. Imagine this one fact alone: man's terror is but for a short time, but God's terror is *forever*. It never ends. The point is clear: before caving in to man's persecution, we need to remember the "fear of God."
3) The destruction of the soul comes from God, not from man. The power to destroy the soul is God's power alone. How fearful we need to be of God, even we who are believers!

"And if the righteous scarcely be saved, where shall the ungodly and the sinner appear?" (1 Pt.4:18).

QUESTIONS:
1. You are not to fear men who persecute you. What struggles do you face with those who do persecute you?
2. What practical things can you do to keep from fearing men?

A CLOSER LOOK #1
(10:28) **Destroy**: to lose one's *well-being* (not to lose one's being), to waste, to ruin, to have a worthless existence. "To destroy both body and soul in hell" does not mean that a person would cease to exist, but that he would live a worthless existence, suffering waste and ruin forever and ever.

4. DO NOT FEAR—GOD CARES—SUPREMELY SO (v.29-31).

The third word of encouragement is this: do not fear, for God cares. Christ is clear: if God cares for the common sparrow, how much more He cares for man! He cares for every event and every detail in a man's life. Therefore, there is no need to fear.

"Casting all your care upon him; for he careth for you" (1 Pt.5:7).

APPLICATION 1:
There is something very precious here, yet there is a revelation of power as well.

1) There is a preciousness in the thought that every sparrow—no matter how common or seemingly insignificant or unnoticed by man—is very dear to God.
2) There is power and care in that God knows every single sparrow on the earth. Not a single sparrow falls that He is unaware of. The idea is that the injury to the sparrow causes pain and hurt which He feels.

APPLICATION 2:
Christ is pointing out five powerful yet precious facts.

1) God's providence: God sees, knows, cares about and oversees all the events and happenings on earth—just as He knows all about the little sparrow that is so common and unnoticed by man.

2) God's knowledge (omniscience): God knows every little happening and all that is, even to the most precise detail. He knows when a single sparrow falls to the ground. He knows every hair of a person's head, even the number of hairs.
3) God's power (omnipotence): God is able to control the persecution and events that happen to the believer, no matter how detailed or minute. He can control and work them out for good to such an extent that there is no need for the believer to fear.
4) God's love and care: God cares about every hurt inflicted upon the believer by persecutors, even to the smallest injury and hurt. The believer is not to fear, but to put His trust in the love and care of God (1 Pt.5:7).
5) God's purpose: God is able to take all the injuries and pain inflicted by the sin and shame of men and work it all out for the good of the believer. He is able to give purpose, meaning, and significance to it all (Ro.8:28f). Therefore the believer is not to fear.

QUESTIONS:
1. God cares for you like no one else can. Knowing this, why is it still hard to trust God when things get hard?
2. What does it mean to you personally to know that God never takes His eye off of His people?
3. How can you balance the love and care of God in your life with the proper fear of God discussed in the last point?

A CLOSER LOOK #2
(10:29) **Fear**: this word means dread, terror. In relation to God, it means to be afraid; to show reverence, to sense a reverential fear; to stand in awe because of a holy fear. It means we fear God because He is God: holy, righteous, pure, just. It means that we fear and stand in awe and reverence of God who will reveal His holiness and execute His justice in some future day of judgment.

5. THE CONCLUSION: LOYALTY IS ESSENTIAL (v.32-33).

Note a crucial point: Christ is talking about confessing Him in the most difficult moment imaginable—while being persecuted. We are sometimes called upon to confess Christ by those who reproach, sneer, mock, curse, question, slander, abuse, and avoid us because of our witness for Christ.

> **"That if thou shalt confess with thy mouth the Lord Jesus, and shall believe in thine heart that God hath raised him from the dead, thou shalt be saved" (Ro.10:9).**

APPLICATION 1:
Note three double things here.
1) There is a double confession: our confession of Christ before men, and the Lord's confession of us before His Father.
2) There is a double day of glory: the Lord's day of glory when He hears us confess His name before men, and our day of glory when we hear Him confess our name before His Father.
3) There is a double privilege: our privilege in confessing the Lord before men, and the Lord's privilege in confessing us before His Father.

APPLICATION 2:
Christ can be denied in three ways:
1) We can deny Christ by word. Our words either confess or deny Christ. Our

ordinary conversation either witnesses for Christ and righteousness or for evil and unrighteousness. Our words either confess or deny that Christ is our Lord.

2) We can deny Christ by act. Our behavior either confesses or denies Christ. We are not to be conformed to the world, but transformed by the renewing of our mind (Ro.12:1-2; cp. 2 Cor.6:17-18; 1 Jn.2:15-16).
3) We can deny Christ by silence. Failing to speak up for Christ to protest evil denies Christ. Silence is probably the greatest denial of Christ committed by believers.

APPLICATION 3:
Denying Christ is the most dangerous thing we can do. Why?

1) Because there is a day coming when we will need Christ to confess us before God.
2) Because Christ has already foretold what He will do if we deny Him: He will deny us. He will tell the truth—He never knew us (Mt.7:23; 25:41).

ILLUSTRATION:
When persecution comes into the life of a believer, it becomes the true test of devotion to the Lord. Anyone can trust Him when things are easy. But when the hard times comes, can you be fully trusted?

Chuck Swindoll tells the story of a house church in the former Soviet Union several years ago. They had to meet in secret to avoid reprisals from the communist government.

One Sunday these believers arrived inconspicuously in small groups throughout the day so as not to arouse the suspicion of KGB informers. By dusk they were all safely inside, windows closed, and doors locked. They began by singing a hymn quietly but with deep emotion. Suddenly, the door was pushed open and in walked two soldiers with loaded automatic weapons at the ready. One shouted, "All right—everybody line up against the wall. If you wish to renounce your commitment to Jesus Christ, leave now!"

Two or three quickly left, then another. After a few more seconds, two more. "This is your last chance. Either turn against your faith in Christ," he ordered, "or stay and suffer the consequences."

Another left. Finally, two more in embarrassed silence with their faces covered slipped out into the night. No one else moved. Parents with small children trembling beside them looked down reassuringly. They fully expected to be gunned down or, at best, be imprisoned.

After a few moments of complete silence, the other soldier closed the door, looked back at those who stood against the wall and said, "Keep your hands up—but this time in praise to our Lord Jesus Christ, brothers and sisters. We, too, are Christians. We were sent to another house church several weeks ago to arrest a group of believers..."

The other soldier interrupted, "But, instead, we were converted! We have learned by experience, however, that unless people are willing to die for their faith, they cannot be fully trusted."

Our commitment to Christ affects all our other relationships. The more devoted we are to Jesus, the more faithful we will be to our church, family, and friends.[2]

---

2 Charles Swindoll. *Living Above the Level of Mediocrity.* As cited in *INFOsearch Sermon Illustrations* (Arlington, TX: The Computer Assistant, 1-888-868-9029, 1986-

MATTHEW 10:24-33

QUESTIONS:

1. If you were persecuted tomorrow and threatened with imprisonment for your faith, how strong and loyal would you be?
2. In what ways can a person deny Christ? What would it take for *you* to deny Him?

SUMMARY:

Many people would like to stick their head in the ground like an ostrich and ignore the reality of the church being persecuted. Ignoring the fact of persecution will not make persecution go away or prevent it from coming to you. When it does come, and it will, our Lord Jesus Christ has encouraged us not to fear, but to heed His challenge.

1. There is the fact of persecution.
2. Do not fear persecutors.
3. Do not fear men who kill the body.
4. Do not fear, for God cares—supremely so.
5. The conclusion: loyalty is essential.

PERSONAL JOURNAL NOTES
(Reflection & Response)

1. The most important thing that I learned from this lesson was:

2. The area that I need to work on the most is:

3. I can apply this lesson to my life by:

4. Closing Statement of Commitment:

F. The Cost of Being the Lord's Disciple, 10:34-42

1. Jesus' purpose
   a. Not to send peace
   b. To send a sword

2. Illustration 1: A person's family
   a. The fact: Christ sets the believer against his family
   b. The demand: Must love Christ supremely
   c. The reward: Counted worthy vs. unworthy

3. Illustration 2: A person's cross
   a. Must follow

34 Think not that I
am come to send
peace on earth: I
came not to send
peace, but a sword.
35 For I am come to
set a man at variance
against his father,
and the daughter
against her mother,
and the daughter in
law against her moth-
er in law.
36 And a man's foes
shall be they of his
own household.
37 He that loveth fa-
ther or mother more
than me is not worthy
of me: and he that
loveth son or daugh-
ter more than me is
not worthy of me.
38 And he that
taketh not his cross,
and followeth after
me, is not worthy of
me.
39 He that findeth
his life shall lose it:
and he that loseth his
life for my sake shall
find it.
40 He that receiveth
you receiveth me,
and he that receiveth
me receiveth him that
sent me.
41 He that receiveth
a prophet in the name
of a prophet shall re-
ceive a prophet's re-
ward; and he that re-
ceiveth a righteous
man in the name of a
righteous man shall
receive a righteous
man's reward.
42 And whosoever
shall give to drink
unto one of these lit-
tle ones a cup of cold
water only in the
name of a disciple,
verily I say unto you,
he shall in no wise
lose his reward

   b. Reward: Counted worthy vs. unworthy

4. Illustration 3: A person's life
   a. Must give up life
   b. Reward: Lose life vs. find life

5. Illustration 4: A person's work & ministry to others
   a. Must welcome a believer & minister to him
   b. Reward: A reciprocal or equal reward
      1) The presence of Christ & of God, (v.40)
      2) The reciprocal or equal reward
      3) The strong assertion: The smallest ministry will not lose its reward

Section VI
THE MESSIAH'S MESSENGERS AND THEIR MISSION, Matthew 9:35-10:42

Study 7: THE COST OF BEING THE LORD'S DISCIPLE

Text: Matthew 10:34-42

Aim: To be aroused to pay the cost of true discipleship.

Memory Verse:

"And he that taketh not his cross, and followeth after me, is not worthy of me. He that findeth his life shall lose it: and he that loseth his life for my sake shall find it" (Mt.10:38-39).

INTRODUCTION

Everything has its price. Nothing in life is ever truly "free." Somewhere along the way, what was offered to you as "free" cost someone something. Whether the offer was "Buy One, Get One Free" or getting something free for 'just an hour of your time' or some other offer, it cost someone…

- labor
- time
- money
- mental energy

MATTHEW 10:34-42

There is also a cost in relation to spiritual things. Our Lord Jesus paid the ultimate cost when He gave His life as payment for our sins. In light of such a great cost, what does it cost us to be His faithful disciples? In this passage Jesus is exact and uncompromising. He lays some heavy demands upon His disciples. He states clearly what it will cost a person to be His disciple, and He describes the cost by using four illustrations.

OUTLINE:

1. Jesus' purpose (v.34).
2. Illustration 1: a person's family (v.35-37).
3. Illustration 2: a person's cross (v.38).
4. Illustration 3: a person's life (v.39).
5. Illustration 4: a person's work and ministry to others (v.40-42).

1. JESUS' PURPOSE (v.34).

Jesus says He did not come to send peace on earth, but a sword. What did He mean? (Cp.Jn.16:33.)

1. He did not come to give His approval or sanction to the physical corruption and decay of the earth. The earth and all that is therein ages, deteriorates, and dies. It all wastes away. Jesus did not come to give God's peace or blessing upon a world that dies. What He came to do was to bring a sword to earth. He came to war against aging and decay and death. He came to slash out, cut away, and put to death the physical dimension of being that condemns everything to decay and death.

2. He did not come to give His approval to the sin and evil of the earth. He could never give God's peace or blessing to a world that is so full of cursing and rebellion against God and so full of selfishness and division between men. He came to bring a sword to earth: to war against sin and evil and to destroy all the evil that is both within and without man.

Jesus' presence automatically causes division. This is because the believer's godly and divine nature is so completely opposite from his fallen human nature inherited from Adam. As certain persons heed the call of Jesus and become one with Him and the way of righteousness, there is suddenly a division both within and without.

a. *Within,* there is division between his old fallen nature and his new divine nature (cp. 2 Cor.5:17; Eph.4:22f; Col.3:8-10; Gal.5:13-17, esp. 16-17).
b. *Without,* there is a division between him and those who choose to reject Jesus and follow the way of darkness

The division often occurs among family members and friends when one person accepts Jesus and the other person does not. The saved person becomes a totally new creature, born of God with new ideals and a righteous behavior; but the unsaved family member or friend remains in darkness, continuing to desire the things which please his flesh.

APPLICATION 1:
The world is full of hurt, pain, and suffering—not peace. The truth cannot be denied. However, we can be of good cheer, for Christ has overcome the world.

> **"These things I have spoken unto you, that in me ye might have peace. In the world ye shall have tribulation: but be of good cheer; I have overcome the world" (Jn.16:33).**

APPLICATION 2:
Christ came to give the sword of His Word to the world. His Word, sharper than any two-edged sword, pierces the soul and spirit of a person, discerning the

thoughts and intents of his heart. It convicts the person to become a follower of God and His righteousness (cp. Heb.4:12).

QUESTIONS:
1. Are you using God's Word as a sword to convince others to follow Christ?
2. God does not give His blessings or approval to the evil of the world. Do you find yourself consciously or unconsciously doing so at times, or perhaps just turning your head the other way? How can you be more conscious of taking a stand against evil and wrongdoing?

2. ILLUSTRATION 1: A PERSON'S FAMILY (v.35-37).

The believer is to note three things about his family.

1. First, Jesus sets the believer against his family. It is important to see that it is Jesus who causes the division. Jesus calls a person out of the world and separates him from the world so that he can go about correcting the evil of the world. If a family member continues to live in sin and to walk ever onward toward the grave without turning to God, two things usually happen.

a. The believer struggles to see his loved one saved, no matter what opposition he may face.
b. The family member rebels against the righteousness and efforts of the believer.

> **"Suppose ye that I am come to give peace on earth? I tell you, Nay; but rather division: for from henceforth there shall be five in one house divided, three against two, and two against three" (Lk.12:51-52).**

APPLICATION 1:
The believer is called to a life of righteousness and to a warfare against sin and evil. If a member of his family is engaged on the side of sin and evil, there is *a natural conflict* between the believer and the family member.

1) The family member is still of the earth, seeking the pleasures and possessions of the world, and still living primarily to satisfy his earthly desires. He represses and subdues the thought of God so that he can pursue his own natural appetites.
2) The believer is of the earth, but he is also of heaven. He is physical and spiritual, and he is living primarily for God and His righteousness, living to reach men with the glorious gospel of Christ.

   The two natures differ drastically. They are diametrically opposed to one another. The person of the world talks primarily about the world and lives for the world. The person of the spirit makes God the primary force of his life: talking about and living for God and His righteousness.

APPLICATION 2:
Jesus is honest with man. He means business. He *came*, and He intends for His purpose to achieve its end even if it causes division within a family. Those who will be saved and who stand for righteousness will be saved by Christ even at the expense of family unity.

2. Second, Jesus demands supreme love. Note the words "more than me." Believers are to love their families, but they are to love God more; He is to be first and foremost. Their first loyalty is to be to God. Two terrible things happen when a family is put before God.

a. Families cannot be what they should be without God. No family can reach its full potential without God. Without God a family will lack spiritual growth and strength, conviction and commitment, confidence and assurance, purpose and meaning for all eternity. There will be no prospect and no hope of eternal life, no assurance of anything beyond this life.

b. Families cannot be looked after and overseen by God unless God is given His rightful place in the family. If the family takes control over its own life, ignoring God and His control, then what happens to the family is in its own hands. God is put off to the side, excluded, and shut out. He is given no voice in the life of the family. All kinds of trouble can and usually does follow. There is a lack of spiritual strength to face the trials and crises that confront the family during its life together. If the family puts God first, however, the family is assured of being everything it should be and of being looked after and cared for by God (Mt.6:33).

"But seek ye first the kingdom of God, and his righteousness; and all these things shall be added unto you" (Mt.6:33).

The point is this: we must love God supremely, putting Him before all others, even before our families. Therefore a man's decision to follow Christ, no matter the sacrifice to his family, is a wise decision; in fact, it is the only reasonable decision (Ro.12:1-2).

APPLICATION:
Sometimes a man loves his family so much that he turns from Christ, choosing his family over Christ. There is usually one of two reasons for this decision.

1) The opposition to his following Christ is too strong. The division within the family is too deep.
2) The sacrifice demanded is too great. It may be that God is calling the man to some ministry, to some field of service, to some act of giving; but he decides the financial and emotional strain would be too much. He decides that God is demanding too much of a sacrifice for his family.

When we allow our families to keep us from serving God and from doing what we should, we are making our families the supreme love of our lives. We are worshipping them, looking after them and their welfare first instead of worshipping and putting God first. When we put our families first, we are allowing our families to become our idols.

3. Third, Jesus warns the believer that he shall be counted either worthy or unworthy of Him.

a. There is a great reward for loving Christ supremely. If we count Christ worthy of our first love, He will count us worthy of Him. We are assured: we shall receive *the great salvation* in Him (cp. Mt.10:32).
b. There is a terrible loss for not loving Christ supremely. If we love our family more than Christ, He will count us unworthy of Him. We are assured that we shall not receive the great salvation in Him (cp.10:Mt.33).

"Whosoever therefore shall be ashamed of me and of my words in this adulterous and sinful generation; of him also shall the Son of man be ashamed, when he cometh in the glory of his Father with the holy angels" (Mk.8:38).

APPLICATION:
A person's family is to be the strongest and most precious relationship among human beings. A person is to love his family as much as he loves any others on earth. However, there is one relationship that is to supersede a person's relationship with his family: that is his relationship to Jesus Christ. He is to love Christ supremely, counting Him more worthy than all, even more worthy than his own

family. There are at least three reasons why Christ is to be counted preeminent.

1) Christ is the Supreme Being of the universe. He is the Creator, Sustainer, and Protector of life throughout the course of our walk upon earth. Our time and our care are in His hands. Our families can sustain and protect us only to a certain point and only for a short time. They do not control life, but Christ can. He is the Supreme Being of the universe; therefore, He is the only One who is worthy of our supreme love.
2) Christ is the Supreme Savior. He is the Giver and Provider of life, both abundant and eternal life. Our families can bring some happiness and pleasure to our lives, and they can protect us to some degree in this life—but not ultimately. Accidents and disease are beyond their power. They can save us in only a few situations and only for a brief time. Christ is the Supreme Savior; therefore, He alone is worthy of our supreme love.
3) With Christ we have the supreme relationship. Christ is totally unselfish and He loves us perfectly. Of course we are not completely unselfish nor do we love perfectly, but to have the privilege of being loved perfectly and treated completely unselfishly (all the time) is the ultimate relationship—the very most a person could ever ask or hope for (Jn.3:16; Mt.7:25-34).

QUESTIONS:

1. How do you feel when you are around a lost family member or close friend? Do you have feelings of…
   - not fitting in?
   - being perceived as a fanatic?
   - being scorned?
   - being made fun of?
   - being misunderstood?

   Do you hold your tongue to avoid causing disturbance or do you risk disturbance by taking a stand?
2. No matter how much we love our families, our love for them must not be greater than our love for Christ. What are some ways we put family first? How could those things be handled differently?
3. What are the great benefits that come to the believer who loves Christ supremely?

3. ILLUSTRATION 2: A PERSON'S CROSS (v.38).

1. Christ again made a strong demand. Note the words "He that taketh not his cross." Every man has "his cross." The cross is the symbol of death and of execution. Every man must die to self day by day. He must count himself dead to sin and follow after Christ.

"Then said Jesus unto his disciples, If any man will come after me, let him deny himself, and take up his cross, and follow me" (Mt.16:24).

2. The reward again is being counted either worthy or unworthy of Christ. If we do not put ourselves to death, that is, die to self, we are not worthy of Christ. He will deny us.

APPLICATION:
What Christ says is strong. A man must die to self, sacrificing his own will, ambition, and desires. Whatever it is that a person wants—comfort, ease, wealth, fame, power, family—all must be placed behind Christ and His will.

ILLUSTRATION:
When Christ calls us to take up our cross, it is not an invitation to negotiate for a better time and place.

> *"Lord, I'll go anywhere and do anything for You-just give me some time to get my affairs in order." This seemed a reasonable enough request to the young man. After all, he was just out of school and had lots of time left to serve Christ. Then he went to work. Taking a position as a salesman at his father's business, he fit right in-right into the rat race. And Christ was pushed aside again. It wasn't long before the growing business took more and more of his time and efforts. "Now Lord, I haven't forgotten about serving You-just give me a little more time to get things settled." Then, he met the girl of his dreams. "Uh, Lord, I'll still go anywhere and do anything for You-just let me get my family started and some bills paid and then we'll get things in order." And so on and so on and so on. And the Lord waited...and waited...and waited....*

We all have places to go and people to see and things to do. And we all have crosses to bear. But these things can hinder us from taking up the most important cross of all: the cross of Christ. Have you saved enough strength to carry all your crosses?

QUESTIONS:
1. We often think of only the *big* or *obvious* sins as needing to be nailed to the cross. But what are some not-so-obvious sins that believers need to nail to the cross?
2. How does a person die to self? What does it really mean for you to carry your cross?

4. ILLUSTRATION 3: A PERSON'S LIFE (v.39).

1. Jesus demands a person's life. Note the unique way He words this.
    a. "He that findeth his life shall lose it." The phrase "finding one's life" means that a person seeks his own pleasure and passions in life. It is a selfish life, finding out what pleases self and going after it.
    b. "He that loseth his life...shall find it." The phrase "loseth one's life" means that a person seeks to lose his life on this earth in order to find God. It means that a person gives up the right to order his own life, and he lets Christ control his life. It means that a person's pursuit must be all-consuming, that a person diligently seeks after God. When a person is consumed with finding God, the things of the world just fade away. But the person who refuses to relinquish this right to the Lord misses out on the life God purposed for him. He fails to experience the fulfillment of completing his mission on earth; whereas the person who gives the Lord the right to order his life experiences that deep sense of fulfillment, satisfaction, and pleasure with his life—even in the face of difficulties and hardships. In addition, Christ says that he will find life, both abundant and eternal.

2. The reward is *losing* life vs. *finding* life, life that is abundant and eternal. Life, the very thing which a person seeks, is found only in Christ. If a person never finds Christ or if he rejects Christ, he loses that life. If he denies himself and follows Christ, he finds life (see A CLOSER LOOK # 1—Mt.10:39).

APPLICATION 1:
A person must not search for his life on this earth. If he finds life on this earth, he will lose his life. Why? Because all that is on this earth is corruptible: aging,

decaying, deteriorating, dying. Nothing on this earth lasts. This fact clearly says something: true and eternal life cannot be found on this earth; only death can be found.

APPLICATION 2:
What men call life is not real life.
⇒ The flesh, with all its goose pimples and chills and butterflies, is not life.
⇒ Wealth, with all the things it can purchase, is not life.
⇒ Recognition and fame, with all the ego it can boost, is not life.
⇒ Power, with all the rights and pomp it can give, is not life.
⇒ Pride, with all the self image it can build, is not life.

All this and all else on the earth fades and passes away. It just does not last. How can life, real life, be something that ends so quickly and leaves one so empty?

ILLUSTRATION:
The so-called "blessings" of this world are temporary; they do not last for long. No matter how good it looks at first glance, what this world offers is not real.

Jeff Ferrera of Waukegan, Illinois, was reconciling his checkbook and called First National Bank of Chicago to get his current balance.

"Your primary checking account currently has a balance of $924,844,204.32," droned the electronic voice. Ferrera was one of 826 customers who were almost billionaires for a day because of the biggest error in the history of U.S. banking. The goof amounted to almost $764 billion, more than six times the total assets of First Chicago NBD Corporation.

"I had a lot of people saying in jest to transfer it to the Cayman Islands and run for it," Ferrera said. But, like most of the others, he simply reported the error to bank officials, who could say only that it was a "computer programming error."—story cited in the Chicago Tribune (5/18/96).

"It pays to remember that all earthly wealth is just as temporal."[2]

A CLOSER LOOK #1
(10:39) **Life—Eternal Life**: real life is found only by giving up one's life to Jesus. The person who refuses to relinquish this right to the Lord Jesus misses out on the life God intended for him. He fails to experience the fulfillment of completing his mission on earth, whereas the person who gives the Lord the right to order his life experiences real life. He experiences that deep sense of fulfillment, satisfaction, and pleasure with his life—even in the face of difficulties and hardships. In addition, he is given that special quality of life called eternal life.

QUESTIONS:
1. Think about it for a moment. How much of your day, your life, is focused upon self, upon earthly matters, upon achieving, getting, and doing what pleases yourself? How can you keep yourself from being caught up in the selfish pursuits of the world?
2. What does it mean to you personally to find your life as you lose it?

2 *Fresh Illustrations for Preaching and Teaching,* Edward K. Rowell, p.222, 1997.

5. ILLUSTRATION 4: A PERSON'S WORK AND MINISTRY TO OTHERS (v.40-42).

1. Christ demands that we welcome and minister to all His servants. Imagine this! The person who ministers to God's messenger is said to minister to the following…
- to Christ Himself (v.40)
- to God the Father (v.40)
- to a prophet (v.41)
- to a righteous man (v.41)
- to a little one (v.42)

> **"And into whatsoever city or town ye shall enter, inquire who in it is worthy; and there abide till ye go thence. And when ye come into an house, salute it. And if the house be worthy, let your peace come upon it: but if it be not worthy, let your peace return to you" (Mt.10:11-13).**

2. The reward is astounding. The person who welcomes and receives God's servant shall receive a reciprocal or an equal reward.
   a. The person who welcomes and ministers shall receive the presence of Christ and of God Himself. He reflects honor upon the Lord and even upon God Himself. In fact, Jesus says that welcoming and ministering to others is the same as entertaining Him and His Father (Mt.10:40).
   b. The person who welcomes and ministers shall receive a reciprocal or an equal reward with God's servant. Perhaps a person cannot be a prophet or a shining example of a righteous man, but he can receive the reward of both. How? By simply welcoming and supporting and caring for God's servant. This is an astounding truth: the person actually shares in the work of God's messenger when he receives and helps him. Christ puts an enormous value on how his messenger is received and treated. If the messenger is welcomed, Christ will give an equal reward for the kindness and care shown to his messenger. (What a lesson for churches as to how they receive and treat their ministers!)
   c. Christ declares that the smallest ministry will not lose its reward. A person will be rewarded for the smallest ministry done for God's messenger. Just giving a cup of water to a messenger is extremely significant to God. It causes God to say emphatically that a person will be rewarded for such an act. The person needs to know that he is ministering to someone who is very, very dear to God. Christ calls His messengers "little ones," which is a term of endearment.

> **"His lord said unto him, Well done, good and faithful servant; thou hast been faithful over a few things, I will make thee ruler over many things: enter thou into the joy of thy lord" (Mt.25:23).**

APPLICATION:
There is great confidence and assurance here for the messenger of God. It is implied that some *will* receive and welcome the messenger of the Lord. There will be some who will open their hearts and homes to him, and they will receive his message.

QUESTIONS:
1. No act of service is just "a little thing" to God. What can you do to reach out and minister to one of God's servants? How does your treatment of this person affect God?
2. What rewards have you reaped because of your treatment of God's servants?

MATTHEW 10:34-42

SUMMARY:

Our Lord Jesus paid the ultimate price when He gave His life as payment for our sins. In light of so great a sacrifice, what does it cost us to be His faithful disciples? The payment is not cheap. It will cost you everything you have in this life. Is the sacrifice worth it? Only you can decide.

1. Jesus' purpose: He did not come to send peace on earth, but a sword.
2. Illustration 1: a person's family. Remember what Christ said about a believer's family.
   ⇒ Jesus sets the believer against his family.
   ⇒ Jesus demands supreme love.
   ⇒ Jesus warns the believer that he will be counted worthy or unworthy of Him.
3. Illustration 2: a person's cross—each one's personal cross—must be taken up to follow Christ.
4. Illustration 3: a person's life. Jesus demands a person's life, rewarding the person who follows Him with abundant and eternal life.
5. Illustration 4: a person's work and ministry to others. This is not an option, but a clear commandment.

PERSONAL JOURNAL NOTES
(Reflection & Response)

1. The most important thing that I learned from this lesson was:

2. The area that I need to work on the most is:

3. I can apply this lesson to my life by:

4. Closing Statement of Commitment:

	CHAPTER 11 **VII. THE MESSIAH'S VINDICATION OF HIS MESSIAHSHIP, 11:1-30** **A. The Assurance: Given to A Questioning Disciple, John the Baptist, 11:1-6** (Lk.7:18-23)	Christ, he sent two of his disciples, 3 And said unto him, Art thou he that should come, or do we look for another?	a. Jesus' works were works of love b. John questioned: Expected a Messiah of judgment, not love
1. Jesus ended the commissioning of His disciples a. He sent them out b. He began to minister again—alone **2. John's perplexity: Pictured a stern Messiah**	And it came to pass, when Jesus had made an end of commanding his twelve disciples, he departed thence to teach and to preach in their cities. 2 Now when John had heard in the prison the works of	4 Jesus answered and said unto them, Go and show John again those things which ye do hear and see: 5 The blind receive their sight, and the lame walk, the lepers are cleansed, and the deaf hear, the dead are raised up, and the poor have the gospel preached to them. 6 And blessed is he, whosoever shall not be offended in me.	**3. Jesus' assurance: He was beyond question the Messiah** a. He spoke as the Messiah b. He demonstrated the power & works of the Messiah c. He fulfilled prophecies of the Messiah d. He preached the gospel of the Messiah e. He promised both the blessing & judgment of the Messiah

Section VII
THE MESSIAH'S VINDICATION OF HIS MESSIAHSHIP, Matthew 11:1-30

Study 1: THE ASSURANCE: GIVEN TO A QUESTIONING DISCIPLE, JOHN THE BAPTIST

Text: Matthew 11:1-6

Aim: To learn how to gain assurance during times of great doubt.

Memory Verse:

"And blessed is *he,* whosoever shall not be offended in me" (Matthew 11:6).

INTRODUCTION

Problems, difficulties, accidents, disease, all kinds of trials happen that make us question:

⇒ Why do bad things happen to good people?
⇒ Why does life seem to be so unfair?
⇒ Why does God allow suffering?
⇒ Why is evil so rampant in the world today?
⇒ Where is God when I need Him the most?

Most of these questions have crossed every believer's mind. And if we are honest, probably more than one of these questions has given rise to brief moments of doubt here and there. When the silence of God becomes louder than our pleas for an explanation, doubt settles in until we can think through the issue and what God is trying to say to us. Contrary to the opinions of some, God is not threatened or intimidated by our thinking. In fact, He welcomes it. As Oswald Chambers once said,

> *Doubt is not always a sign that a man is wrong; it may be a sign that he is thinking.*[1]

John heard about the works of Christ. He had predicted the coming of the Messiah just as the prophets of old had predicted. In his mind, the Messiah was coming to baptize people with the Spirit of God and with fire. Christ had appeared upon the scene and was baptizing people with the Spirit of God, and the people were flocking around Him as though He was the Messiah. But He was doing nothing about baptizing people with fire, the Messianic fire of judgment. To John's mind, Christ was fulfilling only half of the prophecies concerning the Messiah. John was confused. Was Jesus really the Messiah? He had to know. His whole life had been given over to the belief that Jesus was the Messiah. He sent two disciples to ask, and Jesus used the opportunity to vindicate His Messiahship.

OUTLINE:
1. Jesus ended the commissioning of His disciples (v.1).
2. John's perplexity: he pictured a stern Messiah (v.2-3).
3. Jesus' assurance: He was beyond question the Messiah (v.4-6).

1. JESUS ENDED THE COMMISSIONING OF HIS DISCIPLES (v.1).

The idea is that Jesus sent the disciples out alone without Him. They were to learn to minister, and the way they were to learn was through practical experience, while they were actually out ministering. Note that Jesus began to minister again all alone, and the present event happened to Him during this time.

QUESTIONS:
1. What has been your most valuable learning experience as a believer?
2. Why is it so important to gain practical experience as a servant of Christ? Where is the best place for you to gain this experience?

2. JOHN'S PERPLEXITY WAS CAUSED BY HIS PICTURE OF A STERN MESSIAH (v.2-3).

John was in prison and he heard about the works of Christ. Note two points.

1. What John had heard was that the works of Christ were works of love. He knew that the Messiah was to baptize with both the Spirit and fire—the Messianic fire of judgment. He had heard that Jesus was doing the loving works of the Spirit and that people were mobilizing around Him in huge throngs, but he had heard nothing about the fire of Messianic judgment. It seemed that Jesus was fulfilling only half of the Messianic prophecies. He was perplexed and questioning, so he sent two emissaries to Jesus for an answer. Note: despite John's puzzlement and questioning, he still believed in the truth.

⇒ He believed in the promises of Scripture concerning the Messiah: "Art thou He?" (cp. Ps.118:26).

---

[1] Oswald Chambers (1874-1917) in *Draper's Book of Quotations for the Christian World.* Edythe Draper. (Wheaton, IL: Tyndale House Publishers, Inc., 1992). Entry 2933.

⇒ He was committed to seek after God's Messiah: "Do we look for another?"
⇒ He was willing to have his faith confirmed in Jesus as the true Messiah. The fact that he asked the questions shows this.

2. John was questioning Jesus' Messiahship. John was the one who sent two of his disciples to question Jesus (v.2), and it was *to John* that Jesus sent His answer (v.4). John wondered if Jesus was the true Messiah. There were several reasons for his questioning Jesus.

a. John was perplexed. His idea of the Messiah did not match what Jesus was doing. Jesus was not mobilizing people into a great army to free Israel from Roman domination. He was not the stern Messiah pictured by the prophets.
b. John was in prison. He expected to be involved in the overthrow of the Roman conquerors and in the establishment of Israel as a free nation, yet he was languishing in prison. He could not understand why the Messiah did not free him. Had he not been the prominent forerunner for the expected Messiah?
c. John needed assurance. He needed his faith strengthened. The saints of the Scriptures were mere men with passions like we experience. They, too, occasionally needed the Lord to confirm their faith. Even the strongest sometimes need the word and presence of the Lord in a special way. Picture John's concept of the Messiah and his languishing in prison, and his need is clearly understood.

"There hath no temptation taken you but such as is common to man: but God is faithful, who will not suffer you to be tempted above that ye are able; but will with the temptation also make a way to escape, that ye may be able to bear it" (1 Cor.10:13).

APPLICATION:

Note several significant lessons.

1) John did not fully understand Jesus, and to be honest, we all lack understanding; yet what is needed is for us to do what John did:
   ⇒ He trusted Christ anyway.
   ⇒ He committed his life to proclaiming that Jesus was the Messiah and continued to proclaim the message even though he did not fully understand.
   ⇒ He sought answers to what he did not understand.
   ⇒ He did not let his questions destroy his faith.

2) John believed the Scripture and looked for the Messiah's first coming. We are to believe the Scriptures: He has come and He is coming again (Jn.14:2-3;1 Th.4:13f; Tit.2:12-13).
3) We should not fear nor be ashamed because we may not understand or have questions about Jesus. In fact, it is good to make absolutely sure in all matters concerning our salvation. We should seek and ask unashamedly (Jas.1:5).
4) Note a critical fact: John was not weary in looking for the Messiah. He said he would keep on looking if Jesus was not the Messiah. We must not become weary and doubting because Jesus has not yet returned (cp. 2 Pt.3:3-4, 8-18).
5) John's questioning began when he was in prison facing great trouble and trial. It is sometimes difficult to understand why we have to go through so much trouble. We need to approach Christ in those times, coming to Him through His Word and through prayer (1 Pt.4:11-12; Jas.1:5; Is.1:18).
6) John had questions arise in his mind. Even the strongest have moments of weakness, no matter who they are (Mt.26:36-46, 69-75; Gal.2:11f). Severe trials are often a great strain upon our faith. In such times, we need a very special presence of the Lord; we need His strength and assurance.

"Beloved, think it not strange concerning the fiery trial which is to try you, as though some strange thing happened unto you: but

rejoice, inasmuch as ye are partakers of Christ's sufferings; that, when his glory shall be revealed, ye may be glad also with exceeding joy" (1 Pt.4:12-13).

ILLUSTRATION:

Sometimes it is impossible to explain what God is doing. Faith in God helps us trust when we cannot see God's hand at work.

A twelve-year-old boy became a Christian during a revival. The next week at school his friends questioned him about the experience. "Did you see a vision?" asked one friend. "Did you hear God speak?" asked another. The youngster answered no to all these questions. "Well, how did you know you were saved?" they asked. The boy searched for an answer and finally he said: "It's like when you catch a fish, you can't see the fish or hear the fish; you just feel him tugging on your line. I just felt God tugging on my heart."[2]

QUESTIONS:

1. Are you ever confused or doubtful about something God has said or done or allowed to happen? How do you work through those times of personal doubt?
2. When do you most often need God's assurance to keep trusting in Him?

3. JESUS' ASSURANCE: HE WAS BEYOND QUESTION THE MESSIAH (v.4-6).

Jesus gave five assurances to John.

1. Jesus spoke as the Messiah, as one having authority. His words and the power of His message were evidences that Jesus was the Messiah. There were no greater words and no greater lessons than those of Christ. He is recognized as one of the greatest, if not the greatest, teachers of all times. This is one of the proofs that He is beyond question the Messiah.

"Heaven and earth shall pass away: but my words shall not pass away" (Mk.13:31).

2. Jesus demonstrated the power and works of the Messiah. Jesus was saying that His works and concern (love) were the works and concern predicted for the Messiah, and both are unlimited.

   a. He gave sight to the blind. The blind saw physically and spiritually. They not only knew the truth of the world, but of God as well.
   b. He made the lame to walk. He caused men to walk physically and spiritually. They moved strongly about, serving both God and man.
   c. He cleansed the lepers. He made them pure physically and spiritually. They were accepted both by men and God.
   d. He opened the ears of the deaf. He caused the deaf to hear physically and spiritually. They could hear both the voices of men and of God.
   e. He raised the dead to life. They were given life again physically and spiritually. Whereas they had been dead, they now walked as new creatures before men and God.
   f. He preached the gospel to the poor. They who had been so neglected and possessed so little were now receiving the good news of salvation from God Himself.

---

2 *Illustrations Unlimited.* James S. Hewett, Editor, p.188.

"But I have greater witness than that of John: for the works which the Father hath given me to finish, the same works that I do, bear witness of me, that the Father hath sent me" (Jn.5:36).

APPLICATION 1:
Note that Christ did not just profess to be the Messiah, He proved it (Jn.14:10-11). He proved it by ministering to people *in the power of God.* He showed that God had sent Him to demonstrate two things:
1) That God is (exists) and that He is sovereign. He is above and beyond all, and He has the power to override the laws of nature.
2) That God loves man and has provided a way for man to be saved and to live forever.

Every time Jesus ministered to and healed a person, He demonstrated both things: the sovereign power and the great love of God.

APPLICATION 2:
Note a critical point: Christ's miracles are the seal of God. He is God's Son, the Messiah, just who He claims to be. His works are beyond question the works of God (Jn.5:36; 10:25f, 32, 37-38; 14:11).

3. Jesus fulfilled the prophecies of the Messiah.

APPLICATION:
The works of Christ agree with the works predicted for the Messiah. No man has to wait any longer for the Savior and Deliverer. He has come in the Person of Jesus Christ.

QUESTIONS:
1. Jesus assured John that He was the Messiah by speaking to him as the Messiah. When you pray for direction or guidance or understanding, how can you sense that same assurance that John received?
2. What is the greatest miracle you have ever witnessed or heard about? How does this prove that Jesus Christ is the Messiah?
3. Jesus fulfilled *every* prophecy that concerned the Messiah. What does this tell you about the trustworthiness of the Scriptures?

4. Jesus preached the gospel of the Messiah. There is a much needed lesson here. Jesus went to the poor. He neither avoided nor neglected anyone, no matter his social status.
   a. This is a sign of the enormous compassion and mercy of God: that His Son would go to those so often overlooked, neglected, and despised as lazy and shiftless. (Throughout the world, some men undoubtedly are lazy and shiftless, but most men certainly are not.)
   b. The poor have needs, many needs. The person who senses that need turns to Christ much sooner than the person who senses no need. Being self-sufficient and independent can be good in achieving goals, but, when facing God, they are damning and lead to eternal doom. Only those who confess their need for God's care can expect to have God caring for them and saving them.
   c. This is a fulfillment of prophecy: that the Messiah would minister especially to the poor (Ps.72:2, 4, 12-13; Zech.11:11).

"And Jesus went about all Galilee, teaching in their synagogues, and preaching the gospel of the kingdom, and healing all manner of sickness and all manner of disease among the people" (Mt.4:23).

APPLICATION:
Christ preached the gospel to everyone who would listen, no matter what his social status or position.

5. Jesus promised both the blessing and the judgment of the Messiah (see A CLOSER LOOK # 2—Mt.11:6). Note the two facets of what Jesus promised—the two areas of work predicted about the Messiah.

a. There was the area of blessing, of the Spirit, of salvation, of God's care and love for people. This is the area Christ covered in this passage. Today is the day of blessing and of salvation (Mt.11:4-5).

"For he saith, I have heard thee in a time accepted, and in the day of salvation have I succoured thee: behold, now is the accepted time; behold, now is the day of salvation" (2 Cor.6:2).

b. There was the area of fire, of wrath, of judgment. The Messiah is to fulfill His judgment of fire when He returns (see notes—11:1-6; 11:2-3; A CLOSER LOOK # 2—11:6).

"But Israel, which followed after the law of righteousness, hath not attained to the law of righteousness. Wherefore? Because they sought it not by faith, but as it were by the works of the law. For they stumbled at that stumblingstone" (Ro.9:31-32).

APPLICATION:
Note three lessons.

1) Jesus encouraged John not to be offended by Him. He encourages all of us not to be offended by Him, but to believe and trust that He is "of a truth, the Son of God," the Messiah.
2) Many are offended by Christ:
   ⇒ by the idea of and belief in miracles
   ⇒ by His death, the shedding of His blood
   ⇒ by His incarnation and virgin birth
   ⇒ by His demand for self-denial and strict behavior

   Because many are unable to understand the demands of Christ, they question just as John did. However, they fail to follow through like John did; they fail to make a total commitment despite questions.
3) Christ says one of two judgments awaits us. (1) The judgment of blessing, or (2) the judgment of being offended. He is the true Messiah who is to execute both. Right now is the day of blessing and of the Spirit. When He returns, that will be the day of fire and judgment.

ILLUSTRATION:
Every person has an eternal destiny: either with Christ in heaven forever or separated from His presence in a never-ending hell. It is up to us to plan ahead for that inevitable day.

In the days of the pioneers, when men saw that a prairie fire was coming, what would they do? Since not even the fastest of horses could outrun it, the pioneers took a match and burned the grass in a designated area around them. Then they would take their stand in the burned area and be safe from the threatening prairie fire. As the roar of the flames approached, they would not be afraid. Even as the ocean of fire surged around them there was no fear, because fire had already passed over the place where they stood.

When the judgment of God comes to sweep men and women into hell for eternity, there is one spot that is safe. Nearly two thousand years ago the wrath of God was poured on Calvary. There the Son of God took the wrath that should have fallen on us. Now, if we take our stand by the cross, we are safe for time and eternity.[3]

QUESTIONS:

1. Jesus preached the gospel to everyone, the rich and poor alike. But why did Christ have such a burden for the poor? What should His example show the church as a whole? Show us as individuals?
2. The Messiah blesses people, but He also executes judgment. What kind of person will experience His blessing? His judgment?

A CLOSER LOOK #1

(11:5) **Prophecy, Fulfilled**: Jesus was referring to Scripture here. He was telling John that He was fulfilling the predictions of the prophets (Is.35:5-6; 61:1-2; cp. Ps.72:2; 146:8; Zech.11:11). Note, however, that Jesus stressed the personal ministry and *not the political*. He omitted the phrases of Is. 61:1 that could be interpreted that He was a political leader: "proclaiming liberty to the captives, and the opening of the prisons." He needed to get John's attention away from the wrong concept of the Messiah to the true concept. He was reaching out in the power of the Spirit to individuals, saving and restoring them, not reaching out to mobilize people for the deliverance of Israel from Roman enslavement.

A CLOSER LOOK #2

(11:6) **Messiah, Judgment**: Jesus was saying that the Messianic blessing and judgment were coming. Today is the day of salvation, the day of Messianic blessing. Tomorrow will be the day of Messianic fire, the day of judgment against all those who are offended in Christ. The Messianic fire of judgment was John's concern. He did not see Christ judging the world. But Christ assured John: "Blessing is coming; and judgment is coming. Do not be offended because you do not understand everything about me." (See note—11:2-3; A CLOSER LOOK # 1—11:5.)

SUMMARY:

We live in very unsure times and often are tempted to doubt God's control over world events. This uncertainty comes closer to home when we are directly affected by things we cannot yet understand. When doubt comes, we need to reflect upon the important lessons from these points:

1. Jesus ended the commissioning of His disciples and sent them out to minister to the world.
2. John's perplexity: he pictured a stern Messiah, but sought answers to what he did not understand.
3. Jesus' assurance: He demonstrated that He was beyond question the Messiah.

---

3 *Illustrations for Biblical Preaching.* Michael P. Green, Editor. (Grand Rapids, MI: Baker Book House, 1996), p.207.

MATTHEW 11:1-6

PERSONAL JOURNAL NOTES
(Reflection & Response)

1. The most important thing that I learned from this lesson was:

2. The area that I need to work on the most is:

3. I can apply this lesson to my life by:

4. Closing Statement of Commitment:

	B. The Reminder: Given to a Forgetful & Fickle People, 11:7-15 (Lk.7:24-28)	messenger before thy face, which shall prepare thy way before thee.	**true King**
1. People wondered about John's questioning **2. John was not a wavering reed, but a man firm in his conviction**	7 And as they departed, Jesus began to say unto the multitudes concerning John, What went ye out into the wilderness to see? A reed shaken with the wind?	11 Verily I say unto you, Among them that are born of women there hath not risen a greater than John the Baptist: notwithstanding he that is least in the kingdom of heaven is greater than he.	**6. John was the greatest of natural men, yet not as great as the least in the Kingdom of Heaven**
3. John was not a man of soft raiment, but a man of discipline & self-denial	8 But what went ye out for to see? A man clothed in soft raiment? behold, they that wear soft clothing are in kings' houses.	12 And from the days of John the Baptist until now the kingdom of heaven suffereth violence, and the violent take it by force.	**7. John launched a violent overthrow of the kingdom**
4. John was a prophet & more	9 But what went ye out for to see? A prophet? yea, I say unto you, and more than a prophet.	13 For all the prophets and the law prophesied until John. 14 And if ye will receive it, this is Elias, which was for to come.	**8. John was the last of an age, the age predicting the Messiah** **9. John was the promised Elijah, the one to precede the Messiah**
5. John was the Messiah's forerunner, the herald of the	10 For this is he, of whom it is written, Behold, I send my	15 He that hath ears to hear, let him hear.	**10.The conclusion: A person must hear**

Section VII
THE MESSIAH'S VINDICATION OF HIS MESSIAHSHIP, Matthew 11:1-30

Study 2: THE REMINDER: GIVEN TO A FORGETFUL AND FICKLE PEOPLE

Text: **Matthew 11:7-15**

Aim: To guard against being spiritually forgetful and fickle.

Memory Verse:

"He that hath ears to hear, let him hear" (Matthew 11:15).

INTRODUCTION

Why are people so forgetful and fickle? We live in a world that says to its leaders or heroes, "What have you done for me lately?"

⇒ The successful sports coach who experiences a losing streak is suddenly ousted from his position.

⇒ The politician who has truly made a difference for good is suddenly voted out because of his stance on a controversial matter.

⇒ The minister whose healthy church takes a drop in attendance is suddenly blamed for all the problems within the fellowship.

MATTHEW 11:7-15

The modern method of taking the public's pulse on an issue is done through polls. There are polls for everything imaginable. But like the weather, the results of survey polls change often—according to how the wind blows.

John had just questioned if Jesus was the true Messiah (cp. Mt.11:1-6). The questions had been asked in the presence of the people present. Some thought John was wavering in his faith, that he was weak and inconsistent.

Jesus immediately reprimanded the crowd. He vindicated John and his mission, reminding the forgetful and fickle people that John was the forerunner and that He (Jesus) was the true Messiah.

OUTLINE:

1. People wondered about John's questioning (v.7).
2. John was not a wavering reed, but a man firm in his convictions (v.7).
3. John was not a man of soft raiment, but a man disciplined and self-denying (v.8).
4. John was a prophet and more (v.9).
5. John was the Messiah's forerunner, the herald of the true King (v.10).
6. John was the greatest of natural men, yet not as great as the least in the Kingdom of Heaven (v.11).
7. John launched a violent overthrow of the kingdom (v.12).
8. John was the last of an age, the age predicting the Messiah (v.13).
9. John was the promised Elijah, the one to precede the Messiah (v.14).
10. The conclusion: a person must hear (v.15).

1. PEOPLE WONDERED ABOUT JOHN'S QUESTIONING (v.7).

If the people were allowed to think that John was weak and inconsistent, they would soon question if John was the real prophet who was to pave the way for the Messiah. Then following upon the heels of this question would be the questioning of Jesus: Was He the true Messiah? If this kind of talk and questioning had begun, it would have affected not only the crowd, but also those who already believed. It would have been devastating to the Lord's mission. Note how fickle people really are and how easily they forget a prophet's calling when they hear news of his weak moments.

ILLUSTRATION:

People can turn so quickly. All the good that a person is and has done is often easily forgotten. John's experience illustrates the fickleness of people, as does the following illustration.

A man writing at the post office desk was approached by an older fellow who had a post card in his hand. The old man said, "Sir, could you please address this post card for me?" The man gladly did so, and he agreed to write a short message on the post card, and he even signed it for the man, too.

Finally the man doing the writing said to the older man, "Now, is there anything else I can do for you?"

The old fellow thought about it for a minute, and he said, "Yes, at the end could you just put, 'P.S. Please excuse the sloppy handwriting.'"[1]

QUESTIONS:

1. It has been said that a public figure's most recent act is the one that is most remembered. Do you find this to be true of others? Of yourself?
2. How should this knowledge impact your response to gossip or doubt or questioning of others?

---

1 John Yates. *An Attitude of Gratitude. Preaching Today*. (Carol Streal, IL: Christianity Today, Inc.), Tape No. 110.

2. JOHN WAS NOT A WAVERING REED, BUT A MAN FIRM IN HIS CONVICTION (v.7).

Questioning does not necessarily mean that a person is wavering in his beliefs or behavior. John was not a vacillator, a reed swaying with the winds of change. He did not sway nor weaken because of the displeasure and terror of Herod. He was not a man who preached with force when he had the applause of men and weakened when he had the disapproval of men. He was God's servant and he knew it. He served God faithfully in His calling despite having to deal with some questions.
Despite his questioning John was still...

- believing in the Messiah
- strong in spirit
- consistent in his behavior

As stated, John was unwavering in dealing with the problems and temptations that arose in his life: the recognition and praise of the crowds, the rage and imprisonment by Herod, the thought that Jesus was perhaps a mistaken Messiah. Despite all, John was unwavering. He stuck with two things.

⇒ He held firm to his faith in God and in God's Messiah.
⇒ He held firm to his call:

> **"I am not the Christ, but...I am sent before Him" (Jn.3:28, cp. Jn.1:20).**

APPLICATION:
John did not sway with every breeze of change or trial or opposition or crowd. He stood firm in his own calling. Applause or frowns, approval or disapproval, appreciation or disagreement—so much affects us and our work. We must learn and learn quickly that no matter what, we are to go on for Christ and keep on going.

> **"That we henceforth be no more children, tossed to and fro, and carried about with every wind of doctrine, by the sleight of men, and cunning craftiness, whereby they lie in wait to deceive" (Eph.4:14).**

QUESTIONS:
1. What is the difference between a person who is full of doubt and unbelief and the person who asks a lot of hard questions? What kind of person are you—the doubter or the inquirer?
2. When you are trying to understand the difficult circumstances of life, where do you put your trust?

3. JOHN WAS NOT A MAN OF SOFT RAIMENT, BUT A MAN OF DISCIPLINE AND SELF-DENIAL (v.8).

John was dead to the world with its fame and power and ease. He was not worldly nor soft but disciplined and self-denying. He was not a man who was out to save what he had nor to save himself. He was not crumbling under the weight of opposition as a soft and materialistic-minded person would be. He was not a compromiser. John was a man sent by God to proclaim the truth, and he proclaimed it no matter the cost. Christ was saying, "When you look at John you do not see a man of the world with the soft raiments of the world on his mind, but you see an ambassador for God." What a lesson on self-denial and faithfulness in the face of opposition!

APPLICATION:
A life of discipline and self-denial better prepares us to stand against all trials. If we live for God, denying ourselves, then...
- trials will work patience (endurance),
- endurance will work experience,
- experience will work hope, and
- hope will not shame us (Ro.5:3-5).

> **"And he said to them all, If any man will come after me, let him deny himself, and take up his cross daily, and follow me" (Lk.9:23).**

QUESTIONS:
1. There was nothing in this world that impressed John more than Christ. How do you think John came to this point in his life? How can you reach this same point—not allowing anything to distract you from following Christ?
2. What is the greatest challenge you face in attempting to live a life of discipline and self-denial?

4. JOHN WAS A PROPHET AND MORE (v.9).

A prophet is a *foreteller*, a proclaimer of God's message. The message may deal with the past, the present, or the future. Note several things about the prophet:
- ⇒ He is chosen by God.
- ⇒ He is chosen to proclaim the message of God.
- ⇒ He is a man who must be trustworthy—faithful to his mission and courageous in proclaiming God's Word (1 Tim.1:12).

John was such a man. He was a prophet, but note: Jesus said that John was more than a prophet. What does this mean? Very simply, his message included more than the message of the other prophets. His message was the heralding, the actual proclamation, that the Messiah had come. In this, John excelled above all the other prophets. They only *foresaw* the Messiah's coming, but John *saw* Him come. Therefore, it was his responsibility to proclaim Christ's coming.

Note that John's preeminence over the other prophets had to do with duty and responsibility, not with privilege. Some are called by God to excel and to take the lead in responsibility. What a lesson on the *need for humility and fear*—fear lest we come short!

> **"The voice of him that crieth in the wilderness, Prepare ye the way of the LORD, make straight in the desert a highway for our God" (Is.40:3).**

QUESTIONS:
1. What are the main distinctives of a prophetic minister of God? If someone does not exhibit these marks, what conclusions should you make about the person who claims to be a minister of God?
2. Every believer has a duty and responsibility to proclaim God's message. How and where can you do your part?

5. JOHN WAS THE MESSIAH'S FORERUNNER, THE HERALD OF THE TRUE KING (v.10).

Note this: when God chose a person to run ahead and herald the coming of the Messiah, He did not choose a king or any other person of power or fame. He chose *a simple man* and called him *to preach* the coming of the Messiah. This conveyed a powerful message: God's kingdom is not based on earthly pomp or earthly power. It is based on God's Spirit and God's power. It was not brought about by man's hands, but by the hand of God. Thus, God's kingdom is a lasting, eternal kingdom, not a temporary kingdom that eventually will pass away.

APPLICATION:
Christ applied this prophecy to Himself; that is, He *claimed to be the Messiah* before whom John the Baptist ran and prepared the way. Note two things.
1) He and John were the fulfillment of prophecy. He was the Messiah and John was the forerunner who prepared the way by proclaiming His coming.
2) All believers, preachers and laymen alike, are to be preparing the way of the Lord. How? By proclaiming (1) that He has come and (2) that He is coming again. Remember: Christ came the first time, so He will come again.

QUESTIONS:
1. Why do you think God chose John for his position as a prophet? Could God trust you with an equal amount of responsibility?
2. How are you to prepare the way of the Lord? What do you need to do to be more faithful in preparing the way for Him?

6. JOHN WAS THE GREATEST OF NATURAL MEN, YET NOT AS GREAT AS THE LEAST IN THE KINGDOM (v.11).

John did not have the advantages that believers have today. In knowledge, he did not have the full revelation of salvation which God has given believers in the Lord Jesus Christ. In experience, he did not have the Holy Spirit's indwelling in the sense that New Testament believers do.

1. Believers have the opportunity for more knowledge about God than John had. In the kingdom that God is building, those who believe in Jesus have access to the full revelation of God. The believer sees the cross. He knows that the Messiah has come, died, risen, and ascended into heaven. The believer knows the full scope of salvation. He sees the cross, the symbol of the great love of God. He can know the love of God in a way that John and others before John never could have known. Just imagine! The humblest believer can know more about God than the greatest of the Old Testament saints! He can know more than Abraham, Moses, Elijah, or Isaiah! It should be noted, however, that this is not favoritism. On the contrary, it is a heavier responsibility for which followers of Christ will be held more accountable.

2. Believers have the opportunity of more experience with God than John had. The basic difference between believers before Christ and believers after Christ is the Holy Spirit. Believers after Christ have the opportunity to experience God more fully through the indwelling presence of the Holy Spirit. They also understand God's revelation more clearly by knowing the Lord Jesus Christ personally and following Him.

Positionally, both the Old Testament and New Testament believers stand justified before God. Abraham, a believer before Christ, believed God and was counted righteous or justified (Ro.4:3). The Philippian jailer, a believer after Christ, believed God and was saved or justified (Acts. 16:31). Positionally, those in the Kingdom of Heaven today stand no more justified before God than John the Baptist. But having the opportunity to know and experience the full revelation of God, the believer of today is unsurpassed in privilege. However, for this privilege, the world today stands much more responsible and accountable.

APPLICATION 1:
In God's estimation John was the greatest man ever born of a woman. John was neither a prince nor a king. He was not a man of wealth, fame, or power. Who

was he? He was simply a man who believed in the Messiah and who totally committed his life to that belief. Note: God does not value a man by his birth or earthly attainments, but by his relation and commitment to the Messiah.

APPLICATION 2:
John's eminence was probably due to two things.

1) His dedication and commitment to God were most unusual. He was self-denying in his commitment to the Messiah, and although there had been many disciplined people who had served God, John's heart was probably closer to true self-denial than any others. Only God (Christ) would know this. At any rate, Christ declares John's eminence over all men; and in John, we have a blazing example of self-denial and commitment to God.
2) His preaching was repentance and the coming of the Messiah. Many had preached the same message; however, there was probably a difference. John's heart was perhaps more intense and intimate with the presence of God. Only God knows, but Christ did say John was the greatest man ever born. In John there is certainly an example of intense commitment to God's calling.

> **"For he shall be great in the sight of the Lord, and shall drink neither wine nor strong drink; and he shall be filled with the Holy Ghost, even from his mother's womb" (Lk.1:15).**

QUESTIONS:

1. Knowing God is a journey that every believer is expected to experience. How would you evaluate your journey to this point:
   _____It's at a standstill.
   _____It's inch by inch, cautious steps measured by faith.
   _____It's one step forward...two steps back.
   _____It's growing by leaps and bounds.
2. What role does the Holy Spirit play in your knowledge of God?
3. What advantages do you have over believers who lived and died before the death of Christ? Do you bear testimony to those undeniable facts?

7. JOHN LAUNCHED A VIOLENT OVERTHROW OF THE KINGDOM (v.12).

This means at least three things.

1. He stirred people to storm and rush into the kingdom just as an army storms or rushes into a city. In covering the beginning of John's ministry, Luke says:

> **"The kingdom of God is preached, and every man presseth into it" (Lk.16:16).**

2. A person must storm the kingdom to enter it. He must have the spirit of a soldier who storms a city (2 Tim.2:3-4). He cannot be half-hearted, lacking spirit or energy. He cannot be complacent, indulgent, or at ease. He cannot expect simply to slip into heaven. There has to be a real interest and desire, a vigorous stirring and struggle, a diligent seeking after God to enter heaven:

> **"He that cometh to God must believe that He is, and...diligently seek Him" (Heb.11:6).**

3. A person who *really* wishes to enter heaven will storm it; that is, he will endure anything to enter heaven. He will deny himself and change his behavior; he will turn from sin to God (repent). He will subject his desires to God's will and alter his mind in order to enter heaven.

"And be not conformed to this world: but be ye transformed by the renewing of your mind, that ye may prove what is that good, and acceptable, and perfect, will of God" (Ro.12:2).

QUESTIONS:
1. What does it mean to take the Kingdom of Heaven by storm or by force? How does this apply to your life as a believer?
2. There is no place for passivity, lethargy, or complacency in entering heaven. What does God require of a person to enter the Kingdom of Heaven? What have you done to meet these requirements?

8. JOHN WAS THE LAST OF AN AGE—THE AGE PREDICTING THE MESSIAH (v.13).

John ended the age of Old Testament prophecy. He was the last of a long line of prophets who predicted the coming of the Messiah. He was the bridge that spanned from the predictions of the Messiah to the coming of the Messiah; the bridge that spanned the Old Testament to the New Testament. He was the one whom God raised up to be the end of one era and the beginning of a new era, the era of a long line of new prophets who would introduce the Messiah.

"And for this cause he is the mediator of the new testament, that by means of death, for the redemption of the transgressions that were under the first testament, they which are called might receive the promise of eternal inheritance" (Heb.9:15).

QUESTIONS:
1. John was the last of the Old Testament prophets—all who prophesied about the coming of the Messiah. What does this tell you about God's faithfulness? What lessons can you apply from the unifying theme seen in the Old Testament prophets?
2. Think back in time for a moment and make a mental list of the Old Testament prophets who spoke of Christ. Which one of these prophets sticks out the most in your mind? Why?

9. JOHN WAS THE PROMISED ELIJAH, THE FORERUNNER WHO WAS TO PRECEDE THE MESSIAH (v.14).

He was Elijah, the fulfillment of the last prophecy of the Old Testament: "Behold, I will send you Elijah" (Mal.4:5-6; cp. Mal. 3:1). Note, John was not Elijah in person, but he was like Elijah in spirit and power and work (Jn.1:21-23).

Some believe that John was the promised Elijah and some do not. It is a matter of belief. This is what Jesus was talking about: "If ye will receive it." To receive the fact means that a person also has to receive Jesus as the Messiah, the One whom John predicted.

QUESTIONS:
1. John was compared to the prophet Elijah. Which Biblical character would your friends compare you with? Why?
2. John was a true prophet who predicted the coming of the Messiah. In the face of his religious peers, John spoke forcefully. Who do you know who speaks with the same kind of authority, as a person who points others to Christ?

10. THE CONCLUSION: A PERSON MUST HEAR (v.15).

A man has ears in order to hear; let him hear this message.

> **"But blessed are your eyes, for they see: and your ears, for they hear" (Mt.13:16; see also Pr.18:15).**

APPLICATION:
God expects us to use the faculties we have in order to receive His message: we have eyes to see His work; ears to hear His message; minds to reason the truth; hands to work His works; feet to go where He wishes. We are to be as committed to the Messiah as John was.

ILLUSTRATION:
Note a warning: a man with ears can fail to hear. One thing God cannot do is make you listen. Therefore, the great blessing of a free will demands that a person hear what God commands. In a world that is filled with so many distorted sounds, we need to sharpen our listening skills.

Phil Stevenson was out for his morning exercise. He was jogging along when all of a sudden another runner appeared by his side. Phil didn't know where he had come from. As he fell into step, he asked Phil a question.

Since he had trouble even thinking while jogging much less speaking, Phil couldn't believe this guy wanted to talk while he ran. "Where's La Quinta?" he asked, hardly even breathing hard. At first Phil thought he meant a street and couldn't think of one by that name. Then he realized he meant the hotel.

"Just take a left at the next light," Phil said and gestured with his index finger. He wanted the guy to think he was in excellent shape.

"Thanks," said the runner and took off. He easily left Phil behind. When he got to the corner where Phil had told him to turn, however, he went the opposite direction. Phil was frustrated. Here he had expended his precious oxygen to give the guy directions, and then he ignored them. He had given him good directions which would have gotten him to the destination he wanted. You try to help somebody and they just don't seem to hear you.

But what about us? Don't we do the same thing when we ignore God's prompting to call a certain friend, to write a letter, or to ask forgiveness? Maybe we need to run alongside God and get those directions one more time.[2]

QUESTIONS:
1. It is possible for a person to hear the gospel but fail to listen to it. Will God hold this person responsible for what he has heard?
2. What do you need to do to become more disciplined in hearing what the Lord is saying through His Word?

SUMMARY:

Even the strongest believer needs to guard against becoming spiritually forgetful and fickle. The path of spiritual forgetfulness and fickleness is a slippery slope that leads to doubt and unbelief. From time to time we all need reinforcement of what the truth is and what it is not. Jesus made a striking point in this very important passage: people are forgetful and fickle. But we can take comfort in this fact: even a great man like John the Baptist had to be vindicated by Christ.

---

2 *Vista.* Mar 23, 1997. Page 2. SOURCE: *INFOsearch Sermon Illustrations* (Arlington, TX: The Computer Assistant, 1-888-868-9029, 1986-1996).

MATTHEW 11:7-15

1. People wondered about John's questioning.
2. John was not a wavering reed, but a man firm in his convictions.
3. John was not a man of soft raiment, but a man disciplined and self-denying.
4. John was a prophet and more.
5. John was the Messiah's forerunner, the herald of the true King.
6. John was the greatest of natural men, yet not as great as the least in the Kingdom of Heaven.
7. John launched a violent overthrow of the kingdom.
8. John was the last of an age, the age predicting the Messiah.
9. John was the promised Elijah, the one to precede the Messiah.
10. The conclusion: a person must hear.

PERSONAL JOURNAL NOTES
(Reflection & Response)

1. The most important thing that I learned from this lesson was:

2. The area that I need to work on the most is:

3. I can apply this lesson to my life by:

4. Closing Statement of Commitment:

C. The Message: Given to a Childish Generation, 11:16-27
(Lk.7:31-35; 10:12-15, 21-22)

1. The childishness of this generation

16 But whereunto shall I liken this generation? It is like unto children sitting in the markets, and calling unto their fellows,

a. They were contrary, mindless, playful: Faultfinders who could not be pleased

17 And saying, We have piped unto you, and ye have not danced; we have mourned unto you, and ye have not lamented.

1) Accused John of separation

18 For John came neither eating nor drinking, and they say, He hath a devil.

2) Accused Jesus of worldliness

19 The Son of man came eating and drinking, and they say, Behold a man gluttonous, and a winebibber, a friend of publicans and sinners.

b. They justified their inconsistencies

But wisdom is justified of her children.

2. The judgment of this generation

20 Then began he to upbraid the cities wherein most of his mighty works were done, because they repented not:

a. The judgment of 2 privileged cities
1) Because they were privileged
2) Because they did not repent
3) Because they ignored Christ

21 Woe unto thee, Chorazin! woe unto thee, Bethsaida! for if the mighty works, which were done in you, had been done in Tyre and Sidon, they would have repented long ago in sackcloth and ashes.

4) The degree of their judgment: To be greater than most

22 But I say unto you, It shall be more tolerable for Tyre and Sidon at the day of judgment, than for you.

b. The judgment of the most privileged city
1) Because it had the greatest opportunity
2) Because it did not repent
3) Because it neglected Christ

23 And thou, Capernaum, which art exalted unto heaven, shalt be brought down to hell: for if the mighty works, which have been done in thee, had been done in Sodom, it would have remained until this day.

4) The degree of its judgment: To be the greatest

24 But I say unto you, That it shall be more tolerable for the land of Sodom in the day of judgment, than for thee.

3. The blindness of this generation

a. Blind to God's truth
1) The wise are blind: Self-sufficient
2) The babes are not blind: Teachable

25 At that time Jesus answered and said, I thank thee, O Father, Lord of heaven and earth, because thou hast hid these things from the wise and prudent, and hast revealed them unto babes.

b. Blind to God's will & purpose

26 Even so, Father: for so it seemed good in thy sight.

c. Blind to the Messiah
1) He is of God, His very own Son
2) He has been given all things
3) He is the Mediator
4) He alone reveals God

27 All things are delivered unto me of my Father: and no man knoweth the Son, but the Father; neither knoweth any man the Father, save the Son, and he to whomsoever the Son will reveal him.

Section VII
THE MESSIAH'S VINDICATION OF HIS MESSIAHSHIP, Matthew 11:1-30

MATTHEW 11:16-27

Study 1: THE MESSAGE: GIVEN TO A CHILDISH GENERATION

Text: Matthew 11:16-27

Aim: To expose the foolishness of a person who rejects the gospel.

Memory Verse:

> **"All things are delivered unto me of my Father: and no man knoweth the Son, but the Father; neither knoweth any man the Father, save the Son, and *he* to whomsoever the Son will reveal *him*" (Matthew 11:27).**

INTRODUCTION

The pages of history are filled with people who thought they knew more than God, people who acted like spoiled brats, blinded by their own way. It was the inspirational Helen Keller, a woman who was both blind and deaf from the age of two, who was asked by a young boy,

> *"Isn't it the worst thing in the world to be blind?" Smiling, she replied, "Not half so bad as to have two good eyes and see nothing."*[1]

Every generation has its privileges. The privileges are used by some and ignored and abused by others. Since the coming of Christ, the greatest privilege in all the world is that of knowing Him personally, for it is Christ who makes us acceptable to God. And there is no greater privilege than knowing God face to face. However, the vast majority have ignored and abused Christ; therefore, they do not know God, not personally.

When looking at His own generation, Jesus asked: "Whereunto [to what] shall I liken this generation?" And the most adequate illustration He could come up with was that of children (see note 1—Mt.11:16-19). He was saying that His own generation was a *childish generation*. By *childish* He meant *perverse*. They had turned away from that which was right and good to that which was corruptible. They acted contrary to the evidence. They were opposed to the reasonable and acceptable and were obstinate in their opposition. They were simply foolish and contrary. They did not want the truth, so they made excuses for not receiving the truth.

Jesus had a message for such a *childish* and *perverse* generation. It is applicable to every generation.

OUTLINE:

1. The childishness of this generation (v.16-19).
2. The judgment of this generation (v.20-24).
3. The blindness of this generation (v.25-27).

1. THE CHILDISHNESS OF THIS GENERATION (v.16-19).

The illustration is clearly understood. Children are playing in the market place. A few begin to play wedding music on their pipes and cry out to others, "Let's march and play 'wedding'." The others shout back, "No. We don't want to dance around today." So the first group, still wanting to play, begins to play funeral music and shout back, "Well, let's play 'funeral'." "No. We don't want to play funeral either. We don't feel like acting sad."

---

[1] *INFOsearch Sermon Illustrations* (Arlington, TX: The Computer Assistant, 1-888-868-9029, 1986-1996).

1. The generation is contrary, mindless, playful. They are fault-finders who cannot be pleased. They find fault with whatever is suggested. They cannot accept and be pleased with anything that puts restrictions upon their loose play. They find fault with a separatist or nonconformist approach to the gospel, and they also find fault with a sociable approach to the gospel.

a. They accused John of separation. John came neither eating nor drinking. He was a separatist. He was from the desert and lived a strict, austere life, being highly disciplined. He did not associate with people or make friends. Instead, he withdrew from society, cutting himself off from everyone. His message was a gospel of repentance and separation from the things of the world. Therefore, he was accused of having a *devil*, that is, of being mad and insane for choosing to live that way.

b. They accused Jesus of worldliness. Jesus was the very opposite of John. Jesus lived and preached a gospel of liberty. He ate and associated with the people and shared in their social affairs. He moved among all sorts of people, mixing and making Himself accessible to all no matter how terrible they were thought to be. Therefore, He was accused of being a sinner Himself: a glutton, a winebibber, and an immoral friend of sinners. (It must be remembered that when Jesus moved about in the social functions of society, it was for the purpose of witnessing to them, not to be a part of the worldly fellowship.)

2. The childish generation justifies its inconsistencies. John lived and preached a gospel of repentance and separation. Jesus lived and preached a gospel of liberty. The people were like children: they found fault with both and accepted neither. They merely wanted to do their own thing. The final act of childishness was that they justified their inconsistency. This is probably an accusing statement by Jesus. Children usually justify their *wisdom and ideas* even if their wisdom and ideas do not make good sense.

> **"For my people is foolish, they have not known me; they are sottish children, and they have none understanding: they are wise to do evil, but to do good they have no knowledge" (Jer.4:22).**

APPLICATION:

Note several lessons.

1) There are two approaches to righteousness: the separatist approach of John, and the sociable approach of Jesus. The majority of people reject both approaches. They are as children at play, fault-finders who cannot be pleased.
    a) Some are playful. They are having a good time and do not want to be interrupted and bothered. They want to go on *doing their own thing*.
    b) Some are foolish and thoughtless. They do not think about the reason and logic behind God's glorious plan and the Messiah. They refuse to face the reality of the evil, sin, and depravity of the world, the existence of a personal God, and the desperate need for God to save the world.
    c) Some are contrary. Their minds are made up. They are not going to listen to any other view. They have their own thoughts about the world and morality, and they are comfortable living as they wish. Therefore, they stubbornly reject any other view, no matter the reasonableness of what was presented.
2) Most people reject any attempt to restrict their own play. They wish to continue doing their own thing—whether it be seeking pleasure, intellectual pursuit, secular interest, or religious commitment. Most are willing to go only so far in restricting their own desires, will, and way. Few are willing to deny self completely.
3) God clearly used both approaches to righteousness (cp. 1 Cor.12:6-7). Jesus did not condemn John's approach, and John did not condemn Jesus' approach. They supported each other. What a lesson for believers! There is no room for

a judgmental spirit. Men have different temperaments and need to be approached by different methods.

QUESTIONS:

1. Every society is corrupted by people who are quick to judge God's people on the basis of worldly values. Have you ever been judged wrongly when you were doing the *right* thing for God? How did you respond to your accusers?
2. There is a saying that states you cannot please everyone. For the childish generation of this world, this is particularly true. No believer who serves Christ will ever please the childish. What should be your attitude toward these people?
3. Have you ever been accused of spoiling the fun for those who wanted you to join in their loose living? What is the believer to do in such a circumstance?

2. THE JUDGMENT OF THIS GENERATION (v.20-24).

1. There is the judgment of two privileged cities, Chorazin and Bethsaida (see A CLOSER LOOK # 1—Mt.11:20-22). Note why they were judged.

a. They were privileged to have the gospel available. They had the presence of Christ, of believers, and of the gospel. Such exposure condemns a person if he does not respond. Why? Because he has the opportunity to know Christ.
b. They refused to repent. A person who continues to live as he wills and refuses to turn to God condemns himself. God demands repentance.
c. They ignored and neglected Christ. Even in Jesus' day most people paid no attention to Him. Note: judgment is to be based not only upon doing wrong, but also upon not doing right. Just sitting around doing nothing does not free a person from judgment. God expects commitment and diligence in serving Christ.
d. The degree of judgment for the two cities was to be greater than for most, greater than for Tyre and Sidon. Tyre and Sidon never had the opportunity of Christ's ministry. But Chorazin and Bethsaida did, and they *neglected and rejected* Christ. Therefore, their judgment was to be much more severe.

2. There is the judgment of the most privileged city, Capernaum. This was the headquarters of Christ from where He launched His ministry. The degree of judgment upon Capernaum was to be even greater than the judgment upon Sodom (see A CLOSER LOOK # 2—Mt.11:23). Why? Because it was the very center of the Lord's ministry and the people still neglected and rejected Christ.

> **"Whosoever therefore shall be ashamed of me and of my words in this adulterous and sinful generation; of him also shall the Son of man be ashamed, when he cometh in the glory of his Father with the holy angels" (Mk.8:38).**

APPLICATION:

Note four lessons.

1) There is to be a day of judgment, and Christ says there are to be degrees of judgment. Some judgment is to be more "intolerable" than other judgments. Note two things.
   ⇒ There are degrees of privilege. There is much more witness for Christ in some areas than in others. People who live in these areas are more privileged and will be held more accountable than people who had less witness.
   ⇒ There are degrees of judgment. Our response to the message of Christ determines how severely we will be judged.

"But he that knew not, and did commit things worthy of stripes, shall be beaten with few stripes. For unto whosoever much is given, of him shall be much required: and to whom men have committed much, of him they will ask the more" (Lk.12:48).

2) Severe judgment will fall upon all who have had the opportunity to receive Christ and did not.
3) Our eternal state is determined by our response to Jesus Christ, and our state cannot be altered. The doom of Tyre and Sidon could not be altered, neither could the doom of Sodom. Their doom was set, having been determined while they were on earth. However note: Sodom will answer for much in the day of judgment, but not for having neglected Christ. How much greater shall our judgment be because we have neglected and rejected Christ!
4) God forgives sin no matter how terrible. The sins of Sodom would have been forgiven if the people had repented. Judgment can be averted and escaped by repentance of sin.

ILLUSTRATION:
God stays or delays final judgment every day for those who have yet to repent and trust Him. Judgment can be avoided if sinners make the right kind of preparations and heed the rumblings.

The May 1984 National Geographic showed through color photos and drawings the swift and terrible destruction that wiped out the Roman Cities of Pompeii and Herculaneum in A.D. 79. The explosion of Mount Vesuvius was so sudden, the residents were killed while in their routine: men and women were at the market, the rich in their luxurious baths, slaves at toil. They died amid volcanic ash and superheated gasses. Even family pets suffered the same quick and final fate. It takes little imagination to picture the panic of that terrible day.

The saddest part is that these people did not have to die. Scientists confirm what ancient Roman writers record—weeks of rumblings and shakings preceded the actual explosion. Even an ominous plume of smoke was clearly visible from the mountain days before the eruption. If only they had been able to read and respond to Vesuvius's warning!

There are similar "rumblings" in our world: warfare, earthquakes, the nuclear threat, economic woes, breakdown of the family and moral standards. While not exactly new, these things do point to a coming day of Judgment (Matt. 24). People need not be caught unprepared. God warns and provides an escape to those who will heed the rumblings.[2]

A CLOSER LOOK #1
(11:20-22) **Chorazin—Bethsaida**: Jesus did many "mighty works" in these cities, yet there is no record of the works. We must always remember that what we have in the New Testament are only a small number of the miracles and works that Christ did. As John says, "There are also many other things which Jesus did, the which, if they should be written every one, I suppose that even the world itself could not contain the books that should be written" (Jn.21:25).

2 Michael Bogart. Lemoore, California. *Leadership Journal.* (Carol Streal, IL: Christianity Today, Inc.), Vol. 6, no. 4.

A CLOSER LOOK #2
(11:23) **Sodom**: note four things about Sodom in the Bible.

1. Sodom is a symbol of the depth of sin and judgment.
2. Sodom could have been forgiven its sin if the people had repented.
3. Sodom was judged and destroyed because of sin. It would not have been destroyed if its people had repented.
4. Sodom and its people will answer for much in the day of judgment, but not for having neglected and rejected Christ.

QUESTIONS:

1. As you think about the cities and towns around you, can any compare with Chorazin and Bethsaida or Capernaum? In what ways do they compare—good and bad?
2. If Christ came to your town or city, how would He be received?
3. What is being done in your town or city to bring about repentance? What has God promised to do to a community that repents of its sin? What has God promised to do if a sinful community fails to repent?

3. THE BLINDNESS OF THIS GENERATION (v.25-27).

The generation was blind to three things.

1. The people were blind to God's truth. Note the words, "these things," that is, the truth of Christ that the cities missed (see A CLOSER LOOK # 3, Truth—Mt.11:25-27).

2. The people were blind to God's will, to His purpose. God has purposed to save the world through His Son, Jesus Christ. He has also purposed that the wise (the wise in their own eyes, the self-sufficient) shall not see the truth, but the babe (the needful) will have the truth revealed to him. (See A CLOSER LOOK # 4 and 5—Mt.11:25.)

> **"But their minds were blinded: for until this day remaineth the same vail untaken away in the reading of the old testament; which vail is done away in Christ" (2 Cor.3:14).**

3. The people were blind to the Messiah. Note: man is blind to four facts about the Messiah:

a. Man is blind to the fact that Jesus Christ is of God. But note: Christ declares emphatically that He is of God. He calls God, "My Father."

b. Man is blind to the fact that Jesus Christ has received all things from God. But note: Christ declares emphatically that He has been given "all things" by God. *All things have been delivered* into the hands of Christ. He is to oversee and rule the universe. All things have been made for God's Son.

> **"And Jesus came and spake unto them, saying, All power is given unto me in heaven and in earth" (Mt.28:18).**

c. Man is blind to the fact that Jesus Christ is the Mediator. But note: Christ declares emphatically that He is the Mediator. He alone *knows* and is *known* by the Father.

> **"Jesus saith unto him, I am the way, the truth, and the life: no man cometh unto the Father, but by me" (Jn.14:6).**

d. Man is blind to the fact that Jesus Christ alone can reveal the Father. But note: Christ declares emphatically that He alone reveals the Father. No man can know God apart from Christ. A person who wishes to see God and to see what God is like must come to Jesus Christ.

> **"I and my Father are one....If I do not the works of my Father, believe me not....though ye believe not me, believe the works: that ye may know, and believe, that the Father is in me, and I in him" (Jn.10:30, 38).**

ILLUSTRATION:
One of the cruelest consequences of spiritual blindness is the inability to see the ministry of Jesus Christ. Instead of seeing what Christ is doing, the spiritually blind person races toward a Christ-less religion. Author Max Lucado illustrates this with a tale of the famous Taj Mahal.

The favorite wife of the Mogul emperor Shah Jahan died. Devastated, he resolved to honor her by constructing a temple that would serve as her tomb. Her coffin was placed in the center of a large parcel of land, and construction of the temple began around it. No expense would be spared to make her final resting place magnificent.

But as the weeks turned into months, the Shah's grief was eclipsed by his passion for the project. He no longer mourned her absence. The construction consumed him. One day, while walking from one side of the construction site to the other, his leg bumped against a wooden box. The prince brushed the dust off his leg and ordered the worker to throw the box out.

Shah Jahan didn't know he had ordered the disposal of the coffin—now forgotten—hidden beneath layers of dust and time. The one the temple was intended to honor was forgotten, but the temple was erected anyway. Could someone build a temple and forget why? Could someone construct a palace, yet forget the king?

The next time you enter an assembly of worship, position yourself where you can see the people. Then decide. You can tell ones who remember the slain one. They're wide-eyed and expectant. They're children watching the unwrapping of a gift. They're servants standing still as a king passes. You don't doze in the presence of royalty. And you don't yawn while receiving a gift, especially when the giver is the king himself!

You can also tell the ones who see only the temple. Their eyes wander. Their feet shuffle. Their hands doodle, and their mouths open—not to sing, but to yawn. For no matter how hard they try to stay amazed, their eyes start to glaze over. All temples, even the Taj Mahal, lose their luster after a while.

The temple gazers don't mean to be bored. They love the church. They don't mean to grow stale. They put on hats and hose and coats and ties and come every week. But still, something is missing. The One they once planned to honor hasn't been seen in a while.

But those who have seen Him can't seem to forget Him. They find Him, often in spite of the temple rather than because of it. They brush the dust away and stand ever impressed before His tomb—His empty tomb.[3]

---

3 Max Lucado. *Spirit of Revival*, Apr 1994. Pages 4-5. SOURCE: *INFOsearch Sermon Illustrations* (Arlington, TX: The Computer Assistant, 1-888-868-9029, 1986-1996).

A CLOSER LOOK #3
(11:25-27) **Truth—World, Wisdom of**: spiritual truth is "hid." Where? In God. God has done the logical thing. He has taken spiritual truth and locked it up in Himself. Therefore, the only way to access truth is to come to Him. The only key to spiritual truth is faith and trust in God.

It is reasonable. The man who considers himself wise and intelligent and sufficient enough without God never comes to God. Therefore, a personal relationship with God is never known. The man does not come to know God nor the spiritual truth "hid" in God (Ro.1:18-22). God and His presence and His plan for the ages are foreign to the self-sufficient man. The "wise" do not believe God, not enough to come to Him. Therefore, the things of the Spirit and of the gospel are hid from him. But God's heart and truths are open to the person who comes in dependence and trust upon Him.

What Christ condemns is not intelligence and wisdom, but intellectual pride and self-sufficiency. God made man to think, reason, seek, and search in order to discover and build. But God expects man "not to think of himself too highly" (Ro.12:3; cp. Ph.2:3-4). A man is to walk humbly during his short stay on earth, knowing from whom he has come and to whom he is going. He is to trust God, putting his time and destiny in God's hands.

> **"Let nothing be done through strife or vainglory; but in lowliness of mind let each esteem other better than themselves. Look not every man on his own things, but every man also on the things of others" (Ph.2:3-4).**

A CLOSER LOOK #4
(11:25) **The Wise**: those who think of themselves as wise and intelligent; the self-sufficient; the rationalists; the wise of this world (1 Cor.1:21, 25-29; 2:14). The wise are blind to the Lord of heaven and earth and to the truth. By their very nature, the proud and self-sufficient sense no need for help and refuse to receive help. They rest in their own ability and achievements. Therefore, God is helpless in revealing the truth to them.

A CLOSER LOOK #5
(11:25) **The Babe**: the humble and receptive; the teachable.

> **"Verily I say unto you, Whosoever shall not receive the kingdom of God as a little child, he shall not enter therein" (Mk.10:15).**

QUESTIONS:

1. Why is it impossible for an unbeliever to see and understand the truth of God's Word?
2. You have probably heard the phrase, "It's like the blind leading the blind." Why is this especially true for the lost who are seeking direction from the world…
   - for important family decisions?
   - for employment decisions?
   - for other life decisions?
3. What is it that causes a person to be spiritually blind? What is the only way a blind person can gain spiritual sight?

MATTHEW 11:16-27

SUMMARY:

What a great day in which we live. We have the complete revelation of God in two events: in the coming of Christ and in the presence of His Holy Word. In addition to these two great events, we have been born after Christ's coming, death, and resurrection. We also have the empowerment of the Holy Spirit. And we have the hope of His coming again to take us home to heaven—for all eternity. We must never brush aside the wonderful privileges as the unbelievers of this generation have done. We must guard against...

1. The childishness of this generation.
2. The judgment of this generation.
3. The blindness of this generation.

PERSONAL JOURNAL NOTES
(Reflection & Response)

1. The most important thing that I learned from this lesson was:

2. The area that I need to work on the most is:

3. I can apply this lesson to my life by:

4. Closing Statement of Commitment:

MATTHEW 11:28-30

1. Come unto Me a. Who: The weary b. Why: Gives rest c. Condition: Must come	**D. The Great Invitation: Given to This Generation, 11:28-30** 28 Come unto me, all ye that labour and are heavy laden, and I will give you rest.	29 Take my yoke upon you, and learn of me; for I am meek and lowly in heart: and ye shall find rest unto your souls. 30 For my yoke is easy, and my burden is light.	**2. Take my yoke—learn** a. Why: 1) He is meek, lowly 2) We will find rest 3) His yoke is easy, His burden light b. Condition: Must take

Section VII
THE MESSIAH'S VINDICATION OF HIS MESSIAHSHIP, Matthew 11:1-30

Study 4: **THE GREAT INVITATION: GIVEN TO THIS GENERATION**

Text: **Matthew 11:28-30**

Aim: To respond to the great invitation of Christ, the invitation to rest in Him.

Memory Verse:
"Come unto me, all *ye* that labour and are heavy laden, and I will give you rest" (Mt.11:28).

INTRODUCTION
Two of the most important gauges on a car are the fuel gauge and the temperature gauge. If these two gauges are ignored, the consequences are predictable:

⇒ If the fuel gauge goes to empty, the energy needed to keep the engine going will disappear and the car will coast to a stop.

⇒ If the temperature gauge goes to hot, the radiator will boil over and ruin the engine.

In a similar sense, this is what Christ was talking about to His disciples. He knew that believers often run on empty and lose their spiritual energy to serve Him. They become extremely weary—not wanting to go on. Christ knew that believers can boil over when circumstances get too hot, when the stresses of life become too great.

Running out of energy. Being overcome by stress. In this context, Christ comes to the believer and offers a great invitation. Christ paints two pictures in this passage. One picture is of *extreme weariness*. This is the person who has gone as far as he can; he can go no farther—he cannot take another step. The other picture is of *extreme pressure*. This is the person who is about to explode; he cannot take anymore. Christ does not say what caused the weariness or pressure (heavy burdens). It does not matter, for His invitation is open to all. It is a simple invitation, requiring so little and offering so much.

OUTLINE:
1. Come unto Me (v.28).
2. Take my yoke—learn of Me (v.29-30).

1. THE FIRST GREAT INVITATION: "COME UNTO ME" (v.28).

1. Who is to come? The weary and the burdened—those who are laboring and heavy laden, weighed down and despairing, ready to give up and collapse.

APPLICATION:
Some of the things that exhaust us are…
- work: being overburdened with too much to do
- worldliness and carnality (fleshly pleasure)
- sin and guilt and the power of both to destroy
- money and material possessions and the lack of true satisfaction from both
- fame and the emptiness of it
- power and the loneliness of it
- the rituals and traditions of religion
- rules and regulations

Note this: not knowing the truth of life is one of the major causes of exhaustion. Searching for truth but never coming to the truth discourages, exasperates, exhausts, and burdens us. It causes us to whip ourselves in conscience, leaving us empty, uncertain, and insecure about the future.

2. Why should the weary and the heavy laden come to Christ? Very simply, Christ *will give them rest*. Christ will give rest to the *struggling and despairing* soul, to the empty and lonely soul—no matter how intense the experience. No person has gone too far for Christ to inject His rest into him—if the person will only call upon Christ.

3. What are the conditions for receiving this rest? There is only one condition: a person must simply come to Christ. Note that the answer to *rest*…
- is not searching after truth through religion (as important as it is).
- is not positive thinking (as important as it is).
- is not seeking the counsel of true and reliable friends (as important as it is).

The answer to *rest* is coming to Jesus Christ. Rest is available, but we have to come to Jesus Christ in order to receive the rest of God.

> **"Ho, every one that thirsteth, come ye to the waters, and he that hath no money; come ye, buy, and eat; yea, come, buy wine and milk without money and without price" (Is.55:1).**

ILLUSTRATION:
Many people feel pressured or tired, consumed or wounded by the world. Christ invites the weary and wounded to come to Him to find rest. Author Greg Laurie reminds us of this very thing.

> *We all want to feel safe. We want to feel protected. We want to feel secure. We want to feel rested.*
>
> *Then he [Laurie] tells this story: In 1930 an unusual event took place. It still represents an open case in the FBI missing-person files. On August 15, after dining out with his family, a New York State Supreme Court Justice named Joseph Carter hailed a taxi and was never seen or heard from again. The FBI thought the disappearance might be work-related as the judge had heard many mob cases. But there was no real evidence to support that theory. All investigations led to dead-ends. The only clue was a note he left for his wife and family. It said, "I am very, very tired. Love, Joe." That was it. That was the last anyone ever heard from him.*
>
> *"I think many of us," says Pastor Laurie, "feel that way today. Jesus has something to say to the person who is exhausted, to the person who is worn out, chewed up and spit out by life. He offers rest to those who are frustrated, hurting, and tired."*[1]

Are you tired enough to come to Christ and rest?

---

1 Greg Laurie. *Life. Any Questions?* (Dallas, TX: Word Publishing, 1995), p.165.

A CLOSER LOOK #1

(11:28-29) **Christian's Rest**: note the difference between the two rests promised by Jesus Christ. They are the two greatest *rests* imaginable.

1. "I will give you rest" (v.28): first, there is the rest of salvation or justification. This is the rest of deliverance from the slavery and bondage of sin, the power of Christ to conquer the enslaving habits that damage the human body and destroy the human soul. It is the rest of conscience that comes to a person's soul when he ceases his struggle in the wilderness of sin. It is the rest of conquest and triumph that a person experiences when he conquers the enemies of sin and evil through the power of Christ—day by day. It is the rest of victory through the daily storms of life.

2. "Ye shall find rest unto your souls" (v.29): second, there is the rest of sanctification or of pleasure and satisfaction, of confidence and completeness. The rest is not a rest of inactivity, of no work, of an endless slumber, of the right to laziness. It is a rest of three things.

   a. It is a rest of refreshment: a rest of refreshing one's body, mind, and spirit.
   b. It is a rest that fits one for life: a rest that infuses a person with true purpose, meaning, and significance.
   c. It is a rest of encouragement and motivation of soul: a rest that stirs a person to live and undertake his God-given task with enthusiasm, vigor, and endurance.

"And to you who are troubled rest with us, when the Lord Jesus shall be revealed from heaven with his mighty angels" (2 Th.1:7).

QUESTIONS:

1. What are the three greatest burdens you have failed to give to the Lord? How can He do a better job of handling these burdens than you? What are you waiting for?
2. Why do so many believers choose to keep their burdens instead of giving them to the Lord?
3. In what way does Christ give the believer rest? How real is His rest to you

2. THE SECOND GREAT INVITATION IS "TAKE MY YOKE—LEARN OF ME" (v.29-30).

1. Why should a person take up the yoke of Christ? Why should a person begin to learn of Christ? There are three reasons.

   a. Christ is meek and lowly. Some owners of oxen were mean and harsh both in their training and in their working of the oxen, but not Christ. He was meek and lowly, considerate and understanding, mild and gentle, long-suffering and encouraging to every person who came to Him.
   b. We will find rest (v.29). (See A CLOSER LOOK # 1—Mt.11:28-29.)
   c. Christ's yoke is easy; His burden is light (v.30). The "yoke" refers to an oxen's yoke. The yoke was a wooden collar-like instrument placed on the neck and shoulders of the oxen. It was used for tying the ropes of a plow to the oxen or for tying whatever load he had to pull. It was extremely important that the yoke be fitted to the shoulders of the oxen to prevent rubbing the flesh raw and causing sores. At first the oxen might have rebelled against the yoke, but he soon learned that it eased the burden of pulling. The yoke refers to a man's *life and task* while on earth.

      The word "easy" can also mean *well-fitting*. Christ is saying that His yoke, His life and task, are fitted to a person. It is just what a person needs, and it is easy, the least pressuring and the most energizing, fulfilling and satisfying life and task the person could live and undertake.

"Wherefore in all things it behooved him to be made like unto his brethren, that he might be a merciful and faithful high priest in things pertaining to God, to make reconciliation for the sins of the people. For in that he himself hath suffered being tempted, he is able to succour them that are tempted" (Heb.2:17-18).

2. What are the conditions for *finding this rest*? There is only one condition. A person must simply take Christ's yoke and begin to learn of Him. This simply means that we are to learn how to live and labor under His leadership, direction, guidance, and care.

Every man has his yoke, that is, his life to live and his task to do while on earth. From birth he learns from others how to live and how to do his task. Some teachers are hard taskmasters, and most courses in life lead to exhaustion and the weight of heavy burdens. The only taskmaster who can teach and assure *true rest* (of body, mind, and spirit) is Christ; and the only yoke that really fits and proves to be easy is the yoke or life and task of Christ.

"And he said to them all, If any man will come after me, let him deny himself, and take up his cross daily, and follow me" (Lk.9:23).

ILLUSTRATION:
The Christian life is full of paradoxes. Just think about these for a moment:
⇒ We are to walk by faith and not by sight. (2 Cor.5:7)
⇒ We become great leaders by how greatly we serve others. (Mk.10:45; Gal.5:13; Eph.6:7)
⇒ We become wise after we become fools. (1 Cor.4:10)
⇒ We overcome the world by yielding to Christ. (1 Jn.5:4)
⇒ We gain everything by having nothing. (Ph.3:7-8)
⇒ We become strong once we are weak.(2 Cor.12:9)
⇒ We are exalted by being humble. (1 Pt.5:6)
⇒ We live by dying. (Ph.1:21)
⇒ We find rest by taking up a yoke. (Mt.11:29)

And if you take Christ's yoke, you will find rest for your weary soul.

QUESTIONS:
1. In practical terms, what does it mean for you to take up the yoke of Christ?
2. Christ has promised that His yoke will fit you perfectly. Are there yokes you have worn before that did not fit? Why are so many believers willing to wear their own yokes and not the Lord's yoke?

SUMMARY:

In order to live for Christ, a believer's energy must be fueled by a relationship with Him. The stress and pressure and the trials and temptations of life should drive us toward the Savior, not away from Him. His invitation stands; He cries out: if you are tired and weary, if you are heavy laden...

1. Come unto Me.
2. Take my yoke—learn of Me.

MATTHEW 11:28-30

PERSONAL JOURNAL NOTES
(Reflection & Response)

1. The most important thing that I learned from this lesson was:

2. The area that I need to work on the most is:

3. I can apply this lesson to my life by:

4. Closing Statement of Commitment:

	CHAPTER 12 **VIII. MESSIAH'S DEFENSE OF HIMSELF AGAINST OPPONENTS, 12:1-50** **A. Defense 1: The Messiah is Greater Than Religion, 12:1-8** (Mk.2:23-28; Lk.6:1-5)	read what David did, when he was an hun- gred, and they that were with him; 4 How he entered into the house of God, and did eat the showbread, which was not lawful for him to eat, neither for them which were with him, but only for the priests? 5 Or have ye not read in the law, how that on the sabbath days the priests in the	**tradition &** **(cp. David** **3. Step 2: Necessary work has precedence over the Sabbath, that is, over religion**
1. A questionable act—breaking the Sabbath law	At that time Jesus went on the sabbath day through the corn; and his disciples were an hungred, and began to pluck the ears of corn, and to eat.	temple profane the sabbath, and are blameless? 6 But I say unto you, That in this place is one greater than the temple.	**4. Step 3: He, the Messiah, is greater than the temple**
a. The religionists' accusation b. Jesus' progressive argument & defense	2 But when the Pharisees saw it, they said unto him, Be- hold, thy disciples do that which is not law- ful to do upon the sabbath day.	7 But if ye had known what this meaneth, I will have mercy, and not sacri- fice, ye would not have condemned the guiltless.	**5. Step 4: He, the Messiah, will have a religion of mercy & not sacrifice**
2. Step 1: Need has precedence over	3 But he said unto them, Have ye not	8 For the Son of man is Lord even of the sabbath day.	**6. Step 5: He, the Messiah, is Lord of the Sabbath & of religion**

Section VIII
THE MESSIAH'S DEFENSE OF HIMSELF AGAINST OPPONENTS, Matthew 12:1-50

Study 1: DEFENSE 1: MESSIAH IS GREATER THAN RELIGION

Text: Matthew 12:1-8

Aim: To understand the true value of a personal relationship with Christ.

Memory Verse:

"For the Son of man is Lord even of the sabbath day" (Matthew 12:8).

SECTION OVERVIEW:

Note that Chapter 12 deals with the rising opposition to Christ both from the religionists (Mt.12:1-45) and from His own family (Mt.12:46-50). Christ confronted attack after attack, vindicating His Messiahship against each one.

Suspicion, rejection, and fear of Christ were growing at a rapid pace. He could not allow such to go unchecked lest it destroy those who were hanging on to the truth. He had to confront the arguments and denials against His Messiahship. He had to face those who did not believe and were opposed to Him. He had to continue to proclaim the truth for the sake of every generation, for He was the true Messiah, the Savior of all who would believe and surrender to God.

INTRODUCTION

There is a vast difference between the traditions of the church and the traditions of men. Note the contrast of these examples:

God says...	Man says...
⇒ He answers prayer.	⇒ God will answer prayer if I use the correct, traditional formula.
⇒ What He has cleansed is holy (Acts 10:15).	⇒ He will never dare to partake of anything he considers to be unclean (i.e. certain foods, drinks, music, dress, hairstyle, people).
⇒ He can be approached on the basis of Christ's work on the cross.	⇒ God can only be approached if I go to church (my church) on a certain day (on Sunday), at a certain time (around 11:00 am).
⇒ He looks upon the heart of a person and not upon the outward appearance.	⇒ A person must have the right education, the right title, the right association, the right denomination, the right race, the right culture, the right economic status in order to be used by God
⇒ He has bridged the gap between a holy God and sinful man through Jesus Christ, the Messiah.	⇒ Man must work his way into God's favor and presence; to become acceptable to God he must do good works

Far too often, believers get lured into replacing the legitimate traditions of the church with the traditions of men—hurting the very people God has called them to minister to.

Christ used this opportunity to show that He Himself was the Messiah and that both He and man were greater than the Sabbath or religion.

OUTLINE:

1. A questionable act—breaking the Sabbath (v.1-3).
2. Step 1: need has precedence over tradition and ritual (cp. David) (v.3-4).
3. Step 2: necessary work has precedence over the Sabbath, that is, over religion (v.5).
4. Step 3: He, the Messiah, is greater than the temple (v.6).
5. Step 4: He, the Messiah, will have a religion of mercy and not sacrifice (v.7).
6. Step 5: He, the Messiah, is Lord of the Sabbath and of religion (v.8).

MATTHEW 12:1-8

1. A QUESTIONABLE ACT—BREAKING THE SABBATH LAW (v.1-3).

The disciples were hungry. As they walked along the footpath that ran alongside a corn field, they plucked some corn to eat. By law a traveler was allowed to do this. It was not stealing, but there was a problem. It was the Sabbath and the law prohibited work (in this case, plucking corn) on the Sabbath. Note two things.

1. The religionists immediately accused Jesus, condemning Him for letting His disciples break the religious rule (see A CLOSER LOOK # 1—Mt.12:1).

APPLICATION 1:
The religionists (Jewish teachers) corrupted God's Word (Rev.22:18-19; Pr.30:6).

1) A person corrupts God's Word by taking away from the words of Scripture. A person takes away from God's Word...
   - by denying sections that he does not like or understand.
   - by neglecting to live the whole counsel of God.
   - by interpreting some commandments too loosely.

2) A person corrupts God's Word by adding to the words of Scripture. A person adds to God's Word by interpreting and living too strictly. Such exalts the flesh and is nothing more than extreme discipline and self-control. Of course, both discipline and self-control are commendable and are qualities demanded by God's Word, but they are not an end in themselves.

   God's Word is practical and leads to an abundant life, to real living. It is not cold, harsh, restrictive, monastic, unrealistic, or impractical. God did not give His Word for a select group (clergy); He gave it for the common man. "His commandments are not grievous" (1 Jn.5:3).

   The Sadducees were especially guilty of taking away from God's Word. The Pharisees and Scribes were especially guilty of adding to God's Word.

APPLICATION 2:
Note two things.

1) There are beliefs, religious practices, and traditions that are not of God. Men do add to God's Word and put restrictions upon people that God never intended.
2) There is a judgmental and censoring spirit in the heart of religionists when their beliefs are broken.

2. Jesus defended Himself and His disciples. Jesus used the questioning of the religionists to do two primary things.

a. To teach that human need and necessary work have precedence over the Sabbath and religion. Religious ritual and tradition are not as important as people, not to God.
b. To proclaim His Messiahship, His right to set straight the man-made beliefs surrounding God's Word and the *unscriptural restrictions* placed upon man.

QUESTIONS:

1. Do modern-day religionists still make up rules or traditions? What are some of them? What is the underlying purpose of these non-Biblical rules?
2. Have you ever been accused of breaking any of these religious rules? How did you respond to your accusers?

A CLOSER LOOK #1:
(12:1-8) **Religious Laws**: the disciples were not stealing the corn. A hungry traveler was permitted by law to eat a few ears of corn when passing a field (Dt.23:25). The crime was that the disciples *worked*, plucking the ears of corn, *on the Sabbath day*.

This was a serious matter to the orthodox Jew. Just how serious it was can be seen in the strict demands governing the Sabbath. Law after law was written to govern all activity on the Sabbath. A person could not travel, fast, cook, buy, sell, draw water, walk beyond a certain distance, lift anything, fight in a war or heal on the Sabbath unless life was at stake. A person was not to contemplate any kind of work or activity on the Sabbath. A good example of the people's loyalty to the law is seen in the women who witnessed Jesus' crucifixion. They would not even walk to His tomb to prepare the body for burial until the Sabbath was over (Mk.16:1f; Mt.28:1f). It was a serious matter to break the Sabbath law. A person was condemned, and if the offense was serious enough, the person was to die.

This may seem harsh to some, but when dealing with the Jewish nation, one must remember that *it was their religion* that held them together as a nation through centuries and centuries of exile. Their religion (in particular their beliefs about God's call to their nation, the temple, and the Sabbath) became the *binding force* that kept Jews together and maintained their distinctiveness as a people. It protected them from alien beliefs and from being swallowed up by other people through intermarriage. No matter where they were, they met and worshipped together and held on to their beliefs. A picture of this can be seen in the insistence of Nehemiah when he led some Jews back to Jerusalem (Neh.13:15-22 cp. Jer.17:19-27; Ezk.46:1-7).

All the above explains to some degree why the religionists opposed Jesus with such hostility. Their problem was this: they had allowed religion and ritual, ceremony and liturgy (and in some cases position, security, and recognition) to become more important than the basic essentials of human life: personal need, compassion, and the true worship and mercy of God. This is an important note for this point.)

A CLOSER LOOK #2

(12:1) **Sabbath—Sunday**: the word means rest, cessation of labor. The Sabbath is the seventh day of each week (Saturday). It was the day Israel celebrated by resting and doing absolutely no work. It was based upon the seventh day when God rested following His six days of creation (Gen.2:2-3).

So far as is known, there was no Sabbath from creation until Moses. The Sabbath was first instituted under Moses' leadership (Ex.16:23; Neh.9:13-14); thereafter it became a part of Israel's law (Ex.20:8-11).

The Sabbath was kept as a sign to distinguish Israel as God's peculiar people. It was never a day of worship or religious service. It was simply a day of complete rest for man and beast. Christ is accused of violating man-made rules encrusted around the Sabbath.

There is a difference between the Sabbath as observed by the Jews and others and Sunday as observed by Christian believers. The Sabbath is the last day of the week. It was a day when Jesus the Messiah was in the tomb, a day of great sadness for the Christian. However, Sunday is the first day of the week. It is a day of great joy, for it was the day of Jesus' resurrection, the day that He triumphed over death. It is called the *Lord's Day* and is celebrated as a day of rest and joy, a glorious day for searching the soul and meditating upon God. It is the day of worship and of Christian fellowship celebrated by believers worldwide (Acts 20:7; 1 Cor.16:2).

⇒ It was Jesus' custom to worship on the Sabbath (Lk.4:16).
⇒ It was Paul's custom to worship on Sunday (Acts 17:2).
⇒ God's people are not to neglect worship (Heb.10:25; cp. Acts 16:13).
⇒ God's people are to remember the Sabbath day, to keep it holy (Ex.20:8; 31:14, 34:21).
⇒ God's people are promised a special blessing for keeping the Sabbath day holy (Is.56:2; 58:13-14).
⇒ Polluting the Sabbath will bring the judgment of God upon a people (Ezk.20:13; 22:15; cp. Num.15:32-35; Jer.17:27; Ezk.22).

⇒ Buying and selling are not to take place on the Sabbath (Neh.10:31; 13:15).
⇒ Helping the needy is lawful on the Sabbath (Mt.12:12; cp. Jn.7:23; 9:14).
⇒ Early believers worshipped on the day that Christ arose from the dead, that is, on Sunday, the first day of the week (Acts 20:7; 1 Cor.16:2).

QUESTIONS:
1. What is the primary difference between the Sabbath that was celebrated by the Jews and the Sabbath that is celebrated by Christian believers?
2. For the Christian, the Sabbath is a day set aside for worship and for rest. What routine do you normally keep on the Sabbath? How much time do you allow for worship and rest?

2. STEP 1: NEED HAS PRECEDENCE OVER TRADITION AND RITUAL (cp. DAVID) (v.3-4).

The first step in Christ's argument is that need has precedence over religion and its tradition and ritual. This truth is illustrated by David's eating the showbread in the Tabernacle when he was hungry (see A CLOSER LOOK # 3, Showbread—Mt.12:3-4). Despite the religious law, David was held blameless for eating the showbread given to him by the priest (1 Sam.21:1-6). Why? Because he had need. Human need took precedence over religious tradition and ritual.

APPLICATION 1:
Note two things.
1) David broke the law not to indulge a lust, but to meet a genuine need. We are to meet the genuine needs of men. God's call and concern is to meet human need, not *religion* and religious beliefs, not religious practices, rituals, ceremonies, rules, and regulations.
2) The law which was broken to meet David's need still stood. It was a needed law for men to practice, yet it was broken to meet human need. Human need and compassion took precedence over the law.

APPLICATION 2:
There is criteria to determine if a religious belief, law, custom, ritual, ceremony, or rule should be broken: Is it being broken to indulge a lust or to meet a genuine need? An honest answer to this question will tell a person what to do. (Cp. civil law. Speed limits are broken by ambulance drivers to rush a critical patient to the hospital or by policemen to meet emergencies.)

"Even as the Son of man came not to be ministered unto, but to minister, and to give his life a ransom for many" (Mt.20:28).

ILLUSTRATION:
Jesus held the belief that the needs of people were more important than any religious tradition and ritual. Why? Because every single person is of more value to God than all the traditions and wealth in the world.

A gem dealer was strolling the aisles at the Tucson Gem and Mineral Show when he noticed a blue-violet stone the size and shape of a potato. He looked it over, then, as calmly as possible, asked the vendor, "You want $15 for this?" The seller, realizing the rock wasn't as pretty as others in the bin, lowered the price to $10.

The stone has since been certified as a 1,905-carat natural star sapphire, about 800 carats larger than the largest stone of its kind. It was appraised at $2.28 million.

It took a lover of stones to recognize the sapphire's worth. It took the Lover of Souls to recognize the true value of ordinary-looking people like us.[1]

QUESTIONS:
1. What motivates people to place religious tradition and ritual over the needs of people?
2. What criteria should you use to determine if a religious tradition or ritual should be broken? Have you had to break any religious traditions or rituals since you came to know Christ? What were the circumstances and consequences of your action?

A CLOSER LOOK #3
(12:3-4) **Showbread**: the word means *the bread of the face* or *the bread of the Presence*. It symbolized the presence of God who is the Bread of Life. The showbread was twelve loaves of bread that were brought to the house of God as a symbolic offering to God. It was a thanksgiving offering given to express gratitude to God for sustaining food. The loaves were to be taken to the Holy Place by the priest and placed on the table before the Lord. The loaves symbolized an everlasting covenant between God and His people: that He would always see to it that His people had whatever food was necessary to sustain them. The loaves were to be changed every week. The old loaves became food for the priests and were to be eaten by them alone.

3. STEP 2: NECESSARY WORK HAS PRECEDENCE OVER THE SABBATH, THAT IS, OVER RELIGION (v.5).

There was always work to be done in the temple: the handling of animals, the offering of sacrifices, the handling of people, the leading of worship. The *worship of God* and *necessary work* always took precedence over rules and regulations of religion, and the religious workers were always held blameless.

The Sabbath or Sunday has two purposes: rest and worship (see A CLOSER LOOK # 2, Sunday—Mt.12:1). Some work is necessary to carry on the functions of rest and worship. Note two things.

1. Necessary work is any work that is needed to sustain life and worship and meditate upon God. Christ said that doing good for man supersedes religious and Sabbath rules. We are to help a person who has needs before we worry about keeping the rituals and rules of religion.

APPLICATION:
There are many ways for us to go about doing good on the Lord's Day:
⇒ worshipping
⇒ visiting the lost and needy
⇒ feeding the hungry
⇒ bringing others to worship
⇒ helping those caught in unexpected distress
⇒ caring for those who are sick and hurting

[1] Wanda Vassallo. Dallas, TX. *Leadership Journal.* (Carol Streal, IL: Christianity Today, Inc.), Vol. 17, No. 1.

2. Sabbath or Sunday rest is not to hinder the worship of God, but to give time for it and to encourage it. What is allowed on the Sabbath or Sunday, the day set aside for rest and worship? God's Son says, "It is lawful to do well [good] on the sabbath days"; that is, it is lawful to *truly* help a person who has a *real* need.

> **"It is lawful to do well on the sabbath days" (Mt.12:12; see also Heb.10:25; Ex.20:8; Neh.10:31; Neh.13:15).**

QUESTIONS:
1. What are some examples of *necessary* work that must be done on the Sabbath? Explain why these examples are necessary.
2. Is it possible to worship God on the Sabbath by doing acts of service for Him?

4. STEP 3: HE, THE MESSIAH, IS GREATER THAN THE TEMPLE (v.6).

The priests were allowed to work on the Sabbath because it was done for the temple (cp. 2 Chron. 6:18; Is.66:1-2). Christ was saying that His disciples were allowed to work (pluck the ears of corn) because it was done for Him (to meet His hunger). This was a unique opportunity for Christ to proclaim that He was the Messiah, the Son of God, the great source and object of the temple, its founder and the subject of its worship.

Note that Christ was standing in the corn field when He said, "In this place [the corn field] is One greater than the temple [your place of worship]." There is no question what He was doing. He was proclaiming that He was the Messiah.

APPLICATION:
The temple possessed only the *symbolic* presence of God. Christ possessed "all the fulness of the Godhead bodily" (Col.2:9).

> **"The queen of the south shall rise up in the judgment with the men of this generation, and condemn them: for she came from the utmost parts of the earth to hear the wisdom of Solomon; and, behold, a greater than Solomon is here" (Lk.11:31).**

QUESTIONS:
1. Many believers wrongly put the emphasis on the place of worship [the church building] instead of upon the object of our worship [Jesus Christ]. How can individuals ensure that this does not happen to them or to their church body?
2. Can you worship God just as easily outside church walls? If so, is it as acceptable to God?

5. STEP 4: HE, THE MESSIAH, WILL HAVE A RELIGION OF MERCY AND NOT SACRIFICE (v.7).

The supreme law is love, a love that reaches out to any person in need—not religious sacrifice (cp. 1 Sam.15:22; Hos.6:6). Religious practices and rituals may help, but the first thing is love and mercy.

APPLICATION:
These religionists were guilty of the most serious offense.
1) They did not have merciful hearts; they were not compassionate and understanding of human need. How much mercy and compassion are needed in all our dealings!

2) They did not understand "what this meaneth," did not know the true meaning of God's Word nor understand God's heart. They knew God's Word but did not know its meaning. What a message to us!
3) They judged and censored others, again because they did not know the meaning of God's Word nor understand His heart. God's heart and Word never allow censoring anyone.

"Therefore judge nothing before the time, until the Lord come, who both will bring to light the hidden things of darkness, and will make manifest the counsels of the hearts: and then shall every man have praise of God" (1 Cor.4:5).

QUESTIONS:
1. Have you ever witnessed religious ritual taking precedence over compassion and mercy? What effect did it have on the individuals involved?
2. What produces a merciful heart in the Christian believer? In what ways could you be more merciful?

6. STEP 5: HE, THE MESSIAH, IS LORD OF THE SABBATH AND OF RELIGION (v.8).

As Lord, He is the One who determines what true religion is:
⇒ True religion is loving God by believing in the name of His Son Jesus Christ (1 Jn.1:3).
⇒ True religion is loving our neighbors as ourselves—ministering to them and caring for them.

Man should not try to add to or take away from God's Word. Taking away from it denies God and adding to God's Word misrepresents Him. Both dethrone Him and exalt man as Lord.

"But to us there is but one God, the Father, of whom are all things, and we in him; and one Lord Jesus Christ, by whom are all things, and we by him" (1 Cor.8:6).

ILLUSTRATION:
What kind of religion do you practice? It is quite easy to get caught up in what the world calls religion and never do what God has called you to do: to practice true religion.

One summer Larry Mitchell took a group of teenagers to Jamaica on a mission trip. They were working at an orphanage. One day Larry walked into a room, and the smell of human waste just about knocked him over. In a crib in the corner of the room was a little boy whose diaper had been needing to be changed for a long time. Larry had spent a good part of the previous day scrubbing down that crib and the walls around it because the same thing had obviously happened many times before.

Larry felt he had reached his limit. He wasn't sure he could do any more. He had cleaned up the mess, but did he care enough to pick up the child and take care of his needs? While he wrestled with this decision, a 15-year-old girl from their team brushed by him as she came into the room. She went right over to the boy without hesitating and took him out of the crib, bathed him, put clean clothes on him, and just comforted him.

Later in the day, as Larry talked with this girl, he couldn't help but notice the dark stain on the front of her blouse. Yes, it was you-know-what, but it was also a symbol of what James calls true religion: "Religion that God our Father accepts as pure and faultless is this: to look after orphans and widows in their distress and to keep oneself from being polluted by the world" (Jas. 1:27).[2]

Have you been 'stained' with true religion or are you busy keeping your hands clean?

QUESTIONS:

1. In terms of everyday life, what did Jesus mean when He said that He was Lord of the Sabbath?
2. What are some consequences for the person who makes his religion more important than his relationship with the Lord?

SUMMARY:

The lesson is striking: we must never put empty traditions and meaningless rituals before the needs of people. Christ has laid out some very clear steps to help keep believers on track:

1. There was a questionable act—breaking the Sabbath.
2. Step 1: need has precedence over tradition and ritual (cp. David).
3. Step 2: necessary work has precedence over the Sabbath, that is, over religion.
4. Step 3: He, the Messiah, is greater than the temple.
5. Step 4: He, the Messiah, will have a religion of mercy and not sacrifice.
6. Step 5: He, the Messiah, is Lord of the Sabbath and of religion.

PERSONAL JOURNAL NOTES
(Reflection & Response)

1. The most important thing that I learned from this lesson was:

2. The area that I need to work on the most is:

3. I can apply this lesson to my life by:

4. Closing Statement of Commitment:

---

2 *Wesleyan Advocate*, Mar 1997, p.15. SOURCE: *INFOsearch Sermon Illustrations* (Arlington, TX: The Computer Assistant, 1-888-868-9029, 1986-1996).

	B. Defense 2: Man is Greater Than Religion, 12:9-13 (Mk.3:1-6; Lk.6:6-11)	them, What man shall there be among you, that shall have one sheep, and if it fall into a pit on the sabbath day, will he	**trated** a. Is an animal's welfare not put before religious rules? b. Is a man not of
1. Jesus departed a. Entered the synagogue	9 And when he was departed thence, he went into their synagogue:	not lay hold on it, and lift it out? 12 How much then	more value than an animal? **4. The truth stated: Doing good for**
b. Confronted a man with a withered hand	10 And, behold, there was a man which had his hand	is a man better than a sheep? Wherefore it is lawful to do well on the sabbath days.	**man supersedes religious rules**
2. The truth questioned: Is a man more important than religion—than Sabbath rules?	withered. And they asked him, saying, Is it lawful to heal on the sabbath days? That they might accuse him.	13 Then saith he to the man, Stretch forth thine hand. And he stretched it forth; and it was restored whole, like as the	**5. The truth demonstrated: Man & his needs are put before religious rules—man is greater**
3. The truth illus-	11 And he said unto	other.	

Section VIII
THE MESSIAH'S DEFENSE OF HIMSELF AGAINST OPPONENTS, Matthew 12:1-50

Study 2: **DEFENSE 2: MAN IS GREATER THAN RELIGION**

Text: **Matthew 12:9-13**

Aim: To keep your focus upon what is really important: Treating people as more important than religion.

Memory Verse:

"How much then is a man better than a sheep? Wherefore it is lawful to do well on the sabbath days" (Matthew 12:12).

INTRODUCTION

A lot can be learned from people's priorities, from what is really valued by them.

⇒ There are communities that condone gambling for such causes as lower taxes and better schools—when in most cases the revenues just end up supporting those devastated by gambling and other functions of the state.

⇒ There are some environmental groups that actually endanger man's life when trying to protect an endangered species of animal or tree or insect.

⇒ There are religious leaders who do more to support the organization that supports them than to meet the needs of hurting people.

Unless the believer stays focused upon the Lord and His agenda, it is too easy to drift away and lose sight of the goal. Once we lose sight of the desperate needs of people, we become trapped in a religious system that devours them instead of helping them.

Christ used this event to prove His Messiahship and to show that man is greater than religion.

MATTHEW 12:9-13

OUTLINE:

1. Jesus departed (v.9-10).
2. The truth questioned: Is a man more important than religion—than Sabbath rules (v.10)?
3. The truth illustrated (v.11).
4. The truth stated: doing good for man supersedes religious rules (v.12).
5. The truth demonstrated: man and his needs are put before religious rules—man is greater (v.13).

1. JESUS DEPARTED (v.9-10).

This passage is not referring to Jesus leaving the cornfield where He had just been debating with the religionists (v.1-8). It means that He left the town He was in for another town. It was "on another Sabbath" that He entered their synagogue (cp. Lk.6:6).

1. Christ entered their synagogue. Note that discord, disputes, and opposition did not cause Christ to withdraw from worship nor prevent Him from doing what He should (cp. Mt.12:1-8).

APPLICATION:

Note two striking lessons.

1) Jesus was worshipping on the Sabbath. He was where He belonged on the Lord's Day.
2) Conflict and discord should not cause us to forsake the Lord's house. Our first obligation is to love and worship the Lord with our whole being.

2. Christ confronted a man with a withered hand. Note that Jesus had not yet begun to heal the man. The religionists apparently noticed Jesus eyeing the man or else sensed Jesus' compassion and movement to heal the man. The religionists were disturbed, deeply so, for Jesus was about to disregard their beliefs and Sabbath rules again.

APPLICATION:

This man was in the synagogue. He was a man who sensed his dependency upon God. Note two things.

1) A physical handicap does not necessarily keep a person from being strong. A person can be handicapped and still be wonderfully strong. He can be strong spiritually and strong mentally, strong in confidence and strong in assurance, strong in a sense of God's presence and strong in a sense of purpose and meaning. God can give this kind of strength. In fact, physical health is useless and sometimes destructive without the spiritual strength of God. This man with the withered hand evidently knew God's strength, yet he had a need. These two facts touched Jesus' heart.
2) A physical handicap can be used by God—greatly so. God uses handicaps...
   - to demonstrate great faith
   - to set a vibrant example of trust before loved ones, neighbors, and acquaintances
   - to be a dynamic testimony of God's saving grace
   - to cause a person's own salvation
   - to draw a person close to God in a very, very special way
   - to cause a person to become a prayer warrior, an intercessor for both God's people and for a world reeling from a restless and warring spirit, lost and trying to find its way

ILLUSTRATION:

When bad things happen, we often forget that God has a greater purpose that we cannot always see. It is easy to focus upon the pain instead of the beauty of His eternal plan.

MATTHEW 12:9-13

The great French painter Pierre Renoir gradually became crippled by arthritis, and he was eventually confined to a wheelchair. Although his hands were twisted and deformed, he still continued to paint. He could hold the brush only by his fingertips, and he endured excruciating agony with every stroke. A friend watching him work asked, "How can you paint at the expense of such torture?" Renoir replied, "The pain passes, but the beauty remains."[1]

QUESTIONS:

1. Most people will readily admit that there is no "perfect" church. Yet many use strife or discord in the church as an excuse not to attend services or worship God. What can you learn from Jesus' example of worshipping despite conflict and discord?
2. In what way have you seen God use someone's physical handicap to glorify Himself? What does this tell you about God's sovereign plan for a person who is physically handicapped?

A CLOSER LOOK #1

(12:9-13) **Man with the withered hand**: we know nothing about the man with the withered hand. The gospels say nothing else about him. However, William Barclay tells us that there is a dramatic background given by one of the books which was never accepted into the New Testament, *The Gospel According to the Hebrews*. This gospel says that the man was a carpenter who made his living with his hands. It adds that the man pleaded with Jesus to heal him that he might not have to beg for food in shame.[2]

2. THE TRUTH QUESTIONED: IS A MAN MORE IMPORTANT THAN RELIGION—THAN SABBATH RULES (v.10)?

The law said that persons could not be healed or helped on the Sabbath unless life itself was threatened. However, there sat the man and he desperately needed help. Jesus had the power to help him, but should He? If He healed the man, He would be breaking the religious rule. Should Jesus put the man or the ritual first? (See A Closer Look# 2—Mt.12:10 for more discussion.)

> **"Master, which is the great commandment in the law? Jesus said unto him, Thou shalt love the Lord thy God with all thy heart, and with all thy soul, and with all thy mind. This is the first and great commandment. And the second is like unto it, Thou shalt love thy neighbour as thyself" (Mt.22:36-39).**

APPLICATION:

Several lessons are evident in this point.

1) Note the reasons why we put religious custom and the present order of things before man and the meeting of his real needs.
   a) We slip into a routine, a way of doing things, and we continue in it because it is comfortable.
   b) We fear change lest we lose some people and their support.
   c) We fear the loss of position and security.

---

1 *INFOsearch Sermon Illustrations* (Arlington, TX: The Computer Assistant, 1-888-868-9029, 1986-1996).

2 William Barclay. *The Gospel of Matthew,* Vol.2, p.331.

d) We fear failure, the weakening of what we already have, of losing the loyalty of others to our religious position and practices.

2) Every man has need. He needs salvation, a true worship experience, a personal relationship with God day by day, a sense of the Spirit's presence and direction moment by moment. He needs to know how to live in a world that pulls him away from God, a world that pulls him toward every worldly thing imaginable. Yet, everything is too often put before man: maintaining the religious organization, form, ritual, ceremony, custom, service, order, liturgy, rules, and regulations—all seem to be more important than meeting man's needs.

3) Nothing should keep us from meeting man's needs, from putting him and his needs first before all religious ritual and form.
   a) It is the only way the heart of man can be reached and satisfied (Col.2:9-10; Jn.10:10).
   b) It is the only way the church can stop the loss of people who are falling away by the droves. As we have so often heard: they come in the front door and slip out the back door. Why? Their spiritual needs are not being met.

   We need to courageously come before the Lord, searching our hearts and asking several questions. Are we really reaching that many for Christ? Are people really accepting Christ through our ministry? Why not, when the Lord said the fields are white unto harvest? Could it be we are steeped in religion so much that we are putting religion before meeting the needs of people?

4) Man's basic need is to know and worship God in a personal way. Yet, too often we fail to reach out to man by putting worship, form, order, ritual, and rules before meeting his need. Too often, we act as though...
   - man exists for religion, instead of religion existing for man
   - man exists for worship services, instead of worship services existing for man
   - man exists for maintaining the organization, instead of the organization existing for man
   - man exists for the rules and rituals, instead of the rules and rituals existing for man

QUESTIONS:

1. What religious customs do you know about that are harmful to people? Why do these customs have so much power over people who have desperate needs?
2. When a church places more emphasis on its financial needs or problems than on meeting the needs of people, everyone suffers. What harmful consequences can you list?

A CLOSER LOOK #2

(12:10) **Religionists**: the religionists' conflict with Jesus over religious beliefs and rules is sometimes thought by modern man to be petty and harsh, or else such conflicts are just not understood. Three facts will help a person in understanding why the conflicts happened and why they were life-threatening, ending in the murder of Jesus Christ.

1. The Jewish nation had been held together by their religious beliefs. Through the centuries, the Jewish people had been conquered by army after army, and by the millions they had been deported and scattered over the world. Even in the day of Jesus they were enslaved by Rome. Their religion was the binding force that kept Jews together, in particular...

- their belief that God had called them to be a distinctive people (who wor-

shipped the only true and living God).
- their rules governing the Sabbath and the temple, intermarriage, worship and cleansing, and what foods they could and could not eat.

This belief and these rules protected them from alien beliefs and from being swallowed up by other peoples through intermarriage. Their religion was what maintained their distinctiveness as a people and as a nation.

Jewish leaders knew this. They knew that *their religion* was the binding force that held their nation together. Therefore, they opposed anyone or anything that threatened to *break or weaken* the laws of their religion and nation.

2. The religionists were men of deep, deep conviction. They were strong in their beliefs; therefore, they became steeped in religious belief and practice. To break any law or rule governing belief or practice was a serious offense, for it taught *loose* behavior. And loose behavior, once it had spread enough, would weaken their religion. This is the reason Jesus was committing a great offense by breaking their law. In their minds, He was weakening their religion and threatening their nation.

3. The religionists were men who had profession, position, recognition, esteem, livelihood, and security. Anyone who went contrary to what they believed and taught was a threat to all they had. Some religionists undoubtedly felt that Jesus was a threat to them. Every time Jesus broke their law, He was undermining their very position and security.

The errors of the religionists were fourfold.

1. They misinterpreted and corrupted God's Word (cp. Ro.9:4).
2. They committed one serious sin after another in God's eyes (cp. Ro.2:17-29).
3. They rejected God's way of righteousness, God's Messiah, which is Jesus Christ (cp. Ro.10:1-21, esp. 1-4, 19-21).
4. They allowed religion in its tradition and ritual to become more important than meeting the basic needs of human life: the need for God and the need for spiritual, mental, and physical health. Christ, being the true Messiah, was bound to expose such error. Thus the battle lines were drawn.
   ⇒ The Messiah knew that He had to liberate people from such enslaving behavior. He had to save them so they could worship God in freedom of spirit.
   ⇒ The religionists felt that they had to oppose Christ because He was a threat to their nation and to their own personal position and security.

The religionists' attack took two forms.

1. First, they tried to discredit Christ so the multitudes would stop following Him (cp. Mt.21:46).

> **"And they asked him, saying; Is it lawful to heal on the Sabbath days? that they might accuse Him" (Mt.12:10; see also Lk.6:7).**

2. Second, failing to discredit Him, they sought some way to kill Him.

> **"The Pharisees went out, and held a council against Him, how they might destroy Him" (Mt.12:14).**

QUESTIONS:

1. Why is the strict religionist such a dangerous influence upon the life of the local church?
2. There are few things more dangerous than spiritual power that falls into the wrong hands. What damage can the person who misuses his position or influence do to others?
3. Does this same kind of religious hypocrisy still go on today?

3. THE TRUTH ILLUSTRATED (v.11).

The truth was illustrated to prove that man is greater than religion. Jesus asked: If a man had only one sheep, and it fell into a pit on the Sabbath day, would the man not rescue it? Imagine the force of the Lord's question. It showed just how *unreasonable and illogical* the religionists were in their thinking. It exposed them as *ignorant and blind* to real spiritual truth.

The Lord's question had two points…
- Is an animal's welfare not put before religious rules?
- Is a man not of more value than an animal?

> **"If a man on the sabbath day receive circumcision, that the law of Moses should not be broken; are ye angry at me, because I have made a man every whit whole on the sabbath day?" (Jn.7:23).**

APPLICATION 1:
Two questions need to be asked, questions that should search our hearts.
1) Is an animal of more value than a man and his needs?
2) Can things (ritual and order) ever be said to be of more value than compassion for man?

How deceived and irresponsible we so often live and act! How often we oppose Jesus Christ and His true mission just as the religionists of His day opposed Him! And we do it for the same reasons (see A Closer Look # 2—Mt.12:10). The truth needs to be known and lived. Priorities need to be established.

APPLICATION 2:
Man is not only more rational than animals, he is spirit, capable of worshipping and living forever with God. Animals are not spiritual beings; therefore, man and his needs should be placed before animals. If a person has a problem with this fact, it reveals a deceived heart and blinded mind. How many of us follow religious form before reaching out to man and meeting his real needs? How many of us have deceived hearts and blinded minds in our practice of religion?

QUESTION:
In many cases in today's society, more value is placed upon endangered species of animals and plants than upon human life itself. Likewise, in some religious circles, more value is placed upon endangered programs than upon the needs of people. As you look at your own church, what programs are doing the best job of meeting the needs of people? Are there any programs that are more important than the needs of the people?

4. THE TRUTH STATED: DOING GOOD FOR MAN SUPERSEDES RELIGIOUS RULES (v.12).

We are to help a person who has needs before we worry about keeping the rituals and rules of religion.

APPLICATION:
There are many ways for us to go about doing good on the Lord's Day:
⇒ worshipping
⇒ visiting the lost and needy
⇒ feeding the hungry
⇒ bringing others to worship
⇒ helping those caught in unexpected distress
⇒ caring for those who are sick and hurting

MATTHEW 12:9-13

"For I was an hungred, and ye gave me meat: I was thirsty, and ye gave me drink: I was a stranger, and ye took me in: naked, and ye clothed me: I was sick, and ye visited me: I was in prison, and ye came unto me" (Mt.25:35-36; see also Gal.6:2).

QUESTIONS:

1. If you are given the opportunity to help someone in need, what is the first thing that comes to your mind:
   ___"How involved do I have to be?"
   ___"What do I have to gain by helping?"
   ___"What if this backfires?"
   ___"I need to help no matter what."
2. What practical things can you do to minister to the needy? What do you need to do *today*?

A CLOSER LOOK #3
(12:12) **Sabbath—Sunday**: the Sabbath or Sunday is for rest and worship. What is allowed on the Sabbath or Sunday, the day set aside for rest and worship? God's Son says. "It is lawful to do well [good] on the sabbath days"; that is, it is lawful to *truly* help a person who has a *real* need.

5. THE TRUTH DEMONSTRATED: MAN AND HIS NEEDS ARE PUT BEFORE RELIGIOUS RULES—MAN IS GREATER (v.13).

Man is greater; he is much more important. When Jesus healed the man, He demonstrated in no uncertain terms that there is nothing more sacred to God than man. Man is to be *reached* and *brought* into a personal relationship with Him (Lk.19:10), and he is to be helped and brought into a state of abundant living—as much as possible (Jn.10:10).

"For the Son of man is come to seek and to save that which was lost" (Lk.19:10).

APPLICATION:
What a lesson for us as we reach out to lead men to God week by week and day by day! How much we need to correct our deceived hearts and blinded minds! How much we need to be freed from being enslaved to our religious order and forms and our own personal position and security!
1) We live only a short time and then we shall give an account to God.
2) We have only a few short years to go about doing the task of the Lord.

ILLUSTRATION:
There is a time and place for form and ritual. But there is also a time to put our faith into action.

A company of Christians once gathered to pray for a family that had suffered a severe financial setback and was in desperate need. While one of the men was offering a fervent petition on their behalf, a loud knock was heard at the door. The visitor proved to be the sturdy young son of one of the local farmers. "What do you want?" they inquired. "Well, Pa says he can't join you at this time, but he asked me to bring his prayers in the wagon!" "What do you mean?" asked the leader of the group. "If you'll come out and help me bring in what he wanted me to deliver, you'll soon understand," replied the teenager. When they reached the wagon, they saw that "Pa's prayers" consisted of potatoes, flour, beef, oatmeal, turnips, apples, jars of jelly and fruit, and a bundle of clothing. With new understanding in their hearts, the others decided to take the hint and do likewise. Each pledged a generous amount from his own abundant supplies, and the meeting quickly adjourned on a note of praise.[3]

Are you busy *being* religious or busy *doing* good?

QUESTIONS:

1. Why is a person treasured by God above an animal or any other created thing? What does this tell you about God's love and care for you?
2. What is the most important thing you can do for your fellow man?

SUMMARY:

Man is greater than religion. For some people, this statement is paramount to blasphemy. This idea bothered the Pharisees of Jesus' day, and it is still bothering modern-day Pharisees who put men down. But the gap of time does not change the meaning of Jesus' words: man is greater than religion.

1. Jesus departed to another town where He entered the synagogue.
2. The truth questioned: Is a man more important than religion—than Sabbath rules? The law said that persons could not be healed or helped on the Sabbath unless life itself was threatened. However, there sat the man and he desperately needed help.
3. The truth was illustrated to prove that man is greater than religion.
4. The truth was stated: doing good for man supersedes religious rules.
5. The truth was demonstrated: man and his needs are put before religious rules—man is greater.

PERSONAL JOURNAL NOTES
(Reflection & Response)

1. The most important thing that I learned from this lesson was:

2. The area that I need to work on the most is:

3. I can apply this lesson to my life by:

4. Closing Statement of Commitment:

---

3 *INFOsearch Sermon Illustrations* (Arlington, TX: The Computer Assistant, 1-888-868-9029, 1986-1996).

MATTHEW 12:14-21

	C. Defense 3: Messiah Is the Chosen Servant of God, 12:14-21 (Mk.3:7-12)	prophet, saying, 18 Behold my servant, whom I have chosen; my beloved, in whom my soul is well pleased: I will put my spirit	a. God's Chosen Servant b. God's Beloved Son c. God's Spirit was upon Him—fully
1. Two attitudes a. First attitude: The Pharisees plotted against Jesus, so He withdrew b. Second attitude: Multitudes followed Jesus, so He healed c. Jesus requested no publicity	14 Then the Pharisees went out, and held a council against him, how they might destroy him. 15 But when Jesus knew it, he withdrew himself from thence: and great multitudes followed him, and he healed them all; 16 And charged them that they should not make him known:	upon him, and he shall show judgment to the Gentiles. 19 He shall not strive, nor cry; neither shall any man hear his voice in the streets. 20 A bruised reed shall he not break, and smoking flax shall he not quench, till he send forth judgment unto victory.	**3. Jesus' work** a. He proclaims justice to all peoples b. He shows humility 1) Not strife: Arguing 2) Not crying: Reacting 3) Not fussing c. He loves and encourages d. He leads justice to victory
2. Jesus' person	17 That it might be fulfilled which was spoken by Esaias the	21 And in his name shall the Gentiles trust.	e. He gives hope to all

Section VIII
THE MESSIAH'S DEFENSE OF HIMSELF AGAINST OPPONENTS,
Matthew 12:1-50

Study 3: **DEFENSE 3: MESSIAH IS THE CHOSEN SERVANT OF GOD**

Text: **Matthew 12:14-21**

Aim: A twofold aim: (1) To learn the glorious truth that Jesus Christ is God's chosen servant. (2) To imitate Christ in His role as God's chosen servant.

Memory Verse:

"Behold my servant, whom I have chosen; my beloved, in whom my soul is well pleased: I will put my spirit upon him, and he shall show judgment to the Gentiles" (Matthew 12:18).

INTRODUCTION

When something needs to be repaired in your home whom do you call on?

⇒ When your kitchen sink springs a leak?
⇒ When ants or termites infest your home?
⇒ When your electrical wiring is shorting out?

You call on an expert, someone who can fix the problem. Or at least this is what you *should* do! In the same sense, this world was in need of repair.

⇒ It was infested by the corruption of sin.
⇒ It was falling short of what God intended.

MATTHEW 12:14-21

God saw the world in disrepair and sent His Servant, His very own Son who alone could repair man's brokenness. The Old Testament predicted who the Messiah would be and what His work would be. This passage proves that Jesus fulfilled what was predicted of the Messiah.

OUTLINE:

1. Two attitudes toward Jesus and His response (v.14-16). (His response to the way people treated Him proved that He was the Messiah.)
2. Jesus' person (v.17-18).
3. Jesus' work (v.18-21). (What Jesus did and the quiet, tender way He went about doing it proved His Messiahship.)

1. TWO ATTITUDES TOWARD JESUS (v.14-16).

The religionists and the multitudes demonstrate the two attitudes.

1. The religionists rejected and plotted against Jesus. They represent those who rebel against the Lordship of Christ, rebel against His having any control over their lives. There was warning in Jesus' response to the religionists (Pharisees). They had one opportunity after another, and they continually rejected Christ's appeal. They rejected Him so much that their hearts became encrusted and hardened, apparently beyond reach. Christ was forced to withdraw from them.

APPLICATION:
God says, "My spirit shall not always strive with man" (Gen.6:3; cp. Pr.29:1). This is a needful warning, for when we feel pulled to make a decision and put the decision off for an hour or two (a half day or a day at most), the pull fades and eventually dies completely. God's Spirit does not continue to strive with us. Most of us have experienced such movements and killed the Spirit's pull or striving.

2. The multitudes (many of them) believed and trusted and followed Jesus, so He healed them.

APPLICATION:
Jesus heals, responding to any who *truly* follow Him.

3. Jesus requested no publicity (see A CLOSER LOOK # 1—Mt.12:16 for discussion).

A CLOSER LOOK #1
(12:16) **Jesus—No Publicity**: Why did Jesus withdraw and charge the people not to make Him known?

1. Jesus wished to avoid confrontation with those who sought His life. His hour had not yet come. He did not wish to provoke the religionists to a deliberate conflict, putting Himself in premature peril.

2. Jesus did not wish to be pushed forward by public acclaim to assume kingship of the nation. He understood His mission. He had come first to be the Suffering Servant, and He knew that the people were inflammable, aching for deliverance from the Roman conquerors. Too much promotion of His miracles might cause an uprising. He had to prevent an uprising so that He might carry out His mission of dying for the world as the Suffering Servant.

3. Jesus needed time to teach the people what true Messiahship meant. The people thought the Messiah was to overthrow the Roman conquerors and establish Israel as one of the great nations of the world. Jesus had to show that the Messiah's kingdom

was spiritual, not material; present and future, not just present; permanent and eternal, not just mortal and temporal.

4. Jesus needed to teach humility. He refused to make a spectacle, to "be seen of men" (v.19).

5. Jesus wished to give an example of the principle He had laid down: "When they persecute you in this city, flee to another" (Mt.10:23).

QUESTIONS:
1. It is a serious thing to reject the commands of the Lord. How many times will Christ allow a person to reject Him before He withdraws His presence?
2. Jesus will respond to those who follow Him. How has this truth become a reality in your life?

2. JESUS' PERSON (v.17-18).

The person of Jesus Christ is spelled out clearly in these two verses. Note this is a quotation from Isaiah's prediction concerning the person of the Messiah (Is.42:1-4).

1. Jesus Christ is *the Chosen Servant* of God. Christ humbled Himself to do God's will. And He did God's will *perfectly* (2 Cor.5:21; Heb.4:15). Therefore He is *The Ideal Servant* of God. He is the pattern, the picture, the ideal of how every man should serve God. Jesus was God's chosen servant in the great work of redemption.

> **"[Christ Jesus] who, being in the form of God, thought it not robbery to be equal with God: but made himself of no reputation, and took upon him the form of a servant, and was made in the likeness of men: and being found in fashion as a man, he humbled himself, and became obedient unto death, even the death of the cross" (Ph.2:6-8).**

APPLICATION:
Note three strong lessons for us.
⇒ Christ *submitted Himself* to do God's will; therefore,
⇒ He was given *a great work* to do;
⇒ He experienced *the great trust* of God.

2. Jesus Christ is God's beloved Son. There are two precious thoughts here.
   a. Christ has been "in the bosom of the Father" throughout all eternity; that is, His mission to earth and the great salvation He was to bring to man have been in the recesses of God's heart forever. God has always held Christ to be very dear and very precious to Him.
   b. Christ "was daily His [God's] delight, rejoicing always before Him" (Pr.8:30 cp. Pr.8:22-31). Throughout all eternity there has been an inconceivable relationship of love and sharing between the Father and the Son that goes well beyond our finite minds. Christ has always been God's *beloved* Son.

> **"His [God's] dear Son: In whom we have redemption through His blood, even the forgiveness of sins...." (Col.1:13-14. See also 1:13-20 for a beautiful description of the work of Christ and the pleasure of God in that work.)**

3. God's Spirit fully endowed Jesus Christ. Jesus Christ was qualified for the work God sent Him to do. He had an unlimited measure of God's Spirit.

> **"For He [Christ] whom God hath sent speaketh the words of God: for God giveth not the Spirit by measure unto Him" (Jn.3:34; see also Heb.1:9 where "the oil of gladness" refers to the Holy Spirit).**

APPLICATION:
God puts His Spirit upon everyone whom He chooses. This means at least two things.
1) God gives spiritual gifts and power to every chosen vessel. He equips every person to do just what He calls that person to do. (Cp. Ro.12:5-8; 1 Cor.12:7-11, 27-31; Eph.4:11-16.)
2) God also bestows some of His image, some of His likeness upon every chosen person (2 Cor.3:18).

ILLUSTRATION:
Potential. We all have it, but we do not always act like it. God created man in His own image, but we often settle for a watered-down image. The challenge for each believer is to rise up and be what God created him to be: an eagle that soars toward the sun.

A certain man went through a forest seeking any bird of interest he might find. He caught a young eagle, brought it home, and put it among the fowls and ducks and turkeys, and gave it chicken food to eat even though it was an eagle, the king of birds.

Five years later, a naturalist came to see him and, after passing through his garden, said, "That bird is an eagle, not a chicken."

"Yes," said the owner, "but I have trained it to be a chicken. It is no longer an eagle, it is a chicken, even though it measures fifteen feet from tip to tip of its wings."

"No," said the naturalist, "it is an eagle still; it has the heart of an eagle, and I will make it soar high up to the heavens."

"No," said the owner, "it is a chicken and it will never fly."

They agreed to test it. The naturalist picked up the eagle, held it up and said with great intensity: 'Eagle, thou art an eagle; thou dost belong to the sky and not to this earth; stretch forth thy wings and fly.'

The eagle turned this way and that, and then looking down, saw the chickens eating their food, and down he jumped.

The owner said, "I told you it was a chicken."

"No," said the naturalist, "it is an eagle. Give it another chance tomorrow."

So the next day he took it to the top of the house and said, :"Eagle, thou art an eagle; stretch forth thy wings and fly." But again the eagle, seeing the chickens feeding, jumped down and fed with them.

Then the owner said, "I told you it was a chicken."

"No," asserted the naturalist, " it is an eagle, and it has the heart of an eagle; only give it one more chance, and I will make it fly tomorrow."

The next morning he rose early and took the eagle outside the city and away from the houses, to the foot of a high mountain. The sun was just rising, gilding the top to the mountain with gold, and every crag was glistening in the joy of the beautiful morning.

He picked up the eagle and said to it: "Eagle, thou art an eagle; thou dost belong to the sky and not to the earth; stretch forth thy wings and fly."

The eagle looked around and trembled as if new life were coming to it. Yet it did not fly. The naturalist then made it look straight at the sun. Suddenly it stretched out its wings and, with the screech of an eagle, it mounted higher and higher and never returned. It was an eagle, though it had been kept and tamed as a chicken.

We have been created in the image of God, but men have made us think that we are chickens, and so we think we are; but we are eagles. Stretch forth your wings and fly! Don't be content with the food of chickens![1]

QUESTIONS:
1. How would your life be different if you decided to completely submit yourself to God's will?
2. What is the greatest task God has ever entrusted you to do? Why did God choose you for this task? Were you faithful to do what God asked you to do?
3. God always equips His servants to do His work. When has this been particularly evident in your life?

A CLOSER LOOK #2
(12:17-21) **Jesus Christ, Scripture Fulfilled**: note the exact description of the Messiah's ministry.

> **"Behold my servant, whom I uphold; mine elect, *in whom* my soul delighteth; I have put my spirit upon him: he shall bring forth judgment to the Gentiles. He shall not cry, nor lift up, nor cause his voice to be heard in the street. A bruised reed shall he not break, and the smoking flax shall he not quench: he shall bring forth judgment unto truth. He shall not fail nor be discouraged, till he have set judgment in the earth: and the isles shall wait for his law" (Is.42:1-4).**

3. JESUS' WORK (v.18-21).

The work of Jesus Christ is spelled out clearly in these verses.

1. Jesus Christ proclaimed justice to all people. Justice means doing what is right toward God and man. It is living right and doing right. Jesus Christ came to show all men, both Jew and Gentile, how to live and behave toward God and toward man. He came to proclaim *the right way* for man to live out his years on earth.

APPLICATION:
Christ shuts no man out, but men do shun and avoid, exclude and shut one another out. Christ reaches out to the Gentiles no matter how ungodly and corruptible they may be. He reaches out to all, and He shows all how to live just and righteous lives.

> **"Jesus saith unto him, I am the way, the truth, and the life: no man cometh unto the Father, but by me" (Jn.14:6).**

2. Jesus Christ showed humility. The picture is twofold.
   a. Jesus Christ did not come making noise:
      ⇒ *striving* (arguing, quarreling, debating)
      ⇒ *crying* (loudly challenging and reacting against opposition)
      ⇒ *fussing* (brawling and creating an uproar in the streets).

      Jesus Christ came quietly and peacefully to conquer men by loving them and warning them to flee the terrible results of selfishness and sin.
   b. Jesus Christ did not come in the pomp and ceremony which the people had expected of the Messiah. He did not come in the force and violence which the people had expected of the Son of David. He came in peace, humbling and denying Himself and offering peace to all men no matter how selfish and

1 James Aggrey in *Illustrations Unlimited.* James S. Hewett, Editor, p.160-161.

wicked they might be. He came with the voice of appeal and invitation to be saved, not with the voice of argument, terror, and condemnation.

APPLICATION:
This is a strong lesson for every believer. How greatly the life and ministry of so many differ from Christ. So many talk about, put forth, stress, argue, and fuss over promotion and publicity, position and importance, ministry and results.

> **"And the work of righteousness shall be peace; and the effect of righteousness quietness and assurance for ever" (Is.32:17).**

3. Jesus Christ loved and encouraged men. Christ came to encourage.
   a. He did not come to destroy but to heal the "bruised reed": those who were hurt, battered, crushed, discouraged, depressed, down, insecure, inferior, shy. He came to heal all who were bruised.
   b. He did not come to condemn those with a flickering wick (light) nor to cut them off and cast them away; but He came to encourage the flickering: the weak (light), unmotivated, half-hearted, and lazy.

> **"Even as the Son of man came not to be ministered unto, but to minister, and to give his life a ransom for many" (Mt.20:28).**

4. Jesus Christ will lead justice to victory. He will cause justice to triumph throughout the world. A day of victory is coming. Hearts and lives will turn more and more to Him; men will begin to do right and behave as they should toward God and toward men. There is a glorious day of redemption coming, a climactic day of human history when all believers shall be perfected in justice and glory.

> **"Then cometh the end, when he shall have delivered up the kingdom to God, even the father; when he shall have put down all rule and all authority and power" (1 Cor.15:24).**

5. Jesus Christ gives hope to all. This verse, written somewhere between 50-70 AD, was a prediction. History has proven the fulfillment of the prophecy: the people who would trust Jesus were to be the Gentiles. The great purpose of God is for men to trust in "His name" (Ro.10:13). Therefore, the great hope of man is "His name."

> **"That the Gentiles should be fellowheirs, and of the same body, and partakers of his promise in Christ by the gospel" (Eph.3:6).**

APPLICATION:
Christ gives hope to all, no matter how unclean, dirty, or polluted they may be. Trusting Him is all He requires.

> **"For the Son of man is come to seek and to save that which was lost" (Lk.19:10).**

ILLUSTRATION:
God's Word is clear: He wants us to place our trust in Him and in Him alone. This is easy enough to do when things are predictable or manageable, but the challenge comes when we have to walk by faith, not by sight.

> *A church member was having trouble with the concept of tithing. One day he revealed his doubts to his minister: "Pastor, I just don't see how I can give 10 percent of my income to the church when I can't even keep on top of our bills."*

The pastor replied, "John, if I promise to make up the difference in your bills if you should fall short, do you think you could try tithing for just one month?"

After a moment's pause, John responded, "Sure, if you promise to make up any shortage, I guess I could try tithing for one month."

"Now, what do you think of that," mused the pastor. "You say you'd be willing to put your trust in a mere man like myself who possesses so little materially, but you couldn't trust your Heavenly Father who owns the whole universe! The next Sunday, John gave his tithe, and has been doing so faithfully ever since."[2]

No matter what our need may be, we can trust and hope in the name of the Lord.

QUESTIONS:

1. What can you learn from Christ's treatment of other people? What is the first thing you need to work on?
2. Jesus Christ was the most humble man to walk on the face of this earth. What do you need to do to become more like Christ?

SUMMARY:

Only Jesus Christ, God's Chosen Servant, is capable of fixing the brokenness of mankind. He and He alone is the true Messiah. His person and work prove His Messiahship. Remember:

1. There were two attitudes toward Jesus. His response to the way people treated Him proved that He was the Messiah.
2. There was Jesus' person. His fulfillment of prophecy proved He was the Messiah.
3. There was Jesus' work. What Jesus did, and the quiet, tender way He went about doing it proved He was the Messiah.

PERSONAL JOURNAL NOTES
(Reflection & Response)

1. The most important thing that I learned from this lesson was:

2. The area that I need to work on the most is:

3. I can apply this lesson to my life by:

4. Closing Statement of Commitment:

---

2 *Illustrations Unlimited.* James S. Hewett, Editor, p. 461.

MATTHEW 12:22-30

	D. Defense 4: Messiah is of God's Kingdom & House, 12:22-30 (Mk.3:22-30; Lk.11:14-23)
1. Jesus proved His Messianic power a. The proof: A devil-possessed man was healed b. Two reactions	22 Then was brought unto him one possessed with a devil, blind, and dumb: and he healed him, insomuch that the blind and dumb both spake and saw.
1) The people: They hoped that He was the Messiah	23 And all the people were amazed, and said, Is not this the son of David?
2) The religionists: They said that He was of the devil c. Jesus' answer: Four logical & irrefutable arguments	24 But when the Pharisees heard it, they said, This fellow doth not cast out devils, but by Beelzebub the prince of the devils.
2. Argument 1: A divided allegiance destroys a. A kingdom divided destroys itself b. A city or house divided cannot stand c. Satan's kingdom divided cannot stand	25 And Jesus knew their thoughts, and said unto them, Every kingdom divided against itself is brought to desolalation; and every city or house divided against itself shall not stand:
3. Argument 2: Denying Him is inconsistent & illogical a. Why deny His works while the works of others are accepted? b. His works are a sign 1) Of God's Spirit 2) Of God's kingdom coming to man	26 And if Satan cast out Satan, he is divided against himself; how shall then his kingdom stand? 27 And if I by Beelzebub cast out devils, by whom do your children cast them out? therefore they shall be your judges. 28 But if I cast out devils by the Spirit of God, then the kingdom of God is come unto you.
4. Argument 3: A strong man has to be bound before his property can be taken a. Jesus has invaded Satan's house & taken his property b. Jesus has bound Satan	29 Or else how can one enter into a strong man's house, and spoil his goods, except he first bind the strong man? and then he will spoil his house.
5. Argument 4: Neutrality is impossible—one is either with Christ or against Christ	30 He that is not with me is against me; and he that gathereth not with me scattereth abroad.

Section VIII
THE MESSIAH'S DEFENSE OF HIMSELF AGAINST OPPONENTS, Matthew 12:1-50

Study 3: **DEFENSE 4: MESSIAH IS OF GOD'S KINGDOM AND HOUSE**

Text: **Matthew 12:22-30**

Aim: To grow in your conviction that Christ is the Messiah.

Memory Verse:
"He that is not with me is against me; and he that gathereth not with me scattereth abroad" (Matthew 12:30).

INTRODUCTION

Think for a moment. Have you ever been accused of something that was not true? There are few feelings worse than that caused by being slandered. The only antidote for such a vicious attack is the truth. It is the truth that will vindicate us.

MATTHEW 12:22-30

According to the United Press International, as the Vietnam war was nearing its end, a nightmare began for the family of private first class Alan Barton. Barton was killed by a land mine just outside his base in Vietnam. The army was unable to identify the remains. Meanwhile Barton was unaccounted for. Somehow the officers in charge did not see the relationship between these two events, and classified Barton as a deserter...Alan Barton's mother did not believe her son had deserted. She insisted on his innocence. For thirteen years her son's unidentified remains lay in a military morgue in Hawaii as she fought to clear his name. Finally the army rechecked the morgue records, and this time they correctly identified Alan Barton's remains. In February 1983 the army honored the soldier it had wronged...In this world, even heroes may be wrongly incriminated. But just as this soldier's name was cleared and honored, so God promises to vindicate His servants."[1]

Jesus gave a firm response to those who falsely accused Him. We can learn much from His example. The opposition to Christ reached its height in this event. Christ was scorned and diabolically attacked. He was blasphemed, not only accused, but *charged* with being of the devil. Again He kept calm and remained level-headed, going about proving that He was of God, the true Messiah. He answered the monstrous charge by giving four logical and irrefutable arguments.

OUTLINE:

1. Jesus proved His Messianic power (v.22-24).
2. Argument 1: a divided allegiance destroys (v.25-26).
3. Argument 2: denying Him is inconsistent and illogical (v.27-28).
4. Argument 3: a strong man has to be bound before his property can be taken (v.29).
5. Argument 4: neutrality is impossible—one is either with Christ or against Christ (v.30).

1. JESUS PROVED HIS MESSIANIC POWER (v.22-24).

1. The proof: a devil-possessed man (blind and dumb) was healed. Note three things.
   a. The man was "brought to Jesus." Family or friends cared enough to bring him. How desperately some people need family and friends who care enough to help them.
   b. Jesus has compassion on the most evil, even on a man thought to be so evil that he was "possessed with a devil." The devil made the man both blind and dumb, yet Jesus had compassion upon him.
   c. Jesus has the power "to deliver and heal" immediately. The one necessity is coming to Him or being brought to Him.

   APPLICATION 1:
   Christ's very purpose for coming to earth was to conquer Satan and break his power over men. In some cases Satan's power was imagined; in other cases it was real (and still is). When a man is held in bondage by anything, Christ cares for and craves to deliver the man (cp. Heb.2:14-15).

   APPLICATION 2:
   A man without Christ is "blind and dumb" to the things of God.

2. There are two reactions to Jesus' Messianic power.
   a. The people were amazed. They wondered *in hope*, "Is this the Son of David,

---

1 *Contemporary Illustrations for Preachers, Teachers, and Writers.* Craig B. Larson, Editor. (Grand Rapids, MI: Baker Books, 1996), p.275.

the promised Messiah?" They thought He might be, yet they were not quite sure. He was not doing the things they had been taught the Messiah was to do. He seemed to have no concern for political or national affairs. He had neither mobilized an army nor led an uprising against the Romans as the Son of David. Contrariwise, He was demonstrating compassion and love for needy persons who were destitute in spirit and hurting in body. He was proclaiming a message of personal salvation instead of national deliverance.

Such behavior was so different from what they had always believed and been taught. He claimed to be the Messiah; He even claimed to be the Son of God. They wanted to believe; they even hoped, but they were not sure.

b. The religionists (Pharisees) denied Jesus. When they saw the people turning to Jesus, they did two things: (a) they set out to *shatter* the people's hope and belief lest they lose their own position and hold on the people, and (b) they charged Jesus with being from the devil and possessing the power of the devil (see A Closer Look # 4—Mt.12:24).

APPLICATION 1:
The people were open to the possibility that Jesus might be the Messiah, but the religionists were not. Why? Why are some minds and hearts open and others closed to Christ? Too often the difference has to do with peer acceptance or pressure, reputation, pride, wealth, possessions, fame, power, livelihood, public esteem, applause, praise, or position (1 Jn. 2:15-16; cp. 2 Cor.6:17-18).

APPLICATION 2:
Obstinate unbelief is serious, critically serious (see A Closer Look # 4—Mt.12:24). In every generation there are those who cling to their unbelief despite witness after witness. The evidence of the Lord's presence in lives builds up to an undeniable point, yet still they persist in unbelief. They attribute any change in a human life to the power of the mind or to some psychological power of suggestion or to human faith. And they attribute any change in natural events to a fluke in nature or to an unexplainable and yet unknown or undiscovered cause. They will attribute the unexplained to anything just to keep from having to confess Christ and to surrender themselves to Him.

3. Jesus' answer was to give four logical and irrefutable arguments for His Messiahship. The open heart and honest mind must admit four arguments (see outline—pts.2-5).

QUESTIONS:
1. Who is the most evil person you can think of? Do you think Christ has the power to deliver and heal him or her? Do you pray to that end?
2. What can you do to reach a person who *refuses* to believe the claims of Christ?

A CLOSER LOOK #1
(12:22) **Devils—Evil Spirits**: evil spirits are demons. There is only one devil. However, there are many evil or unclean spirits or demons, and the New Testament has much to say about them.

The characteristics of demons other than the ones given in the outline above are said to be as follows:

1. They are spirits (Mt.12:43-45).
2. They are Satan's emissaries (Mt.12:26-27).
3. They know their fate is to be eternal doom (Mt.8:29; Lk.8:31).
4. They affect man's health (Mt.12:22; Mt.17:15-18; Lk.13:16). Apparently, demon-possession is to be distinguished from mental illness.
5. They seduce men to a false religion of harshness or asceticism (1 Tim. 4:1-3).

6. They seduce men to depart from the faith (1 Tim. 4:1).
7. They are cast out of people (exorcism) in the name of Jesus Christ (Acts 16:18).
8. They shall participate in the apocalyptic or ill-fated judgment which is coming upon the earth (Rev.9:1-11, 20).

A CLOSER LOOK #2

(12:23) **Christ—Messiah**: the word for "Christ" and "Messiah" is the same word: *christos*. Messiah is the Hebrew word and Christ is the Greek word. Both words refer to the same Person and mean the same thing: *the Anointed One*. The Messiah is *the Anointed One* of God. Matthew says that Jesus "is called Christ" (Matthew 1:16); that is, He is recognized as *the Anointed One* of God, the Messiah Himself.

In the day of Jesus Christ, people feverishly panted for the coming of the long promised Messiah. The weight of life was harsh, oppressive, and heavy with burdens. Under the Romans, people felt that God could not wait much longer to fulfill His promise. Such longings for deliverance left the people gullible. Many arose who claimed to be the Messiah and led the gullible followers into rebellion against the Roman State. The insurrectionist Barabbas, who was set free in the place of Jesus at Jesus' trial, is an example (Mark 15:6f).

The Messiah was thought to be several things:

1. Nationally, He was to be the leader from David's line who would free the Jewish state and establish it as an independent nation, leading it to be the greatest nation the world had ever known.
2. Militarily, He was to be a great military leader who would lead Jewish armies victoriously over all the world.
3. Religiously, He was to be a supernatural figure straight from God who would bring righteousness over all the earth.
4. Personally, He was to be the One who would bring peace to the whole world.

Jesus Christ accepted the title of Messiah on three different occasions (Mt.16:17; Mk.14:61; Jn.4:26). The name *Jesus* shows Him to be man. The name *Christ* shows Him to be God's anointed, God's very own Son. *Christ* is Jesus' official title. It identifies Him officially as:

⇒ Prophet (Dt.18:15-19.)
⇒ Priest (Ps.110:4.)
⇒ King (2 Sam.7:12-13.)

These officials were always anointed with oil, a symbol of the Holy Spirit who was to perfectly anoint the Christ, the Messiah (Mt.3:16; Mk.1:10-11; Lk.3:21-22; Jn.1:32-33).

A CLOSER LOOK #3

(12:24) **Religionists—Unbelief**: the religionists were bitter, stinging, rough, and cutting in their accusations against Jesus. "He hath a devil and is mad" (Jn.10:20). He is a "Samaritan and has a devil" (Jn.8:48); He is born out of wedlock (Jn.8:41). He is "greedy, alcoholic, a friend of sinners" (Lk.7:34).

Why did the religionists (Pharisees, Sadducees, and Scribes) oppose Jesus so vehemently? There were several reasons.

1. Religion gives a sense of security. It is the opium of the people, as Karl Marx said. It makes a person secure and comfortable with himself. Therefore, a truly professional and committed religionist opposes anything that threatens the security he has found.

2. Religionists oppose change. Every true religionist believes his way is the way, the truth, and the life; therefore, there is no reason to change so long as his needs are being met.

3. Religion can lead to position, pride, and a sense of importance. One of the most difficult things in the world is for a person to give up his position and admit he is wrong. To do so is to deny his importance. Think about it—for this is exactly what Christ demands of every man (Lk.9:23). This is the reason so many of the gifted and the powerful of the world reject Christ and become hostile toward Him.

A CLOSER LOOK #4

(12:24) **Beelzebub—Satan**: the charge against Jesus was that His power to deliver men from evil was not of God, but of the devil. The idea was that He was sent by the devil to deliberately deceive people and to lead them away from the true traditional religion and beliefs. Note two things.

1. The evidence of supernatural power was clearly seen and even admitted by the enemies of Christ. Some force other than human power was healing people and performing miracles. Jesus' enemies were forced to look for answers elsewhere.

2. The depth of unbelief is seen here. It is *obstinate unbelief, a rooted hostility* that is full of malice and attempts to injure. It is an unbelief that will not surrender to the claims of Christ despite the evidence. The evidence was clear. Lives were changed and miracles did happen, yet some persons still refused to believe and they hardened themselves in that unbelief. They searched out other answers for the miraculous power of Christ. They sought to attribute His power to anything that would keep them from having to confess Christ and surrender their own lives and possessions to Him.

2. ARGUMENT 1: A DIVIDED ALLEGIANCE DESTROYS (v.25-26).

This is a universal truth. Division leads to separation and ruin. A divided kingdom, city, or house cannot stand. It fights and destroys itself. Satan is not going to empower anyone to deliver people from evil—not time after time as Jesus was doing. If he did, Satan would destroy his own kingdom and rule over lives. Jesus was arguing that it was an absolute impossibility that He had come from anywhere other than from God Himself. "What fellowship...hath righteousness with unrightousness? And what communion hath light and darkness? And what concord hath Christ with Belial? (2 Cor.6:14-15).

Christ was saying that His works and power had to be of God. They could not possibly be of Satan nor of any source other than God Himself. Three things show this.

1. His works were too numerous (Jn.21:25).

2. His works were too supernatural—too immense and beyond any known human power—to be explained by any source other than the power of God Himself.

3. His works were too good, too virtuous, and too effective in delivering men to be from any source other than God.

> **"Forasmuch then as the children are partakers of flesh and blood, he also himself likewise took part of the same; that through death he might destroy him that had the power of death, that is, the devil; and deliver them who through fear of death were all their lifetime subject to bondage" (Heb.2:14-15).**

ILLUSTRATION:

The works of Jesus Christ were greater than any man who has ever lived. And yet His work is ignored, denied or downplayed by so many.

Some years ago, the distinguished publishing house of Grosset & Dunlap brought together a panel of 28 educators and historians and asked them to select the hundred most significant events of history, then list those events in order of importance. After months of labor, the panel reported that they considered the most significant event of history to be the discovery of America. In second place was the invention of movable type by Gutenberg. Eleven different events tied for third place, and five events tied for fourth place. The events tying for fourth were the writing of the Constitution of our country, the development of ether, the development of the x-ray, the discovery of the airplane, and the life of Jesus of Nazareth. Jesus tied for fourth.[2]

Do you give Jesus and His works their rightful place in your life?

Christ did not come to build up the kingdom of Satan and of darkness. The only dealings He had with Satan were twofold.

1. Christ broke the power and fear of Satan over lives.

"For this purpose the Son of God was manifested, that he might destroy the works of the devil" (1 Jn.3:8).

2. Christ destroyed the works of Satan as the arch rebel against God.

APPLICATION:
Note the strong lesson on division. No body of people can survive division. A divided people cannot stand. Too many people within churches have ignored the lesson: "If ye bite and devour one another, take heed that ye be not consumed one of another" (Gal.5:15; cp. 1 Cor.1:10f).

QUESTIONS:
1. Today many people still fail to acknowledge the supernatural power of God. Have you ever limited God's power by showing a lack of faith?
2. What is the greatest miracle that you have experienced or been touched by? Without this display of God's power, how would your life have been different?
3. What effect does a divided community of believers have upon the witness of Christ?

3. ARGUMENT 2: DENYING HIM IS INCONSISTENT AND ILLOGICAL (v.27-28).

1. Why are Jesus' claims and works denied while the claims and works of others are accepted? There were those who "cast out devils" in Jesus' day; there were exorcists who practiced the casting out of demons.

a. There were those who cast out devils in Christ's name, yet they did not follow Him (Mk.9:38).
b. There were Jewish exorcists who traveled about using the name of Jesus in a magical way (Acts 19:13f).
c. There were exorcists who were unfaithful to Christ (Mt.7:22).

Jesus was saying that to deny Him was inconsistent and illogical. The *good works* of other men were acknowledged, yet His *good works* were denied and attributed to evil. His works were the greatest works ever performed for men, and they far outnumbered the works of any man (Jn.21:25). How could His power and His works be of *evil* and

---

2 Bruce Thielemann. "*Christus Imperator.*" *Preaching Today.* (Carol Stream, IL: Christianity Today, Inc.), Tape 55.

the works of others be of *good*? His works were bound to be of God. If His works were the *good works* of God, then His claim to be the Messiah was bound to be true, for God would not give His power to a liar and a deceiver.

There is only one logical and consistent conclusion: Jesus' works are of the Spirit of God. This points to a critical fact: His claim is true. He is the Messiah and the kingdom of God has come to men. Any other position is illogical and inconsistent.

2. Christ's works are a sign of His Messiahship. His works are a sign that God's Spirit rests upon Him and that God's kingdom has come to man.

APPLICATION:
Christ pulls no punches in this argument. He is very clear and pointed: all unbelievers are inconsistent and illogical in their unbelief.

If we ascribe good works to others and say that they are blessed by God, why do we not do the same with Christ, especially when He did so many great works with such phenomenal power? Why do we not say that He is of God and blessed as no other person is blessed by God? Some do profess such. Why then do so many say His claim to be the Savior is not true?

Christ is saying that such a position is illogical and inconsistent, for God could not bless a liar and a deceiver—especially with such supernatural and phenomenal power.

"But I have greater witness than that of John: for the works which the Father hath given me to finish, the same works that I do, bear witness of me, that the Father hath sent me" (Jn.5:36).

QUESTIONS:
1. An unbeliever who opposes Christ refuses to adequately credit Him for His good works. Why are these same people quick to heap praise on other men who do good things?
2. People who claim to live according to "logic' miss the mark if they deny Christ. What are the differences between God's logic and man's logic?

4. ARGUMENT 3: A STRONG MAN HAS TO BE BOUND BEFORE HIS PROPERTY CAN BE TAKEN (v.29).

Satan is the strong man; Christ is the invader who enters Satan's house to free those imprisoned by Satan. Note: Christ is arguing that He is far from being in alliance with Satan; He is actually in opposition to him. He is entering the "evil house" or domain (territory) of Satan and taking his (human) goods. He is turning men "from darkness to light, and from the power of Satan to God, that they may receive forgiveness of sin" (Acts 26:18). God "delivers us from the power of darkness" (Col.1:13).

When did Christ invade Satan's house and bind him?

1. Satan was bound somewhat during Jesus' temptations in the wilderness. For the first time in history, Satan confronted Someone whom he could not lead away from God. After the wilderness experience Satan was set back, His power shaken. The Man Christ Jesus had withstood the heaviest barrage of temptation ever launched. Satan was bound to sense the impending *binding* that was to come.

"For this purpose the Son of God was manifested, that he might destroy the works of the devil" (1 Jn.3:8).

2. Satan was bound even more as He confronted Jesus throughout His life with temptation after temptation (Mt.16:23). Jesus stood fast, resisted, and overcame the temptations, conquering and binding Satan more and more each time.

"Which of you convinceth me of sin? And if I say the truth, why do ye not believe me?" (Jn.8:46).

3. Satan was bound dramatically after Jesus' Garden of Gethsemane experience. Jesus was tempted to take another route other than the cross, yet He obeyed God perfectly.

"For consider him that endured such contradiction of sinners against himself, lest ye be wearied and faint in your minds. Ye have not yet resisted unto blood, striving against sin [the Garden of Gethsemane]" (Heb.12:3-4).

4. Satan was bound in a completed sense at the cross. Christ had secured *perfect righteousness*—He had never sinned. Therefore He was the Ideal Man, the Perfect Man. As the Ideal Man His righteousness and death could stand for and embrace all men who would place their lives into His keeping. Satan's house of evil and sin was broken, completely broken.

"For he hath made him to be sin for us, who knew no sin; that we might be made the righteousness of God in him" (2 Cor.5:21).

5. Satan shall be bound climactically and forever at the end of time. Both the earth and the heavens shall be made anew and established forever in perfection—established without Satan and his "evil house" carrying on their evil work. (Cp. 2 Pt.3:3-18.)

"And then shall that Wicked be revealed, whom the Lord shall consume with the spirit of his mouth, and shall destroy with the brightness of his coming" (2 Th.2:8).

QUESTIONS:
1. As you study Scripture, note that Christ bound Satan step by step. What lessons can you draw from this as you resist Satan's power?
2. If Christ bound Satan at the cross, why does Satan appear to be unbound in the world today?

5. ARGUMENT 4: NEUTRALITY IS IMPOSSIBLE—ONE IS EITHER WITH CHRIST OR AGAINST CHRIST (v.30).

A person is either with Christ or against Christ. This could be a picture of a shepherd or a farmer. Each is involved in gathering—the one gathering sheep and the other gathering the harvest. Each can also become guilty of scattering—the one scattering the sheep and the other scattering the harvest.

Christ says two things.
1. A person stands with Him, believing and trusting Him, or else a person stands against Him in unbelief and distrust.
2. A person works with Him in gathering others, or else works against Him by scattering others (see note—Mt.12:22-24).

Note two significant facts.
1. Neutrality is impossible. There are only two sides: with Christ or against Christ.
2. Refraining from evil is not enough. A person must gather with Christ. A person must constantly be doing good. If we do not gather, we scatter.

"For he that is not against us is on our part" (Mk.9:40).

MATTHEW 12:22-30

ILLUSTRATION:

Think about this: the most loving thing God can do for the unrepentant unbeliever who dies without Christ is to sentence him to hell. Why? Because heaven would be so uncomfortable for him. A great preacher of a former generation, Charles Spurgeon, stated it so well:

> *Let me imagine a man entering heaven without a change of heart. He comes within the gates. He hears a sonnet. He's shocked! It is to the praise of his enemy. He sees a throne, and on it sits One who is glorious; but it is his enemy. He walks streets of gold, but those streets belong to his enemy. He sees hosts of angels, but those hosts are the servants of his enemy. He is in an enemy's house, for he is at enmity with God. He could not join the song, for he would not know the tune. There he would stand, silent, motionless, till Christ would say, with a voice louder then ten thousand thunders, "What doest thou here? Enemies at a marriage banquet? Enemies in the children's house? Enemies in heaven? Get thee gone! Depart, ye cursed, into the everlasting fires of hell!"*[3]

God allows no fence sitters—either you are for Him or against Him.

QUESTIONS:

1. A person cannot sit on the fence of compromise. Each person must choose to stand either for or against Christ. On which side of the fence have you chosen to stand? Why?
2. Some people want to be true Christian believers, but they are hesitant to take sides against the world. What is the fate of a life of neutrality?

SUMMARY:

For nearly two-thousand years, people have been slandering Jesus Christ. They refuse to believe the truth about Him, that He is the Messiah. Like Christ, we also need to keep calm and remain level-headed as we go about proving that He is of God, the true Messiah. It is important that every believer be able to answer any attacks against the deity of Christ.

1. Jesus proved His Messianic power by healing a devil-possessed man who was both blind and dumb.
2. Argument 1: a divided allegiance destroys. This is a universal truth. Division leads to separation and ruin. A divided kingdom, city, or house cannot stand. It fights and destroys itself. Satan is not going to empower anyone to deliver people from evil—not time after time as Jesus was doing. If he did, Satan would destroy his own kingdom and rule over lives.
3. Argument 2: denying Him is inconsistent and illogical. Jesus was saying that to deny Him was inconsistent and illogical. The *good works* of other men were acknowledged, yet His *good works* were denied and attributed to evil. His works were the greatest works ever performed for men, and they far outnumbered the works of any man (Jn.21:25).
4. Argument 3: a strong man has to be bound before his property can be taken. Satan is the strong man; Christ is the invader who enters Satan's house to free those imprisoned by Satan.
5. Argument 4: neutrality is impossible—one is either with Christ or against Christ.

---

3 *INFOsearch Sermon Illustrations* (Arlington, TX: The Computer Assistant, 1-888-868-9029, 1986-1996).

MATTHEW 12:22-30

PERSONAL JOURNAL NOTES
(Reflection & Response)

1. The most important thing that I learned from this lesson was:

2. The area that I need to work on the most is:

3. I can apply this lesson to my life by:

4. Closing Statement of Commitment:

E. Defense 5: A Man's Words Determine His Destiny, 12:31-37
(Mk.3:28-30; Lk.11:14-16)

31 Wherefore I say unto you, All manner of sin and blasphemy shall be forgiven unto men: but the blasphemy against the Holy Ghost shall not be forgiven unto men.

32 And whosoever speaketh a word against the Son of man, it shall be forgiven him: but whosoever speaketh against the Holy Ghost, it shall not be forgiven him, neither in this world, neither in the world to come.

33 Either make the tree good, and his fruit good; or else make the tree corrupt, and his fruit corrupt: for the tree is known by his fruit.

34 O generation of vipers, how can ye, being evil, speak good things? for out of the abundance of the heart the mouth speaketh.

35 A good man out of the good treasure of the heart bringeth forth good things: and an evil man out of the evil treasure bringeth forth evil things.

36 But I say unto you, That every idle word that men shall speak, they shall give account thereof in the day of judgment.

37 For by thy words thou shalt be justified, and by thy words thou shalt be condemned.

1. Blasphemous words against the Holy Spirit are unforgiven
- a. The warning
  - 1) All is forgiven except this one sin
  - 2. Even sin against Christ is forgiven
- b. The terrible result
  - 1) Unforgiven in this world
  - 2) Unforgiven in the next world

2. Words either confess or deny Christ
- a. A demand: Make Christ good or bad
- b. Christ is known by His fruit

3. Words expose the heart
- a. Expose some as vipers
  - 1) Bc. they are evil
  - 2) Bc. words are out of the heart
- b. Expose a good man: A good heart that does good things
- c. Expose an evil man: An evil heart that does evil things

4. Words must be accounted for
- a. Every idle word
- b. In the day of judgment

5. Words determine a man's destiny
- a. Words justify him
- b. Words condemn him

Section VIII
THE MESSIAH'S DEFENSE OF HIMSELF AGAINST OPPONENTS, Matthew 12:1-50

Study 5: **DEFENSE 5: A MAN'S WORDS DETERMINE HIS DESTINY**

Text: **Matthew 12:31-37**

Aim: To carefully measure each word you speak, using Christ as your role model.

Memory Verse:

"But I say unto you, That every idle word that men shall speak, they shall give account thereof in the day of judgment" (Matthew 12:36).

INTRODUCTION

Everyone has experienced the embarrassment of speaking out of turn, of saying something that aroused discomfort. Who has not…

- said unkind words about someone who accidentally overheard it
- said words that were spoken in anger and cut the heart of the listener
- said something that betrayed a confidence

- said words that were regretted because they could not be taken back before the damage was done

The urgent goal of every believer must be to control what comes out of the mouth. Words are extremely important, in fact so important that they determine a man's destiny (Mt.12:37). Our words either bless God or curse God; bless men or curse men (Jas.3:9). The tongue is said to be "a world of iniquity," a "fire," and "an unruly evil, full of deadly poison" (Jas.3:6, 8). Christ said, "Not that which goeth into the mouth defileth a man; but [the words] which cometh out of the mouth, this defileth a man" (Mt.15:11).

There is a heavy responsibility placed upon man for the words he speaks.

OUTLINE:

1. Blasphemous words against the Holy Spirit are unforgiven (v.31-32).
2. Words either confess or deny Christ (v.33).
3. Words expose the heart (v.34-35).
4. Words must be accounted for (v.36).
5. Words determine a man's destiny (v.37).

1. BLASPHEMOUS WORDS AGAINST THE HOLY SPIRIT ARE UNFORGIVEN (v.31-32).

The warning is unmistakable. Note these facts.

1. It is a *sin of the tongue* that is unpardonable. This fact alone points to the seriousness of all *sins of the tongue*.

2. Note why Christ gave the warning. He warns...

- to strike fear in the hearts of those who border on committing the unpardonable sin (Mt.12:23-24; cp. 23:13)
- to stir a reverence and repentance toward God (Mt.12:33, 37)

3. The one sin for which there is no forgiveness is not a sin against Christ, but a sin against the Holy Spirit (Mt.12:31-32). Why? There is one simple reason given in Scripture. The Holy Spirit is the Person who works in the heart of man; it is He who "convicts the world of sin, and of righteousness, and of judgment...." (Jn.16:8-11). There is a single word that is very descriptive of His work: *conviction*. A man sees, feels, or hears about God's goodness and love and of his own need to surrender to God. The Spirit takes those evidences and uses them as convictions. He convicts a man's heart to believe. A man may go on and on...

- insisting on his own way
- refusing to acknowledge God and surrender his life to God
- choosing to be blind to what he sees, feels, and hears (the convictions of the Spirit)

Such a man eventually becomes so hardened that he cannot recognize God's truth and goodness. He reaches a point of such hardness that he no longer sees God or feels God or hears God. This man has blasphemed God's Spirit and counted His convictions as worthless. He has abused, reviled, neglected, ignored, and hardened his heart to the promptings of God's Spirit permanently. He has blasphemed God's Spirit and such blasphemy is unforgivable, Christ says.

4. Note what the unpardonable sin is. In the simplest and clearest of terms, it is *stubborn rejection, stiff-necked refusal, obstinate unbelief*. This results in *a dead spirit* and apparently *a rooted malice* (Mt.12:23-24; cp. 23:13.)

When the Spirit convicts a man to turn to God, and that man...

- continually rejects the conviction, his rejection becomes stubborn
- continually refuses, his refusal becomes stiff-necked
- continually disbelieves, his unbelief becomes obstinate

That man deadens his spirit against the convictions of the Spirit and develops a rooted malice against God. He insists on his own way too long and refuses to surrender to God while his heart is still soft enough to be touched.

What a warning to creatures of conditioning and habit—a warning against conditioning ourselves to reject God over and over again. And what a call to stir a reverence and repentance toward God! How much we need to surrender to God while our hearts are soft enough to be touched!

5. In trying to determine just who it is that commits the unpardonable sin, two things are known.

⇒ The blood of Christ cleanses from every sin. There is not a single sin that cannot be forgiven—except obstinate unbelief against the convictions of the Holy Spirit (Mt.12:31-32).

⇒ There is no hope for salvation except through Christ and the convicting power of the Holy Spirit.

Therefore, to reject or blaspheme the convicting power of the Holy Spirit is to deprive a person of salvation through Christ. Of course, a man who is concerned about having committed the unpardonable sin has not. His very concern shows that he can still come to Christ.

APPLICATION:
This is the glorious grace of God: all manner of sin (any sin, every sin, even blasphemy—even a word spoken against Christ) will be forgiven. This shows the humiliation that both Christ and the Father are willing to bear through the denial and cursing of men. Paul, the *old* Saul of Tarsus who was a blasphemer and murderer of early believers, was forgiven by God and greatly used by God (Acts 9:1; cp. 8:1).

"In whom we have redemption through his blood, the forgiveness of sins, according to the riches of his grace" (Eph.1:7).

6. The terrible result is unmistakable. All sin is forgiven—*EXCEPT ONE*. Blasphemy against the Spirit of God is not forgiven. It is not forgiven in this world nor in the next world. In this world, there will be no *peace of conscience*, no *sense of forgiveness, no absolution*. In the next world, a man will stand guilty before God.

"But he that shall blaspheme against the Holy Ghost hath never forgiveness, but is in danger of eternal damnation" (Mk.3:29; see also Heb.6:6; 10:26; 12:17).

QUESTIONS:
1. What traits might you find in a person's heart who sins against the Holy Spirit? What can you do to guard yourself from allowing any of these things to enter your heart?
2. In simple terms, exactly what is "the unpardonable sin"? Why is it called "the unpardonable sin"?
3. Why is it impossible for a born-again believer to commit the unpardonable sin? When you sin, what solution has God offered?

2. WORDS EITHER CONFESS OR DENY CHRIST (v.33).

Christ is the tree in this verse, referring back to verses 27-28. What Christ was saying is twofold.

1. Christ was making a demand: "Decide. Make Christ [Messiah] either good or bad. Quit vacillating and swaying with the wind. Judge me to be good and my fruit

good, or else judge me to be corrupt and my fruit corrupt. I am either good, that is, I am who I say I am, the Messiah, the Savior of the world; or else I am bad, a deceiver and a liar, out to lead people away from God into another path of human reasoning. Who am I? Judge. Decide. For I am known by my works even as a tree is known by its fruits."

2. Christ is known by His fruit. He was saying, "There is no middle ground. Neutrality is impossible (v.29). You are either with me or against me, so quit playing the hypocrite and being half-hearted about me. Make a decision. Make and declare me *good* [of value] for you and your life or else declare me *corrupt* [a deceiver and liar] for you and your life, I am known by my fruit, so either speak for me as good or else speak for me as corrupt."

Note how strong Christ was in this demand, in fact, how strong He was throughout this whole passage. How thin the ice upon which so many of us stand! How close to the precipice we are with our thoughts of waiting and indecision.

> **"No servant can serve two masters: for either he will hate the one, and love the other; or else he will hold to the one, and despise the other. Ye cannot serve God and mammon" (Lk.16:13).**

QUESTIONS:

1. Every person has to make a decision concerning his or her relationship with Christ. Why is it impossible for a person to "sit on the fence" and seek out the middle ground of compromise?
2. What fruit have you observed in Christ's life that would convince you to choose Him above all else?

3. WORDS EXPOSE THE HEART (v.34-35).

Christ says that a man's words expose his heart, the kind of man he is. A man's words expose one of three things about him:

⇒ that he has the heart of a viper (v.34)
⇒ that he has the heart of a good man (v.35)
⇒ that he has the heart of an evil man (v.35)

The idea is that words come out of an overflowing heart: "Out of the abundance [overflow] of the heart the mouth speaketh."

⇒ A man's words expose his true nature: what he is like beneath the surface.
⇒ A man's words expose what he is down deep within his heart: his motives, desires, and ambitions.
⇒ A man's words expose his true character: good or bad, kind or cruel.
⇒ A man's words expose his mind, what he thinks: pure or impure thoughts, clean or dirty thoughts.
⇒ A man's words expose his spirit, what he believes and pursues: the legitimate or illegitimate, the intelligent or ignorant, the true or false, the beneficial or wasteful.

> **"Take heed, brethren, lest there be in any of you an evil heart of unbelief, in departing from the living God" (Heb.3:12).**

ILLUSTRATION:

Without fail, the heart will eventually reveal what is inside a person.

> *She had never been fishing before, but to spend time with Willie, Lucy told him she loved to fish. He was happy to find a woman who could share his obsession with fishing gear, drop-offs, and water temperature.*
>
> *When they got to Willie's favorite fishing spot, the fish weren't biting but*

Lucy didn't care. The sun was shining and the water lapped gently at the sides of the boat. To be with Willie was all that mattered. After an hour of sharing his fishing patience, Lucy said, "Willie, you know that red and white thing you put on my line?" "You mean the bobber?" he replied. "Yeah, how much did it cost?" "Oh, about 50 cents." "Well, I owe you 50 cents because mine just sank." The truth was out. Lucy's words revealed that she actually knew very little about fishing.

Sooner or later our words unmask the true condition of our heart.[1]

APPLICATION:
As the old saying goes, "What's down in the well comes up in the bucket!" We act and behave and do things because of what we are within. Our hearts (what we are within) determine our behavior. This says something extremely important. *Reformation*—reforming behavior and changing the outside—is not the answer to the ills of human nature or of society. *Transformation* of the heart, of the *inner being* of man, is the answer. Human nature cannot be *made* good; it has to be transformed, that is, regenerated or born again. Only God can reach into the inner recesses of man's spirit and change his heart.

Note: the answer to the world's problems is not political, legal, military, or even religious. It is spiritual—a spiritual change of man's heart.

"But that on the good ground are they, which in an honest and good heart, having heard the word, keep it, and bring forth fruit with patience" (Lk.8:15).

QUESTIONS:
1. Looking back over the previous week, what have you said that you wish could be taken back? Why is it impossible to retrieve words that have been spoken in haste?
2. What can you tell about a person's life when his words are examined?
3. If a machine could be hooked up to your heart and to your mouth, what would it reveal about you?
   ___I tend to speak before I think.
   ___I tend to think before I speak.
   ___I don't really mean most of what I say.
   ___I'm very good at saying one thing but thinking or doing another.
   ___I'm transparent—what you hear is what I'm thinking.

4. WORDS MUST BE ACCOUNTED FOR (v.36).

All idle words must be accounted for in the day of judgment. Idle means negative, unfruitful, barren, ineffective. The term "idle words" conveys very well what Christ means.

APPLICATION:
Note several lessons.
1) God hears and records every idle word that we speak.

"There is not a word in my tongue, but, lo, O Lord, thou knowest it altogether" (Ps.139:4).

2) Unprofitable words make us, and show us to be, unprofitable servants.

---

1 *INFOsearch Sermon Illustrations* (Arlington, TX: The Computer Assistant, 1-888-868-9029, 1986-1996).

3) Our idle words must be confessed to God and His mercy must be requested, for we are guilty of this unprofitable and wasteful sin.
4) Scripture flows with charge after charge governing the tongue.

"Let us therefore follow after the things which make for peace, and things wherewith one may edify another" (Ro.14:19).

QUESTIONS:

1. On an average day, how many idle words (negative, unfruitful, barren, ineffective) do you speak?
   ___Few to none.
   ___More than a few.
   ___I can't count that high.
2. Why are idle words so hard to control? What kinds of situations tend to cause you to speak idle words?
3. Can you think of the idle words that you speak most often? What practical thing can you do to control idle words in your life?

5. WORDS DETERMINE A MAN'S DESTINY (v.37).

Our words will either justify or condemn us.

APPLICATION 1:

This same law given by God is common to man's law. A man is judged to be guilty or not guilty based on testimony, that is, by his words.

Kind, gracious, loving, edifying, profitable words will testify for us and justify us in the day of judgment. Ugly, dirty, filthy, angry, spiteful, gossiping, grumbling, murmuring words will testify against us and condemn us in the day of judgment.

"Death and life are in the power of the tongue" (Pr.18:21).

APPLICATION 2:

Two things are said about a man who "bridleth not his tongue" (Jas.1:26).
1) His religion is vain, false, empty, a lie, hypocritical.
2) He deceives his own heart.

"If any man among you seem to be religious, and bridleth not his tongue, but deceiveth his own heart, this man's religion is vain" (Jas.1:26).

ILLUSTRATION:

It takes a wise person to know when to keep his mouth closed. No matter how much a person knows, how many languages he speaks, how important he is, the wise person knows how to control his words. Is it any wonder that silence is golden?

In his book with Ken Blanchard, Everyone's a Coach, Don Shula tells of losing his temper near an open microphone during a televised game with the Los Angeles Rams. Millions of viewers were surprised and shocked by Shula's explicit profanity. Letters soon arrived from all over the country, voicing the disappointment of many who had respected the coach for his integrity.

Shula could have given excuses, but he didn't. Everyone who included a return address received a personal apology. He closed each letter by stating, "I value your respect and will do my best to earn it again."

MATTHEW 12:31-37

There are two ways to gain respect. One is to act nobly. The other is, when you fail to do so, to make no excuses.[2]

QUESTIONS:

1. What is the relationship between your tongue and respect? Why do your words have the power to either justify or condemn you?
2. If words are so powerful, why do people use words so carelessly? Do you have the control of your tongue that you should have? How can you get better control?

SUMMARY:

Do you control your tongue? This is one of the greatest tests of spiritual maturity. Far too many people settle for lives that are characterized by loose tongues—tongues that are careless, negative, condemning. But the words we speak are a matter of life and death, determining our destiny. Jesus reminds us of this very thing. We need to remember…

1. Blasphemous words against the Holy Spirit are unforgiven.
2. Words either confess or deny Christ.
3. Words expose the heart.
4. All idle words must be accounted for.
5. Words determine a man's destiny.

PERSONAL JOURNAL NOTES
(Reflection & Response)

1. The most important thing that I learned from this lesson was:

2. The area that I need to work on the most is:

3. I can apply this lesson to my life by:

4. Closing Statement of Commitment:

---

[2] *Leadership Journal.* (Carol Streal, IL: Christianity Today, Inc.), Vol.17, No.1.

F. Defense 6: Messiah's Answer to an Evil Generation or to Apostates, 12:38-45
(Lk.11:24-26; 29-32)

1 An evil generation sought a sign
- a. Jesus condemned His generation as evil & adulterous
- b. Jesus gave one sign
    - 1) The sign: Symbolized by Jonah
    - 2) The sign: His death & resurrection

2 An evil generation was condemned because it did not repent
- a. Nineveh will testify against
- b. Why: There is now a greater messenger than Jonah
- c. Result: Condemnation

38 Then certain of the scribes and of the Pharisees answered, saying, Master, we would see a sign from thee.

39 But he answered and said unto them, An evil and adulterous generation seeketh after a sign; and there shall no sign be given to it, but the sign of the prophet Jonas:

40 For as Jonas was three days and three nights in the whale's belly; so shall the Son of man be three days and three nights in the heart of the earth.

41 The men of Nineveh shall rise in judgment with this generation, and shall condemn it: because they repented at the preaching of Jonas; and, behold, a greater than Jonas is here.

42 The queen of the south shall rise up in the judgment with this generation, and shall condemn it: for she came from the uttermost parts of the earth to hear the wisdom of Solomon; and, behold, a greater than Solomon is here.

43 When the unclean spirit is gone out of a man, he walketh through dry places, seeking rest, and findeth none.

44 Then he saith, I will return into my house from whence I came out; and when he is come, he findeth it empty, swept, and garnished.

45 Then goeth he, and taketh with himself seven other spirits more wicked than himself, and they enter in and dwell there: and the last state of that man is worse than the first. Even so shall it be also unto this wicked generation.

3 An evil generation was condemned because it did not seek the greater wisdom
- a. The queen of Sheba will testify against
- b. Why: There is now a greater One than Solomon to impart the truth

4 An evil generation followed a false religion—that of self-reformation
- a. Illustration: A parable
    - 1) Man reforms his life
    - 2) Man fails to fill his life with Christ
- b. Result
    - 1) Greater depravity
    - 2) End condition is worse
- c. Point: A generation that rejects Christ is fit for the takeover of evil

Section VIII
THE MESSIAH'S DEFENSE OF HIMSELF AGAINST OPPONENTS, Matthew 12:1-50

Study 6: **DEFENSE 6: MESSIAH'S ANSWER TO AN EVIL GENERATION OR TO APOSTATES**

Text: **Matthew 12:38-45**

Aim: To be strong and clear in your motives for following Christ.

Memory Verse:

"But without faith *it is* impossible to please *him:* for he that cometh to God must believe that he is, and *that* he is a rewarder of them that diligently seek him" (Hebrews 11:6).

MATTHEW 12:38-45

INTRODUCTION

"Lord, just give me a sign and I'll believe you!" This negotiating point is used by countless people around the world every day. Not willing to accept what God has already revealed, the skeptic always wants more proof.

> *A traveler was driving down a back road and came face to face with a sign that read, "Road Closed." The road ahead looked fine to him, so he quickly concluded that the sign was no longer valid and drove on. After a few miles he came to a bridge that was washed out, so he had to turn around and retrace his route. When he reached the point where the warning sign stood he read these words scrawled on the back: "Welcome Back. See other side for further instructions!"*

Such is the nature of man. Even when things are clearly spelled out, men frequently brush aside the obvious, expecting to get special instructions that apply just to them.

There is within the heart of every person a desire to be special and to be treated specially. This desire can be good or it can be bad. What is within the heart makes the difference.

For example, in dealing with God it is good to want a special relationship with Him or a special call or a special gift. However, it is evil to seek special or spectacular signs. Christ is very clear on this point. Why? Because God has given every sign that could be needed in Christ Himself.

OUTLINE:

1. An evil generation sought a sign (v.38-40).
2. An evil generation was condemned because it did not repent (v.41).
3. An evil generation was condemned because it did not seek the greater wisdom (v.42).
4. An evil generation followed a false religion—that of reformation (v.43-45).

1. AN EVIL GENERATION SOUGHT A SIGN (v.38-40).

Paul said, "The Jews require a sign" (1 Cor.1:22). And they did; they always required supernatural signs from any prophet or messenger who claimed to be from God. Six things should be noted.

1. This is the same type of situation that Jesus faced in His wilderness experience: the temptation to prove His Messiahship by some spectacular sign.

2. The Jews wanted more than the signs of miracles. They wanted *a sign from heaven*, apparently some sensational event occurring in the sky which would reveal beyond doubt that Christ was the promised Messiah (Mt.16:1; Mk.8:11; Lk.11:16). Note the words "from thee." They wanted the sign to appear at a given moment by His command, not some freak spectacular event happening accidentally in the future that He might claim as a sign.

3. There were at least two reasons why the Jews required a sign.
   a. Their religion was one of signs and miracles. Their religion had been given by God Himself and established by the miraculous acts of the prophets of God. A quick survey of the Old Testament will show this. Thus, anyone who claimed to be of God had to prove his credentials by what the Jews considered some "sign" from God.
   b. Jesus had come to supersede or fulfill the religion that had been built upon supernatural signs (Mt.5:17). The Jews were asking what His signs or credentials were to do this.

> **"And others, tempting him, sought of him a sign from heaven" (Lk.11:16).**

4. The Jews were totally unjustified in seeking additional signs from Jesus. There had been sign after sign, miracle after miracle, work after work—sufficient to lead any man to the firm belief: "Truly, this man is the Son of God" (Mk.15:39; cp. Acts 2:22). A lack of signs was not their problem. Their problem was twofold.

a. They just did not believe and did not want to believe. They were obstinate in their unbelief.
b. They did not understand the love and the faith of God, that is, the true religion of God. They failed to see what God was after: faith and love, not signs and works. God wants a man simply to believe and love Him because of who He is and because of what He has done for man. The true religion of God is not a religion of works and signs, but of faith and love in Christ Jesus, His own Son.

5. Those who sought a sign were called an evil and adulterous generation. The reason is simple. They were apostates, going after the false gods of works and signs instead of seeking the God of faith and love. In seeking after signs and works, they were committing spiritual whoredom, that is, turning from the true God and His Messiah to the false gods of signs and works. (Note: it is human reason that seeks after signs and works and proofs. But the spirit of man seeks after belief and trust and love—the spiritual qualities that bind life together and make sense of life in all its facets.)

6. No sign whatsoever will be given to any generation to prove conclusively that Jesus is the Messiah but one: the sign of Jonah. The sign of Jonah pointed to the resurrection of Christ from the dead (Mt.12:39-40.) The resurrection is the *great proof* that Jesus is the Messiah, the Savior of the world. He is "declared to be the son of God with power...by the resurrection from the dead" (Ro.1:4).

APPLICATION 1:

Note two significant lessons.

1) Christ will hear and answer prayer, meeting the true needs of His people. But He will not fulfill the selfish lusts of people nor satisfy the curiosity of the carnal. He will not answer the arguments of the unbelieving by spectacular signs (Jas.4:1-3). God is through with signs. He has given the ultimate in signs; He has given His Son: His death, burial, and resurrection.

> **"Him, being delivered by the determinate counsel and foreknowledge of God, ye have taken, and by wicked hands have crucified and slain: whom God hath raised up, having loosed the pains of death: because it was not possible that he should be holden of it" (Acts 2:23-24).**

2) Note the word "Master." Not all who call Him, "Lord, Lord," shall enter into the kingdom of heaven. Many profess, but few possess. "Many are called, but few are chosen" (Mt.22:14; cp. 20:16.)

APPLICATION 2:

Men try to *prescribe* how God should act. They insist and beg God to do something, to give a sign; and if God will do it, they promise to serve God with renewed commitment. Note two things.

1) God does not work by signs. He works by faith and love. He wants men to believe Him because He has promised, not because some spectacular sign occurs. He may sometimes grant a sign because the issue is not covered in the Word of God or because of the weakness of a believer, but signs are not His way of dealing with men.
2) We should not prescribe to God, trying to dictate how He is to deal with us. God has given us *three enormous helps* that are more than sufficient in meeting our needs: His Word, prayer, and the Holy Spirit. Think—what more can God do?

MATTHEW 12:38-45

QUESTIONS:

1. Have you ever been tempted to demand that God "prove" something to you? Why is it wrong to demand anything of God? Is it ever acceptable to ask for a sign?
2. People of all generations have experimented with the supernatural—seeking and finding false gods. Why have their experiences failed to meet their spiritual needs?

A CLOSER LOOK #1
(12:39) **Adulterous**: spiritual adultery and unfaithfulness; apostate; spiritual whoredom; seeking and carousing with other gods; worshipping and giving one's love to false gods. The generation was committing spiritual adultery against God. However, the word "adultery" could also mean that the people of the day were so given over to sexual sins that they could be characterized as an *adulterous* generation. (Cp. Judg.2:17; 1 Chron.5:25; Ps.106:39; Ezk.6:9; 20:30; 23:35; Hos.4:12; 5:4; 9:1.)

A CLOSER LOOK #2
(12:40) **Heart of the Earth**: the place of departed spirits; the abode of the dead.

2. AN EVIL GENERATION WAS CONDEMNED BECAUSE IT DID NOT REPENT (v.41).

Note several things.

1. A whole generation can be evil and adulterous—so much so that its very lifestyle can be characterized as "evil and adulterous" (v.39).

2. The Ninevites are a prime example of *repentance* and of just how essential repentance is. A person must repent or else he will be condemned.

3. There is a day of judgment out in the future. Note the words "in judgment" (v.41) and "in the judgment" (v.42). Both phrases point to a definite day of judgment.

4. The Ninevites' repentance will be used as a testimony in the day of judgment. The people of Nineveh are the prime example of people turning to God from the depth of sin. They had sunk into the pit of sin, as deeply as a people can sink, yet they repented at the preaching of Jonah.

5. The Ninevites' repentance leaves all *without excuse*. Why? There is no one who has stooped any lower into sin than they did, yet they repented. They show that anyone can turn to God from sin no matter how terrible the sin is. No man has any excuse for not turning to God.

6. Christ claims to be greater than Jonah. He claims to be the greatest messenger who has ever come, the Messiah Himself. Therefore, all men are definitely without excuse. The worst sinners in history repented at the preaching of a mere man, the prophet Jonah. Now the Messiah Himself, God's own Son, has come; and He has preached and announced: "the kingdom of God" itself is at hand. Every person is now, beyond question, without excuse.

> **"I tell you, Nay: but, except ye repent, ye shall all likewise perish" (Lk.13:3).**

APPLICATION 1:
Note several things about Nineveh.
1) Nineveh was an ungodly and wicked city (Jonah 1:2).
2) God sent a prophet (Jonah) to warn Nineveh.

3) "The people of Nineveh believed God" and repented when the prophet preached.

Christ applies the experience of Nineveh to the world.
1) The world is an ungodly and wicked place.
2) God sent His prophet (Jesus Christ, His own Son) to warn the world in love.
3) The people of the world "do not believe God" and do not repent when the message of Christ is preached.

APPLICATION 2:
Note what Christ is saying. "You asked for a sign. I am God's sign."
1) "The Ninevites recognized God's message when Jonah preached, and they believed God and repented."
2) "You do not recognize me. You are so blind, evil, and adulterous that you cannot even see One who is greater than Jonah. God has given you the greater sign, the Messiah Himself; yet you do not see or hear."
3) "The Ninevites will rise up in judgment and be used as a testimony against you."

QUESTIONS:
1. In simple terms, what is repentance?
2. Why is repentance such a challenge to a person living in sin?
   a. Looking back at history, what happened to nations who refused to repent?
   b. Can you think of any nations that did repent before God?
   c. Where does your nation stand in regards to repentance?

3. AN EVIL GENERATION IS CONDEMNED BECAUSE IT DID NOT SEEK THE GREATER WISDOM (v.42).

There are several important lessons about the Queen of Sheba and Christ in this verse.

1. The Queen of Sheba is a prime example of an individual *seeking after* some person who knows the truth. She demonstrates just how important it is to seek someone who can *share the truth*. In her search, she had to seek as diligently and go through as much as anyone else ever had to in seeking after the truth.
   a. She had a long and perilous search. She had to travel from "the uttermost parts of the earth" to seek the truth.
   b. She had heavy responsibilities. She was a queen with enormous duties and a busy schedule. As the Head of State, duty after duty demanded her time and presence and a whole kingdom depended upon her care; yet she let nothing stop her search for the truth.
   c. She was uncertain about her seeking. Her search was a gamble, uncertain in at least two senses.
      1) She could not be absolutely certain that Solomon was as wise in the truth as he was said to be. Reputations become exaggerated when spread by word of mouth. She knew this just as any wise person would know.
      2) She had no personal invitation to visit Solomon. Fame flatters men and causes them to become inaccessible in order to enhance their reputation of *busyness, heavy responsibility,* and *greatness*. She could not be sure he would see her or grant much time to her.
   d. She had to bear terrible prejudice. She was a woman in a man's world. In her day, women were nothing more than chattel property, possessed and used by men for their own pleasure as they so desired.

2. The Queen of Sheba's seeking will be used as a testimony in the day of judgment. Her diligent seeking—the unbelievable extremes and difficulties she overcame to find

one who knew the truth—stands as a testimony against all who fail to seek the truth.

3. The Queen of Sheba's seeking leaves all without excuse. There is no distance too far or perilous, no responsibility so important, no question or uncertainty so weighty, no prejudice or opposition so strong—nothing any greater than what the Queen of Sheba faced. Yet despite all, she sought the truth. It was the primary drive of her life. Thus, everyone is left without excuse.

> **"And I say unto you, Ask, and it shall be given you; seek, and ye shall find; knock, and it shall be opened unto you. For every one that asketh receiveth; and he that seeketh findeth; and to him that knocketh it shall be opened" (Lk.11:9-10).**

4. Christ claims to be greater than and superior to Solomon. He claims to be the Way, the Truth, and the Life—just imagine, *life itself* (Jn.14:6). He claims to be the One whom all men should seek and find—at any price—or else face condemnation.

Since Christ has come, all men are definitely without excuse. The most improbable person in all the world, the Queen of Sheba, went to the farthest extremes possible to seek after the truth. And she was seeking truth from a mere man, Solomon. Now the Messiah, the One who is "the truth" Himself, has come and revealed the truth of God. Every person is now, beyond question, without excuse.

> **"And the Word was made flesh, and dwelt among us, (and we beheld his glory, the glory as of the only begotten of the Father,) full of grace and truth" (Jn.1:14).**

APPLICATION:

The Queen of Sheba went to the farthest extremes humanly possible to seek one (Solomon) who might share the truth with her. She is a dynamic example that no effort, energy, or suffering should be spared in seeking the One who is the very embodiment of truth itself. If we are to know God, diligent seeking is demanded:

> **"He that cometh to God must believe that He is, and that He is a rewarder of them that diligently seek Him" (Heb.11:6. Cp. Mt.7:7; Pr.8:17).**

ILLUSTRATION:

Only those who really want to know the Lord will seek Him out. Likewise, those who want nothing to do with God will find what they are seeking: excuses.

> *Jim Smith went to church on Sunday morning. He heard the organist miss a note during the prelude, and he winced. He saw a teenager talking when everybody was supposed to be bowed in silent prayer. He felt like the usher was watching to see what he put in the offering plate and it made him boil. He caught the preacher making a slip of the tongue five times in the sermon by actual count. As he slipped out through the side door during the closing hymn, he muttered to himself, "Never again, what a bunch of clods and hypocrites!"*
>
> *Ron Jones went to church one Sunday morning. He heard the organist play an arrangement of "A Mighty Fortress" and he thrilled at the majesty of it. He heard a young girl take a moment in the service to speak her simple moving message of the difference her faith makes in her life. He was glad to see that this church was sharing in a special offering for the hungry children of Nigeria. He especially appreciated the sermon that Sunday—it answered a question that had bothered him for a long time. He thought as he walked out the doors of the church, "How can a man come here and not feel the presence of God?"*

Both men went to the same church, on the same Sunday morning. Each found what he was looking for.[1]

QUESTIONS:
1. What obstacles (either real or imagined) hinder people from seeking God's wisdom?
2. What practical traits can you glean from the Queen of Sheba's diligent search?
3. Every day, people ignore Christ and look for more modern ways to find the truth. What are some shortcomings of other pursuits—whether persons or reli-

4. AN EVIL GENERATION FOLLOWED A FALSE RELIGION—THAT OF REFORMATION (v.43-45).

How descriptive this picture is of a man who reforms and does not clean up his life!

1. Note what happens when a man casts the evil (spirit) out of his life.
   a. Many dry places are experienced. No matter where a person goes or what he does, there are many moments of dryness. No matter how diligently a person seeks, nothing seems to fill the void of the evil (spirit) put out of his life. There is always some dryness.
   b. The evil (spirit) that was in man and has been put aside seeks rest, but finds none. Man's evil spirit, when it is subdued or cast aside, becomes restless. It goes about in *restless wanderings*, yet it finds no rest.
   c. A man always experiences the craving of the evil to return. The evil (spirit) says, "I will return." Note the words "into my house." His house was the place that was so comfortable, that made him feel so secure and so at ease. The evil spirit is saying, "I will return to that which always looked so good and tasted so good and made me feel so good."

2. All the above has to do with a man reforming and cleaning up his life for a period of time. But note what happens when the evil (spirit) returns to the man and knocks on the door of his thoughts and pries at the windows of his desires.
   a. He finds the house empty *and unoccupied*.
   b. He finds the house swept and clean and put in order—ready for occupancy. The man has removed all the rubbish and swept out all the dirt. He has cleaned the house of his life, but he has not invited the *tenant* (the Lord Jesus Christ) to move in and occupy the premises.
3. Note what happens when the evil (spirit) finds the house empty and unoccupied.
   a. He swarms in and floods with more force than ever. The man indulges much more than before.
   b. He brings more evil with him—launching out and doing more evil than ever.
   c. He "dwells" there. It is unlikely he will ever clean his house again.

The reader should note that Jesus applies the truth of this parable not only to individuals, but to whole generations and societies as well. The answer to the evil and ills of society is not reformation—not the changing of the outside and external—but the transformation and regeneration of man's heart. It is the filling of the human heart with Christ Himself and with the acts of Christian love and care. The message and acts of love and care are to be carried to a world that is suffering and reeling in pain and war, and doomed to die without God.

> **"Howbeit then, when ye knew not God, ye did service unto them which by nature are no gods. But now, after that ye have known God, or rather are known of God, how turn ye again to the weak and beg-**

---

[1] *Illustrations Unlimited.* James S. Hewett, Editor, p. 409.

garly elements, whereunto ye desire again to be in bondage? Ye observe days, and months, and times, and years [religious ritual]" (Gal.4:8-10).

APPLICATION:
Note four lessons.

1) Evil can be conquered through Christ. It can be expelled, pushed back, and cast out of our lives; *but it cannot be destroyed or eliminated—not in this life*. Evil, even when put out of a life and turned away from, will always attack again. What is needed is *a supernatural power* to turn away from evil. That power is in Jesus Christ.
2) When evil is put out of a life, something else must be put in to take its place. What is that something? Jesus Christ. The love of Christ and His mission of redemption are to fill a man's heart and life. The world is weighed down with prejudice, war, wickedness, selfishness, pride, and power; and so many people are so needful. A man must cast the evil out of his life and replace it with Christ. When a man truly gives his life to Christ, he is filled with so much to do that he does not have time to think evil or do evil.
3) The church's answer to keep from losing people is true conversion and Christian action. A person must be truly converted *from* evil *to* Christ and then put to work. The converted believer must be *shown* and *directed* to his task in the Lord's church, then he must be led to serve Christ.
4) The church's task is twofold.
    a) To show people the desperate needs of the world and community, both nationally and internationally (Acts 1:8).
    b) To challenge and lead people to become personally involved in meeting those needs.

ILLUSTRATION:
The world's solution for dealing with sin is to paint over it, to call it something different, or ignore it by focusing upon other things. But no matter how hard the world tries to solve the problem of sin, sin continues to own multitudes of sinners.

Professor Cornelius Plantinga writes:

In a famous incident, the World Health Organization once tried to assist the residents of Borneo in the extermination of houseflies, which were widely suspected of spreading disease there. Officials sprayed the insides of Borneo houses with large quantities of DDT, an action that triggered an unforeseen and nearly disastrous sequence of events.

As the flies died, the local gecko lizards feasted on the fly corpses and sickened from the DDT concentrated in them. Their sick condition made the geckos easy prey for housecats, who ate their fill of the DDT-poisoned geckos and likewise sickened and died. The loss of the cats gave rats free run of people's houses.

When the rats began to devour house food and to threaten people with serious disease—in particular with bubonic plague—panicky government officials scrambled for solutions. At last they resorted to arranging for large numbers of foreign cats to be parachuted into the area in order to mend the break in the food chain.

Dr. Neil Anderson says "it's better to get rid of the garbage than to try to kill off the flies."[2]

---

2 *First Things*, Oct. 1994, p.26. SOURCE: *INFOsearch Sermon Illustrations* (Arlington, TX: The Computer Assistant, 1-888-868-9029, 1986-1996).

MATTHEW 12:38-45

Have you allowed garbage to accumulate in your life? If you are not careful, it will take over and ruin your life.

QUESTIONS:

1. What kind of *housecleaning* do you need to do in your heart to make it unappealing to an evil spirit?
2. Keeping a house clean involves many things: sweeping, dusting, washing, etc. What cleaning tools has God given to help you clean your heart?
3. Satan will quickly come and make himself at home in any life where Christ is not in residence. How would you describe your relationship with Satan?
   ___He is the owner of my heart (house).
   ___He is a renter with a long-term lease.
   ___He is a pesky houseguest who continues to make unwanted visits.
   ___He has no place in my heart (house).

SUMMARY:

Is your walk with the Lord hindered by seeking special signs from Him? The trip of faith is never based upon confirming signs. Instead, our eyes are to be on Christ. He is the only sign we will ever need. Note how others have failed to keep their eyes upon Christ:

1. An evil generation sought a sign.
2. An evil generation was condemned because it did not repent.
3. An evil generation was condemned because it did not seek the greater wisdom.
4. An evil generation followed a false religion—that of reformation.

PERSONAL JOURNAL NOTES
(Reflection & Response)

1. The most important thing that I learned from this lesson was:

2. The area that I need to work on the most is:

3. I can apply this lesson to my life by:

4. Closing Statement of Commitment:

MATTHEW 12:46-50

	G. Defense 7: Messiah's Answer to Doubting Relatives, 12:46-50 (Mk.3:31-35; Lk.8:19-21)	out, desiring to speak with thee.	
		48 But he answered and said unto him that told him, Who is my mother? and who are my brethren?	**2 He proclaimed the existence of a unique family** a. It is not based on blood relationships
1 He was misunderstood by His family a. They "stood without": Disturbed by His claims	46 While he yet talked to the people, behold, his mother and his brethren stood without, desiring to speak with him.	49 And he stretched forth his hand toward his disciples, and said, Behold my mother and my brethren!	b. It is based on discipleship
b. They tried to interrupt His ministry	47 Then one said unto him, Behold, thy mother and thy brethren stand with-	50 For whosoever shall do the will of my Father which is in heaven, the same is my brother, and sister, and mother.	c. It is based on doing God's will d. It is based on a heavenly, spiritual relationship with God as Father

Section VIII
THE MESSIAH'S DEFENSE OF HIMSELF AGAINST OPPONENTS, Matthew 12:1-50

Study 7: **DEFENSE 7: MESSIAH'S ANSWER TO DOUBTING RELATIVES**

Text: **Matthew 12:46-50**

Aim: To learn how to maintain your focus, even when others misunderstand and oppose you.

Memory Verse:

"For whosoever shall do the will of my Father which is in heaven, the same is my brother, and sister, and mother" (Matthew 12:50).

INTRODUCTION

What kind of world would we be living in if our great leaders were hindered by their mothers and fathers who stood in the way? Imagine if the parents of these historical giants had tried to stand in the way…

- of the great explorer Christopher Columbus: "I'm sorry Chris. No more sailing lessons for you. I want you to learn how to herd sheep."
- of the great inventor Thomas Edison: "Stop wasting your time on every foolish idea you get."
- of the great musician and composer Handel: "Come out of your room and give us a break. All we hear is 'Messiah, Messiah, Messiah.'"

Fortunately for the world, the families of these great men did not stand in the way of their destiny. But one only has to wonder aloud how many people have *not* become great because of opposition from within their families. On more than one occasion…

- parents have quenched the zeal of children who have come to know the Lord.
- parents have fought God by encouraging their children to pursue worldly careers instead of becoming missionaries to the foreign fields.
- parents have over-protected their children from the daily challenges of life, handicapping them terribly.

MATTHEW 12:46-50

The family can be a subtle but powerful opposition. In fact, there is no stronger opposition than a family that misunderstands or stands against one of its own members who has accepted Christ. Jesus had declared, "A man's foes shall be they of his own household" (Mt.10:34-39). He was now experiencing this opposition Himself.

Note that Mary was acting out of a mother's love and a sense of responsibility for her son. Nevertheless, she was wrong.

OUTLINE:

1. Jesus was misunderstood by His own family (v.46-47).
2. Jesus proclaimed the existence of a unique family relationship—a spiritual family (v.48-50).

1. JESUS CHRIST WAS MISUNDERSTOOD BY HIS FAMILY (v.46-47).

Apparently Jesus' family was disturbed by His claims and all the rumors being buzzed about the country.

Jesus was not disowning His family; He was not reacting because He was hurt by their disbelief. Jesus held His family close to His heart just as He did every soul and every home. This is clearly seen in Scripture.

1. His thoughts were tenderly upon His mother and her care while He was dying upon the cross (Jn.19:27).

2. He was probably experiencing a deep longing for His family's support when He uttered the despairing truth: "The Son of man hath not where to lay his head" (Mt.8:20; Lk.9:58).

3. He was constantly talking about the family relationship by referring to His *Father*, God Himself.

4. He, God's very own Son, was sent into the world through the body of a woman and reared in the environment of a home. God thereby sanctified the family and the home beyond human esteem.

In this passage Jesus is not disowning His family nor relegating the family to a position of less importance nor teaching that the human family matters little to God. What, then, is He doing? He is proclaiming the existence of a unique family—a spiritual family (see note 2—Mt.12:48-50).

> **"But if any provide not for his own, and specially for those of his own house, he hath denied the faith, and is worse than an infidel" (1 Tim.5:8).**

ILLUSTRATION:

Interruptions are to be expected. The key lesson for the believer is not to be distracted when interruptions come his way.

> *Up near the dangerous front, an Army chaplain was conducting worship services. Artillery explosions were heard nearby, right in the middle of the chaplain's prayer. He paused in mid-sentence and spoke louder. "Is that outgoing or incoming?"*
>
> *Together the reverent soldiers answered, "Outgoing, sir."*
>
> *The chaplain reverently resumed his prayer right in the middle of the sentence where he had stopped."*[1]

---

1 *INFOsearch Sermon Illustrations* (Arlington, TX: The Computer Assistant, 1-888-868-9029, 1986-1996).

APPLICATION 1:
Note several things.
1) Jesus was preaching when His family interrupted Him. Think of the different ways He could have reacted, yet notice how He controlled the situation. Every servant confronts interruption sometime. We should learn to control our reactions when we are interrupted, as difficult as it may be.
2) Jesus' family felt close enough to Him to interrupt Him. Easy access and familiarity do sometimes breed less respect and esteem.
3) Jesus uses the interruption to teach a great lesson: God is building a unique family—a spiritual family

APPLICATION 2:
Jesus' family had the opportunity to be with Him daily, the privilege of supporting Him and of learning from Him, yet they were not with Him. Why? Easy access and familiarity often breed...

- less respect ·
- ess esteem
- neglect
- unbelief
- contempt

We often neglect that which we can have anytime we desire it: parents, children, spouse, friends, worship, Bible study, prayer.

APPLICATION 3:
Opposition, even from our family, should not cause us to forsake our calling and mission. Christ continued on fulfilling all that God had called Him to do.

QUESTIONS:
1. How does your immediate family view your relationship to Christ?
   ___As a "fanatic"
   ___As someone who is narrow-minded
   ___As a hypocrite
   ___As a person who has been changed by the gospel
   ___Other:____
2. Make a list of unsaved family members. What kind of witness have you been to them? How much do you *really* pray for their salvation?
3. Would you consider your family to be a support or a hindrance to your personal spiritual growth? Why?

2. JESUS CHRIST PROCLAIMED THE EXISTENCE OF A UNIQUE FAMILY—A SPIRITUAL FAMILY (v.48-50).

Jesus proclaimed a family relationship so bound together spiritually that it supersedes the human family.

Jesus said four things about the spiritual family.

1. The spiritual family is not based on blood relationships. The human family is not downgraded, but a superior family relationship is proclaimed. It is a true personal relationship with God the Father, a relationship that is spiritual and eternal.

It is a relationship that is above the physical and temporal. The human family is important, but the human family breaks down. It breaks down in all its relationships. Children rebel and turn against parents and against one another. Parents oppose children and too often reject them. Spouses mistreat and turn from one another, allowing barriers to build.

New families are often rebuilt after the death of a spouse or after divorce. Human families are temporal and ever so fragile because of selfishness and evil and the sin of the human heart. The human family is important, but it is only a type of the true family, the family of God Himself.

The true spiritual family—those who genuinely know God in a personal way—know *a stronger and closer union, a more binding force* than blood relationships. They know a true spiritual relationship with God the Father and His true followers, a spiritual relationship that is...

- more loyal
- more secure
- more understanding
- more loving
- more tender
- more binding
- more meaningful
- more purposeful
- more challenging
- more fulfilling

Of course, God's great desire is for the human family to be part of His eternal family. There should be no closer bond than a human family spiritually united in Christ Jesus our Lord.

2. The spiritual family is based on discipleship—true discipleship to Jesus Christ. One of the clearest descriptions of what it means to be a true disciple of Christ is found in Luke.

a. In order to become a disciple of Christ a man must put Christ first: before family—before self.

"If any man come to me, and hate not his father, and mother, and wife, and children, and brethren, and sisters, yea, and his own life also, he cannot be my disciple" (Lk.14:26).

b. In order to become a disciple of Christ a man must bear the cross of death—to self.

"And whosoever doth not bear his cross, and come after me, cannot be my disciple" (Lk.14:27).

c. In order to become a disciple of Christ a man must give thought to discipleship—count the cost and the consequences.

"For which of you, intending to build a tower, sitteth not down first, and counteth the cost, whether he have sufficient to finish it? Lest haply, after he hath laid the foundation, and is not able to finish it, all that behold it begin to mock him, saying, This man began to build, and was not able to finish. Or what king, going to make war against another king, sitteth not down first, and consulteth whether he be able with ten thousand to meet him that cometh against him with twenty thousand? Or else, while the other is yet a great way off, he sendeth an ambassage, and desireth conditions of peace" (Lk.14:28-32).

d. In order to become a disciple of Christ a man must pay the ultimate price—forsaking all.

"So likewise, whosoever he be of you that forsaketh not all that he hath, he cannot be my disciple" (Lk.14:33).

e. In order to become a disciple of Christ a man must demonstrate love to others.

"A new commandment I give unto you, That ye love one another; as I have loved you, that ye also love one another. By this shall all men know that ye are my disciples, if ye have love one to another" (Jn.13:34-35).

f. In order to become a disciple of Christ a man must be steadfast in his loyalty to Jesus Christ.

"Then said Jesus to those Jews which believed on him, If ye continue in my word, then are ye my disciples indeed" (Jn.8:31).

g. In order to become a disciple of Christ a man must be fruitful in serving Christ.

"Herein is my Father glorified, that ye bear much fruit; so shall ye be my disciples" (Jn.15:8).

Note that discipleship is centered around Jesus Christ. He is the central figure around whom all disciples live and move and have their being. Thus, it is discipleship to Christ that brings about the family of God. The family of God is a spiritual family based on true discipleship to Jesus Christ.

3. The spiritual family is based on doing God's will. Christ clearly says that doing God's will results in several things.

a. Doing the will of God establishes the family of God: a unique, spiritual family built by the Father and the Son. The family of God is built around the will of God, with the family members committed to doing His will.

"And he answered and said unto them, My mother and my brethren are these which hear the word of God, and do it" (Lk.8:21).

b. Doing the will of God secures fellowship with God and His people: it secures a unique fellowship—a spiritual fellowship with both the Father and the Son.

"Jesus answered and said unto him, If a man love me, he will keep my words: and my Father will love him, and we will come unto him, and make our abode with him. He that loveth me not keepeth not my sayings: and the word which ye hear is not mine, but the Father's which sent me" (Jn.14:23-24).

c. Doing the will of God proves that a person has become a member of God's family: that a person has entered into the Kingdom of Heaven, that is, into the spiritual world or dimension of being.

"Not every one that saith unto me, Lord, Lord, shall enter into the kingdom of heaven; but he that doeth the will of my Father which is in heaven" (Mt.7:21).

d. Doing the will of God proves a unique fact: that God's family does exist—that what Christ claims is true.

"If any man will do his will, he shall know of the doctrine, whether it be of God, or whether I speak of myself" (Jn.7:17; cp. 16-18).

4. The spiritual family is based on a heavenly or spiritual relationship with God as Father. Christ very clearly says: "Whosoever shall do the will of *my Father which is in heaven*, the same is my brother, and sister, and mother." A person who seeks after God,

who seeks to do His will, is the person who develops a relationship with God. That person becomes God's adopted child within God's family, a brother or sister to Christ.

Several unique things create this spiritual family of sons and daughters of God, of brothers and sisters to Christ.

a. The spiritual family is created by a unique rebirth of one's spirit—brought about by the Spirit of God.

> **"Jesus answered and said unto him, Verily, verily, I say unto thee, Except a man be born again, he cannot see the kingdom of God....Jesus answered and said unto him, Verily, verily, I say unto thee, Except a man be born of water and of the Spirit, he cannot enter into the kingdom of God" (Jn.3:3, 5).**

b. The spiritual family is created by a unique adoption into the family of God—witnessed to by the Spirit of God.

> **"But when the fulness of the time was come, God sent forth his Son, made of a woman, made under the law, to redeem them that were under the law, that we might receive the adoption of sons. And because ye are sons, God hath sent forth the Spirit of his Son into your hearts, crying, Abba, Father" (Gal.4:4-6).**

c. The spiritual family is created by a unique fellowship created by the Spirit of God.

> **"And they continued stedfastly in the apostles' doctrine and fellowship, and in breaking of bread, and in prayers" (Acts 2:42).**

d. The spiritual family is created by a unique commitment to Jesus Christ, that is, by becoming disciples of His—stirred by the love of Christ. (See pt.2 this note—Mt.12:48-50.)

> **"For the love of Christ constraineth us; because we thus judge, that if one died for all, then were all dead: and that he died for all, that they which live should not henceforth live unto themselves, but unto him which died for them, and rose again" (2 Cor.5:14-15).**

e. The spiritual family is created by a unique experience as one worships and serves God daily.

> **"And he said to them all, If any man will come after me, let him deny himself, and take up his cross daily, and follow me" (Lk.9:23).**

APPLICATION 1:
Christ sets the supreme example of loyalty to God and to the family of God.

APPLICATION 2:
Family and friends need to tread carefully in their response to the person who is called to serve God.
1) God expects support and encouragement, not questioning and opposition.
2) God expects understanding, not feelings of being neglected and uncared for.

ILLUSTRATION:
Believers are being created by God in a way that makes every believer a member of the body of Christ. By His Holy Spirit, God has adopted each one of us into

this very special family, fusing us together as one. Noted author Max Lucado reminds us of this necessary unity.

> *We are much like Ruth and Verena Cady. Since their birth in 1984 they have shared much. Just like any twins, they have shared a bike, a bed, a room, and toys. They've shared meals and stories and TV shows and birthdays. They shared the same womb before they were born and the same room after they were born. But the bond between Ruthie and Verena goes even further. They share more than toys and treats; they share the same heart.*
>
> *Their bodies are fused together from the sternum to the waist. Though they have separate nervous systems and distinctive personalities, they are sustained by the same, singular three-chambered heart. Neither could survive without the other. Since separation is not an option, cooperation becomes an obligation.*
>
> *They have learned to work together. Take walking, for example. Their mother assumed they would take turns walking forward or backwards. It made sense to her that they would alternate; one facing the front and the other the back. The girls had a better idea. They learned to walk sideways, almost like dancing. And they dance in the same direction.*
>
> *They've learned to make up for each other's weaknesses. Verena loves to eat, but Ruthie finds sitting at the table too dull. Ruthie may eat only a half cup of fruit a day. No problem, her sister will eat enough for both. It's not unusual for her to have three bowls of cereal, two yogurts and two pieces of toast for breakfast. Ruthie tends to get restless while her sister eats and has been known to throw a bowl of ice cream across the room. This could lead to discipline for her, but also has consequences for her sister.*[2]

A spiritual family that is united by the Spirit of God can overcome any obstacle.

QUESTIONS:

1. It should come as no surprise that a believer often feels closer to another believer than to an unsaved family member. Is this true or false in your life? Why?
2. What does it really mean to be a disciple of Jesus Christ? How would you evaluate your own commitment to these traits of being a disciple?
3. What does it really mean for a person to do the will of God? How do you know what the will of God is?

SUMMARY:

A person who loves the Lord has no greater earthly blessing than to have his family support him. So much can be achieved when a believer is supported. But when a family opposes the believer, he can receive encouragement by remembering that...

1. Jesus was misunderstood by His own family.
2. Jesus proclaimed the existence of a unique family relationship—a spiritual family.

---

2 Max Lucado. *The Great House of God.* (Dallas, TX: Word Publishing, 1997), p.133-134.

MATTHEW 12:46-50

PERSONAL JOURNAL NOTES
(Reflection & Response)

1. The most important thing that I learned from this lesson was:

2. The area that I need to work on the most is:

3. I can apply this lesson to my life by:

4. Closing Statement of Commitment:

	IX. THE MESSIAH'S PARABLES DESCRIBING THE KINGDOM OF HEAVEN, 13:1-52 **A. The Parable of the Sower: How a Man Receives the Gospel, 13:1-9** (cp.13:18-23; Mk. 4:1-9; Lk.8:4-15)	4 And when he sowed, some seeds fell by the way side, and the fowls came and devoured them up: 5 Some fell upon stony places, where they had not much earth: and forthwith they sprung up, because they had no deepness of earth: 6 And when the sun was up, they were scorched; and because they had no root, they withered away. 7 And some fell among thorns; and the thorns sprung up, and choked them: 8 But other fell into good ground, and brought forth fruit, some an hundred-fold, some sixty-fold, some thirty-fold. 9 Who hath ears to hear, let him hear.	a. Some dwelt by the wayside b. Some received the Word in stony places c. Some received the Word among thorns **4 Only a small number allowed the Word to take permanent root** **5 Only a few allowed the Word to bear 100% fruit** **6 A strong call: Hear**
1 Christ preached a parable a. On the Sabbath b. By the seashore c. Multitudes gathered d. They pressed Him into a boat **2. A sower went forth to sow** **3 A large number did not allow the Word to take permanent root**	The same day went Jesus out of the house, and sat by the seaside. 2 And great multitudes were gathered together unto him, so that he went into a ship, and sat; and the whole multitude stood on the shore. 3 And he spake many things unto them in parables, saying, Behold, a sower went forth to sow;		

PLEASE NOTE: *THE EXPLANATION FOR THE PARABLE OF THE SOWER IS GIVEN IN MT.13:18-23. IT IS BEST TO STUDY THIS PARABLE AND ITS EXPLANATION TOGETHER. FOR THIS REASON BOTH SCRIPTURES AND OUTLINES ARE GIVEN HERE.*

	C. The Parable of the Sower Explained, 13:18-23 (Mk.4:13-20)	which received seed by the way side. 20 But he that received the seed into stony places, the same is he that heareth the word, and anon with joy receiveth it; 21 Yet hath he not root in himself, but dureth for a while: for when tribulation or persecution ariseth because of the word, by and by he is offended.	c. Result: Satan snatches the seed away **3 The seed on stony ground** a. Identity: A person who experiences a quick, dramatic conversion b. Problem: He has little root & is unprepared to face the trials & persecution of life c. Result: He falls away
1 Describes the kingdom of heaven **2 The seed by the wayside** a. Identity: A person who is hard & closed-minded b. Problem: His heart is not soft; the seed is unable to penetrate	18 Hear ye therefore the parable of the sower. 19 When any one heareth the word of the kingdom, and understandeth it not, then cometh the wicked one, and catcheth away that which was own in his heart. This is he		

4 The seed among thorns a. Identity: A person who is religious & worldly-minded b. Problem: Worldliness c. Result: Word is choked & he bears no fruit	22 He also that received seed among the thorns is he that heareth the word; and the care of this world, and the deceitfulness of riches, choke the word, and he becometh unfruitful. 23 But he that re-	ceived seed into the good ground is he that heareth the word, and understandeth it; which also beareth fruit, and bringeth forth, some an hundredfold, some sixty, some thirty.	**5 The seed on good ground** a. Identity: A person who hears & understands the Word b. Result: He bears fruit, but these bear different percentages

Section IX
THE MESSIAH'S PARABLES DESCRIBING THE KINGDOM OF HEAVEN,
Matthew 13:1-52

Study 1: **THE PARABLE OF THE SOWER: HOW A MAN RECEIVES THE GOSPEL**

Text: **Matthew 13:1-9, 18-23**

Aim: To understand the unique relationship between the Word of God and a person's heart.

Memory Verse:

"But he that received seed into the good ground is he that heareth the word, and understandeth it; which also beareth fruit, and bringeth forth, some an hundredfold, some sixty, some thirty" (Matthew 13:23).

SECTION OVERVIEW:

The eight parables of Mt.13 have to do with the "mysteries of the kingdom of heaven" (Mt.13:11). By *mystery* Jesus does not mean something mysterious, but rather something unknown and not revealed until this present time. What is the mystery, the new revelation? It is twofold.

1. Jesus pictured modern-day Christianity. He said the kingdom of heaven is a mixture of good and bad. It includes *professing* believers as well as *genuine* believers; *false* doctrine as well as *true* doctrine; *false* ritual as well as *true* ritual; *hypocritical* worship as well as *genuine* worship; *professing* belief as well as *real* belief. (Cp. the Sower and the Seed, the Wheat and the Tares, the Mustard Seed, and the Leaven.)

2. Jesus pictured the world and its priceless value. He said that He had come to seek and sacrificially purchase the world. He said that His followers were to laboriously work, seeking to pull men into the kingdom. He said they were unusually privileged: they had received the new revelation of God to add to their knowledge of the old revelation. Therefore, they were now responsible for teaching the new as well as the old (cp. the Hidden Treasure, the Pearl, the Net, and the Householder).

INTRODUCTION

Anyone who has ever planted a garden knows that several things are needed in order to enjoy the fruits of their labor.

⇒ There must be good soil.
⇒ There must be good seed.

⇒ There must be good work habits—plowing up the ground, sowin[g], weeding the garden, and providing sufficient water.
⇒ Lastly, there must be time to harvest.

A person who is serious about getting results will work hard at it, doing the best job possible. In the same way, those who are serious about spreading the Gospel must be even more ambitious in sowing the Word of God into the hearts of people.

Christ tells the parable of the sower in verses 1-9. He interprets this parable in verses 18-23. *The sower* is either the Lord Jesus Christ or a servant of His (v.37). (The servants of the Lord, ministers or laymen, are "laborers together with God," 1 Cor.3:9). *The seed* is the Word of God or the Word of the kingdom (v.19). It is called (1) the "incorruptible seed" (1 Pt.1:23), and (2) "the gospel which...bringeth forth fruit" (Col.1:5-6).

The ground upon which the seed is sown is the heart of the hearer. Christ says two significant things about the ground:

⇒ There are different ways for the ground to hear and receive the Word (seed).
⇒ The fate of the Word, how well it grows, depends upon the ground, that is, the hearer.

Each hearer is personally responsible for how he receives the Word of God.

OUTLINE:

1. Christ preached a parable (v.1-2).
2. A sower went forth to sow (v.3, 18).
3. A large number did not allow the Word to take permanent root (v.4-7).
4. Only a small number allowed the Word to take permanent root (v.8, 23).
5. Only a few allowed the Word to bear 100 percent fruit (v.8, 23).
6. A strong call: hear (v.9).

1. CHRIST PREACHED A PARABLE (v.1-2)

⇒ He preached on the Sabbath.
⇒ He preached by the seashore.
⇒ He preached as the multitudes gathered.
⇒ The multitudes pressed Him into a boat.
⇒ He preached from the boat.

QUESTION:
Jesus was not constricted in His preaching by the day of the week, by the location, or by the size of the crowd. What lessons can you learn from His example?

2. A SOWER WENT FORTH TO SOW (v.3).

Note two things.

⇒ First, the sower did go forth.
⇒ Second, the sower did sow the seed (the Word of God) or the Word of the Kingdom (v.19).

ILLUSTRATION:
When we teach the Word of God, our concern is not to be who will or who will not respond. Our task is simple: to sow the seed.

When it comes to sharing the gospel, it is not our responsibility to deter-

mine in advance who will be receptive....Fred Craddock illustrates this with an incident he remembered from his shy teenage years:

"A pretty girl had moved into our town and into our school. She was immediately popular. Admiring her from a distance, I asked her, in the privacy of my mind, to go with me to the movies. I looked at her, then looked at myself, and, in the privacy of my mind, she said no. For days afterward I was both hurt and angry at her rejection of me, a decision she was never allowed to make.

"It may be that when we speak to many, only a few will hear, but we have not been called to speak to a few and then complain that there are not many."[1]

QUESTIONS:

1. There are people who sow all kinds of things in life—some good and some bad. What can you do to be receptive to only the good seed and protect yourself from the bad seed?
2. Thinking very practically, what results can you expect when you sow the seed of God's Word into another person's life? How does a person sow God's Word into the life of another?

3. A LARGE NUMBER DID NOT ALLOW THE WORD TO TAKE PERMANENT ROOT (v.4-7).

Note something very important: these people did hear the Word of God. They were in church or Bible study or exposed to the Word somewhere—*regularly*. The Word did fall upon them, but they did not allow the Word to penetrate their hearts—not permanently.

Note that the number of persons who rejected the Word was far greater than the one's who received it. They did not all obey the gospel...

"Lord, who hath believed our report" (Ro.10:16; see also Mt.22:14).

APPLICATION:

A person is held accountable for the kind of heart he has: hard, emotional, superficial, thorny, or soft and tender.

QUESTIONS:

1. Some people are repeatedly exposed to the Word of God, yet they are still shallow in their faith. How can you explain this?
2. What effect do trials and tribulations have upon the person whose spiritual roots are weak?

Carefully examine the reason *why* the seed did not take permanent root:

1. Some dwelt by the wayside (13:4, 19). In the day of Christ there were no fences to separate property lines. Instead, long narrow foot paths were used for the traveling public. These paths were trodden down as hard as pavement by the constant use of those passing through. This is the hard wayside ground referred to by Christ.

Note: these hear the Word but they do not understand it (v.19). They are exposed to the Word of God somewhere on a regular basis. The Word definitely does fall upon them. Some have made public decisions, and some have not; but no matter, they are all

---

[1] *Overhearing the Gospel.* Fred B. Craddock. (Abington, 1978), p.39. *INFOsearch Sermon Illustrations* (Arlington, TX: The Computer Assistant, 1-888-868-9029, 1986-1996).

still off to the side, paying little attention to what is going on. Even those who have made decisions are not genuine. They are hard, very hard, with closed minds and concrete hearts; therefore, they pay no attention and give no heed to the Word. Their minds are elsewhere. They have no interest and are indifferent, failing to realize how important the Word is to life. They feel they can get along without the Word of God, that it is not needed in life.

Christ said "the wicked one" comes and snatches away whatever Word is sown. People whose hearts are not open and soft are easy prey for the devil. The Word always remains on the surface of their hearts, thereby exposing it to whatever the devil may wish to grab.

There are at least four reasons why people become hardened to the gospel.

a. They continuously rebel. They react because of some tragedy or unfortunate circumstance and then blame God.
b. They do not stay awake or alert; they do not pay attention. They do not consider the gospel important enough to merit their attention. In their minds, other things need their attention more than the gospel.
c. They are careless in handling the gospel. They treat the gospel as an *item*, an *additive*, a *part of life* instead of life itself. When needed and when time is available, the gospel is acceptable. Their attitude is that the gospel has its place, but it is not the permeating factor of life that so many make it.
d. They are deceived. What matters to them is attendance, being present in *worship services* and associating with other Christians. A change of heart and life is meaningless. The gospel is merely a matter of religion to them, a matter of form and ceremony, not a matter of life.

"For the heart of this people is waxed gross, and their ears are dull of hearing, and their eyes have they closed; lest they should see with their eyes, and hear with their ears, and understand with their heart, and should be converted, and I should heal them" (Acts 28:27).

APPLICATION:

Scripture gives a clear warning: "We ought to give the more earnest heed to the things which we have heard, lest at any time we should let them slip" (Heb.2:1f).

QUESTIONS:

1. In some countries the message of the gospel has saturated communities through the airways and the printed media. It seems there are churches on every street corner. Yet so many people live on in their sins. What causes people to harden their hearts to the gospel?
2. What is the most important thing you can do to keep your heart soft and open to the gospel?

2. Some received the Word in stony places (13:5-6, 20-21). In some parts of Palestine, lying right beneath the ground is a layer of limestone. When seed falls upon this ground, something dramatic happens. The limestone holds the rain and heat from the sunlight right under the surface; therefore, the fallen seed sprouts quickly and dramatically. But it has no root.

The application is clear: this person has what appears to be a dramatic conversion. He makes a decision for Christ, and he stands out as an example of a changed life and quick growth. However, the change lasts only for a season, perhaps an extended season, but in the end it fails.

Note four things about this person (v.20-21):

⇒ he hears the Word
⇒ he receives the Word immediately

⇒ he receives the Word with joy
⇒ he endures for a while

Note why this person fails.

a. He has no true roots (v.21). He has not rooted and grounded himself in the Word and in prayer. He has not learned the doctrines and principles of Christianity. He began in the *emotional joy* of the Word and in his decision to reform his life, but he has continued to live in the emotions of his experience and his newly found Christian friends. He does little about the hard demands of Christ that come only through diligent study and disciplined prayer. He knows little about sacrificial obedience: "Study to show thyself approved" (2 Tim. 2:15).
b. He has little spiritual strength to withstand the trials and persecutions of life. Pressure from circumstances or former friends of the world—mockery, abuse, or whatever—causes him to cave in.

"And Jesus said unto him, No man, having put his hand to the plough, and looking back, is fit for the kingdom of God" (Lk.9:62).

APPLICATION:
Hearing the Word preached and taught will not get a person into heaven. A person has to receive the Word, to truly take it into his life. A great mistake is sometimes made with a person experiencing a dramatic conversion. The person is pushed forward as a strong testimony long before he has proven the genuineness of his conversion (1 Tim.3:10). But note a sobering fact: it is "he that endureth to the end [who] shall be saved" (Mt.10:22).

QUESTIONS:
1. What kinds of things dull your ability to hear God's call to you? Or His instructions? Or His chastisement? Or His promises?
2. How can you be more sensitive or alert to God's voice in your life?

3. Some received the Word among thorns (13:7, 22). The thorny ground is deceptive ground. It looks good and clean, appearing to be clear of weeds and thorns, but it is not. Right under the surface of the soil is a chain of roots ready to spring up. The fact that the roots are already there means that the thorns will be stronger and grow faster than the *good seed*. They will choke the life out of the good seed.

Thorns represent those who receive the Word as an addition to their life. The Word is merely added on, not allowed to replace the world and the things of it. These do not truly repent; they simply try to take God and add Him as another compartment in their lives. They make God only a small part of their affairs; consequently, the Word is always choked to death. (1 Jn.2:15-16).

Note what the thorns are.

a. Thorns are "the cares of this world" (v.22). They *prick and prick* away at the Word. They *entangle* a person in the world and the things of the world (2 Tim. 2:3-4). They irritate, aggravate, trouble, and hinder a person from pursuing his task. When a person's mind is on *the cares of the world*, his mind is not on God and the things of the Word or Spirit. He is carnal-minded, not spiritual-minded (Ro.8:5-8; 2 Cor.10:3-5).
b. Thorns are "the deceitfulness of riches" (v.22). Note: it is not wealth itself that is worldly (thorny); it is the *deceit* of wealth. Wealth deceives in several ways.
   1) Wealth tends to make a person *self-confident* and *self-dependent*. It makes him feel comfortable and secure in this world. Such tends to keep him from trusting and calling upon God.
   2) Wealth tends to make a person *overly comfortable*, *extravagant*, and *indulgent*. It makes him live sumptuously, beyond what is needed. He sometimes

feels that he can spend to get a little more and a little better than is necessary. This feeling arises especially if he has already given to meet the needs of the world.

3) Wealth tends to *consume a person's mind*. It arouses the urge and passion to keep and protect all that a person has and to make more and more. A wealthy person often finds himself more and more centered around his wealth and less and less centered around the things of God and His Word.

4) Wealth tends to *misinterpret the blessings of God*. It leads a person to the false idea and security that *to have is to be blessed by God*, and not to have is to be blessed less by God. This is a false concept that has prevailed since the beginning of time: that to receive and have anything in this world is a blessing from God, and the more a person has the more he is *especially blessed*. God has promised the necessities of life in this material world, but His great blessings are spiritual (Mt.6:25-34).

Note: these four deceptions show clearly why it is so difficult for a rich man to enter the kingdom of heaven.

> **"And the cares of this world, and the deceitfulness of riches, and the lusts of other things entering in, choke the word, and it becometh unfruitful" (Mk.4:19).**

QUESTIONS:
1. What are the most common things—the thorns—that tend to choke God out of your life?
2. What is the key thing you can do to overcome the influence of the cares or things of the world?

4. ONLY A SMALL NUMBER ALLOWED THE WORD TO TAKE PERMANENT ROOT (v.8, 23).

A person who allows the Word to take permanent root represents the honest and good heart (Lk.8:15). Christ says two things about him.

1. He hears the Word of God and understands it. His heart is soft and tender toward God, so he listens, meditates, concentrates, and thinks. He is not hypocritical, wasting his time and being present physically, but absent mentally. He does not allow his thoughts to wander off when the Word of God is being preached. He is responsible and behaves intelligently. He listens to God's Word, studies and receives it.

2. He is fruitful. He bears the fruit of God's Word and Spirit in his own life (Gal.5:22-23). And he reproduces himself by reaching out to lead others to a saving knowledge of the Lord.

Note that John chapter 15 categorizes fruit-bearing as "no fruit" (Jn.15:1), "fruit" (Jn.15:2), "more fruit" (Jn.15:3), and "much fruit" (Jn.15:5, 8).

> **"Therefore if any man be in Christ, he is a new creature: old things are passed away; behold, all things are become new" (2 Cor. 5:17).**

APPLICATION:
God's Word will never return to Him void (Is.55:11). This is a glorious encouragement to the minister or teacher or believers who shares the gospel. If the gospel is truly preached or taught or shared, fruit will be borne. And bearing fruit is that which distinguishes the true believer from the hypocrite.

QUESTIONS:
1. What does it mean for you to be spiritually fruitful?
2. What effect does God's Word have upon...
   - your spiritual life?
   - your family life?
   - your business life?

5. ONLY A FEW ALLOWED THE WORD TO BEAR 100 PERCENT FRUIT (v.8, 23).

This is a shocking truth! Not all believers are equal. Some bear only 30 percent fruit; some 60 percent fruit; and shockingly, only a very small number bear 100 percent fruit. Frankly, most people are not willing to give 100 percent of their energy, effort, strength, time, or possessions to the Lord's work—whether in or outside of the ministry. There is not the willingness to pay the price—not within most men.

QUESTIONS:
1. As you examine your life, in what area do you see the greatest fruit? The least? Are you doing all you can do?
2. Every person's call and place of ministry are different. But God equips every person to do what He calls him to do. What things are holding you back from bearing 100 percent fruit in your calling?

6. A STRONG CALL: HEAR (v.9).

Christ issues a strong call, "Hear. The person who has ears to hear, let him hear" (v.9). The ear has no greater purpose than to hear the message of God.

> **"Not every one that saith unto me, Lord, Lord, shall enter into the kingdom of heaven; but he that doeth the will of my Father which is in heaven" (Mt.7:21).**

ILLUSTRATION:
Sometimes we become so caught up in our day-to-day routine that we miss out on what God is saying to our hearts:

> *Patricia Goldman, the vice chairman of the National Transportation Safety Board, tells a story about a stewardess who, frustrated by passenger inattentiveness during her what-to-do-in-an-emergency talk at the beginning of each flight, changed the wording and said, "When the mask drops down in front of you, place it over your navel and continue to breathe normally." Not a single passenger noticed.*[2]

QUESTIONS:
1. What kinds of things do you sink your roots into that hurt your faith?
2. If your faith were challenged today, would you be able to stand and not fall? What can you do to assure victory in the face of trials and temptations?

---

2 *Illustrations Unlimited.* James S. Hewett, Editor, p. 319.

MATTHEW 13:1-9, 18-23

SUMMARY:

The gospel of Jesus Christ is the most powerful message ever given to mankind. If a person receives the gospel and allows it to take permanent root, he will be gloriously saved by the power of God. On the other hand, if the gospel is sown upon a heart that will not receive it, that same gospel has the power to banish a person from God's presence forever. This is the message that is so clearly seen in the points of this Scripture:

1. Christ preached a parable, a parable of the sower.
2. A sower went forth to sow.
3. A large number did not allow the Word to take permanent root.
4. Only a small number allowed the Word to take permanent root.
5. Only a few allowed the Word to bear 100 percent fruit.
6. A strong call: "Hear. The person who has ears to hear, let him hear." The ear has no greater purpose than to hear the message of God.

PERSONAL JOURNAL NOTES
(Reflection & Response)

1. The most important thing that I learned from this lesson was:

2. The area that I need to work on the most is:

3. I can apply this lesson to my life by:

4. Closing Statement of Commitment:

MATTHEW 13:10-17

B. The Messiah's Reasons for Speaking in Parables: Who Receives & Who Loses, 13:10-17
(Mk.4:10-12; Lk. 8:9-10; 10:23-24)

1 Why Jesus spoke in parables
- a. The disciples questioned Jesus
- b. The general statement
  - 1) Mysteries are given to believers
  - 2) Mysteries are not given to unbelievers

2 Reason 1: Seekers & achievers receive more
- a. Some seek & have
- b. Some do not seek & lose

3 Reason 2: Unbelievers reject & lose
- a. Their willful rejection
  - 1) Do see & hear, yet refuse to really see & hear
  - 2) Refuse to understand
- b. Their rejection prophesied
- c. Their rejection described
  - 1) Harden their hearts
  - 2) Deafen their ears
  - 3) Close their eyes
  - 4) Deny what they see
  - 5) Refuse understanding
  - 6) Fight conversion & healing

4 Reason 3: Believers receive & are blessed
- a. They see & hear
- b. They are especially privileged—privileged over Old Testament believers

10 And the disciples
came, and said unto
him, Why speakest
thou unto them in
parables?
11 He answered and
said unto them, Because it is given unto you to know the
mysteries of the
kingdom of heaven,
but to them it is not
given.
12 For whosoever
hath, to him shall be
given, and he shall
have more abundance: but whosoever hath not, from him
shall be taken away
even that he hath.
13 Therefore speak I
to them in parables:
because they seeing
see not; and hearing
they hear not, neither
do they understand.
14 And in them is
fulfilled the prophecy
of Esaias, which
saith, By hearing ye
shall hear, and shall
not understand; and
seeing ye shall see,
and shall not perceive:
15 For this peoples'
heart is waxed gross,
and their ears are dull
of hearing, and their
eyes they have
closed; lest at any
time they should see
with their eyes, and
hear with their ears,
and should understand with their
heart, and should be
converted, and I
should heal them.
16 But blessed are
your eyes, for they
see: and your ears,
for they hear.
17 For verily I say
unto you, That many
prophets and righteous men have desired to see those
things which ye see,
and have not seen
them; and to hear
those things which ye
hear, and have not
heard them.

Section IX
THE MESSIAH'S PARABLES DESCRIBING THE KINGDOM OF HEAVEN,
Matthew 13:1-52

Study 2: THE MESSIAH'S REASONS FOR SPEAKING IN PARABLES: WHO RECEIVES AND WHO LOSES

Text: **Matthew 13:10-17**

Aim: To hear Christ with spiritual ears and see Him through spiritual eyes.

Memory Verse:

"For whosoever hath, to him shall be given, and he shall have more abundance: but whosoever hath not, from him shall be taken away even that he hath" (Matthew 13:12).

MATTHEW 13:10-17

INTRODUCTION
Who are the real winners and losers in life? It depends on a person's perspective.

The world says you are a winner...
- if you have a lot of money
- if you are famous
- if you own bigger and better things
- if you do your own thing, no matter how perverse

The world says you are a loser...
- if you are poor
- if you are meek and submissive
- if you are content with what you have
- if you are old-fashioned and have a moral conscience

On the other hand,

The Word of God says you are a winner...
- if you seek first the Kingdom of God and His righteousness (Mt.6:33)
- if you humble yourself before God (Jas.4:10)
- if you put your treasures in heaven (Mt.6:20)
- if you confess your sins (1 Jn.1:9)

The Word of God says you are a loser...
- if you seek your own empty ways (Is.53:6)
- if pride overcomes you (Pr.16:18)
- if the pursuit of the world becomes your goal (1 Jn.2:16)
- if you continue to practice sin, never repenting (1 Jn.2:8)

At this point in Jesus' ministry, He made a significant change in His method of teaching. He began to speak in parables that were difficult to understand—especially when unbelievers were present. Why would He speak so His audience could not understand what He was saying? Three conclusions can be drawn from what Jesus said.

1. The unbelieving crowds were deliberately shutting their eyes and ears to His claim, refusing to be converted and healed spiritually (v.13-15).
2. It was time to teach the "mysteries of the kingdom of heaven" to true disciples. The mysteries would be understood by true disciples, but they would be misunderstood by those who deliberately blinded their eyes and deafened their ears.
3. The "mysteries of the kingdom of heaven" cannot be understood without first recognizing Jesus as the Messiah and as the One who brings the kingdom of heaven to men.

Jesus had always used illustrations and sometimes the illustrations had been parables, but the parables had always been clearly understood. But now the parables were different, totally different. They were not clear, and the change in Jesus' method shocked the disciples. Therefore, they questioned Him: "Why?" His answer was a strong warning to some and a great promise to others.

OUTLINE:
1. Why Jesus spoke in parables (v.10-11).
2. Reason 1: seekers and achievers receive more (v.12).
3. Reason 2: unbelievers reject and lose (v.13-15).
4. Reason 3: believers receive and are blessed (v.16-17).

1. WHY JESUS SPOKE IN PARABLES (v.10-11).

Why did Jesus speak in parables? Note four points.

1. Consider the words, "Why speakest thou *unto them* in parables?" The disciples knew the people did not understand, and Jesus was not explaining the parables to them. The disciples were concerned lest the people miss the lessons.

APPLICATION 1:
We should always be concerned about the way the Word is preached and taught and how people are receiving the Word. Are they listening and growing or are they disinterested and stymied?

APPLICATION 2:
Note: the same preaching turned some off (the unbelieving crowds) and stirred some to seek more (the believing disciples). There is encouragement here for the preacher and teacher and warning to the unbeliever.

2. Jesus made a very general statement. God gives believers the understanding of spiritual things, the mysteries of the kingdom, but the mysteries of the kingdom are not given to unbelievers. This is logical, exactly what would be expected. The reasons given by Christ explain even more why believers alone see and understand what God reveals (v.12-15).

Common sense tells us that God will reveal things to a person who really believes in Him and draws near to Him—things that He cannot reveal to a person who ignores, neglects, and scoffs at God. Therefore, Christ puts it very simply: "It is given unto you to know the mysteries of the kingdom of heaven, but to them [unbelievers] it is not given." God does not reward unbelief; He rewards belief and trust (cp. Mt. 13:35).

3. There are "mysteries" in the kingdom of heaven:

⇒ the incarnation and virgin birth of Christ
⇒ the ideal and perfect righteousness of Christ secured by His living a sinless life while on earth
⇒ the death of Christ on the cross for man (Mt.27:26-56)
⇒ the intercessory work of Christ going on right now (Heb.3:1)
⇒ the Holy Spirit and His presence in the believer (Jn.14:16-21)
⇒ the material world and the spiritual world, or the physical and spiritual di mension of being
⇒ man's sinfulness and his dead spirit due to sin (Ro.3:9-19; Eph.2:1-3)
⇒ the church, both local and universal, and the mixture of both good and evil in it
⇒ the future resurrection (1 Cor.15:51)
⇒ the destruction and remaking of the heavens and earth into a perfect universe 2 Pt.3:10-13)

4. The mysteries of heaven have to be revealed by God. Man cannot know them by human reason; they have to be *given*, that is, revealed.

> **"But the Comforter, which is the Holy Ghost, whom the Father will send in my name, he shall teach you all things, and bring all things to your remembrance, whatsoever I have said unto you" (Jn.14:26).**

QUESTIONS:

1. What are some things God reveals to His people that unbelievers do not understand? Why are these things kept from the unbeliever?
2. What is the most profound thing God has ever shown you?
3. Should you ever be concerned about "turning off" an unbeliever by sharing the gospel? Why or why not?

2. REASON 1: SEEKERS AND ACHIEVERS RECEIVE MORE (v.12).

The first reason Christ spoke in parables is that seekers and achievers receive more. Therefore, He wanted to stir all men to seek and to achieve more and more. Seekers and achievers do receive and get more. The indifferent and complacent receive little and get less. This is a law of every realm.

MATTHEW 13:10-17

1. It is the law of nature: the early bird gets the worm; he gets; therefore, he survives; the late get little and suffer.

2. It is the law of man: men reward energy and effort, results and production. They threaten and often take away from the lazy and inactive. Those who labor and practice and are diligent and persistent see, hear, and get. They are in a position to get more and more and to be given more and more. But the neglectful, lazy, and unfaithful lose.

All through life a man either gains or loses. He seldom, if ever, stands still. It all depends on the dreams, the effort, and the energy he is willing to exert.

3. It is the law of God.

> **"Blessed are they which do hunger and thirst after righteousness: for they shall be filled" (Mt.5:6).**

APPLICATION 1:
A short formula says it all:
Perspective + initiative = success
Perspective - initiative = lost opportunity
Initiative - perspective = nothing

Perspective means the ability to see, envision, dream, understand. It is the ability to see clearly; to envision opportunity; to dream dreams; to conceive visions; to look through. A person who has the capacity to dream dreams and envision visions and see what is necessary to reach the vision has perspective. It is the capacity to measure the importance of the vision and the steps to achieve it in all its relationships. Very simply, it is a person with a vision who can measure its importance and who can see its various parts.

Initiative means taking the first step. A person must act, but he must act at the right time. Therefore, a person who has...

- *Perspective* (seeing opportunity) + *initiative* (acting at the right time) = success
- *Perspective* (seeing opportunity) - *initiative* (failing to act at the right time) = lost opportunity
- *Initiative - perspective* = nothing. The person strikes out aimlessly, beginning project after project and ending up with nothing. Why? Because he lacks perspective or vision.

It is the person who has God's perspective (vision) and God's energy (spirit) who achieves and has all and does all that God purposes for him.

APPLICATION 2:
The person who continually seeks to achieve will receive more. This passage is both a great encouragement and a realistic and understandable threat.

1) It is a great encouragement to the person who is...

- faithful
- diligent
- steadfast
- persevering
- consistent
- enduring
- hard-working
- an initiator and finalizer
- a beginner and finisher

2) It is a realistic and understandable threat to the person who is...

- lazy
- idle
- complacent
- inconsistent
- misguided
- closed-minded
- closed-eyed
- closed-eared
- self-satisfied
- sluggish
- slothful
- shiftless
- purposeless
- a time-waster
- a late starter

QUESTION:
How would you apply the short formula from *Application 1* to your life? Think in terms of your life as…

- a believer:
  - _____Success
  - _____Lost opportunity
  - _____Nothing
- an employee or employer:
  - _____Success
  - _____Lost opportunity
  - _____Nothing
- a parent or a child:
  - _____Success
  - _____Lost opportunity
  - _____Nothing
- a friend:
  - _____Success
  - _____Lost opportunity
  - _____Nothing
- a witness for Christ:
  - _____Success
  - _____Lost opportunity
  - _____Nothing

3. REASON 2: UNBELIEVERS REJECT AND LOSE (v.13-15).

The second reason Christ spoke in parables is that unbelievers reject and lose more. Note three things.

1. The unbeliever's rejection is willful, always deliberate. He sees and hears, yet he refuses to really open his eyes and ears. He refuses to understand. But why? Why does a person act so illogically, rebelling and refusing to understand? Christ said, "This people's heart is waxed gross" (v.15). The Greek is "this people's heart has grown fat [overweight]." Being fat indicates carnality, an unhealthy appetite, and senselessness. To eat constantly, adding ever more weight, is living after the flesh and makes no sense at all. It is gluttonous and senseless. Christ was therefore saying this: the unbeliever has become so greedy and senseless that he rebels and refuses to understand the mysteries of God. His greed is due to worldliness and lust for the things of the world (Ro.8:5-8; 1 Jn.2:15-16), and his senselessness is due to being deceived by the evil one (2 Cor.4:3-4).

2. The unbeliever's rejection is prophesied (Is.6:9-10; cp. Jn.12:40; Acts 28:26f). A man who willfully rejects God experiences a *judicial blindness and rejection* by God. The person who deliberately chooses to be blind and who rejects understanding is given over to a *just punishment*. His obstinate unbelief and constant sin and continual rejection lead to a judicial blindness and to being rejected by God.

> **"Wherefore God also gave them up to uncleanness….For this cause God gave them up unto…vile affections….God gave them over to a reprobate mind" (Ro.1:24, 26, 28.)**

3. The unbeliever's rejection is clearly and strongly described:
   ⇒ They harden their hearts.
   ⇒ They deafen their ears.
   ⇒ They close their eyes.

⇒ They deny what they see.
⇒ They refuse understanding.
⇒ They fight conversion and healing.

APPLICATION 1:
Why do men reject Christ? Why do they harden their hearts, deafen their ears, and close their eyes?

> **"Men loved darkness rather than light, because their deeds were evil" (Jn.3:19).**

APPLICATION 2:
One of the most tragic sights in all the world is to see people sitting under or exposed to the most glorious message and falling asleep—being listless, inattentive, disinterested, or willfully hardened and closed-minded. God will "give them up" to their slumber and deliberate hardness.

ILLUSTRATION:
There is nothing more dangerous than a hard heart. The very nature of a hard heart makes sin more desirable than repentance. The unbeliever constantly chooses sin and asks God to leave him alone.

> *Aaron Burr, the third Vice President of the United States, was reared in a godly home and admonished to accept Christ by his grandfather Jonathan Edwards. But he refused to listen. Instead, he declared that he wanted nothing to do with God and said he wished the Lord would leave him alone. He did achieve a measure of political success in spite of repeated disappointments. But he was also involved in continuous strife, and when he was 48 years old, he killed Alexander Hamilton in a duel. He lived for 32 more years, but through all this time he was unhappy and unproductive. It was during this sad chapter in his life that he declared to a group of friends, 'Sixty years ago I told God that if He would let me alone, I would let Him alone, and God has not bothered about me since.' Aaron Burr got what he wanted.*[1]

The lesson for the unbeliever: be careful what you ask of God—you just might get it!

QUESTIONS:
1. Think of your own life. What kinds of things caused you to reject Christ before you were saved? Do you know others who are making the same mistakes? What practical things can you do to keep them from making a fatal mistake?
2. What role does Satan play in a person's rejection of Christ?

4. REASON 3: BELIEVERS RECEIVE AND ARE BLESSED (v.16-17).

The third reason Christ spoke in parables is that believers receive and are blessed with more. The blessings of God include the greatest possessions imaginable: love, joy, peace, confidence, assurance, and eternal security. The blessings of God come from seeing and hearing, that is, from *conversion and spiritual healing*, not from the things that men desire (Jn.10:10; 14:27; 15:11; 16:33; Ph.4:6-7).

---

1 *INFOsearch Sermon Illustrations* (Arlington, TX: The Computer Assistant, 1-888-868-9029, 1986-1996).

MATTHEW 13:10-17

> **"Repent ye therefore, and be converted, that your sins may be blotted out, when the times of refreshing shall come from the presence of the Lord" (Acts 3:19).**

New Testament believers are much more privileged than Old Testament believers because of Christ (Hebrews is an epistle that really shows the New Testament believers' great privilege in Christ.)

> **"But as it is written, Eye hath not seen, nor ear heard, neither have entered into the heart of man, the things which God hath prepared for them that love him. But God hath revealed them unto us by his Spirit: for the Spirit searcheth all things, yea, the deep things of God" (1 Cor.2:9-10).**

QUESTION:
An unbeliever will see something in a true believer that he wishes he had: love, joy, peace, confidence, assurance, and eternal security. Is your life a testimony to that fact?

SUMMARY:

Despite all the categories into which men place each other—age, race, religion, gender, nationality, political persuasion—life is really made up of just two kinds of people: winners and losers. The winners are those who receive Christ into their lives. The losers are those who reject His invitation to eternal life. In the final analysis, will *you* be a winner or a loser? Jesus tells us to hear His strong warning and to claim His great promise of eternal life.

1. Why Jesus spoke in parables.
2. Reason 1: seekers and achievers receive more.
3. Reason 2: unbelievers reject and lose.
4. Reason 3: believers receive and are blessed.

PERSONAL JOURNAL NOTES
(Reflection & Response)

1. The most important thing that I learned from this lesson was:

2. The area that I need to work on the most is:

3. I can apply this lesson to my life by:

4. Closing Statement of Commitment:

MATTHEW 13:18-23

C. The Parable of the Sower Explained, 13:18-23 (Mk.4:13-20)

18 Hear ye therefore the parable of the sower.

19 When any one heareth the word of the kingdom, and understandeth it not, then cometh the wicked one, and catcheth away that which was sown in his heart. This is he which received seed by the way side.

20 But he that received the seed into stony places, the same is he that heareth the word, and anon with joy receiveth it;

21 Yet hath he not root in himself, but dureth for a while: for when tribulation or persecution ariseth because of the word, by and by he is offended.

22 He also that received seed among the thorns is he that heareth the word; and the care of this world, and the deceitfulness of riches, choke the word, and he becometh unfruitful.

23 But he that received seed into the good ground is he that heareth the word, and understandeth it; which also beareth fruit, and bringeth forth, some an hundredfold, some sixty, some thirty.

1. **Describes the kingdom of heaven**
2. **The seed by the wayside**
   a. Identity: A person who is hard & closed-minded
   b. Problem: His heart is not soft; the seed is unable to penetrate
   c. Result: Satan snatches the seed away
3. **The seed on stony ground**
   a. Identity: A person who experiences a quick, dramatic conversion
   b. Problem: He has little root & is unprepared to face the trials & persecution of life
   c. The result: He falls away
4. **The seed among thorns**
   a. Identity: A person who is religious & worldly minded
   b. Problem: Worldliness
   c. Result: Word is choked & he bears no fruit
5. **The seed on good ground**
   a. Identity: Those who hear & understand the Word
   b. Result: They bear fruit, but they bear different percentages

PLEASE NOTE: *THIS PASSAGE IS THE EXPLANATION OF THE PARABLE OF THE SOWER AND THE SEED COVERED IN MT.13:1-9. FOR THIS REASON, THE COMMENTARY IS BEING COMBINED WITH THAT OUTLINE. (PLEASE SEE OUTLINE—MATTHEW 13:1-9, 18-23 FOR DISCUSSION.)*

D. The Parable of the Wheat & the Tares: The Question of Evil, Why It Exists, 13:24-30
(cp.Mt.13:36-43)

1. Describes the kingdom of heaven

2. A man sows good seed
   a. He does sow
   b. He owns the field

3. An enemy sows tares
   a. He sows secretly
   b. He sows in the same field

4. A day for fruit comes
   a. Wheat appears
   b. Tares appear

5. A day of questioning comes
   a. Question 1: Where do the tares come from?
   b. The answer: An enemy sows them
   c. Question 2: Shall we judge & root up the tares?
   d. The answer
      1) Do not judge: Will root up some wheat along with tares
      2) Let both grow together

6. A day of harvest is coming
   a. Tares: Will be bundled & burned
   b. Wheat: Will be gathered into the owner's barn

24 Another parable put he forth unto them, saying, The kingdom of heaven is likened unto a man which sowed good seed in his field:
25 But while men slept, his enemy came and sowed tares among the wheat, and went his way.
26 But when the blade was sprung up, and brought forth fruit, then appeared the tares also.
27 So the servants of the householder came and said unto him, Sir, didst not thou sow good seed in thy field? from whence then hath it tares?
28 He said unto them, An enemy hath done this. The servants said unto him, Wilt thou then that we go and gather them up?
29 But he said, Nay; lest while ye gather up the tares, ye root up also the wheat with them.
30 Let both grow together until the harvest: and in the time of harvest I will say to the reapers, Gather ye together first the tares, and bind them in bundles to burn them: but gather the wheat into my barn.

PLEASE NOTE: *THE EXPLANATION FOR THE PARABLE OF THE WHEAT AND TARES IS GIVEN IN MT.13:36-43. IT IS BEST TO STUDY THIS PARABLE AND ITS EXPLANATION TOGETHER. FOR THIS REASON BOTH SCRIPTURES AND OUTLINES ARE GIVEN HERE.*

H. The Parable of the Wheat and the Tares Explained, 13:36-43

1. The parable explained
   a. Jesus was alone with His disciples
   b. The disciples asked the meaning of the parable

2. The good seed
   a. The sower: Jesus Christ
   b. The field: The world
   c. The seed: True believers

3. The bad seed
   a. The tares or weeds: Unbelievers
   b. The sower: The devil

4. The harvest
   a. The day: The end of the world
   b. The reapers: Angels

5. The reaping of the tares
   a. Symbolizes judgment
   b. When: In the end of the world
   c. Executed by angels
   d. Who: Those in the kingdom

36 Then Jesus sent the multitude away, and went into the house: and his disciples came unto him, saying, Declare unto us the parable of the tares of the field.
37 He answered and said unto them, He that soweth the good seed is the Son of man;
38 The field is the world; the good seed are the children of the kingdom; but the tares are the children of the wicked one;
39 The enemy that sowed them is the devil; the harvest is the end of the world; and the reapers are the angels.
40 As therefore the tares are gathered and burned in the fire; so shall it be in the end of this world.
41The Son of man shall send forth his angels, and they shall gather out of his

1) Who offend others 2) Who are lawless e. The judgment: Fire & weeping	kingdom all things that offend, and them which do iniquity; 42 And shall cast them into a furnace of fire: there shall be wailing and gnashing	of teeth. 43 Then shall the righteous shine forth as the sun in the kingdom of their Father. Who hath ears to hear, let him hear.	**6. The reaping of the wheat** a. Identity: The righteous b. Position: Glory in the Kingdom **7. The strong call**

Section IX
THE MESSIAH'S PARABLES DESCRIBING THE KINGDOM OF HEAVEN, Matthew 13:1-52

Study 3: **THE PARABLE OF THE WHEAT AND THE TARES: THE QUESTION OF EVIL, WHY IT EXISTS, 13:24-30**

Text: **Matthew 13:24-30, 36-43**

Aim: To discover the underlying reasons why evil exists and how you can stand against it.

Memory Verse:

"Let both grow together until the harvest: and in the time of harvest I will say to the reapers, Gather ye together first the tares, and bind them in bundles to burn them: but gather the wheat into my barn" (Matthew 13:30).

INTRODUCTION

What would you be willing to do for a million dollars? Various polls have been taken over the past few years, trying to chart the kind of people we really are. The results of some of the polling data have been astounding. For a million dollars, some people would be willing…

- to steal something
- to betray a good friend
- to have sex with a stranger
- to leave home and move to a foreign country
- to marry someone without any feelings of love
- to tell a lie that would put someone else in harm's way
- to take a bribe and not point out the corruption of leaders

No one should really be surprised by what some people would do for a million dollars. In fact, people do these very things for a whole lot less every day. Evil has corrupted every fabric of society. Morality is no longer politically correct. The laws of God are being replaced by the subjective whims of fallen man. What is the believer to do in such an evil world? Why does God allow evil to exist?

Some of man's basic questions about the presence of evil in the world and judging others are covered in this parable. It is a parable that has some very practical answers and lessons for man.

1. There are both good and evil people in this world and in the kingdom of heaven (v.24-26).
2. Christ sows the righteous; the devil sows the wicked (v.24-25).
3. Men question why there is evil in the world and in the kingdom (church). Did God plant the evil as well as the good (v.27-28)?
4. Men are not to judge who the wheat and tares—the good and bad—are. Why? Be-

cause it is sometimes difficult to distinguish between the good and bad, and some of the good might be rooted up (v.29).

5. A day of harvest and of judgment is coming (v.29-30).
6. God alone has the wisdom to judge correctly (v.29-30).

Jesus explains the parable in vs.36-43. Glancing at the major points of the parable will help one get an overview of the parable.

OUTLINE:

1. The parable describes the kingdom of heaven (v.24).
2. A man (Christ) sows good seed (the righteous) (v.24, 37, 38).
3. An enemy (the devil) sows tares (the wicked) (v.25, 38, 39).
4. A day for fruit comes (v.26).
5. A day of questioning comes (v.27-30).
6. A day of harvest is coming (v.30).

1. THE PARABLE DESCRIBES THE KINGDOM OF HEAVEN (v.24).

The kingdom of heaven and of God is revealed in four different stages throughout history.

1. There is the spiritual kingdom that is at hand; it is present right now (Mt.4:17; 12:28).

a. The present kingdom refers to God's rule, reign, and authority in the lives of believers.

> **"Who hath delivered us from the power of darkness, and hath translated us into the kingdom of his dear Son" (Col. 1:13).**

b. The present kingdom is offered to the world and to men in the person of Jesus Christ.

c. The present kingdom must be received as a little child.

> **"But when Jesus saw it, he was much displeased, and said unto them, Suffer the little children to come unto me, and forbid them not: for of such is the kingdom of God" (Mk. 10:14-15).**

d. The present kingdom is experienced only by the new birth.

> **"Jesus answered and said unto him, Verily, verily, I say unto thee, Except a man be born again, he cannot see the kingdom of God" (Jn. 3:3).**

e. The present kingdom is entered now and must be received now.

> **"Whether of them twain did the will of his father? They say unto him, The first. Jesus saith unto them, Verily I say unto you, That the publicans and the harlots go into the kingdom of God before you" (Mt. 21:31; see also Mk. 10:15).**

f. The present kingdom is a spiritual, life-changing blessing.

> **"For the kingdom of God is not meat and drink; but righteousness, and peace, and joy in the Holy Ghost" (Ro. 14:17).**

g. The present kingdom is to be the first thing sought by believers.

"But seek ye first the kingdom of God, and his righteousness; and all these things shall be added unto you" (Mt. 6:33).

2. There is the professing kingdom that is also in this present age. It refers to modern-day Christianity in every generation. It pictures what the kingdom of heaven or professing Christianity is like or will be like between Christ's first coming and His return or second coming. This imperfect state is what is called "the mysteries of the kingdom of heaven" (Mt.13:1-52, esp. 13:11).

"Another parable put he forth unto them, saying, The kingdom of heaven is likened unto a man which sowed good seed [good men] in his field: but while men slept, his enemy came and sowed tares [evil men] among the wheat, and went his way" (Mt. 13:24-25).

3. There is the millennial kingdom that is future. It is the actual rule of Christ or the government of Christ that is to come to this earth for a thousand years.

a. The millennial kingdom is the kingdom predicted by Daniel.

"And in the days of these kings shall the God of heaven set up a kingdom, which shall never be destroyed: and the kingdom shall not be left to other people, but it shall break in pieces and consume all these kingdoms, and it shall stand for ever" (Dan. 2:44).

b. The millennial kingdom is the kingdom promised to David.

"I have made a covenant with my chosen, I have sworn unto David my servant, thy seed will I establish for ever, and build up thy throne to all generations" (Ps. 89:3-4).

c. The millennial kingdom is the kingdom pictured by John.

"And I saw thrones, and they sat upon them, and judgment was given unto them: and I saw the souls of them that were beheaded for the witness of Jesus, and for the word of God, and which had not worshipped the beast, neither his image, neither had received his mark upon their foreheads, or in their hands; and they lived and reigned with Christ a thousand years. But the rest of the dead lived not again until the thousand years were finished. This is the first resurrection. Blessed and holy is he that hath part in the first resurrection: on such the second death hath no power, but they shall be priests of God and of Christ, and shall reign with him a thousand years" (Rev. 20:4-6).

4. There is the perfect kingdom of the new heaven and earth that is future.

a. The eternal kingdom is the rule and reign of God in a perfect universe for all eternity.

"Then cometh the end, when he shall have delivered up the kingdom to God, even the Father; when he shall have put down all rule and all authority and power" (1 Cor. 15:24).

b. The eternal kingdom is the perfect state of being for the believer in the future.

"Now this I say, brethren, that flesh and blood cannot inher-

it the kingdom of God; neither doth corruption inherit incorruption" (1 Cor. 15:50).

c. The eternal kingdom is an actual place into which believers are to enter sometime in the future.

"And I say unto you, That many shall come from the east and west, and shall sit down with Abraham, and Isaac, and Jacob, in the kingdom of heaven" (Mt. 8:11).

d. The eternal kingdom is a gift of God that will be given in the future.

"Fear not, little flock; for it is your Father's good pleasure to give you the kingdom" (Lk. 12:32).

QUESTIONS:

1. God's kingdom cannot be experienced in the future if it is not first experienced now. What is the most important thing a person must do to secure entrance into the kingdom of heaven?
2. What are some of the major differences between God's kingdom and man's kingdom? Why are so many people comfortable living in man's kingdom?

2. A MAN (CHRIST) SOWS GOOD SEED (v.24, 37-38).

The man is Christ, the Son of Man (v.37); *the good seed* are the righteous (v.43), the children of the kingdom (v.38). *The field* is the world. Note two things.

1. The man, Christ, does His work. His work is to sow righteous people in the world.

"Even as the Son of man came not to be ministered unto, but to minister, and to give his life a ransom for many" (Mt.20:28).

2. The man, Christ, owns the world. The world is "his field."

"All things were made by him; and without him was not any thing made that was made" (Jn.1:3).

APPLICATION:

Note several lessons.

1) Christ owns the field. The world is His by right because He created it (Jn.1:3; Col.1:16; Heb.1:2).
2) Christ does sow in the world. He works actively. He is not far off in outer space someplace, disinterested and inactive. He is vitally interested in the world, and He works hard at sowing the righteous.
3) Seed is scattered all over the field. God has scattered the seed, the righteous, all over the world. No single nation possesses all the righteous of the earth. No single nation is a favorite of God. God is not a respecter of persons.
4) Seed is to bear fruit. If it does not, it is either *dead* or else it is not real seed.
5) There is no righteous person apart from God. He is *the sower* of the righteous seed.

ILLUSTRATION:

There is a sinister movement at work of intimidating believers. It goes like this:

⇒ Keep the gospel to yourself.
⇒ There is no need to evangelize because everyone is going to heaven anyway.

⇒ It is offensive to push your religion on someone who does not believe as you do.
⇒ What will people think if they find out you are a Christian?
⇒ Why make waves? Just leave well enough alone.

After this kind of pressure, many believers just play it safe and do not witness for Christ—just what Satan wants.

A man once visited a farmer who was an acquaintance of his. He had not seen him for a long while, and from all appearances it seemed that hard times had befallen him. Wondering what had gone wrong, he asked, "Have a poor harvest this year?" The response quickly came, "I didn't have any!" "Oh, I'm sorry," his friend sympathized. "Didn't you even get cotton?" "No, and I didn't plant any. I was afraid of what the boll weevil might do." "Well, what about your corn?" "Didn't put in any of that either," said the farmer. "I thought we wouldn't get enough rain." "But certainly you must have gotten some sweet potatoes." "No, I decided not to have any!" he exclaimed. "I was afraid the bugs would get them." No wonder this poor man didn't reap a harvest! He was so apprehensive that he didn't even try to raise anything.[1]

QUESTIONS:
1. Are there things that prevent you from sowing the seed of the gospel in this lost world?
2. How does a person know whether someone is a "good seed" or "bad?" Why is this such an important issue to today's believer?
3. Into what kind of field or workplace has Christ sown you? What special challenges do you face in this field, your workplace?

3. AN ENEMY (THE DEVIL) SOWS TARES (v.25, 38-39).

The enemy is the devil (v.39), the liar, the deceiver, the one who struggles against the truth. *The tares* are the children of the devil or the wicked one (v.38).

1. Note what the enemy (the devil) does. His work is to sow wicked or lawless people in the world and to do it secretly so they will be unnoticed (v.38, 41). He came while men slept (v.25). They were…

- unconscious
- busy
- unconcerned
- unaware
- preoccupied
- enticed with pleasure and other affairs

The devil operated under the cover of darkness and deception.

"Why do ye not understand my speech? even because ye cannot hear my word. Ye are of your father the devil, and the lusts of your father ye will do. He was a murderer from the beginning, and abode not in the truth, because there is no truth in him. When he speaketh a lie, he speaketh of his own: for he is a liar, and the father of it. And because I tell you the truth, ye believe me not" (Jn.8:43-45).

2. Note that the enemy (the devil) sows in the same field as the Lord. The bad are sown among the good. The devil's method is counterfeit and imitation (cp. 2 Cor.11: 13-15). Some within the world and within the church have not been sown by the Lord.

---

1 *INFOsearch Sermon Illustrations* (Arlington, TX: The Computer Assistant, 1-888-868-9029, 1986-1996).

They may be in the world and in the church; they may even look like they belong to Him, but they do not.

> **"For such are false apostles, deceitful workers, transforming themselves into the apostles of Christ. And no marvel; for Satan himself is transformed into an angel of light. Therefore it is no great thing if his ministers also be transformed as the ministers of righteousness; whose end shall be according to their works" (2 Cor.11:13-15).**

APPLICATION 1:
The devil is a sworn enemy to Christ, to the world, and to all good. He is the sworn enemy of man, to his peace, and to the fulfillment of his purpose and life on earth. Whatever power he uses on earth is the same as the power used by wicked men: it is usurped or stolen and unjust.

APPLICATION 2:
One reason so many tares are sown is because so many righteous are sleeping when they should be watching over the field (v.25). Satan never sleeps; he is ever awake for every opportunity.

> **"Be sober, be vigilant; because your adversary the devil, as a roaring lion, walketh about, seeking whom he may devour" (1 Pt.5:8).**

QUESTIONS:
1. Just as Christ sows good seed, Satan sows tares or weeds. What effect do Satan's tares have upon the world? Upon the church?
2. In what ways can God use you to oppose Satan's work?

4. A DAY FOR FRUIT COMES (v.26).

A day for bearing fruit always comes. It comes for every professing Christian. The tares themselves were called "darnel," some form of plant or wild corn that was slightly poisonous and narcotic. When eaten it would cause dizziness and nausea. It was called the bastard wheat. Its roots became intertwined with the roots of the wheat. If it was rooted up, it would destroy the wheat plant before the fruit became mature. The method used to get rid of it was to let it grow and then to harvest it with the wheat. It was then separated from the wheat, bundled together, and cast into a flaming fire.

Note something: the tares (that is, the unregenerate) looked like wheat when sown and during the growing stage. All men appear the same in religious practices. It is during the fruit-bearing stage that the difference appears. Unregenerate men can imitate true believers for only so long; eventually their true nature begins to show.

> **"Even so every good tree bringeth forth good fruit; but a corrupt tree bringeth forth evil fruit" (Mt.7:17).**

APPLICATION 1:
A tare shows itself when the wheat is harvested. Likewise, a person's true nature always comes out eventually. A wicked person may profess to be righteous, but a life of selfishness and unrighteousness will eventually take hold. The profession may continue, but so will the life of wickedness.

APPLICATION 2:
A fact to note: the tares (wicked) among the wheat (righteous) are hurtful to the wheat.

1) They are an evil reflection upon the wheat. They sometimes make it very difficult for the world to distinguish between *good* and *evil*; therefore they are the primary cause for the charge of hypocrisy leveled against the church.
2) They stymie the growth of the wheat. Their behavior and conversation and thoughts are centered in the world, not on Christ. Therefore, the righteous are not edified when tares are clinging to them.
3) They are a threat to the wheat. They can draw needed nourishment from the wheat. The professing tare can tempt and lead the righteous away from the Lord and His nourishment, tempt and lead the righteous into the world and its delights.
4) They can cause the death of the wheat. The professing tare can persecute and even kill the wheat.

QUESTIONS:
1. What influence do tares, the wicked people of the world, have upon you? What influence do you have upon the tares that are planted close to you?
2. Is it possible for tares to grow in a local church? What is the only way to separate the tares (the professing believer) from the wheat (the true believer)? How is God's wisdom seen in this method of separation?

5. A DAY OF QUESTIONING COMES (v.27-30).

There is the question concerning *tares* or evil in the world.
⇒ Where does evil come from?
⇒ If there is a God, why is evil allowed to continue?

At this particular stage of the disciples' growth, Jesus simply states that evil persons are present—that someone who is an enemy to God plants them. His statement without an explanation is enough, at least for the present time. However, in answering the question of evil, a person needs to consider the full revelation of God that is given in Scripture. Scripture reveals that Jesus Christ, the Son of Man, is the original Sower or Creator. He is the Master and Owner of the field or world. He created man to be perfect (v.43), that is, in His own image; and He planted within man a spirit to do right (Gen.1:26). But immediately after creation, the other sower, the devil, went right to work. He began with Adam and Eve (Gen.3:1f); and ever since he has sown nothing but tares, the unrighteous, among God's "good seed."

There is the question as to why evil is allowed to continue in the world and why hypocrites are allowed to continue in the church instead of being disciplined and expelled. This question, of course, concerns judging others. Jesus' answer to this question needs close attention. A person on this earth is not to judge others (see **A Closer Look #1**—Mt.13:29-30).

1. It is sometimes hard to distinguish between the wheat and the tares, those who are truly righteous and those who profess to be righteous but are not. But note: if a person judges, he may tear out some wheat along with the tares.

2. A day of judgment *is* coming; however, it is not to be executed by men, but by Christ at His return.

APPLICATION 1:
Evil is of great concern to the righteous. We must always be before the Lord dealing with the presence of evil and our responsibility toward it.

APPLICATION 2:
Note who is to blame for wicked people in God's kingdom and church: it is not God's servant but the devil who is responsible. God's servant is not at fault and not to be blamed for the presence of hypocrites in the church.

APPLICATION 3:
Great caution and patience must always be shown in dealing with the sins of men.

> **"For the Son of man is come to seek and to save that which was lost [sinful]" (Lk.19:10).**

QUESTIONS:
1. Who is your real enemy—the people who oppose you or Satan? Why?
2. How should you respond to someone who is wary of going to church because "the church is full of hypocrites."

A CLOSER LOOK #1
(13:29-30) **Judging Others**: there are three very practical reasons why no man should judge another.

1. A person is to be judged for his whole life. He is not to be judged for a single act or for a particular period of his life. No one sees another person's whole life. In fact, very little of a person's life (thought or activity) is seen by any one individual.
2. A person may make a serious mistake or go through a stage of terrible sin. Then, by the eternal mercy and eternal grace of God, he may turn back to Christ and make the rest of his life a wonderful service for God.
3. Any person who is judged to be righteous today may fall into sin later, years later. Only God can see the whole of a life. Only God can see and know all the facts that led the person to sin: facts within his being and facts without; pressures within and pressures without; relationships within and relationships without. Only God can know a person completely and fully—accurately know all the ramifications of every thought and act and stage of life.

> **"Judge not, that ye be not judged" (Mt.7:1).**

QUESTIONS:
1. Is it ever appropriate for you to judge another person? Why or why not?
2. Why must the believer trust God's wisdom in dealing with people?
3. Have you ever been too quick to judge another person? What practical lessons did you learn from your experience?

6. A DAY OF HARVEST IS COMING (v.30).

1. The ones to be judged and condemned are in the kingdom; they include all those who offend others and who do iniquity (are lawless).
2. The Bible unquestionably teaches there is to be a torment for unbelievers in fire. However, it must be remembered that the fire we know is material and temporal; it is not spiritual or eternal. Earthly fire does not last forever. Nothing on earth does. Earthly fire is of the physical dimension of being. The fire of hell, whatever its nature and qualities, is spiritual and eternal. It never ends. And men must face this; they must not shrink from the truth of hell. Why? Because hell, that is, separation from God, is much worse than any experience here on earth. It will be much worse than any physical experience imaginable. This is the teaching of Scripture. This is the point Jesus was making. Man absolutely must flee from hell. Man absolutely must flee to Christ for salvation. (See Mt.5:22, 29; 10:28; 18:9; 23:15, 33; 25:41; Mk.9:43-48; Lk.12:5; 16:23; 2 Th.1:8-9; 2 Pt.2:4; Rev.14:10-11; 16:10; 18:10; 19:20; 20:10-15; 21:8.)

MATTHEW 13:24-30, 36-43

ILLUSTRATION:

The reality of an eternity in hell is nothing to take lightly. But unbelievers obviously do not take it seriously. While a lot of people think they are good enough to go to heaven on their own, a few honest souls confess that they have a good chance of winding up in hell. The sad fact is that the path to hell is a broad one. No one in his right mind should follow the crowd on this path. James Hewett shares this prose:

I am told that an Indiana cemetery has a tombstone (more than a hundred years old) which bears the following epitaph:

"Pause Stranger, when you pass me by,
As you are now, so once was I
As I am now, so you will be,
So prepare for death and follow me."

An unknown passerby read those words and underneath scratched this reply:

"To follow you I'm not content,
Until I know which way you went."[2]

QUESTIONS:

1. How would you respond to a person who does not believe in a real, literal hell?
2. How do you use the reality of hell in sharing the gospel with the lost?
   ___I ignore the subject at all costs.
   ___I subtly hint at the threat of hell.
   ___I warn others of the coming judgment of hell.
   ___Other________________________________

SUMMARY:

Why is there evil in the world today? This question has puzzled the simple as well as the profound thinkers of every generation. But in no way has evil hindered God from accomplishing His will on earth. Always remember that the most terrible act of evil—the crucifixion of the sinless LORD—became the greatest act of triumph over evil. God is in complete control and will one day eradicate evil forever. Until that great day, remember these important points:

1. This parable describes the kingdom of heaven.
2. A man (Christ) sows good seed (the righteous).
3. An enemy (the devil) sows tares (the wicked).
4. A day for fruit is coming.
5. A day of questioning is coming.
6. A day of harvest is coming.

PERSONAL JOURNAL NOTES
(Reflection & Response)

1. The most important thing that I learned from this lesson was:
2. The area that I need to work on the most is:
3. I can apply this lesson to my life by:
4. Closing Statement of Commitment:

---

2 *Illustrations Unlimited.* James S. Hewett, Editor, p. 145.

1. Describes the kingdom (Christianity) **2. A mustard seed was sown**	**E. The Parable of the Mustard Seed: The Growth & Greatness of Christianity, 13:31-32** (Mk.4:30-32 Lk.13:18-19) 31 Another parable put he forth unto them, saying, The kingdom of heaven	is like to a grain of mustard seed, which a man took, and sowed in his field: 32 Which indeed is the least of all seeds: but when it is grown, it is the greatest among herbs, and becometh a tree, so that the birds of the air come and lodge in the branches thereof.	a. A man deliberately took & sowed the seed b. He sowed in his field **3. The mustard seed grew** a. Was the smallest seed b. Grew into the greatest of bushes c. Result: Birds come & lodge in its branches

Section IX
THE MESSIAH'S PARABLES DESCRIBING THE KINGDOM OF HEAVEN, Matthew 13:1-52

Study 4: **THE PARABLE OF THE MUSTARD SEED: THE GROWTH AND GREATNESS OF CHRISTIANITY**

Text: **Matthew 13:31-32**

Aim: To more fully understand the Kingdom of Heaven (Christianity), its growth and its greatness.

Memory Verse:

"But ye shall receive power, after that the Holy Ghost is come upon you: and ye shall be witnesses unto me both in Jerusalem, and in all Judaea, and in Samaria, and unto the uttermost part of the earth" (Acts 1:8).

INTRODUCTION

Think of the word "potential." Exactly what is it? Very simply, potential expresses the idea of possibility. Potential is rooted in the idea that something is possible if certain conditions are met. To put this on a practical level, think about the early days of companies like...

- Microsoft
- General Motors
- IBM
- AT&T

These companies had original investors who contributed small amounts of money (compared to what a share of their stock is worth today) to support an idea they believed in. Each company had the potential to become a great organization and each company realized its potential. On the other hand, other companies began at the same time as Microsoft, General Motors, IBM, and AT&T and failed miserably. What is the difference? Maybe the product. Maybe the delivery or packaging. Maybe the management. All of these are important and so much more. But whatever the reason, some companies simply failed to succeed.

But the organization that has the greatest potential in history is not a business at all. It is not to be found on the world's stock exchanges. This organization is not governed by a board of directors whose job is to keep the stockholders happy. The organization that has the greatest potential and that has already had the greatest impact on the world is the church of Jesus Christ. From the humble beginnings of a few men who invested their very lives, the message of Christianity has swept the world and has influenced kings, governments, businesses, and people of every tribe, tongue, and nation.

Christ is describing the growth and greatness of His kingdom and of Christianity in this parable. He shows how it begins as the smallest of seeds and grows into the greatest of movements.

The parable is a powerful message to individual believers and congregations as well as to Christianity as a whole. The seed of faith begins ever so small, but it grows into the greatest of bushes as it nourishes itself day by day. Mature (grown, v.32) believers and congregations alike provide lodging (comfort and security) for the people of a turbulent world.

OUTLINE:

1. The parable describes the kingdom of heaven (Christianity) (v.31).
2. A mustard seed is sown (v.31).
3. The mustard seed grows and becomes the greatest of bushes (v.32).

1. THE PARABLE DESCRIBES THE KINGDOM (CHRISTIANITY) (v.31).

The parable describes the kingdom of heaven, that is, the kingdom's present state here on earth.

1. There is the spiritual kingdom that is at hand; it is present right now (Mt.4:17; 12:28).
   a. The present kingdom refers to God's rule and reign and authority in the lives of believers.

   > **"Let this mind be in you, which was also in Christ Jesus: who, being in the form of God, thought it not robbery to be equal with God: but made himself of no reputation, and took upon him the form of a servant, and was made in the likeness of men: and being found in fashion as a man, he humbled himself, and became obedient unto death, even the death of the cross. Wherefore God also hath highly exalted him, and given him a name which is above every name: that at the name of Jesus every knee should bow, of things in heaven, and things in earth, and things under the earth; and that every tongue should confess that Jesus Christ is Lord, to the glory of God the Father" (Ph.2:5-11).**

   b. The present kingdom is offered to the world and to men in the person of Jesus Christ.
   c. The present kingdom must be received as a little child.

   > **"But when Jesus saw it, he was much displeased, and said unto them, Suffer the little children to come unto me, and forbid them not: for of such is the kingdom of God" (Mk.10:14-15).**

   d. The present kingdom is experienced only by the new birth.

   > **"Jesus answered and said unto him, Verily, verily, I say unto thee, Except a man be born again, he cannot see the kingdom of God" (Jn.3:3).**

   e. The present kingdom is entered now and must be received now.

"Whether of them twain did the will of his father? They say unto him, The first. Jesus saith unto them, Verily I say unto you, That the publicans and the harlots go into the kingdom of God before you" (Mt.21:31).

f. The present kingdom is a spiritual, life-changing blessing.

"For the kingdom of God is not meat and drink; but righteousness, and peace, and joy in the Holy Ghost" (Ro.14:17).

g. The present kingdom is to be the first thing sought by believers.

"But seek ye first the kingdom of God, and his righteousness; and all these things shall be added unto you" (Mt.6:33).

2. There is the professing kingdom that is also in this present age. It refers to modern-day Christianity in every generation. It pictures what the Kingdom of Heaven or professing Christianity is like, and what professing Christianity will be like between Christ's first coming and His return. This imperfect state is what is called "the mysteries of the kingdom of heaven" (Mt.13:1-52, esp. 13:11).

"Another parable put he forth unto them, saying, The kingdom of heaven is likened unto a man which sowed good seed [good men] in his field: but while men slept, his enemy came and sowed tares [evil men] among the wheat, and went his way" (Mt.13:24-25).

ILLUSTRATION:
To those who seek to live and prosper in the kingdom of heaven, a life of fulfillment awaits them. On the other hand, there are many people who come close but never receive the benefits of the kingdom.

The kingdom of heaven is like a physician who became wealthy, having discovered a cure for a fatal disease. After some time, when he knew he would not be living much longer, he decided to give his wealth to some people in real need.

One day he went out on the street and found a man lying on the sidewalk, hungry, hopeless, and almost naked. The doctor took pity on him and extended to him a bank card. He said to him, "Take this card. It gives you access to a bank account with $100,000,000. You must make withdrawals every day for all your needs and to help others as much as you can."

The outcast looked at the card. He looked at the physician. He looked at the card again. He couldn't believe anything the good man said. "Could it be," he thought, "that this stranger has gone out of his mind?" Angrily, he grabbed the card threw it away, spat on his would-be benefactor, and returned to his sidewalk bed.

The doctor continued his search...[finally, a]...woman caught the famous physician's eye. She was in the greatest need of all: deathly sick, thin, and weak. The rich man made the same offer to her: "Take this card. It represents all that you need and more. You must make withdrawals every day for all your needs and for the needs of those around you." She took the card in her trembling hands and saw her very own name on it. She thanked the rich man and went straightway to the bank. She walked up to the teller, presented the card, and dared to ask for $100. She could not yet fully understand the vast riches at her disposal. The teller was a friend of the wealthy doctor and was aware of his offers. She could see the woman's true distress and kindly responded, "Is that all you need? You'll earn more in interest in the time it takes me to count *it out than what you asked for!" The woman, in total disbelief, then asked for what she thought was a staggering sum—$5,000.*

The woman rented a small apartment, bought food and new clothes, took a badly needed bath, and went to the rich physician for healing of her sickness as well as advice on how to prevent its recurrence. The woman began to live as much like a rich person as she knew how and sought to imitate the only wealthy person with whom she was acquainted—the physician. Following the instructions given her, the woman went to the bank every day to make withdrawals and shared her wealth with others in need.[1]

QUESTIONS:

1. How aware are you of Christianity or the Kingdom of Heaven...
   - when you are tempted to sin?
   - when you are weak in your faith?
   - when you are on the mountain-top of success?
   - when you are in the valley of failure or despair?
   - when you are being persecuted because of your faith?

2. What impact should the Kingdom of Heaven have upon your day-to-day life?

A CLOSER LOOK #1

(13:31-32) **Mustard Seed, Parable of**: there are two interpretations of this parable.

1. Some say the birds are those in the world who find their lodging in the kingdom (the church and Christianity) that had so small a beginning, but is now growing into a stately movement. Many in the world, believers and non-believers alike, have found help and safety under its branches. Laws and institutions of mercy, justice, and honor have to a large extent evolved from this magnificent movement. This interpretation relies heavily upon the picture painted by the Old Testament. A great empire is said to be like a tree and conquered nations are said to be like birds who lodge under its shadow (Ezk.17:22-24; 31:1-6; Dan.4:14).

2. Others say the birds are the children of the evil one who see the lodging facilities and protective covering of the kingdom and seek lodging therein.

Neither interpretation need exhaust the meaning. However, two facts should be noted.

1. Jesus was speaking to the multitudes in the first four parables. His purpose was to teach what the Kingdom of Heaven is like. It is a *mixture of good and evil*. He had just been vindicating His Messiahship to the Pharisees (Mt.12:1-50) who were set upon destroying Him (Mt.12:14). It was the same day that He began to speak in parables, and His purpose was to hide the mysteries from unbelievers and to protect Himself from those who would destroy Him (Mt.13:10-17). They were the evil ones who had penetrated the kingdom. However, this fact needs to be known only by true disciples, not necessarily by those who are evil. Therefore, some say that the very purpose for speaking in parables seems to point to the interpretation of a mixture of good and evil.

2. The birds are used to describe the evil one in the Parable of the Seed (v.4, 19).

2. A MUSTARD SEED IS SOWN (v.31).

The mustard seed was used in proverbial sayings to describe smallness in the day of Jesus. The mustard seed grew to be a great bush, a bush as large as a tree. Its characteristics were loftiness, expansion, and prominence. (See A Closer Look # 2, Mustard Seed—Mt.13:31.)

---

1 *Ministry,* Jun. 1994. Page 20. SOURCE: *INFOsearch Sermon Illustrations* (Arlington, TX: The Computer Assistant, 1-888-868-9029, 1986-1996).

MATTHEW 13:31-32

The Man in the parable is Jesus Christ. The *field* is the world, *His* world. (cp. v.24, 37-38). It is in *His* field or *His* world that Jesus Christ plants the seed.

The word *took* means to deliberately take; to take with purpose and thought. The planting of the seed was not by chance. It did not just happen. Christ *deliberately* planted the seed and nourished the growth of the bush. The bush existed because of *great purpose and thought*.

APPLICATION:
The Man in the parable was active, very active, not lazy or lethargic. He planned and He sowed. This is a great lesson for us as we sow seeds in our lives. What an enormous difference there would be in the world if we would live our lives in such a manner that many could come and find the care they so desperately need!

QUESTIONS:
1. Like the mustard seed, your life as a believer started out small. Has your witness grown beyond yourself since then? If not, why not? If so, how did this growth take place?
2. There is an old saying that we are to bloom where God plants us. Where has God planted you to serve Him? What kind of witness do you have—is your witness…
   - blossoming?
   - stunted and not growing?
   - unfruitful?
   - dead?

A CLOSER LOOK #2
(13:31) **Mustard Seed**: the seed was not actually the smallest seed known in Jesus' day. But the seed was small and the mustard bush grew as large as some trees. It has been reported that a rider on horseback could find shade under its branches. The fact that such a small seed could produce such a huge bush caused people to use the mustard seed as a proverbial expression to describe smallness.

3. THE MUSTARD SEED GREW AND BECAME THE GREATEST OF BUSHES (v.32).

Note three things.

1. There was the beginning of the bush (Christianity). It began as the smallest of seeds. There are several facts that show just how small the beginning of the kingdom or Christianity really was.

a. Christianity began in the soul of a single person. Christ launched the movement all by Himself. The idea and dream were in His soul and no one else's. He moved out alone—in God's strength.

> **"For God so loved the world, that he gave his only begotten Son, that whosoever believeth in him should not perish, but have everlasting life" (Jn.3:16).**

b. Christianity was born in the soul of a carpenter from the obscure villages of Nazareth and Capernaum (Galilee) and from an obscure and despised nation, Israel.

> **"Philip findeth Nathanael, and saith unto him, We have found him, of whom Moses in the law, and the prophets, did write, Jesus of**

Nazareth, the son of Joseph. And Nathanael said unto him, Can there any good thing come out of Nazareth? Philip saith unto him, Come and see" (Jn.1:45-46).

c. Christianity was carried forth by men without position and without prestige. They were not mighty or noble or famous. They were only common folk, some from ordinary professions such as fishing (Mt.4:18-21) and some from despised professions such as tax collecting (Mt.9:9).

"For ye see your calling, brethren, how that not many wise men after the flesh, not many mighty, not many noble, are called: but God hath chosen the foolish things of the world to confound the wise; and God hath chosen the weak things of the world to confound the things which are mighty; and base things of the world, and things which are despised, hath God chosen, yea, and things which are not, to bring to nought things that are: that no flesh should glory in his presence" (1 Cor.1:26-29).

d. Christianity grew from just a few persons who had very "little faith" (cp. Mt.14:31; Lk.12:32).

"Wherefore, if God so clothe the grass of the field, which to day is, and to morrow is cast into the oven, shall he not much more clothe you, O ye of little faith?" (Mt.6:30).

e. Christianity numbered only about one hundred and twenty persons when Christ departed this earth.

"And in those days Peter stood up in the midst of the disciples, and said, (the number of names together were about an hundred and twenty)" (Acts 1:15).

2. There was the growth of the bush (Christianity) into the greatest of bushes. Christ said explicitly that when the kingdom or Christianity is fully grown, it is the greatest of movements.

a. Christianity is the greatest movement socially. It has changed the face of the earth. Liberty and freedom, and the laws and institutions of mercy, justice, and honor have for the most part evolved from Christianity. The movement has set free the enslaved and raised enormously the status of women and children.

b. Christianity is the greatest movement individually and personally. This is true because Christ did for an individual just what a tree does for a bird.

1) Christ gives *rest* to a person just as a tree provides rest for a bird.
2) Christ gives a *home* to a person just as a tree provides a home for a bird
3) Christ gives *food*, physically and spiritually, to a person just as a tree provides food for a bird.

APPLICATION:

This parable is a great encouragement to every believer.

1) It is an encouragement to us in our personal lives and in our ministries. No matter how small we may begin, we must continue on. If we continue, our lives and efforts will grow. We may be like Christ and see little growth in numbers while here on earth, but the growth will take place. Success is assured.

"Say not ye, There are yet four months, and then cometh harvest? behold, I say unto you, Lift up your eyes, and look on the fields; for they are white already to harvest. And he that reapeth receiveth wages, and gathereth fruit unto life eternal: that both he that soweth and he that reapeth may rejoice together" (Jn.4:35-56).

2) It is an encouragement to our hope in eternity. The eternal kingdom will finally come some day and we shall be rewarded for our faithful labor.

> **"And whosoever shall give to drink unto one of these little ones a cup of cold water only in the name of a disciple, verily I say unto you, he shall in no wise lose his reward" (Mt.10:42).**

ILLUSTRATION:
God is growing His kingdom in the hearts of His people all around the earth. It might not look like much to some, but rest assured, the Kingdom of Heaven is growing in us.

> *A little boy came to see a farmer one day. He wanted to buy a big watermelon. "That'll be three dollars," said the farmer. The boy replied, "I've only got 30 cents." Pointing to a very small watermelon in the corner of the field, the farmer said, "How about that one?" "OK, I'll take it," said the little boy. "But leave it on the vine. I'll come back and get it in a month."*[2]

3. There was the result of the bush's presence. The birds come and lodge in its branches. The same two steps are essential for man.

a. First, a person must come.

> **"Come unto me, all ye that labour and are heavy laden, and I will give you rest" (Mt.11:28).**

b. Second, a person must lodge and live and walk in Christ.

> **"As ye have therefore received Christ Jesus the Lord, so walk ye in him" (Col.2:6).**

QUESTIONS:
1. What practical lessons can you draw from the parallel between the mustard seed and Christianity?
2. What impact has Christianity made in your community? How does the Christian life affect…
   - families?
   - the poor?
   - the widows and orphans?
   - the spiritually bankrupt person?

SUMMARY:

There is a great lesson for us in this parable: no matter how small, how insignificant, how trivial we perceive God's Kingdom to be, it is growing right before our eyes. The Kingdom of Heaven is on the move, capturing the hearts of people in every corner of the world. Whenever you begin to doubt the growth of God's kingdom, remember the points taught from this Scripture:

1. The parable describes the Kingdom of Heaven (Christianity).
2. A mustard seed is sown. The planting of the seed was not by chance. It did not just happen. Christ *deliberately* planted the seed and nourished the growth of the bush. The bush existed because of *great purpose and thought*.
3. The mustard seed grows and becomes the greatest of bushes, filling the world with the saving gospel of Jesus Christ.

---

2 *Bit & Pieces*. Vol. M, No. 1D (1991), p.2. SOURCE: *INFOsearch Sermon Illustrations* (Arlington, TX: The Computer Assistant, 1-888-868-9029, 1986-1996).

MATTHEW 13:31-32

PERSONAL JOURNAL NOTES
(Reflection & Response)

1. The most important thing that I learned from this lesson was:

2. The area that I need to work on the most is:

3. I can apply this lesson to my life by:

4. Closing Statement of Commitment:

	F. The Parable of the Leaven: The Transforming Power of the Gospel, 13:33 (Lk.13:20-21)
1. The parable describes the kingdom 2. Leaven is deliberately taken 3. Leaven is mixed in unfinished meal 4. Leaven silently transforms the whole lump	33 Another parable spake he unto them; The kingdom of heaven is like unto leaven, which a woman took, and hid in three measures of meal, till the whole was leavened.

Section IX
THE MESSIAH'S PARABLES DESCRIBING THE KINGDOM OF HEAVEN, Matthew 13:1-52

Study 5: THE PARABLE OF THE LEAVEN: THE TRANSFORMING POWER OF THE GOSPEL

Text: **Matthew 13:33**

Aim: To examine and embrace the transforming power of the gospel.

Memory Verse:

"Therefore if any man be in Christ, he is a new creature: old things are passed away; behold, all things are become new" (2 Cor.5:17).

INTRODUCTION

One of the chief characteristics of the gospel of Christ is that it miraculously transforms people. From the depths of skid row to the hallowed halls of our churches, people are changed by the power of Christ. As people are transformed, it impacts the world around them.

> *The story is told on an English earl who visited the Fiji Islands. Being an infidel, he critically remarked to an elderly chief, "You're a great leader, but it's a pity you've been taken in by those foreign missionaries. They only want to get rich through you. No one believes the Bible anymore. People are tired of the threadbare story of Christ dying on a cross for the sins of mankind. They know better now. I'm sorry you've been so foolish as to accept their story." The old chief's eyes flashed as he answered, "See that great rock over there? On it we smashed the heads of our victims. Notice the furnace next to it? In that oven we formerly roasted the bodies of our enemies. If it hadn't been for those good missionaries and the love of Jesus that changed us from cannibals into Christians, you'd never leave this place alive! You'd better thank the Lord for the Gospel; otherwise we'd already be feasting on you. If it weren't for the Bible, you'd now be our supper!"*[1]

---

1 *INFOsearch Sermon Illustrations* (Arlington, TX: The Computer Assistant, 1-888-868-9029, 1986-1996).

MATTHEW 13:33

There are essentially two interpretations of this parable.

1. Some commentators say the leaven represents evil that penetrates the Kingdom of God and His church. The main arguments of this position are threefold.
   a. Consistency with the Lord's purpose points to this interpretation. That is, His purpose is to teach that the Kingdom is a mixture of good and evil.
   b. The Lord's very choice of words—*leaven taken by a woman and hidden in the meal*—indicates a mixture of evil within the good. Leaven is always used to symbolize evil in Scripture (cp. Mt.16:6, 11). Leaven sours, ferments, and putrefies. It is a picture of corruption which penetrates and permeates the dough (cp. 1 Cor.5:6-8; 2 Cor.7:1; Gal.5:7-9).
   c. The woman had to hide the leaven, camouflage it in the meal.
2. Most commentators say the leaven symbolizes the Kingdom of God that penetrates and works silently to transform men and society.
   a. It is argued that Christ and His gospel alone have *the power* to transform lives, individually and socially, "till the whole [is] leavened." It is felt that evil could never be said to "leaven the whole" of God's kingdom, for such would mean the failure of the kingdom.
   b. It is also argued that the woman took the leaven and acted with purpose and plan. The argument is that no person can be said to deliberately act against God's kingdom until "the whole [is] leavened." If evil works and works until it has "leavened the whole," then evil will succeed in corrupting God's kingdom. Again, such an interpretation would mean that God's kingdom is to fail.

OUTLINE:

1. The parable describes the kingdom of heaven (v.33).
2. Leaven is deliberately taken (v.33).
3. Leaven is mixed in unfinished meal (v.33).
4. Leaven silently transforms the whole lump (v.33).

1. THE PARABLE DESCRIBES THE KINGDOM OF HEAVEN (v.33).

There is the professing kingdom in this present age. It refers to the people who profess Christianity in every generation. It pictures the imperfect state of the kingdom of heaven or professing Christianity, what professing Christianity is like between Christ's first coming and His return. This imperfect state is what is called "the mysteries of the kingdom of heaven" (Matthew 13:1-52, esp. Matthew 13:11).

ILLUSTRATION:

God's kingdom is spread by those who have been changed by the power of the gospel. If you have been transformed, you have no right to keep it to yourself.

Fritz Kreisler (1875-1962), the world-famous violinist, earned a fortune with his concerts and compositions, but he generously gave most of it away. So, when he discovered an exquisite violin on one of his trips, he wasn't able to buy it.

Later, having raised enough money to meet the asking price, he returned to the seller, hoping to purchase that beautiful instrument. But to his great dismay, it had been sold to a collector. Kreisler made his way to the new owner's home and offered to buy the violin. The collector said it had become his prized possession and he would not sell it. Keenly disappointed, Kreisler was about to leave when he had an idea. "Could I play the instrument once before it is consigned to silence?" he asked. Permission was granted, and the great virtuoso filled the room with such heart-moving music that the collector's emotions were deeply stirred. "I have no right to keep that to myself," he exclaimed. "It's yours, Mr. Kreisler. Take it into the world, and let people hear it!"

MATTHEW 13:33

To sinners saved by grace, the gospel is like the rapturous harmonies of heaven. We *have no right to keep it to ourselves. Jesus tells us to take it out into the world and let it be heard.*[2]

QUESTIONS:
1. Why is the kingdom of heaven hard for an unbeliever to understand?
2. What is the most powerful way you can convey the truth of God's Kingdom to an unbeliever?

2. THE LEAVEN IS DELIBERATELY TAKEN (v.33).

In the first interpretation where leaven represents evil, the woman would probably represent the religion of man or what might be called a rationalistic or humanistic religion. Man has always had a religion of some sort, a religion of his own making. He attempts to satisfy the spiritual need of his soul, and just being associated with Christianity and being within the walls of the church make him feel better.

In the second interpretation where leaven represents the Kingdom of God, the woman would probably be the church and the leaven the gospel. The meal would be the world or those without the knowledge of God in the world. This means that the church would have a twofold task.

1. The church would seek to leaven *individuals*: to penetrate an individual with the gospel until the whole person is transformed.

> **"But as many as received him, to them gave he power to become the sons of God, even to them that believe on his name" (Jn.1:12).**

2. The church would seek to leaven *society* as a whole: to penetrate society with the gospel until the whole of society was transformed.

> **"Go ye therefore, and teach all nations, baptizing them in the name of the Father, and of the Son, and of the Holy Ghost: teaching them to observe all things whatsoever I have commanded you: and, lo, I am with you alway, even unto the end of the world" (Mt.28:19-20).**

APPLICATION:
It was the woman's task to leaven the bread and make it as it should be. Note: (1) she did her job, and (2) it took leaven (the gospel) to do the job right.

QUESTIONS:
1. Believers are "leavening" or bearing witness to others every day—either in a good or bad way. What does it mean to "leaven" or bear witness to someone?
2. How comfortable do you feel when you have an opportunity to share the gospel with another person? What do you need to work on, to change, in order to more clearly and confidently share the good news of Jesus Christ?

3. THE LEAVEN IS MIXED IN UNFINISHED MEAL (v.33).

If the leaven is the gospel, then the picture is that of the gospel being placed...
- into the unfinished and imperfect world
- into the unfinished and imperfect church in its earthly state

---

2 *INFOsearch Sermon Illustrations* (Arlington, TX: The Computer Assistant, 1-888-868-9029, 1986-1996).

The gospel (leaven) has to be placed right in the midst of the world and the church (unfinished and imperfect meal) if it is to do its work.

Note another point: meal is not bread, not by itself. By itself it is hard, dry, unsatisfying, and not very nourishing. Using meal by itself to make bread is insufficient and is a misuse of the meal. Yet, how many try to make it through life without the leaven of the gospel. Their lives are thereby misused and incomplete.

APPLICATION:
The gospel is powerful, extremely powerful. Just a "little leaven leaveneth the whole lump" (1 Cor.5:6; Gal.5:9). Note three things.

1) A person who will allow just a little of the gospel to penetrate his life will eventually have his life changed.

   "These were more noble than those in Thessalonica, in that they received the word with all readiness of mind, and searched the scriptures daily, whether those things were so. Therefore many of them believed; also of honourable women which were Greeks, and of men, not a few" (Acts 17:11-12).

2) Believers are to mix the gospel in the world. Just a little leaven will transform much. But observe: the leaven has to be worked and worked in order to be mixed thoroughly. What a lesson for faithfulness in sounding forth the message of the gospel!

   "These things speak, and exhort, and rebuke with all authority. Let no man despise thee" (Tit.2:15).

3) It does not take much leaven to do the work. No matter how little of the gospel a person knows, he should be leavening, that is, working to reach people and to change the world for Christ. There is no excuse for doing nothing.

   "Howbeit Jesus suffered him not, but saith unto him, Go home to thy friends, and tell them how great things the Lord hath done for thee, and hath had compassion on thee" (Mk.5:19).

If a person interprets the leaven to be evil, then the picture is that of the church in its unfinished and imperfect state. Because it is unfinished and not yet perfected, it is permeated with evil. The evil and unbelieving men (leaven) enter the church; they falsely profess to follow Christ.

QUESTIONS:

1. Have you allowed the leaven of the gospel to work its way into your heart and life? Has it finished its work in you or do you still have room to grow?
2. Think for a moment. Who do you know who needs a little leaven (the gospel) in his or her life? In what ways can you plant the seed of the gospel to impact this person's life?

4. LEAVEN SILENTLY TRANSFORMS THE WHOLE LUMP (v.33).

Leaven changes and transforms bread. Bread made from water is hard, dry, and not very nourishing. But leaven mixed in with dough changes and transforms bread tremendously. It does at least four things for bread.

1. Leaven makes bread soft, no longer hard. The leaven of the gospel does the same. It penetrates the heart of a man, softening the hardness of his life. He becomes much more sensitive toward the Lord and toward the needs of others. He becomes a more caring and giving person. Softness is definitely one of the trademarks of a transformed person.

2. Leaven makes bread porous and moist, no longer dry. The leaven of the gospel does the same. It penetrates the dryness of a man's heart and life so he can grow into a fruitful person.

3. Leaven makes bread satisfying, no longer unfulfilling. Again the leaven of the gospel does the same for the man who lives a dissatisfied life with no purpose, meaning, or significance. The gospel leavens or transforms a person's heart, giving purpose and joy and hope—all the satisfaction a person could ever desire.

4. Leaven makes bread nourishing, no longer of little benefit. The leaven of the gospel does the same thing for the man who seems to accomplish so little in life. The gospel not only gives purpose, but it also inspires and causes a person to feed others. A person transformed by the gospel is able to feed the truth to the world—the truth about the emptiness and loneliness of the human heart and God's provision for man's plight.

Note several important facts about how leaven works.

1. Leaven works quietly and silently. It works without fanfare and the spectacular. There is a thoughtful lesson here on how the gospel should be presented.

2. Leaven finishes its work. Once it is inserted into the dough, nothing can stop it or ever pluck it out. It is in the dough forever, and it will transform the dough forever. There is a great lesson here on the security of the person who genuinely allows the gospel to penetrate his heart and life.

> **"And I give unto them eternal life; and they shall never perish, neither shall any man pluck them out of my hand" (Jn.10:28).**

3. Leaven works slowly and gradually, yet consistently. It takes time for it to leaven the whole lump. The believer can learn at least two lessons from this fact.

a. It will take time for him to grow in the gospel. Just as a child grows physically, if the believer receives proper nourishment, his spiritual growth will take time; but it will be consistent and sure.

> **"And now, brethren, I commend you to God, and to the word of his grace, which is able to build you up, and to give you an inheritance among all them which are sanctified" (Acts 20:32).**

b. It will take time for his own witnessing and work to produce bread. Yet his leavening (service and ministry) will leaven the lump of meal, the people with whom he works.

> **"Let your light so shine before men, that they may see your good works, and glorify your Father which is in heaven" (Mt.5:16).**

4. Leaven changes the quality, not the substance, of the dough. It is still dough, yet it is changed. A man who receives the gospel remains a man, but he is a changed man—a man of quality, a man of God.

> **"Therefore if any man be in Christ, he is a new creature: old things are passed away; behold, all things are become new" (2 Cor.5:17).**

APPLICATION:

The gospel, God's Word of hope, is quick and powerful. It is sharp; therefore, it will penetrate and transform lives.

> **"For the word of God is quick, and powerful, and sharper than any twoedged sword, piercing even to the dividing asunder of soul and spirit, and of the joints and marrow, and is a discerner of the thoughts and intents of the heart" (Heb.4:12).**

MATTHEW 13:33

ILLUSTRATION:
The world is dying for the Bread of Life, the One who transforms and gives hope. We need to be careful to provide what the world needs, not what we think they want.

Max Lucado tells the parable of a beggar who came one day and asked for bread. The baker told him he had certainly come to the right bakery and then took his cookbook down off the shelf and proceeded to tell the poor man everything he knew about bread.

He talked about how the wheat was milled into flour, reciting all kinds of interesting statistics and the precise measurements of the recipe. He was pretty impressed with his presentation himself, but when he looked up the beggar wasn't smiling. 'I just want some bread,' he said.

The baker commended him for that desire and offered to show him the bakery. Guiding him down the hallowed halls, he paused to point out the rooms where the dough was prepared and the ovens where it was baked. "No one else has facilities like these," the baker boasted. "But here is the very best part—the room of inspiration." He just knew the beggar would be impressed as he swung open the double doors to the sanctuary with its beautiful stained-glass windows.

When the beggar didn't say a word, the baker assumed that he was in awe. Quickly he stepped behind the pulpit and whispered, "Oh, I know, my friend. I find it overwhelming, too. People come here from all over the city to hear me speak, and I read to them the recipe from the cookbook of life."

The beggar had slipped into a pew and sat down. The baker assumed that he knew what the man wanted. 'Would you like to hear me speak,' he asked, but the shabby old man repeated his original request: "I'd just like some bread."

"A wise choice," the baker said and led him out through the front door of the bakery. "Now what I'm going to tell you is very important. All along this street you'll find other bakeries, but watch out. They don't serve true bread. I know one of them uses two teaspoons of salt instead of one. And at that one over there they heat the ovens three degrees hotter than they should be. Oh," the baker went on, shaking his head, "they may call it bread, but it's not according to the book!"

The beggar silently turned and started to walk away. "I thought you wanted some bread," the baker called after him. With a shrug, he turned and looked back. "I think I lost my appetite."

The baker went back inside lamenting the fact that the world just isn't hungry for bread any more.[3]

QUESTIONS:
1. What are the distinctive qualities of leaven? Can you recall a time when you personally observed the power of leaven (the gospel) in someone's life?
2. The gospel changes people. In what way has this fact been true in your own life? What habits have been changed? What attitudes, prejudices, biases have been overcome?

---

3 *A Gentle Thunder*. Max Lucado. (Nashville, TN: Word Publishing, 1995), p.41-42.

MATTHEW 13:33

SUMMARY:

The gospel of Jesus Christ has the power to change even the hardest heart. God challenges each believer to take this transforming message and share it with the world. Note these important facts:

1. The parable of the leaven describes the kingdom of heaven.
2. The leaven, the gospel, the kingdom of heaven is deliberately taken.
3. The leaven, the gospel, the kingdom of heaven is mixed in unfinished meal, in the world.
4. The leaven, the gospel, the kingdom of heaven silently transforms the whole lump (the believer).

PERSONAL JOURNAL NOTES
(Reflection & Response)

1. The most important thing that I learned from this lesson was:

2. The area that I need to work on the most is:

3. I can apply this lesson to my life by:

4. Closing Statement of Commitment:

	G. The Messiah's Purpose for Speaking in Parables, 13:34-35 (Mk.4:33-34)
1. To reach the multitude **2. To teach "these things"** **3. To fulfill Scripture** **4. To reveal the mystery of the gospel**	34 All these things spake Jesus unto the multitude in parables; and without a parable spake he not unto them: 35 That it might be fulfilled which was spoken by the prophet, saying, I will open my mouth in parables; I will utter things which have been kept secret from the foundation of the world.

Section IX
THE MESSIAH'S PARABLES DESCRIBING THE KINGDOM OF HEAVEN, Matthew 13:1-52

Study #5: THE MESSIAH'S PURPOSE FOR SPEAKING IN PARABLES

Text: **Matthew 13:34-35**

Aim: To understand and benefit from Christ's use of parables.

Memory Verse:

"That it might be fulfilled which was spoken by the prophet, saying, I will open my mouth in parables; I will utter things which have been kept secret from the foundation of the world" (Mt.13:35).

INTRODUCTION

Some of a nation's most important treasures are its secrets. If those secrets fall into the wrong hands, the strength and integrity of the nation are put at risk. Just imagine if the secrets of your nation were exposed to your enemy:

⇒ the military secrets
⇒ the scientific secrets
⇒ the economic secrets
⇒ the political secrets

Every nation has had its traitors through the years, and the ramifications for the nation betrayed were disastrous. Even as a nation's secrets are important, the secrets of God's kingdom are important—but even more so.

A secret is something that is hidden, kept from someone...

- who is not ready to hear
- or who cannot understand
- or who does not deserve to know

MATTHEW 13:34-35

When and with whom does God share His secrets? In these two important verses, Christ reveals His purpose for speaking in parables.

OUTLINE:
1. To reach the multitude (v.34).
2. To teach "these things" (v.34).
3. To fulfill Scripture (v.35).
4. To reveal the mystery of the gospel (v.35).

1. TO REACH THE MULTITUDE (v.34).

There were several reasons why the crowds followed Christ in such numbers throughout His ministry.

1. Some followed Christ because they had great need. They truly believed He could help them.
2. Some followed Christ for what they could get out of Him. Following Him fulfilled, to some degree, their material and physical desires (Jn.6:26).
3. Some followed Christ out of curiosity.
4. Some followed Christ because they thought He was the answer to utopia, to personal and national fulfillment. They thought He might possibly be the Messiah who was to free Israel and meet the needs of its people forever.
5. Some few followed Christ because they honestly believed He was the true Messiah and had the words of eternal life. They desired to be true disciples of His (Jn.6:67-68; cp. 1:29, 34, 40-41, 45, 49; Mt.16:16).

QUESTIONS:
1. People today follow Christ for many different reasons. What is the best reason to follow Him?
2. What events in your life caused you to follow Christ?

2. TO TEACH "THESE THINGS" (v.34).

There are many teachers, ministers and laymen alike who would like to be progressive and creative, to come up with novel ideas, to make some advancement in thought. They want people to recognize and approve them; therefore, they try to impress people. In so doing, they go beyond Christ and what He taught. They twist or branch off from the teachings of Christ. John warns against this: if a person does not follow the teachings of Christ, then he does not have God. He is not saved; he is not truly born of God. The only person who is born of God is the person who stays in the teachings of Christ. This does not mean that believers are not to be creative and thoughtful. It means that we must not move out beyond Christ and His teachings.

ILLUSTRATION:
There are certain laws that can be modified without bringing harm to a person. For example, the law of gravity can be modified by the law of aerodynamics. Through this second law, an airplane can lift off the ground and fly. However, if the law of aerodynamics is ever broken, the plane will revert to the first law, the law of gravity.

There once was an elderly couple who were first-time flyers. Everything about the trip across the vast ocean was new to them. About mid-way through the flight, the captain calmly announced on the public address that one of the three engines had mechanical failure and had to be shut down. "There is no need for concern folks. We have two powerful engines that will get us safely to our destination. We will need to adjust our arrival one hour later than scheduled." That seemed to satisfy the couple and they reclined back into their seats only to hear another, more urgent, message from the captain: "Sorry to disturb you again so quickly, but our number two engine has stopped working. Our time of arrival will be delayed two more hours." The wife looked at her husband with an air of slight irritation and said, "If that third engine goes out, we will be up here forever!"

As long as we stay true to God's Word, true to the teachings of Christ, we will be filled with His power and achieve our goal.

APPLICATION:
Note: it is the teachings of Christ that we are to follow, not teachings about Christ. As A.T. Robertson says in his *Word Pictures in the New Testament* (Vol.6, p.254), our standard is to be Christ. We must be progressive and seek to move forward, but it should be toward Christ, not away from Him. What are the teachings of Christ? The following verses give us the doctrine of Christ.

THE TEACHINGS OF CHRIST

The Doctrine of Christ	Scriptural Basis
The Incarnation of Christ	**"And the word was made flesh, and dwelt among us, (and we beheld his glory, the glory as of the only begotten of the Father,) full of grace and truth" (Jn.1:14).**
The Salvation of Christ	**"And as Moses lifted up the serpent in the wilderness, even so must the Son of man be lifted up: that whosoever believeth in him should not perish, but have eternal life" (Jn.3:14-15).** **"And many other signs truly did Jesus in the presence of his disciples, which are not written in this book: but these are written, that ye might believe that Jesus is the Christ, the Son of God; and that believing ye might have life through his name" (Jn.20:30-31).**
The Deity of Christ	**"That all men should honour the Son, even as they honour the Father. He that honoureth not the Son honoureth not the Father which hath sent him" (Jn.5:23).** **"I and my Father are one" (Jn.10:30).** **"He that hateth me hateth my Father also" (Jn.15:23).**
The Bread of Life	**"And Jesus said unto them, I am the bread of life: he that cometh to me shall never hunger; and he that believeth on me shall never thirst" (Jn.6:35).**
The Source of Eternal Life	**"But there are some of you that believe not. For Jesus knew from the beginning who they were that believed not, and who should betray him. And he said, Therefore said I unto you, that no man can come unto me, except it were given unto him of my Father. From that**

The Doctrine of Christ	Scriptural Basis
	time many of his disciples went back, and walked no more with him. Then said Jesus unto the twelve, Will ye also go away? Then Simon Peter answered him, Lord, to whom shall we go? thou hast the words of eternal life" (Jn.6: 64-68).
The Representative, The Ambassador of God	**"Jesus answered them, and said, My doctrine is not mine, but his that sent me. If any man will do his will, he shall know of the doctrine, whether it be of God, or whether I speak of myself" (Jn.7:16-17).**
The Glory of Christ	**"And this is life eternal, that they might know thee the only true God, and Jesus Christ, whom thou hast sent" (Jn.17:3).**

QUESTIONS:
1. The shift from truth to error is often subtle. What safeguards can you establish in your own life to keep the truth of God's Word before you?
2. Have you grasped the doctrines of Christ? How confident are you in your ability to share these great truths with an unbeliever?
3. Bad doctrine almost always starts out with a grain of truth. Can you think of any examples where the truth of God's Word has been perverted?

3. TO FULFILL SCRIPTURE (v.35).

A person must know that Christ came to fulfill the law. Jesus said He was neither contradicting nor destroying the Old Testament Scriptures, nor was He standing against them. He was fulfilling them, completing them, bringing out what was implied. He was showing what the real meaning of the Old Testament Scripture is, its full meaning—all that God intended the Scripture to say. As God's Son, He is the Revelation of the truth. He is to reveal the true and complete meaning of the Scriptures. There are several ways in which Jesus Christ fulfilled the law.

1. Before Christ, the law described how God wanted man to live. The law was the ideal, the words that told man what he was to do. But Christ fulfilled and completed the law; that is, God gave man more than just mere words to describe how He wants man to live. He gave man the Life, the Person who perfectly pictures and demonstrates the law before the world's very eyes. Jesus Christ is the Picture, the Living Example, the Pattern, the Demonstration of life as it is to be lived. He is the Perfect Picture of God's will, the Ideal Man, the Representative Man, the Pattern for all men.

> **"And the Word was made flesh, and dwelt among us, (and we beheld his glory, the glory as of the only begotten of the Father,) full of grace and truth" (Jn.1:14).**

2. Before Christ, the law was only words and rules. It could only inject the idea of behavior into the mind of a person. It had no spirit, no life, no power to enable a person to do the law. However, Christ fulfilled and completed the law. He was *Spirit and Life*, so He was able to put spirit and life to the words and rules of the law. He was able to live the life described by the words and rules. As such, He was able to inject both

the idea and the power to behave into a person's mind and life. It is now His life that sets the standard and the rule for the believer; it is His Spirit and life that gives the believer power to obey.

> **"There is therefore now no condemnation to them which are in Christ Jesus, who walk not after the flesh, but after the Spirit. For the law of the Spirit of life in Christ Jesus hath made me free from the law of sin and death. For what the law could not do, in that it was weak through the flesh, God sending his own Son in the likeness of sinful flesh, and for sin, condemned sin in the flesh: that the righteousness of the law might be fulfilled in us, who walk not after the flesh, but after the Spirit" (Ro.8:1-4).**

3. Before Christ, the law stated only the rule and the principle of behavior. It did not explain the rule nor the spirit behind the rule. Neither did the law give the full meaning of the rule. The law always had to have an interpreter. But Christ fulfilled and completed the law. He explained the rule and the spirit behind the rule. He interpreted the law. He gave the law its real and full meaning.

> **"But before faith came, we were kept under the law, shut up unto the faith which should afterwards be revealed. Wherefore the law was our schoolmaster to bring us unto Christ, that we might be justified by faith" (Gal.3:23-24; see also Ro.3:20-22).**

4. Before Christ, the law demanded perfect righteousness; it demanded a perfect life. But man failed at certain points. Man just could not obey the law perfectly; he fell short of perfect righteousness. But Christ fulfilled and completed the law. He kept the law in *every detail*. He secured the *perfect righteousness* demanded by the law. He fulfilled all the requirements, all the types, and all the ceremonies of the law—perfectly. As such, He became the Perfect Man, the Ideal Man, the Representative Man for all men. As the Ideal Man, He simply embraced all men; He embodied the righteousness that man must now have.

> **"Therefore by the deeds of the law there shall no flesh be justified in his sight: for by the law is the knowledge of sin. But now the righteousness of God without the law is manifested, being witnessed by the law and the prophets; even the righteousness of God which is by faith of Jesus Christ unto all and upon all them that believe: for there is no difference" (Ro.3:20-22; see also 2 Cor.5:21).**

5. Before Christ, the law demanded punishment for disobedience. If a man broke the law, he was to be punished. But Christ fulfilled and completed the law. In fact, He went to the farthest point possible in fulfilling the law. He paid the maximum price and showed the ultimate love. He bore the punishment of the law for every man's disobedience; He took the punishment of the law upon Himself. As the Ideal Man, He not only embodies the righteousness that must cover all men, He also frees all men from the penalty of the law. And He makes them sons of God. (See Ro.8:15-17; Gal.3:13-14; Gal.4:1-7.)

QUESTIONS:

1. How often do you spend time in the Old Testament? What value is there in having an intimate knowledge of the Old Testament?
2. Jesus Christ *fulfilled* the law. What does this mean to the person who rejects the teachings of the Old Testament?
3. What frustrations does a person face who tries to keep the law without Christ?

4. TO REVEAL THE MYSTERY OF THE GOSPEL (v.35).

God has revealed the mystery of His will to us. Remember: in the Bible a mystery is not something unexplainable or difficult to understand. Rather, it is a truth that has been locked up in God's plan for ages until He was ready to reveal it to man. When the time came, He unlocked the truth and opened it up to man. A mystery is a truth revealed by God that had never before been known. The mystery of God's will can be simply stated: God is to gather together and unify all things in a spirit of peace and harmony—all things, both visible and invisible. All things are to be brought to a peaceful and eternal state under the authority and glorification of Jesus Christ. God is moving history toward that climactic consummation.

⇒ God has an eternal purpose and plan for the world, and it is His pleasure to bring it about. He joys and rejoices to bring it about, and what He does is good. It is all good.

⇒ There is terrible division throughout the universe. The need for God "to gather all things in heaven and earth" indicates division (cp. Eph.6:12). And the fact that God's primary concern through all the ages has been to harmonize the divisions shows how devastating and horrible the division really is.

⇒ There is to be a consummation, a climax of history—a fulness of time, a new order—in which all things will be unified and harmonized and brought to a peaceful state under the authority of Jesus Christ. History is in the hands of God.

⇒ Jesus Christ is God's appointed Head over the new creation and new order. He is God's Head over the church, which is God's new creation in the present world and order of things (Eph.1:22-23). And He is to be God's Head over the new creation in the future world and order of things (Jas.1:18).

⇒ The church is the Lord's instrument of reconciliation and peace, His representative body upon the earth. As the instrument of the Lord, the church is to do two things.

   a. The church is to take Christ and His message of reconciliation and peace to the world. Through "His body, the church," all division and disorder among men are to be condemned, and His message of harmony and peace is to be proclaimed.
   b. The church is to practice reconciliation upon the earth. "In the church," all laws, barriers, and divisions are to be done away with. They are to be nonexistent. The church is to be a speck or embryo of heaven upon the earth.

ILLUSTRATION:

Wherever the church is, it has the awesome responsibility of being God's representative on earth. Far too often, the work of the church is done by a few strong believers. Can you imagine the possibility if every believer worked together for world evangelism?

David Huxley owns a world record in an unusual category: he pulls jetliners.

On October 15, 1997, for example, he broke his own record at Mascot Airport in Sydney, Australia. He strapped around his upper torso a harness that was attached to a steel cable some fifteen yards long. The other end of the steel cable was attached to the front-wheel strut of a 747 jetliner that weighed 187 tons. With his tennis shoes firmly planted on the runway, Huxley leaned forward, pulled with all his might, and remarkably was able to get the jetliner rolling down the runway. In fact, he pulled the 747 one hundred yards in one minute and twenty-one seconds. A superhuman feat indeed.

The church resembles that 747 jetliner. The strength of a few extraordinary humans can pull the institution of the church for very short distances. Or we can pray until God starts up powerful engines that enable his church to fly thousands of miles on the wings of the Holy Spirit.[1]

Is your church "pulling" or "soaring"?

QUESTIONS:
1. What are some mysteries of God that He has opened up to you?
2. What role are you to have in making known the mysteries of God to the world?

SUMMARY:

When does God share His secrets and with whom does He share them? God shares His secrets with those who belong to Him, with those who follow Christ. Through our fellowship with Christ, He trusts us with the very secrets of the kingdom of heaven. This lesson reminds us again of His purpose for speaking in parables:

1. To reach the multitude.
2. To teach "these things," the Word of God itself.
3. To fulfill Scripture.
4. To reveal the mystery of the gospel.

PERSONAL JOURNAL NOTES
(Reflection & Response)

1. The most important thing that I learned from this lesson was:

2. The area that I need to work on the most is:

3. I can apply this lesson to my life by:

4. Closing Statement of Commitment:

1 *Contemporary Stories & Illustrations for Preachers, Teachers, & Writers.* Craig B. Larson, Editor, p.37.

H. The Parable of the Wheat and the Tares Explained, 13:36-43

1. The parable explained
   a. Jesus was alone with His disciples
   b. The disciples asked the meaning of the parable

2. The good seed
   a. The sower: The Son of man
   b. The field: The world
   c. The seed: The children of the kingdom

3. The bad seed
   a. The seed: The children of the devil
   b. The sower: The devil

4. The harvest
   a. The day: The end of the world
   b. The reapers: Angels

5. The reaping of the tares
   a. Symbolizes judgment
   b. When: In the end of the world
   c. Executed by angels
   d. Who: Those in the kingdom
      1) Who offend others
      2) Who are lawless
   e. The judgment: Fire & weeping

6 The reaping of the wheat
   a. Identity: The righteous
   b. Position: Glory in the Kingdom

7. The strong call

36 Then Jesus sent
the multitude away,
and went into the
house: and his disci-
ples came unto him,
saying, Declare unto
us the parable of the
tares of the field.
37 He answered and
said unto them, He
that soweth the good
seed is the Son of
man;
38 The field is the
world; the good seed
are the children of
the kingdom; but
the tares are the chil-
dren of the wicked
one;
39 The enemy that
sowed them is the
devil; the harvest is
the end of the world;
and the reapers are
the angels.
40 As therefore the
tares are gathered
and burned in the
fire; so shall it be
in the end of this
world.
41 The Son of man
shall send forth
his angels, and they
shall gather out of
his kingdom all
things that offend,
and them which do
iniquity;
42 And shall cast
them into a furnace
of fire: there shall be
wailing and gnashing
of teeth.
43 Then shall the
righteous shine forth
as the sun in the
kingdom of their Fa-
ther. Who hath ears
to hear, let him hear.

PLEASE NOTE: *THIS PASSAGE IS THE EXPLANATION OF THE PARABLE OF THE WHEAT AND THE TARES COVERED IN MT.13:24-30. FOR THIS REASON, THE COMMENTARY IS BEING COMBINED WITH THAT OUTLINE. (PLEASE SEE OUTLINE AND NOTES—MT.13:24-30 FOR DISCUSSION.)*

A CLOSER LOOK #1

(13:41) **Judgment**: the ones to be judged and condemned are in the kingdom; they include all those who offend others and who do iniquity (are lawless).

A CLOSER LOOK #2

(13:42) **Hellfire—Weeping—Gnashing**: the Bible unquestionably teaches there is to be a torment for unbelievers in fire. However, it must be remembered that the fire we know is material and temporal; it is not spiritual or eternal. Earthly fire does not last forever. Nothing on earth does. Earthly fire is of the physical dimension of being. The fire of hell, whatever its nature and qualities, is spiritual and eternal. It never ends. And men must face this; they must not shrink from the truth of hell. Why? Because hell, that is, separation from God, is much worse than any experience here on earth. It will be much worse than any physical experience imaginable. This is the teaching of Scripture. This is the point Jesus was making. Man absolutely must flee from hell. Man absolutely must flee to Christ for salvation.

A CLOSER LOOK #3

(13:43) **Reward**: the righteous will be glorified. The promise is given to the righteous, the promise that they will "shine forth as the sun in the kingdom of their Father."

What does this mean? Several things need to be said.

1. It will involve a *glorified* man. But just what a *glorified* man will look like is not known.

> **"Beloved, now are we the sons of God, and it doth not yet appear what we shall be: but we know that, when he shall appear, we shall be like him; for we shall see him as he is" (1 Jn. 3:2).**

2. It will involve a *glorious* body.

> **"Christ who shall change our vile body, that it may be fashioned like unto his glorious body, according to the working whereby he is able even to subdue all things unto himself" (Ph.3:21; see also Ro.8:17; 1 Cor.15:41-44, 48-50, 53).**

3. It will involve "shining forth" as the sun, a reflection of the glory of God.

	I. The Parable of the Hidden Treasure, Giving up All for Christ, 13:44
1. The parable describes the kingdom **2. A treasure is hid in a field** **3. A man finds treasure** a. He hides & protects it b. He goes, sells all, buys the field, & rejoices	44 Again, the kingdom of heaven is like unto treasure hid in a field; the which when a man hath found, he hideth, and for joy thereof goeth and selleth all that he hath, and buyeth that field.

Section IX
THE MESSIAH'S PARABLES DESCRIBING THE KINGDOM OF HEAVEN,
Matthew 13:1-52

Study 7: THE PARABLE OF THE HIDDEN TREASURE: GIVING UP ALL FOR CHRIST

Text: **Matthew 13:44**

Aim: To look deep inside your heart to answer the question: Have I given up all for Christ?

Memory Verse:

"Again, the kingdom of heaven is like unto treasure hid in a field; the which when a man hath found, he hideth, and for joy thereof goeth and selleth all that he hath, and buyeth that field" (Mt.13:44).

INTRODUCTION

If you were given the opportunity to purchase something extremely valuable, but it would cost you everything you had, would you do it?

⇒ There are people who invest their life savings to buy a business.
⇒ There are people who scrimp and save for years to go to college.
⇒ There are people who put everything they have on the line to buy their "dream house."

Why do some people risk everything for a dream or an ideal? Because they want it badly enough and see the great value in it. This is how it should be for the believer. We should want Christ so badly that we are willing to give all we are and have for Christ.

There are two main interpretations of this parable.

1. Some say that Jesus Christ is *the man* (cp. v.24, 37-38) and *the treasure* in the field represents potential believers who are in the world.

2. Others say *the treasure* is the gospel of Christ or Christ Himself, the Messiah who is ever so precious, and *the man* represents believers who take the message of Christ or the gospel to the world.

MATTHEW 13:44

OUTLINE:

1. The parable describes the kingdom (v.44).
2. A treasure is hid in a field (v.44).
3. A man finds the treasure (v.44).

1. THE PARABLE DESCRIBES THE KINGDOM (v.44).

Jesus was now talking only to His disciples. In v.36, He had sent the multitude away; now He shared four parables with the disciples alone. The parable of the Hidden Treasure and The Pearl of Great Price (13:45-46) could possibly be preached or taught together. Their point is the same: the great value of Christ. Here Jesus used a parable to describe the kingdom of heaven and its immense value.

2. A TREASURE IS HID IN A FIELD (v.44).

1. In this interpretation, where the treasure is interpreted to be potential believers, Jesus sees the treasure of men in the world, and seeing them He does four things.

a. He *hides* the treasure: He takes what the Father has given Him and tucks it away in His heart, choosing and protecting them until He can complete the work of salvation.

"I am the good shepherd, and know my sheep, and am known of mine. As the Father knoweth me, even so know I the Father: and I lay down my life for the sheep. And other sheep I have, which are not of this fold: them also I must bring, and they shall hear my voice; and there shall be one fold, and one shepherd....My sheep hear my voice, and I know them, and they follow me: and I give unto them eternal life; and they shall never perish, neither shall any man pluck them out of my hand. My Father, which gave them me, is greater than all; and no man is able to pluck them out of my Father's hand. I and my Father are one" (Jn.10:14-16, 27-30).

b. He *goes*: He comes to the world.

"For the son of man is come to seek and to save that which was lost" (Lk.19:10).

c. He *sells* all: He gives up heaven in all its glory and splendor.

"And she brought forth her firstborn son, and wrapped him in swaddling clothes, and laid him in a manger; because there was no room for them in the inn" (Lk.2:7).

d. He *buys*: He pays the ultimate price. He gives His life for the life of man.

"But God commendeth his love toward us, in that, while we were yet sinners, Christ died for us" (Ro.5:8).

e. He *joys*: He envisions the glorious day when all His treasure shall be possessed by Him.

"Looking unto Jesus the author and finisher of our faith; who for the joy that was set before him endured the cross, despising the

shame, and is set down at the right hand of the throne of God" (Heb.12:2).

2. In this interpretation, a man sees the gospel, the saving message of Christ, as never before; that is, he understands the immense treasure of salvation, or of Christ Himself (see note 3—Mt.13:44).

a. He *hides* the treasure: tucks it away in his heart, protecting it, not letting it loose. He seeks and continues to seek the truth of Christ.
b. He *goes*: approaches Christ and makes a decision.
c. He *sells all*: repents and turns from his former life to God.
d. He *buys*: commits all and gives all to possess the treasure of salvation.
e. He *joys*: experiences the completeness and satisfaction of the treasure, envisioning and hoping for more and more, eternally.

Either is a fitting interpretation, and we are probably safe in saying that neither one exhausts the meaning.

"Who, when he had found one pearl of great price, went and sold all that he had, and bought it" (Mt.13:46; See also Mk.8:36; 1 Tim.6:7).

Jesus Christ is the most valuable treasure a person can possess. No matter what we offer, it will never be enough to purchase our salvation. And yet, salvation is free. But in no way is it cheap. It cost God His only Son.

ILLUSTRATION:
Some people have the idea that God's treasure can be purchased with money or good works. Paul Francisco writes:

When I was a child, our church celebrated the Lord's Supper every first Sunday of the month. At that service, the offering plates were passed twice: before the sermon for regular offerings, and just prior to Communion for benevolences [charities or goodwill offerings]. My family always gave to both, but they passed a dime to me to put in only the regular offering.

One Communion Sunday when I was nine, my mother, for the first time, gave me a dime for the benevolent offering also. A little later when the folks in our pew rose to go to the Communion rail, I got up also. "You can't take Communion yet," Mother told me.

"Why not?" I said. "I paid for it!"[1]

QUESTIONS:
1. Of all of the things you have—material or otherwise—what do you treasure the most? Why is this true with you?
2. What makes Jesus Christ such a valuable treasure?

3. A MAN FINDS THE TREASURE (v.44).

In Jesus' day it was common practice to hide treasure and valuables by burying them in the ground. The earth was the safest place to hide one's valuables; for example, in the "Parable of the Talents," the unprofitable servant hid his talent in the earth to keep from losing it (Mt.25:25).

The field could represent the gospel. The treasure would then be Christ who is "hid" in the gospel. A person cannot find the treasure (Christ) by just scratching the surface of the earth (gospel). One must dig and dig deep (Jn.5:39; 2 Tim.2:15).

---

1 Cited in *Lite Fare*. "The Christian Reader" (March/April 1993), 38. SOURCE: *Contemporary Illustrations for Preachers, Teachers, and Writers*. Craig B. Larson, Editor, p.93.

MATTHEW 13:44

There is an enormous difference between the philosophical treasures of the world and the treasure of Christ and His Word. A person does not learn the world's philosophical treasures by scratching the surface. He has to dig. So it is with the treasure of Christ: a person has to dig into the gospel and dig deep to find the treasures of the gospel.

When the man finds the treasure, he does five things.

1. He *hides and protects* it. A person who has really tasted and learned the value of Christ hides the treasure in his heart. He continually seeks to lay hold of the gospel; he does not let the gospel go. He resolves to possess the treasure.

> **"That they should seek the Lord, if haply they might feel after him, and find him, though he be not far from every one of us" (Acts 17:27).**

2. He *goes*; that is, he approaches Christ and makes a decision. Note two things.
   a. Christ gives invitation after invitation for men to come and seek His mercy.

> **"Come unto me, all ye that labour and are heavy laden, and I will give you rest" (Mt.11:28).**

   b. A decision has to be made by the man to accept the invitation or not.

3. He *sells* all; that is, he repents and turns away from his former life, turning to God. There are two critical points here.
   a. The man is *willing* to sell and to give up all. He is *willing* to turn to God from all. He is *willing* to repent. Why? To gain the priceless treasure.

> **"Repent ye: for the kingdom of heaven is at hand" (Mt.3:2).**

   b. He is not only willing, but he *gives up and denies all*. He lives a life of self-discipline. This involves the sacrifice of personal desires and ambitions, cravings and wants, lusts and possessions. It involves all of one's life.

> **"And fear not them which kill the body, but are not able to kill the soul: but rather fear him which is able to destroy both soul and body in hell" (Mt.10:28).**

4. He *buys*; that is, he commits all and gives all to possess the treasure of salvation. The person knows something: it is worth anything to *lay hold of* Christ. Therefore, the person presents his body as a living sacrifice to Christ.

> **"Jesus said unto him, If thou wilt be perfect, go and sell that thou hast, and give to the poor, and thou shalt have treasure in heaven: and come and follow me" (Mt.19:21).**

5. He *joys* or *rejoices*; that is, he experiences the completeness and satisfaction of the treasure (Christ) (v.44). The person experiences three things.
   a. He experiences abundant life.

> **"I am come that they might have life, and that they might have it more abundantly" (Jn.10:10).**

   b. He experiences completeness.

> **"And ye are complete in him, which is the head of all principality and power" (Col.2:10).**

c. He experiences the fruit of the spirit.

"But the fruit of the Spirit is love, joy, peace, longsuffering, gentleness, goodness, faith, meekness, temperance: against such there is no law" (Gal.5:22-23).

ILLUSTRATION:
Things that appear to be a "dream-come-true" can often become a nightmare. One man's treasure can easily become another man's tragedy, as is the case following:

Lottery millionaire Buddy Post has a winner's story that's a sobering cautionary tale to those who dream of winning the lottery and living the dream: Be careful what you wish for.

In 1988, the ex-carnival worker and cook won $16.2 million in the Pennsylvania Lottery. But as the Associated Press recounts it, that was when his troubles began.

Even before the first check arrived, Post's landlady sued, claiming she owned part of the winning ticket. The courts awarded her one-third of the proceeds. Meanwhile, Post and various relatives opened a bar, a used-car lot and other businesses, using the promise of lottery proceeds to come as capital. All the businesses failed and by now Post is deeply in debt to lawyers and creditors.

It gets worse. In 1993, his brother was convicted of attempting to kill Buddy and his wife in hopes of inheriting the lottery money. Then Buddy was convicted of assault and sentenced to prison. He's free pending appeal and claims he only fired a gun into the air to scare off his stepdaughter's boyfriend, who was pestering him about a failed business venture.

Post's sixth wife left him and filed for divorce and Buddy has been ordered to pay her $40,000 a year in support. He's $50,000 in debt and has filed for bankruptcy. The gas has been shut off at the mansion he bought with lottery winnings. Now he hopes to auction off 17 future lottery payments worth $5 million. But Pennsylvania Lottery officials are threatening to block the action, claiming that future payments can't be sold.

Buddy Post may or may not have learned by now that money can't buy love, happiness, friends, business acumen and a lot of other desirable things. Surely, though, he's learned that it can buy a lot of trouble. Be careful what you wish for.[2]

The only treasure worth sacrificing all for is Jesus Christ and His Word; anything else has the potential for heartbreak, disappointment, and trouble.

QUESTIONS:
1. How willing are you to dig into the gospel to find eternal treasures?
   __ I am not willing. I'm saved; that's all I care about.
   __ I am willing, but I have to be reminded and pushed to do it.

2 *The Florence News Journal*. Florence, SC, Nov.27, 1996, p.6.

MATTHEW 13:44

SUMMARY:

So many people in the world have yet to discover the treasure of Jesus Christ. But once a person discovers for himself the great value of knowing Christ, he is prepared to give all to gain Christ. What treasure have you found in Christ?

1. The parable describes the kingdom. Here Jesus used a parable to describe the kingdom of heaven and its immense value.
2. The treasure is hid in a field.
3. A man finds the treasure.

PERSONAL JOURNAL NOTES
(Reflection & Response)

1. The most important thing that I learned from this lesson was:

2. The area that I need to work on the most is:

3. I can apply this lesson to my life by:

4. Closing Statement of Commitment:

MATTHEW 13:45-46

	J. The Parable of the Merchant Man & the Pearl of Great Price: Giving Up All for Christ, 13:45-46
1. He seeks pearls a. Seeks *many* pearls b. Seeks *fine* pearls	45 Again, the kingdom of heaven is like unto a merchant man, seeking goodly pearls:
2. He finds a priceless pearl a. He goes b. He sells all he has c. He buys the pearl	46 Who, when he had found one pearl of great price, went and sold all that he had, and bought it.

Section IX
THE MESSIAH'S PARABLES DESCRIBING THE KINGDOM OF HEAVEN, Matthew 13:1-52

Study 8: **THE PARABLE OF THE MERCHANT MAN AND THE PEARL OF GREAT PRICE: GIVING UP ALL FOR CHRIST**

Text: **Matthew 13:45-46**

Aim: To weigh the priceless value of Christ against the cheapness of the world—and consider the cost.

Memory Verse:

"Whom have I in heaven *but thee?* and *there is* none upon earth *that* I desire beside thee. My flesh and my heart faileth: *but* God *is* the strength of my heart, and my portion for ever" (Psalm 73:25-26).

INTRODUCTION

Can you tell the difference between an authentic treasure and a fraud or reproduction?

For many centuries genuine pearls commanded a high price because of their scarcity. Great quantities of oysters had to be examined before a few could be found that contained the coveted treasures. Then suddenly the market became flooded with them. After some investigation the mystery of the abundant supply was revealed. Enterprising individuals had discovered that if a foreign object is lodged in its tender flesh, the oyster will form a glistening pearl around the source of discomfort. Deciding to help nature along, these men artificially induced the process by inserting irritants such as tiny beads and buckshot into the shells. When the pearls had formed, they were carefully harvested. Wealthy patrons became suspicious, however, and insisted that the lustrous jewels be subjected to special tests. Though outwardly they seemed perfect, the x-ray showed their impurity, for they had 'false hearts' of lead or glass.[1]

---

1 *INFOsearch Sermon Illustrations* (Arlington, TX: The Computer Assistant, 1-888-868-9029, 1986-1996).

MATTHEW 13:45-46

There are many people and things that draw us away from what is truly to be treasured: a relationship with Jesus Christ. The lesson of this parable is a reminder to us that only Christ is worth giving our lives, our all, to acquire. The point of this parable is the same as the Parable of the Hidden Treasure. They could be preached or taught together. The Parable of the Pearl has two interpretations.

1. Some say the *merchant man* is Jesus Christ. The *many pearls* for which He seeks are potential believers, and the *one great pearl* is the church, the full body of believers (cp. Jn.17:21; 1 Cor.13:12). Note: the pearls are sought after, and the one great pearl is found as a result of seeking for all the pearls.

2. Some say the merchant man represents those who seek after truth (pearls). In the search, some men discover the truth of Jesus Christ, the pearl of great price; and when a person finds a priceless pearl, he takes the three steps outlined by Christ: he goes, sells all he has, and buys the pearl of great price.

OUTLINE:

1. He seeks pearls (v.45).
2. He finds a priceless pearl (v.46).

1. HE SEEKS PEARLS (v.45).

A true pearl is born out of suffering. A speck of sand or parasite makes its way into an oyster shell. The oyster is a living organism, so the intruder hurts the oyster. To protect itself, the oyster secretes a substance called mother-of-pearl, or nacre, to surround the intruder. It is the secretion that gradually forms the pearl. Thus, the pearl is born out of much torment and pain. The same is true of the believer and the church: both are born out of suffering and out of the travail and death of the Lord Jesus Christ.

> **"That whosoever believeth in him should not perish, but have eternal life. For God so loved the world, that he gave his only begotten Son, that whosoever believeth in him should not perish, but have everlasting life" (Jn.3:15-16).**

ILLUSTRATION:

The life of a believer is not always an easy one, but suffering is not to be shunned. It is often the hardships that define a person's character.

> *The following story is about a handicapped high school student. Although the crutches on which he hobbled kept him from being physically active, he excelled in his studies and was well liked by his peers. They saw the problems he had getting around, and they sometimes felt sorry for him, but for a long time nobody asked him why he had this difficulty. One day, however, his closest friend finally did. 'It was polio,' answered the student. The friend responded, 'With so many difficulties, how do you keep from becoming bitter?' Tapping his chest with his hand, the young man replied with a smile, "Oh, it never touched my heart."*[2]

No matter what hardships come along, a person must not let them affect his pursuit of the truth.

Another picture can be seen in the fact that the pearl is embedded in living, but corruptible flesh. It remains there until perfectly formed and purified. Then it is separated from the corruptible flesh as a thing of beauty. It is priceless, fit for the crown of a king.

---

2 *INFOsearch Sermon Illustrations* (Arlington, TX: The Computer Assistant, 1-888-868-9029, 1986-1996).

"But lay up for yourselves treasures in heaven, where neither moth nor rust doth corrupt, and where thieves do not break through nor steal" (Mt.6:20).

Still another picture is seen in the beauty of a pearl. A pearl has a lovely aesthetic value. It is purchased and possessed as much for the *inward satisfaction and enjoyment* as for its monetary value.

"These things have I spoken unto you, that my joy might remain in you, and that your joy might be full" (Jn.15:11).

QUESTIONS:
1. What good things have come from your own experiences in suffering? Was the suffering worth the price of the pearl?
2. As you look back over your life, what "pearls" do you treasure the most? Why?

2. HE FINDS A PRICELESS PEARL (v.46).

The man discovers the pearl of great price while seeking for pearls. Note there are *many* pearls and some of these are *fine* pearls. Pearls are a symbol of truth and of life. Men seek truth and life in such things as philosophy, science, technology, wealth, fame, sensation (the flesh), art, music, literature, and religion. But there is only one pearl that is priceless, only one pearl that is worth more than the world itself—the pearl of Jesus Christ Himself.

ILLUSTRATION:
There are many people who claim to be or to know the source of truth. Ask a scientist what the basis of truth is and he will tell you science. Ask a banker what the basis of truth is and he will tell you economics. There is some truth in both of these theories, but they are not *the source* of truth. Jesus Christ is the *Source of truth* and He *is the Truth*. The person who possesses Christ knows the Source of Truth, as is illustrated in the following story from Haddon Robinson's book Biblical Preaching:

A Chinese boy who wanted to learn about jade went to study with a talented old teacher. This gentleman put a piece of the precious stone into his hand and told him to hold it tight. Then he began to talk of philosophy, men, women, the sun and almost everything under it. After an hour he took back the stone and sent the boy home. The procedure was repeated for several weeks with a different piece of jade. The boy became frustrated. When would he be told about the jade? He was too polite, however, to question the wisdom of his venerable teacher. Then one day, when the old man put a stone into his hands, the boy cried out instinctively, "That's not jade!" He had become so familiar with the genuine that he could immediately detect a counterfeit.[3]

QUESTIONS:
1. Are you familiar enough with the truth that you would recognize a counterfeit?
2. As a believer, what is your responsibility regarding the truth?

---

3 Haddon Robinson. *Biblical Preaching*. (Grand Rapids, MI: Baker Book House, 1980). SOURCE: *INFOsearch Sermon Illustrations* (Arlington, TX: The Computer Assistant, 1-888-868-9029, 1986-1996).

MATTHEW 13:45-46

SUMMARY:

What have you found in the world that is worth keeping and valuing above Christ? Every day, countless people make the same discovery: no matter what the world offers, nothing compares with the treasure of finding and knowing Jesus Christ.

1. He seeks pearls. Why is this true? Because the believer knows that a true pearl is born out of suffering. The same is true of the believer and the church: both are born out of suffering and out of the travail and death of the Lord Jesus Christ..
2. He finds a priceless pearl. There are *many* pearls and some of these are *fine* pearls. But there is only one pearl that is priceless, only one pearl that is worth more than the world itself—the pearl of Jesus Christ Himself.

PERSONAL JOURNAL NOTES
(Reflection & Response)

1. The most important thing that I learned from this lesson was:

2. The area that I need to work on the most is:

3. I can apply this lesson to my life by:

4. Closing Statement of Commitment:

MATTHEW 13:47-50

Outline	Scripture	Scripture	Outline
1. The parable describes the kingdom **2. A net is cast into the sea** a. It gathers every kind b. It is drawn when full c. The good are	**K. The Parable of the Dragnet: Separating the Bad from the Good, 13:47-50** 47 Again, the kingdom of heaven is like unto a net, that was cast into the sea, and gathered of every kind: 48 Which, when it was full, they drew to shore, and sat	down, and gathered the good into vessels, but cast the bad away. 49 So shall it be at the end of the world: the angels shall come forth, and sever the wicked from among the just, 50 And shall cast them into the furnace of fire: there shall be wailing and gnashing of teeth.	gathered into containers d. The bad are cast away **3. The parable is a symbol of the world's end** a. Angels come forth b. Purpose: Separate the wicked from the just 1) To cast into fire 2) Result: Weeping & gnashing

Section IX
THE MESSIAH'S PARABLES DESCRIBING THE KINGDOM OF HEAVEN, Matthew 13:1-52

Study 9: THE PARABLE OF THE DRAGNET: SEPARATING THE BAD FROM THE GOOD

Text: **Matthew 13:47-50**

Aim: To realize the finality of God's judgment upon the lost.

Memory Verse:

"So shall it be at the end of the world: the angels shall come forth, and sever the wicked from among the just, And shall cast them into the furnace of fire: there shall be wailing and gnashing of teeth" (Matthew 13:49-50).

INTRODUCTION

Anyone who has ever fished knows that a hook can latch onto just about anything. Depending on where a person throws his line, he might pull in an old shoe, some weeds, a log, or—with some luck—a fish or two.

Note that the person is not fishing for the old shoe or weeds or a log. The fisherman is trying to catch something that he can use—fish. And only certain kinds of fish will do. They have to be big enough and they have to be edible. But in order to catch the good, he must take the chance of catching the bad also. The possibility of catching something bad has never stopped the committed fisherman from casting his line. What he cannot use, he simply throws out.

The net in this parable is the kingdom of heaven and the gospel is the message of the kingdom. The sea is the world in all the depths of its darkness and its unknown. The fishermen represent Christ and His followers.

Note several things.

1. The followers of Christ worked and worked hard. They cast the gospel, the message of the kingdom, into the world.

2. There is a mixture of good and bad in the kingdom while it is on earth. The net, the gospel and kingdom, gathers both good and bad.

3. The net has a limit as to how many it will hold. Of course, only the Lord knows when it is time to draw the net. There is a set time, a climactic hour coming.

4. Separation of the bad from the good does not take place until the net is full. The Lord has the right and the wisdom to execute judgment at the proper time. (Cp. Mt.5:13; 2 Pt.3:3-4, 8-13.)

OUTLINE:
1. The parable describes the kingdom of heaven (v.47).
2. A net is cast into the sea (v.47-48).
3. The parable is a symbol of the end of the world (v.49-50).

1. THE PARABLE DESCRIBES THE KINGDOM OF HEAVEN (v.47).

We must always remember that the kingdom of Christ already exists. God transferred us into the kingdom of His dear Son, into the kingdom of the Lord Jesus Christ.

⇒ His rule and reign already exist in the spiritual world or spiritual dimension of being, that is, in heaven.

⇒ His rule and reign already exist in the hearts and lives of believers in this physical world or physical dimension of being.

The message of the glorious gospel is that God has transferred the believer from the power of darkness into the kingdom of His dear Son.

> **"Jesus answered and said unto him, Verily, verily, I say unto thee, Except a man be born again, he cannot see the kingdom of God" (Jn.3:3).**

QUESTIONS:
1. When is God's kingdom most real to you? When is it most hard to believe?
2. How has life changed for you since God transferred you out of the darkness and into His light, His kingdom?

2. A NET IS CAST INTO THE SEA (v.47).

Christ and His true followers do cast the net of the gospel into the world. They work hard "fishing for men" (Mt.4:19) (see A CLOSER LOOK # 1—Mt.13:47).

Note what happens when the net is cast into the sea.

1. The net gathers every kind. The visible kingdom or church contains a mixture of both good and bad. There are reasons why some bad (unconverted people) want to be a part of the earthly church.

a. The church stresses *morality, virtue, ethics, and justice*. Civilization and society progress when they are built upon this message, so the church is considered one of the basic institutions of some societies.

b. The church offers *social standing and opportunity*. In some communities it is even expected that a socially acceptable person becomes a church member.

c. The church offers *fellowship*. Many people are lonely and empty for various reasons such as being single, divorced, a newcomer, or shy. The church meets their need.

d. The church instills a sense of *spiritual security* to some. They feel God is pleased and accepts them because they attend and serve the church regularly. Therefore, they *support and work for* the church.

e. The church offers some degree of *authority* and *direction*. The Bible says that "men are as the fish of the sea...that have no ruler over them." Some find in the church the authority they need. There are few people so self-disciplined that they need no authority or direction.

2. The net is drawn when full. Note two encouraging facts.
   a. Sometimes the net catches more than at other times. The catch sometimes goes quickly and sometimes slowly. God's servant should never despair from lack of results, and he should never quit because of slow results (1 Cor.3:6-8).
   b. The gospel is effective: the net (heaven) will be filled. God's Word will not return to Him empty (Is.55:11).

3. The good are gathered into containers. Note the good are already in the kingdom of heaven while on this earth. They have a real relationship with God already.

> **"I am the door: by me if any man enter in, he shall be saved, and shall go in and out, and find pasture" (Jn.10:9).**

4. The bad are cast away. Who are the bad? They are the sea creatures that are...

- the wrong kind
- too small
- unclean
- useless
- unfit
- dead

ILLUSTRATION:

There are some people who love to take risks. Just for fun, these people gamble with their money, their reputations, and their health. In their minds, the worst thing that can happen is to lose a little time or money. As foolish as this is, it is not as foolish as risking eternity. The lack of assurance does not bother some people.

> *In 1994 Northwest Airlines offered some unusual round-trip passages aboard one of their planes. Fifty-nine dollars bought a "Mystery Fare" ticket that provided a one-day trip to an unknown American city. Buyers didn't find out where they were heading until they arrived at the airport the day of the flight. Still, the airline had plenty of takers. In Indianapolis fifteen hundred people crowded the airline counter to buy the Mystery Fare tickets that were sold on a first-come, first-served basis.*
>
> *Not surprisingly, when buyers learned their destination, not all were thrilled. One buyer who was hoping for New Orleans but found he had a ticket for Minneapolis walked through the airport terminal yelling "I've got one ticket to the Mall of America. I'll trade for anything."*
>
> *Mystery Fare tickets may be a fun surprise for a weekend vacation, but normally the last thing you want is a ticket to a mystery destination. And one time you never want a Mystery ticket is on the day of your death. You don't want to face eternity uncertain about whether you will go to heaven or hell.*[1]

QUESTIONS:

1. What things would attract unbelievers to your church for the wrong reasons? What would attract them for the right reasons?
2. It is God's job to cast away the bad people who are swept up in His net. Why is this God's job and His alone? What can happen if people take this job upon themselves?

---

1 *Contemporary Illustrations for Preachers, Teachers, and Writers*. Craig B. Larson, Editor, p.216.

A CLOSER LOOK #1
(13:47) **Dragnet—Seine Net**: the dragnet was actually a large square net that was pulled through the water behind a boat. It was weighted down so that it formed a *cone-shaped drag* catching everything in its path. The fishermen could tell when the net was full by the weight of its pull. When it was full, they drew the net to shore and began the tedious process of separating the good fish from the bad. The bad, of course, were not kept. They were cast away.

3. THE NET (THE PARABLE) IS A SYMBOL OF THE WORLD (v.49-50).

1. The dragnet cannot distinguish between the good and bad as it is pulled through the water—it just gathers the bad with the good. So angels will come forth to execute judgment in behalf of Christ.

   a. Separation occurs when the net is full and has been pulled to shore.
   b. The angels of God will do the separating, not the church or any religious authority.

It is a fact: when man judges, he blunders and makes mistakes.

2. The purpose of the angels' coming forth is to separate the wicked from the just. Note who it is that is cast away: it is people who are in the net, who are in the kingdom of heaven on earth, but they are still bad. They have not changed and become good. Brushing shoulders with and living among, fellowshipping and worshipping with the good will not make a bad person good. A bad person must sincerely change in order not to be cast away.

ILLUSTRATION:
Teaching and preaching about the reality of hell has caused many sinners to change their minds and give their lives to Christ.

A young man in Switzerland had been brought up in a home where God and the Bible were revered. Although the Gospel was often presented to him with loving urgency, he refused to believe and became increasingly rebellious. Finally he said, 'I'm sick and tired of Christians. I'm going to look for a place where I can avoid them.' His mother wept as he packed his suitcase and left home. He boarded a train, only to find that two passengers seated behind him were discussing the Scriptures. 'I'm not going to stay here,' he muttered. At the next stop he left the coach and entered a restaurant. To his dismay, some elderly ladies were talking about the return of the Lord. Knowing a ship was docked nearby, he decided it might be a way to escape the "religious chatter" he encountered at every turn. But when the steamer embarked, he discovered that it was filled with happy young students from a Bible academy. Thoroughly disgusted, he made his way downstairs to find the bar. Approaching the captain, he exclaimed, "Say, can you tell a man where he can get away from all these cursed fanatics?" The skipper looked up and said with a grin, "Yes, just go to Hell. You won't find any Christians there!" These startling words caused him to realize his eternal peril, and when he returned home, he soon found peace by receiving the Savior. Now he seeks to help others by sharing his testimony with them.[2]

APPLICATION 1:
The only time the bad will be in the presence of the good is now. Soon, very soon, the bad will be separated from the good by Christ, taken and cast out of the

2 *INFOsearch Sermon Illustrations* (Arlington, TX: The Computer Assistant, 1-888-868-9029, 1986-1996).

presence of the good. Christ preached and taught *separation* from God time and again.

> **"So shall it be at the end of the world: the angels shall come forth, and sever the wicked from among the just" (Mt.13:49).**

APPLICATION 2:
There is a specific destination for the wicked, and it is a place of *everlasting punishment*. Christ preached and taught *everlasting punishment* time and again.

> **"But I say unto you, That whosoever is angry with his brother without a cause shall be in danger of the judgment: and whosoever shall say to his brother, Raca, shall be in danger of the council: but whosoever shall say, Thou fool, shall be in danger of hell fire" (Mt.5:22).**

A CLOSER LOOK #2
(13:49-50) **Parable**: note that the first part of this parable deals with the present state of the kingdom or the church. The latter part deals only with the future (v.49-50).

A CLOSER LOOK #3
(13:49) **Sever—Separate**: to separate; to set off by bounds. The wicked are to be taken completely away, taken and cast completely out of the presence of the good.

A CLOSER LOOK #4
(13:50) **Hell-Fire**: the word is used eleven or twelve times in the New Testament, and in every case it is spoken by Jesus except in the Epistle of James. It illustrates the terrible truth of the second death, of man's final separation from God. Jesus pointed to the burning, repulsive rubbish dump outside the city limits of Jerusalem and said that it was exactly what hell was like. The dump was called Gehenna. It was in the Valley of Hinnom which served as a public incinerator. Hanging over it was a layer of thick, smoldering smoke arising from what seemed to be an eternal flame. The smell and filth became a breeding cesspool for a loathsome worm that was difficult to kill (Mk.9:44). Thus, Jesus found in Gehenna a description of just what it means to be separated from God eternally and to die the second death. Note several facts about Hell or Gehenna.

⇒ It is the same as the lake of fire (Rev. 19:20; 20:10, 14-15).
⇒ It has to do with the second death (Rev. 21:8; Jn.8:24).
⇒ It is a literal Hell (Mt.5:29-30; 10:28; 23:15, 33; Lk.12:5).
⇒ It is everlasting fire (Mt.18:8).
⇒ It is hell fire (Mt.18:9; Jas.3:6).
⇒ It is unquenchable fire (Mk.9:43-49).

The teaching of Jesus should always be remembered. Remembrance is critical in determining a person's fate. Hell is a definite place, a real place that is specifically located. It was originally prepared for the devil and his angels. But all men who choose to follow self and evil, rejecting God, shall also be sent to hell eternally.

> **"And now also the axe is laid unto the root of the trees: therefore every tree which bringeth not forth good fruit is hewn down, and cast into the fire" (Matthew 3:10).**

A CLOSER LOOK #5

(13:50) **Weeping and Gnashing of Teeth**: the judgment of unbelievers is to be terrible. Note: Jesus predicted that the Jews who persist in unbelief shall perish. They are rejected by God, despite the fact they had been chosen to be the children of God and had been given so many privileges.

1. There will be outer darkness: a region, a place, a habitation, a home of pitch black that forbids any sight whatsoever. A place without light, without gleam or hope of any light whatsoever. It is a place of utter darkness in which one lives completely incapacitated, helpless, and hopeless. It is far away from the splendor and glory and brightness of God's presence. It is being cast into the gloom and blackness of the outer world. It is misery, the misery of a lost soul.

> **"But the children of the kingdom shall be cast out into outer darkness: there shall be weeping and gnashing of teeth" (Mt.8:12).**

2. There will be weeping: grief, loud grief, mourning, groaning, wailing, floods and floods of tears.

3. There will be gnashing of teeth: grinding; biting in hostility and bitterness and indignation; spitefully snapping the teeth. It is rage, fury, and despair because nothing can be done. A person's state is permanently determined.

> **"And shall cast them into a furnace of fire: there shall be wailing and gnashing of teeth" (Mt.13:42).**

QUESTIONS:

1. Judgment is a sure thing. God will judge the world. What conclusions can you draw about God's character as to why He has not yet fully executed His judgment?
2. Heaven and hell are two distinctively different places. What kind of people will spend eternity in heaven? What kind of people will spend eternity in hell? How can you be certain in your answer?

SUMMARY:

God has cast out His net over the earth and is catching people every day. In His net are believers, people who follow and serve Him day by day. But in His net are also bad people, the unbelievers who will be cast into hell, forever separated from God. The question that you and I must answer is this: When God is sorting out the bad from the good, into which category will you and I be placed?

1. This parable describes the kingdom of heaven.
2. A net is cast into the sea. Christ and His true followers are busy casting the net of the gospel into the world. They work hard "fishing for men."
3. The net is a symbol of the end of the world. The dragnet cannot distinguish between the good and bad as it is pulled through the water—it just gathers the bad with the good. Sometime in the future, angels will come forth to execute judgment in behalf of Christ.

MATTHEW 13:47-50

PERSONAL JOURNAL NOTES
(Reflection & Response)

1. The most important thing that I learned from this lesson was:

2. The area that I need to work on the most is:

3. I can apply this lesson to my life by:

4. Closing Statement of Commitment:

	L. The Parable of the Householder: Devotion & Study & Sharing, 13:51-52
1. The disciples are questioned—do they understand the parables?	51 Jesus saith unto them, Have ye understood all these things? They say unto him, Yea, Lord.
2. They are compared to Jewish Scribes a. To imitate their devotion b. To imitate their study **3. They are compared to the head of a house** a. Possess a treasure b. Are responsible to share	52 Then said he unto them, Therefore every scribe which is instructed unto the kingdom of heaven is like unto a man that is an householder, which bringeth forth out of his treasure things new and old.

Section IX
THE MESSIAH'S PARABLES DESCRIBING THE KINGDOM OF HEAVEN, Matthew 13:1-52

Study 10: **THE PARABLE OF THE HOUSEHOLDER: DEVOTION AND STUDY AND SHARING**

Text: **Matthew 13:51-52**

Aim: To take on a fresh challenge to offer supreme devotion to God.

Memory Verse:

"Study to show thyself approved unto God, a workman that needeth not to be ashamed, rightly dividing the word of truth" (2 Timothy 2:15).

INTRODUCTION

Are you devoted to the study of the Scriptures? Before you answer, how would you define the word "devotion"?

⇒ Does devotion mean a quick five-minute reading of an inspirational thought?
⇒ Does devotion mean saying a quick blessing over your lunch?
⇒ Does devotion mean studying your Sunday school lesson for thirty minutes late Saturday night?

These are not what God means by devotion. A believer who is devoted to the Scriptures lives in them and is governed by Biblical principles in everything he does. A devoted person is a person who wants to make a difference in his generation. One such man was Jim Elliot.

MATTHEW 13:51-52

Jim Elliot was martyred in 1956. At the time of his death he was trying to reach the Auca Indians of South America for Christ. Just 3 years earlier, after watching an Indian die in a jungle hut, he had affirmed his willingness to serve God and die if necessary among these people. Then he added this petition: "Lord, let me live until I have declared Thy works to this generation." I'm sure Jim Elliot didn't expect God to answer his prayer by letting him be speared to death before he was 30 years old. But neither did he have any idea that within 3 years his name would be known all over the world, and that his journals would challenge many to give themselves to the Lord's service. He's been in heaven now for [many] years, but he is still "speaking" to hundreds of thousands of people.[1]

This parable teaches a strong truth: the true disciples of Christ had the same privilege and responsibility as Scribes and householders. They were unusually blessed. Throughout their lives they had been instructed in the old counsel, but now they had been taught by Christ, the Messiah Himself. They now knew the new counsel of God. Thus, they were to be responsible disciples and share the whole counsel of God, both the old and the new.

1. The Jewish Scribe had two unusual traits. He was extremely devoted and he studied his religion all the time. Christ wanted the disciples to develop the same devotion. He wanted them to study the kingdom of heaven (the gospel and His Word) with the same kind of unswerving diligence (Acts 17:11; 1 Cor.15:58; 2 Tim.2:15; 2 Pt.2:2-3). Therefore, He questioned them, "Have you understood these things?" No doubt, He was referring to the parables He had just shared, but He was probably also referring to all that He had been teaching throughout His ministry. They answered, "Yes, Lord."

At this point He called them Scribes, hoping to plant an idea that He wanted them to always remember: they must be as devoted as the Scribes. But there was to be one difference: they were not to be devoted to religion, but to Him and His kingdom, His gospel, and His Word (2 Tim.2:15; 3:16; 1 Pt.2:2-3; cp. Dt.17:19; Is.34:16; Jn.5:39; Acts 17:11; Ro.15:4; Col.3:16).

2. The householder or head of a house possessed the treasures of food, both old and new. He had two prime duties in dealing with food. He was to store the old food and keep it fresh, and he was to add the new food to the old, serving both at the appropriate time.

Christ was charging the disciples to share what they had learned. They knew the old truths, the message of the Old Testament; and now, since He had come, they were learning the new truths, the message of the New Testament. They were, therefore, responsible to share both the old and new.

OUTLINE:
1. The disciples are questioned—do they understand the parables (v.51)?
2. They are compared to Jewish Scribes (v.52).
3. They are compared to the head of a house (v.52).

1. CHRIST QUESTIONED THE DISCIPLES—DID THEY UNDERSTAND THE PARABLES (v.51)?

1. Note the extreme concern of Christ in making sure that His audience understood. (Did some seem to be disinterested, daydreaming, falling asleep? Was that the reason for His question?)

---

1 *INFOsearch Sermon Illustrations* (Arlington, TX: The Computer Assistant, 1-888-868-9029, 1986-1996).

2. Note the patience of Christ in His teaching. No doubt, Christ would have gone over and over the parables if the disciples had not understood. What a lesson for us in our preaching and teaching.

APPLICATION:
Note several lessons in this question.
1) Christ wants us to understand His Word, what He teaches us.
2) We should ask for an explanation when we do not understand.
3) There is no disgrace or reproach for not understanding.
4) We should be ready to help others to understand and be so observant that we can tell when they do not understand. We need to know when others are puzzled or have questions.

ILLUSTRATION:
What is it that makes a teacher good? It has been said that some are called to teach; others just do. The thing that really stands out in a person whom God has called to teach is the person's life. The person who is truly called and committed to teach lives for Christ, obeys Him. In addition, the good teacher has the ability to...
- make the complex simple
- help the student understand
- truly convey Christ's message

A good teacher will be patient and not let the students starve for a lack of knowledge and understanding of God's Word.

Several years ago, The British Weekly published this provocative letter:

"Dear Sir: It seems ministers feel their sermons are very important and spend a great deal of time preparing them. I have been attending church quite regularly for 30 years and I have probably heard 3,000 of them. To my consternation, I discovered I cannot remember a single sermon. I wonder if a minister's time might be more profitably spent on something else?"

For weeks a storm of editorial responses ensued ... finally ended by this letter: "Dear Sir: I have been married for 30 years. During that time I have eaten 32,850 meals—mostly my wife's cooking. Suddenly I have discovered I cannot remember the menu of a single meal. And yet ... I have the distinct impression that without them, I would have starved to death long ago."[2]

QUESTIONS:
1. How does Christ help you better understand His Word? How can you take this and help other believers grow in their faith?
2. Are you patient in explaining the gospel to others? What is the key to working with those who have a hard time understanding?

2. THE DISCIPLES WERE COMPARED TO JEWISH SCRIBES (v.52).

What did Christ mean?

1. The disciple is to *imitate* the Scribes' devotion, but there is to be a significant

---

2 John Schletewitz. Poway, CA. *Leadership Journal.* (Carol Stream, IL: Christianity Today, Inc.), Vol. 6, No. 2.

difference. The disciple is to be devoted to Christ, not religion. This means at least three things.

a. He is to be "a living sacrifice":

> **"I beseech you therefore, brethren, by the mercies of God, that ye present your bodies a living sacrifice, holy, acceptable unto God, which is your reasonable service. And be not conformed to this world; but be ye transformed by the renewing of your mind, that ye may prove what is that good, and acceptable, and perfect, will of God" (Ro.12:1-2).**

b. He is to be "crucified with Christ":

> **"I am crucified with Christ: nevertheless I live; yet not I, but Christ liveth in me: and the life which I now live in the flesh I live by the faith of the Son of God, who loved me, and gave himself for me" (Gal.2:20).**

c. He is to love God with all his heart:

> **"Thou shalt love the Lord thy God with all thy heart, and with all thy soul, and with all thy mind" (Mt.22:37).**

2. The disciple is to imitate the Scribes' study. Note three things that characterized the scribes. (Again, there is to be a significant difference. Our study centers around Christ and not religion.)

a. The subject of our study. We are to study the kingdom of heaven. It is the gospel of that kingdom that we are to teach. Other areas of study such as philosophy, psychology, and social justice may help in supporting or illustrating our preaching and teaching; but our prime instruction must be in the Word of our Lord.
b. The need for intellect. We must study what Christ has said before we can understand what He says.
c. The need for personal application. Christ's concern was that each disciple understand to the point that he could apply the lessons learned. If they were to teach, they first had to *understand and live*. We must all have a personal knowledge and understanding of God's kingdom to effectively live, preach, and teach.

APPLICATION:

Note two significant things about Scripture.

1) Scripture was given to help man learn and grow.

> **"All scripture is given by inspiration of God, and is profitable for doctrine, for reproof, for correction, for instruction in righteousness" (2 Tim.3:16).**

2) We are to study and walk in Christ if we want God's approval.

> **"But as we were allowed of God to be put in trust with the gospel, even so we speak; not as pleasing men, but God, which trieth our hearts" (1 Th.2:4).**

QUESTIONS:

1. Explain the difference between serving Christ and serving your religion or church?
2. What challenges do you face in your Bible study time? What practical things can you work on to be a better Bible student?

3. THE DISCIPLES ARE COMPARED TO THE HEAD OF A HOUSE (v.52).

Disciples are like the head of a household—extremely responsible. They are responsible for two things.

1. To share the kingdom of heaven with all of its riches.

> **"Go ye therefore, and teach all nations, baptizing them in the name of the Father, and of the Son, and of the Holy Ghost: teaching them to observe all things whatsoever I have commanded you: and, lo, I am with you alway, even unto the end of the world" (Mt.28:19-20).**

2. To share what they have, both the old and the new. They are to show just how the new fulfills the old.

APPLICATION:

The disciple is like the head of a household.

⇒ The disciple possesses an enormous treasure: the Old and New Testament.

> **"For whatsoever things were written aforetime were written for our learning, that we through patience and comfort of the scriptures might have hope" (Ro.15:4).**

⇒ The disciple possesses an enormous treasure: the old and new revelation.

> **"For the law was given by Moses, but grace and truth came by Jesus Christ. No man hath seen God at any time; the only begotten Son, which is in the bosom of the Father, he hath declared him" (Jn.1:17-18).**

⇒ The disciple possesses an enormous treasure: the old and new truth.

> **"For the law was given by Moses, but grace and truth came by Jesus Christ" (Jn.1:17).**

⇒ The disciple possesses an enormous treasure: the old and new messages of God.

> **"For what the law could not do, in that it was weak through the flesh, God sending his own Son in the likeness of sinful flesh, and for sin, condemned sin in the flesh" (Ro.8:3).**

⇒ The disciple possesses an enormous treasure: the old and new covenants.

> **"But now hath he obtained a more excellent ministry, by how much also he is the mediator of a better covenant, which was established upon better promises" (Heb.8:6).**

APPLICATION 2:
Heritage is critical. The godly past is not to be discarded. It is to be developed, built upon, and fulfilled.

> **"Think not that I am come to destroy the law, or the prophets: I am not come to destroy, but to fulfil" (Mt.5:17).**

ILLUSTRATION:
The richest people in the world are not those with all the money. The richest people in the world are rich because of the treasure that is found in knowing Jesus Christ.

> *The story is told of a wealthy man who lost his wife when their only child was young. A housekeeper was hired to take care of the boy, who lived only into his teens. Heartbroken from this second loss, the father died a short time later. No will could be found; and since there were no relatives, it looked as if the state would get his fortune. The man's personal belongings, including his mansion, were put up for sale. The old housekeeper had very little money, but there was one thing she wanted. It was a picture that had hung on a wall in the house—a photo of the boy she had loved and nurtured. When the items were sold, nobody else wanted the picture, so she bought it for just a few pennies. Taking it home, she began to clean it and polish the glass. As she took it apart, a paper fell out. It was the man's will, and in it he stated that all his wealth should go to the one who loved his son enough to buy that picture.*[3]

Do you share the riches of knowing Christ with those who are spiritually bankrupt?

QUESTIONS:
1. Think about your Christian faith for a moment. How generous are you in sharing the gospel with the lost:
   _____I'm very generous.
   _____I give when asked.
   _____I have nothing to offer.
   What has to happen in your life for you to be generous in sharing the gospel?
2. What kind of Christian heritage do you have? Can your heritage (Christian parents, grandparents, close friends, your denomination, your local church) save you? Why or why not?

SUMMARY:

God has blessed the true believer ever so richly. But with the *blessing* also comes *responsibility*, the responsibility of sharing what you have with the world. God has entrusted each believer with the precious Word of God and the empowering of the Holy Spirit. Coupled with the Good News—the best news—each one of us has a duty to be devoted to God, to study His Word, and to share the priceless treasure within us. This is how the world will be won for Christ. Will you be a devoted servant for Him?

1. The disciples were questioned—did they understand the parables?
2. The disciples were compared to Jewish Scribes. They were to *imitate* the Scribes' devotion, but there was to be a significant difference. The true disciple of Christ is to be devoted to Christ, not religion. The true disciple is to imitate the Scribes'

---

3 *INFOsearch Sermon Illustrations* (Arlington, TX: The Computer Assistant, 1-888-868-9029, 1986-1996).

study. (Again, there is to be a significant difference. Our study centered around Christ and not religion.)

3. The disciples were compared to the head of a house. They were responsible for two things: to share the kingdom of heaven with all of its riches and to share what they had, both the old and the new. They were to show just how the new fulfills the old. So are we.

PERSONAL JOURNAL NOTES
(Reflection & Response)

1. The most important thing that I learned from this lesson was:

2. The area that I need to work on the most is:

3. I can apply this lesson to my life by:

4. Closing Statement of Commitment:

OUTLINE & SUBJECT INDEX

MATTHEW, Volume 2

(Chapters 8-13)

OUTLINE & SUBJECT INDEX

MATTHEW, Volume 2

(Chapters 8-13)

REMEMBER: When you look up a subject and turn to the Scripture reference, you have not only the Scripture, you have *an outline and a discussion* (commentary) of the Scripture and subject.

This is one of the *GREAT VALUES* of *The Teacher's Outline & Study Bible™*. Once you have all the volumes, you will have not only what all other Bible indexes give you (that is, a list of all the subjects and their Scripture references), *BUT* you will also have...

An outline of *every* Scripture and subject in the Bible.
A discussion (commentary) on every Scripture and subject.
Every subject supported by other Scriptures or cross references.

DISCOVER THE GREAT VALUE for yourself. Quickly glance below to the very first subject of the Index of Matthew, Volume 2. It is:

ACCEPTANCE - ACCEPTABLE
Discussed. Receiving and rejecting men. Mt. 8:5-13

Turn to the reference. Glance at the Scripture and outline of the Scripture, then read the commentary. You will immediately see the GREAT VALUE of the INDEX of *The Teacher's Outline & Study Bible™*.

OUTLINE & SUBJECT INDEX

OUTLINE & SUBJECT INDEX

OUTLINE & SUBJECT INDEX

OUTLINE & SUBJECT INDEX

OUTLINE & SUBJECT INDEX

OUTLINE & SUBJECT INDEX

OUTLINE & SUBJECT INDEX

OUTLINE & SUBJECT INDEX

OUTLINE & SUBJECT INDEX

ILLUSTRATION INDEX

MATTHEW, Volume 2

(Chapters 8-13)

ILLUSTRATION INDEX

ILLUSTRATION INDEX

ILLUSTRATION INDEX

ILLUSTRATION INDEX

ILLUSTRATION INDEX

PURPOSE STATEMENT

LEADERSHIP MINISTRIES WORLDWIDE

exists to equip ministers, teachers, and laymen in their understanding, preaching and teaching of God's Word by publishing and distributing worldwide *The Teacher's Outline & Sermon Bible®* and related ***Outline Bible*** materials, to reach & disciple men, women, boys and girls for Jesus Christ.

MISSION STATEMENT

1. To make the Bible so understandable - its truth so clear and plain - that men and women everywhere, whether teacher or student, preacher or hearer, can grasp its message and receive Jesus Christ as Savior, and . . .

2. To place the Bible in the hands of all who will preach and teach God's Holy Word, verse by verse, precept by precept, regardless of the individual's ability to purchase it.

The ***Outline Bible*** materials have been given to LMW for printing and especially distribution worldwide at/below cost, by those who remain anonymous. One fact, however, is as true today as it was in the time of Christ:

THE GOSPEL IS FREE, BUT THE COST OF TAKING IT IS NOT

LMW depends on the generous gifts of believers with a heart for Him and a love for the lost. They help pay for printing, translating and distributing ***Outline Bible*** materials into the hands of God's servants worldwide, who will present the Gospel message with clarity, authority and understanding beyond their own power.

LMW was incorporated in the state of Tennessee in July 1992 and received IRS 501(c)(3) nonprofit status in March 1994. LMW is an international, nondenominational mission organization. All proceeds from USA sales, along with donations from donor partners, go 100% into underwriting our translation and distribution projects of ***Outline Bible*** materials to preachers, church and lay leaders, and Bible students around the world.

LEADERSHIP MINISTRIES WORLDWIDE

Publisher & Distributor of OUTLINE Bible *Materi-*

Currently Available Materials, with New Volumes Releasing Regularly

- **The Preacher's Outline & Sermon Bible® — DELUXE EDITION** 3-Ring, looseleaf binder

Volume 1 . .St. Matthew I (chapters 1-15)
Volume 2 . .St. Matthew II (chapters 16-28)
Volume 3 . .St. Mark
Volume 4 . .St. Luke
Volume 5 . .St. John
Volume 6 . .Acts
Volume 7 . .Romans
Volume 8 . .1 & 2 Corinthians (1 volume)
Volume 9 . .Galatians, Ephesians, Philippians, Colossians (1 volume)
Volume 10 . .1 & 2 Thessalonians, 1 & 2 Timothy, Titus, Philemon (1 volume)
Volume 11 . .Hebrews -James (1 volume)
Volume 12 . .1 & 2 Peter, 1,2 & 3 John, Jude (1 volume)
Volume 13 . .Revelation
Volume 14 . .Master Outline & Subject Index

FULL SET — 14 Volumes

- **The Preacher's Outline & Sermon Bible® — OLD TESTAMENT**

Volume 1 . . . Genesis I (chapters 1-11)
Volume 2 . . . Genesis II (chapters 12-50)
Volume 3 . . . Exodus I (chapters 1-18)
Volume 4 . . . Exodus II (chapters 19-40)
Volume 5 . . . Leviticus
Volume 6 . . . .Numbers
Volume 7 . . . .Deuteronomy
Volume 8 . . . .Joshua New vols release periodically

- **The Preacher's Outline & Sermon Bible® — SOFTBOUND EDITION**
  Identical content as Deluxe. Lightweight, compact, and affordable for overseas & traveling
- **The Preacher's Outline & Sermon Bible® — 3 VOL HARDCOVER w/CD**
- **The Preacher's Outline & Sermon Bible® — NIV SOFTBOUND EDITION**
- **Practical Word Studies In the New Testaament — 2 VOL HARDCOVER SET**
- **The Minister's Personal Handbook - *What the Bible Says . . . to the Minister***
  12 Chapters - 127 Subjects - 400 Verses OUTLINED - Paperback, Leatherette Deluxe
- **The Teacher's Outline & Study Bible™ • New Testament Books •**
  Complete 45 minute lessons - 4 months of studies/book; 200± pages - Student Journal
- **OUTLINE Bible Studies series: 10 Commandments - The Tabernacle**
- **CD-ROM: Preacher, Teacher, and Handbook- (Windows/STEP) - WORDSearch**
- **Translations of Preacher, Teacher, and Minister's Handbook: Limited Quantities**
  Russian - Spanish - Korean - Hindi - Telugu - Tamil - Chinese • *Future: French, Portuguese*

— Contact us for Specific Language Availability and Prices —

For quantity orders and information, please contact either:

LEADERSHIP MINISTRIES WORLDWIDE **or** *Your OUTLINE Bible Bookseller*
PO Box 21310 • Chattanooga, TN 37424-0310
(423) 855-2181 (9am - 5pm Eastern) • FAX (423) 855-8616 (24 hours)
E•Mail - info@outlinebible.org FREE Download Samples & 24 hr Orders: **www.outlinebible.org**

Equipping God's Servants Worldwide with OUTLINE Bible Materials
LMW is a nonprofit, international, nondenominational mission agency

Outline Bible Resources

This material, like similar works, has come from imperfect man and is thus susceptible to human error. We are nevertheless grateful to God for both calling us and empowering us through His Holy Spirit to undertake this task. Because of His goodness and grace, ***The Preacher's Outline & Sermon Bible***® New Testament is complete in 14 volumes, and the Old Testament volumes are releasing periodically.

The Minister's Handbook is available and other OUTLINE Bible materials are releasing electronically on **POSB-CD** and our **Website**.

God has given the strength and stamina to bring us this far. Our confidence is that, as we keep our eyes on Him and grounded in the undeniable truths of the Word, we will continue working through the Old Testament volumes and the second series known as *The Teacher's Outline & Study Bible™*. The future includes other helpful OUTLINE Bible books and **Handbook** materials for God's dear servants.

We offer this material first of all to Him in whose name we labor and serve and for whose glory it has been produced.

Our daily prayer is that each volume will lead thousands, millions, yes even billions, into a better understanding of the Holy Scriptures and a fuller knowledge of Jesus Christ the incarnate Word, of whom the Scriptures so faithfully testify.

You will be pleased to know that a small portion of the purchase price has gone to underwrite and provide similar volumes in other languages (Russian, Korean, Spanish and others yet to come). A preacher, pastor, layleader, or Bible student somewhere around the world will be more able to present God's message with clarity, authority, and understanding beyond his or her own power. *Amen*

LEADERSHIP MINISTRIES WORLDWIDE

P.O. Box 21310 • Chattanooga, TN 37424-0310
(423) 855-2181 FAX (423) 855-8616
Email – info@outlinebible.org
www.outlinebible.org – *FREE* download materials